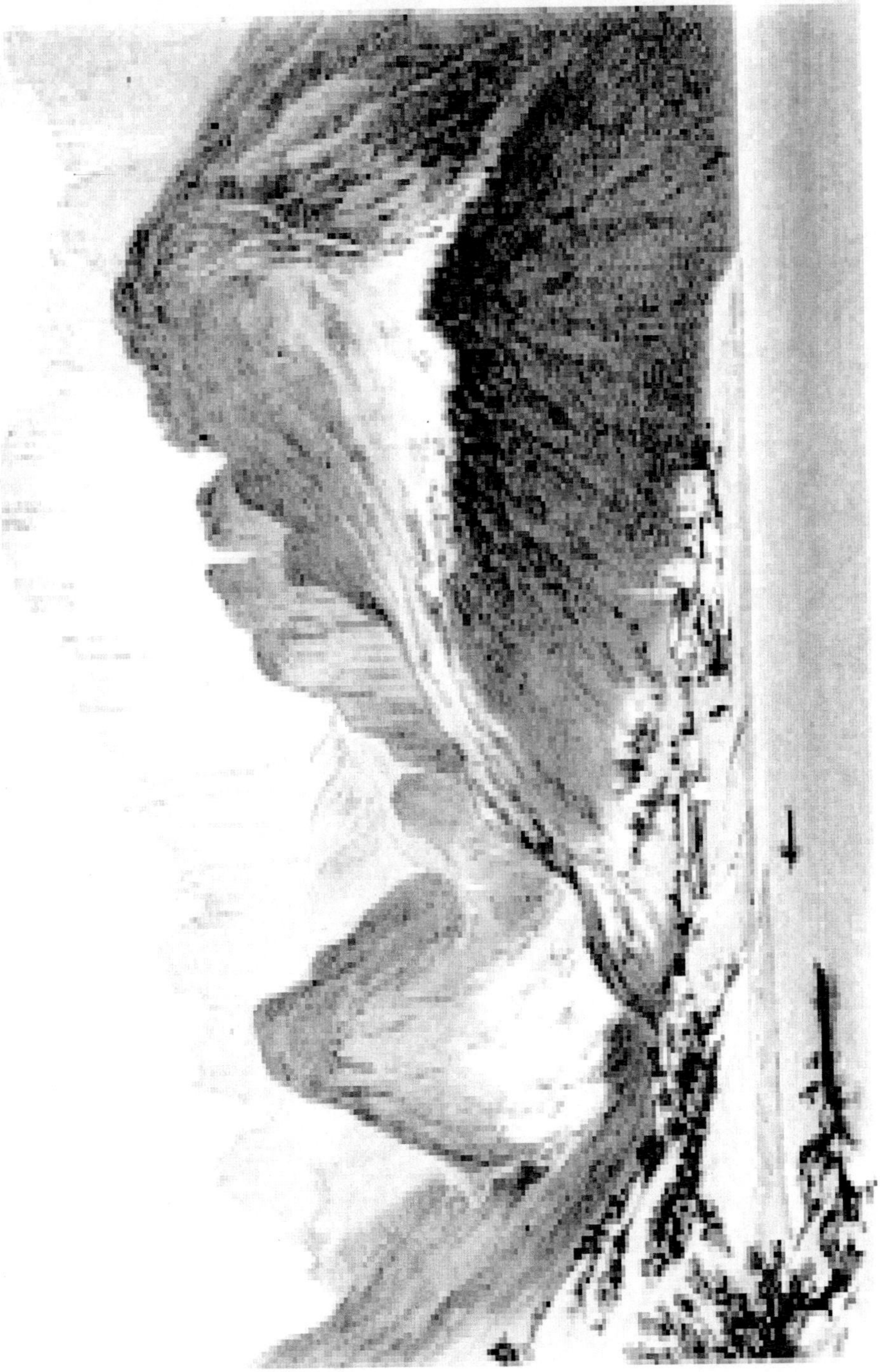

THE DOLOMITE MOUNTAINS

THE DOLOMITE MOUNTAINS

EXCURSIONS THROUGH

TYROL, CARINTHIA, CARNIOLA, & FRIULI

IN

1861, 1862, & 1863.

WITH A GEOLOGICAL CHAPTER, AND PICTORIAL ILLUSTRATIONS
FROM ORIGINAL DRAWINGS ON THE SPOT.

BY

JOSIAH GILBERT AND G. C. CHURCHILL F. G. S.

'Onward, where the rude Carinthian boor
Against the houseless stranger shuts the door.

ISBN: 978-93-5128-625-7

First Published in 1864
Indian Reprint in 2017

Published by

Kalpaz Publications
C-30, Satyawati Nagar,
Delhi – 110052
E-mail: kalpaz@hotmail.com
Website: kalpazpublications.com
Ph.: +91-9212142040

Cataloging in Publication Data—DK
Courtesy: D.K. Agencies (P) Ltd. <docinfo@dkagencies.com>

Gilbert, Josiah, 1814-1892, **author.**
The Dolomite mountains : excursions through Tyrol, Carinthia, Carniola, & Friuli in 1861, 1862, & 1863 : with a geological chapter, and pictorial illustrations from original drawings on the spot / by Josiah Gilbert and G.C. Churchill F.G.S.
pages cm
"First published in 1864"—Title page verso.
ISBN 9789351286257

1. Dolomite Alps (Italy) 2. Geology—Alps. I. Churchill, George Cheetham, author. II. Title.

DG975.D67G55 2017 DDC 914.538 23

PREFACE.

THE great zone of the Alps stretches from the French Mediterranean coast on the west to the borders of Hungary on the east. The western and central portions have been illustrated by numerous books of travel and adventure, but the eastern section has received very partial attention. Partial we may call it, since while Salzburg, the Salzkammergut, and Styria, on its northern side, have been, to a considerable extent, visited and described, the Venetian, Carnic, Julian, and Karawanken Alps, to the south, have been for the most part neglected by English tourists. The few notices of the Save and of the Isonzo valleys in the journals of Sir Humphry Davy, and brief descriptions of the Ampezzo route to Venice in the pleasant pages of Mrs. Trollope and Miss Sewell, are perhaps the only exceptions to this remark. There is, therefore, a distinct blank in Alpine literature, and this deficiency the present work claims in some measure to supply.

We trust it will be seen that through no lack of intrinsic interest the South-Eastern Alps have been left so long unexplored. The title of the volume points to one source of attraction in which these Alps have no competitor. The Dolomite Mountains, filling an extensive district in South Tyrol, and distributed in blocks along the chain eastward, are unique in Europe, both as regards the character of their scenery, and the geological problems connected with them.

All matters personal to the Authors, which it may be desirable to explain, are given in the Introduction to the narrative.

We are indebted to Messrs. Hanhart for the great pains they have taken, with a limited number of colours, to represent the general aspect of Dolomite landscape. Mr. E. Whymper's personal knowledge of mountains has enabled him, with rare delicacy and precision, to render the forms of Dolomite from the original drawings: for his fidelity in this respect, we are under especial obligations.

LONDON: *May* 21, 1864.

CONTENTS.

CHAPTER IV.

RATZES AND THE SEISSER ALP.

CHAPTER V.

RATZES TO CORTINA.

CHAPTER VI.

FROM THE AMPEZZO TO THE GAIL THAL.

CHAPTER VII.

THE GAIL THAL.

CHAPTER VIII

THE ISONZO.

CHAPTER IX.

THE UPPER SAVE.

CHAPTER X.

THE LAKE OF VELDES AND THE WOCHEIN SAVE.

CHAPTER XI.

THE CALDRON OF THE STEINER ALP.

CHAPTER XII.

A——'S LETTERS.

CHAPTER XIII.

MOUNTAINS OF FRIULI, OR CARNIA.

CHAPTER XIV.

TITIAN'S COUNTRY AND THE AMPEZZO.

CHAPTER XV.

THE CRESPENA JOCH AND CAPRILE COUNTRY.

CHAPTER XVI.

PRIMIERO.

CHAPTER XVII.

OUT-OF-THE-WAY SPOTS.

CHAPTER XVIII.

PHYSICAL DESCRIPTION OF THE DOLOMITE DISTRICTS.

LIST OF ILLUSTRATIONS.

MAPS.

CHROMO-LITHOGRAPHS

BY MESSRS. M. AND N. HANHART.

ENGRAVINGS ON WOOD

BY MR. E. WHYMPER.

LIST OF ILLUSTRATIONS.

INTRODUCTION.

Several years ago, when planning an excursion to Tyrol, we were struck by the following passages in 'Murray's Handbook:'—'Here the traveller obtains a view of the Dolomite Mountains. They are unlike any other mountains, and are to be seen nowhere else among the Alps. They arrest the attention by the singularity and picturesqueness of their forms, by their sharp peaks or horns, sometimes rising up in pinnacles and obelisks, at others extending in serrated ridges, teethed like the jaw of an alligator; now fencing in the valley with an escarped precipice many thousand feet high, and often cleft with numerous fissures, all running vertically. They are perfectly barren, destitute of vegetation of any sort, and usually of a light yellow or whitish colour.'

And again: 'They,' the Dolomites, 'form a striking contrast to all other mountains in their dazzling whiteness, in their barren sterility. . . . Sometimes they take the appearance of towers and obelisks divided from one another by cracks some thousand feet deep; at others, the points are so numerous and slender that they put one in mind of a bundle of bayonets or sword-blades. Altogether they impart an air of novelty and sublime grandeur to the scene, which can only be appreciated by those who have viewed it.' *

Our curiosity was excited by these descriptions, yet we did not at that time think of making the district referred to a special object of the journey. Our purpose was to visit the more frequented parts of Tyrol, but we arranged a route which might perhaps afford a glimpse of those singular mountains. We accomplished that journey in 1856, and, in the earlier portion of this volume, have told how we then first saw the Dolomites.

In 1858, some of our party, returning from Venice, directed their course through Tyrol by the Ampezzo road, then, and even now, very little traversed. It intersects a principal portion of the Dolomite region, but offers little more than intimations of the extraordinary scenery enclosed in the valleys, or displayed from the heights on either hand.

These two journeys convinced us there was much to see among the Dolomites, and in 1860 Mr. Churchill undertook to combine with botanical purposes a brief preliminary survey of the district. It was the first time for some years that we had been prevented from arranging our usual summer travelling party, but since circumstances so ruled it, there was some consolation in knowing that the way was being prepared, and information obtained, for the united expedition proposed for the following year.

The tour thus concerted, and in which all again had the happiness of joining, took place in the unexampled summer of 1861. Its splendid weather afforded every advantage, and while exploring those wonderful valleys, the intention, rather vague at first, of describing what we saw for a larger circle than the home readers of

* Southern Germany, pp. 329, 344.

our letters, took definite shape, and we used sketch-book and note-book with that view. We were encouraged to this no less by the peculiarity of the scenery, than by its singular seclusion from the tourist world. During eight weeks, and over a space of more than two hundred miles, we did not meet a solitary member of that restless fraternity—English or foreign—and in many places were the first English people that had been seen.

In that journey we were tempted rather beyond the region of the Dolomites proper, into districts farther to the east, and scarcely less remarkable, as will be seen from our narrative. To the original scene of our researches, however, we determined to return another year, feeling, as learners do in other fields, more conscious of what there remained to know than content with what we had acquired. A route was therefore laid down for the following season, which should utilise and supply the deficiencies of the previous excursions. In 1861 we had passed from west to east, and rather upon the northern side of the principal chain. In 1862 we went from east to west, and southward of our former line. These two journeys form the basis of our volume. In 1863 a final journey was undertaken to complete our knowledge of the district.

The arrangement of the work is then as follows:—

1. First Glimpses of the Dolomites. A Tour in 1856.
2. An Excursion to Val Fassa in 1860. By G. C. Churchill.
3. A Tour through South Tyrol, Carinthia, and Carniola, in 1861.
4. A Tour through Carinthia, Friuli, and the Venetian Alps in 1862.
5. Out-of-the-way Spots. A Supplementary Journey in 1863.
6. A Physical Description of the Dolomite Region.

It will be seen that different hands have been engaged in the composition of the work. Where not otherwise specified, the narratives are from the pen of the first-named of the authors on the title-page. Mr. Churchill contributes the account of his own solitary excursion, and the Physical Description at the end. The earlier portions of the 1862 narrative, referring to parts of Carinthia not strictly connected with our subject, are extracted from the letters of A——.

Of the travellers themselves it may be well to say a little more. They were two holiday-making Englishmen, each accompanied by his wife. This association necessarily affects the character of the narrative. 'Ah!' said Herr Imseng, the climbing curé of Saas, to a friend of ours, 'you have your mother with you; when you come again, leave her at home, and then we can do something.' English ladies—mothers or no—have since then performed exploits which should modify the curé's opinion. Nevertheless, we must at once admit that ours is not a story of Alpine *adventure*. We were not accoutred with hatchet and rope, and cannot boast of perilous ascents, or of spending our nights in sleeping-bags. If such feats are necessary to doing something—then we did nothing. Let it be observed, however, that the Dolomites are not particularly adapted for climbers—as an experienced Alpine Club-man who made the trial confessed, expressing much disgust at their evil qualities in this respect;—and, further, that the peculiar scenery of these mountains can, as we believe, be fully appreciated, and their conformation understood, without such extraordinary efforts; and we have, perhaps, sufficient justification for not attempting them.

S—— and A—— were therefore by no means 'impedimenta' in such excursions as ours. On the contrary, we owe to them many pleasant incidents of travel, and introductions to peasant hearts and homes we should not otherwise have obtained. Had they condescended to tell all the story themselves, we cannot doubt it would have been found more amusing.

We four, then, made the party. Churchill has a vasculum swung at his back, and a press-book under his arm; while, if *en route*, a bulky leather-case, the depôt of his treasures, is a marked object among the baggage. His friend carries sketching apparatus, and fixes his three-legged stool wherever a subject tempts, and time and weather, too often very ungracious, will allow. A——, armed with brush and pencil, attacks quaint costumes and pretty faces. S—— is constituted reader of the party, an important office not only on wet days within doors, but when the sketchers are busy abroad.

Our baggage—a leather bag apiece, and a couple of knapsacks, with the case already mentioned—can all be carried on one stout horse or mule, though more often it is divided among three or four men; with whom, filing up the mountain side, we make a respectable caravan. The tourist alpenstock became far too elegant an appendage for our use. Umbrellas, which will serve for walking-sticks or protection from the sun, and light cloaks strapped to the waist, form our travelling-gear. If need arises, sturdy staves are borrowed for the occasion. Our equipment is therefore very simple, lightness of carriage being a main consideration. After the first journey, two small tea-pots were added, and found extremely useful.

Having so far introduced ourselves, we venture to offer our services to any who may desire to be conducted to the Dolomite valleys. We shall be happy if, in retracing pleasant days of travel, we can make the record of them agreeable to others, and by aid of pen and pencil place before them some dim reflection of those scenes of grandeur. We shall be glad also if we can interest any of our readers in the curious geological questions attaching to the Dolomite district, and, by presenting some of the leading facts and differing theories, secure a permanent value for the volume. Nor, although cherishing the idea of seclusion, shall we grudge to a few select and kindred spirits the pleasure of verifying our descriptions by a personal visit, especially if they feel thereby the more indebted to us for showing the way. But we deprecate the intrusion of the noisy, idle stream of tourists, who, indeed, are little likely to turn aside from the substantial comforts of the high road.

Route of 1861.
D° „ 1862.

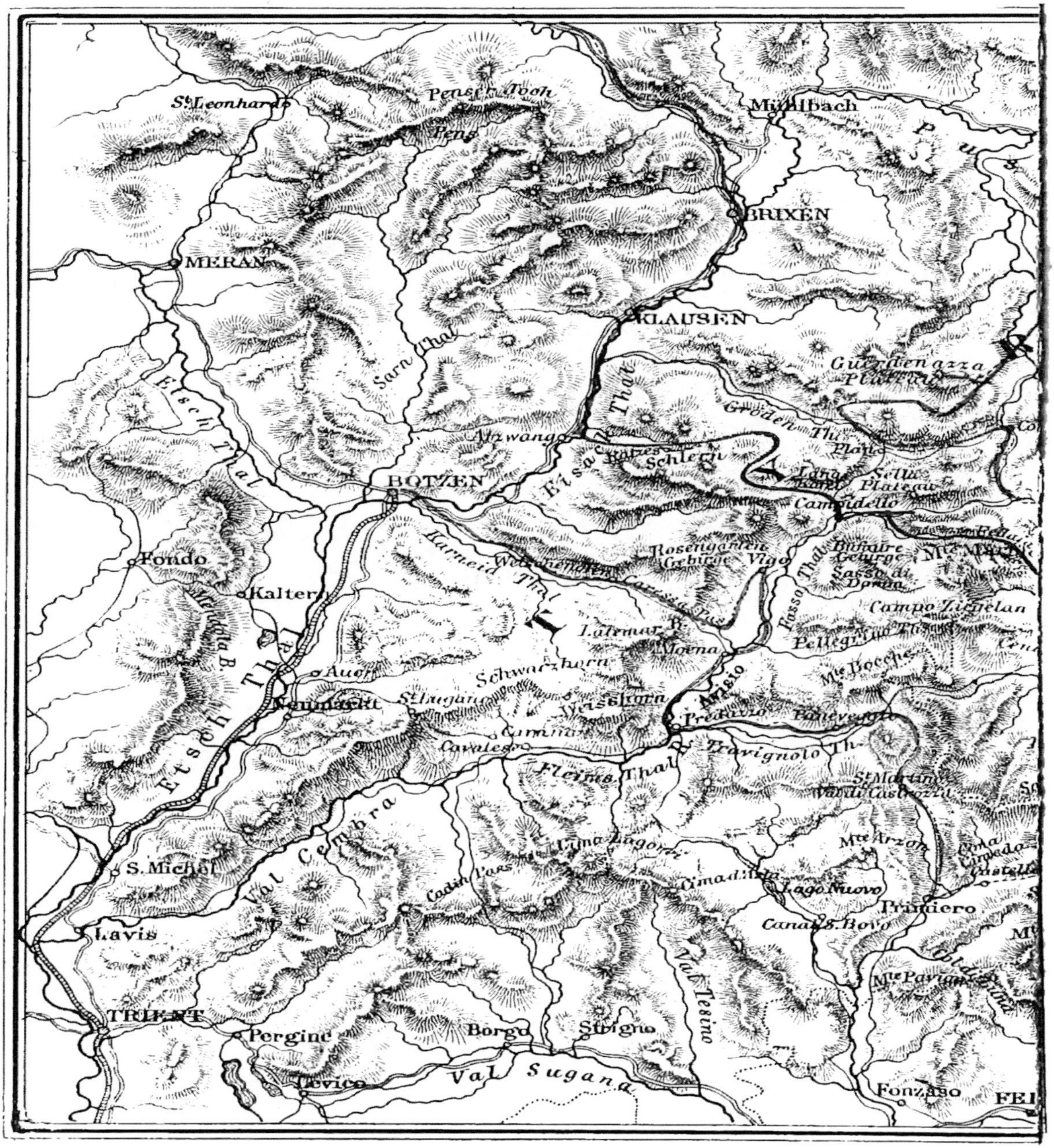

FIRST GLIMPSES OF THE DOLOMITES.

1856.

CHAPTER I.

FROM THE DANUBE TO THE DRAVE.

The Lake of Hallstadt — Goldsmith in Carinthia — Hof and Bad Gastein — Ascent of the Gamskar Kogel — Bochstein and bad Weather — The extortionate Farmer — The Death Pictures and Châlets of Nassfeld — Cloud and Snow — The Tauernhaus, and Descent upon Malnitz. — Ober Villach. — The Pedlar Bedroom. — Winklern and a glimpse of Dolomite.

Onward, where the rude Carinthian boor
Against the houseless stranger shuts the door.

FEW PEOPLE, perhaps, attach any very distinct geographical idea to the above familiar quotation from Goldsmith. We readily confess to a time when we were in that predicament ourselves. Some years ago, we saw 'Nach Kärnthen' on a sign-post, and that naturally brought with it some enlightenment. Afterwards we learnt a little more as from the summit of the Gamskar Kogel, in Salzburg, we surveyed the dark serrated line of the Noric Alps, which forms its northern boundary; at last, having crossed that barrier by the Pass of Nassfeld, behind Gastein, we found ourselves in Carinthia itself. How far the Carinthian boor has improved in his manners since Goldsmith with a travel-worn flute stood at his door, our story will declare; and it will soon be seen how far that first journey was connected with our subsequent explorations of the Dolomites.

It was the summer of 1856. We had left the Danube, with its rapids and gloomy woods, and far-sweeping mountains at Linz, travelling southward by Gmünden and Ischl, till we reached Hallstadt, that little lake town, disturbed by no sound of wheels, on a roadless shore. Here was our first rest. Here, returning one evening at dusk down the staircased footpaths—there are no other—we happened upon an incident well suited to the scene. The lake was full of boats gliding from the deep shadows of the mountains towards a large gondola, occupied by peasant musicians, attired, like everyone else, in conical cockaded hats, and ornamented belts and breeches. They were giving a serenade in honour of a visit from the director of the mines; and the effect was so exquisitely scenic, that one might have expected the dark precipices soon to fall softly asunder, and disclose a bevy of pink-petticoated damsels tripping out for the ballet. The performance ended about ten o'clock with the Austrian National Anthem; and then the crowd of boats separated—some passing back into the shadows—some disappearing along the glistening ripples of the moonlit water. Crossing by Abtenau through solitary gorges of rock and forest into the main south road from Salzburg, we waited for the next morning's diligence at Golling, a small town, full of wagons and wagoners—and merry wagoners too, for from numerous deep-arched inns, there was noise of music and of stamping feet all night long.

As a party of four, we easily obtained a 'separat wagen,' or supplementary carriage—one among seven or eight of all sorts and sizes accompanying the diligence—for the baths of Gastein. In this motley procession of vehicles we descended into the tremendous forest-filled gulf which forms the grandeur of the Pass of Luegg, where white faces of masonry in the woods, and embrasures in rocky buttresses, show that Austria keeps guard against invasion. The town of Werfen succeeds after a few miles, picturesquely perched on a rock in the midst of the valley, with fine backward views of the Tannen Gebirge, a lofty implacable barrier of limestone, whose turret ridges command the landscape in every direction. At St. Johann everybody dined; and at Lend, the next post station, turning abruptly to the left out of the valley of the Salza, we ascended a pass, the Klamm, offering a fair resemblance to the Via Mala. By evening light a wide and verdant basin opened to view, closed at the farther end by that wall of Alps towards which our day's journey of about fifty miles had been conducting us. The Carinthian valleys lay beyond; but there was no passage to them but by foot or horse-paths over the glacier-glistening ridges. Bad Gastein is at the extremity of the *cul de sac*: short of it by five miles is the old mining town of Hof Gastein: and we had contemplated a stroke of shrewdness in securing quarters there at a distance from the gay centre of attraction, though near enough for its scenery, and better situated for the ascent of the Gamskar, a mountain from whose top we hoped to survey the borders of our promised land. Unexpectedly, even Hof Gastein was full: a small inn was the only resource; and our wives, who did not yet know what 'roughing it' was, received their first lesson in that useful acquirement.

Carinthia, or Kärnthen as it is called in German, is a mountain-girdled land. The high range now in front of us formed the eastern limb of that great dividing chain which, stretching longitudinally through Switzerland and Tyrol, takes in the latter country the name of the Noric Alps. They guard Carinthia on the north; and on the south two ranges of almost equal importance, the Carnic and the Karavanken, separate it respectively from Venetia and Carniola. Two or three subordinate ridges divide it lengthways, and render it altogether mountainous in character. The long valley of the Drave intersects the province, and is a leading feature in its geography; but Klagenfurt, the capital, rather singularly, occupies a situation apart, in a plain of its own, northward of the Drave valley, but nearly in the centre of the country. Speaking generally, Carinthia lies directly north of the Gulf of Trieste, and between Tyrol and Hungary, though separated from the latter country by a portion of Styria. It is immediately enclosed by Salzburg and Styria on the north, by Venetia and Carniola on the south, and by Tyrol and Styria on the west and east.

How came Goldsmith—in days before travelling was invented, as we are apt to think, except as regarded the 'Grand Tour,' and when mountains were thought of only as a horror or a plague—how came Goldsmith to visit so remote and mountain-guarded a region? To us its seclusion was an irresistible attraction; but the surrounding countries were not then thronged with his countrymen, and he could have found seclusion at far less cost of shoe-leather. We may find some explanation in the fact that Carinthia was at that period more on a footing with the rest of the empire. All roads were alike then, and those of Carinthia therefore not worse than others, while the chief events of its history were of nearer interest then than now. People had not forgotten the fearful struggles of Germany with the Turks, in the latest of which Eugene, the friend of Marlborough, had obtained so much renown; and the battle of Villach, in 1492, when the Carinthian nobles defeated them with great slaughter, would be more notable to the students of history in the eighteenth than in the nineteenth century. So to Goldsmith, though it led him 'onward' far, Carinthia might have been as much known as Tyrol is to us, and not less accessible, though it is scarcely probable that he took the mountain path by which we entered the country.

We arrived at Hof Gastein on a Tuesday evening, August 19, and it was necessary to gather information, and arrange plans for our future progress. Some of us were then new to mountain travelling—I smile as I think of their ample experience since—and the others found it perplexing to estimate the real amount of difficulty in prospect. We were deprived of the abundant aids which surround the traveller in Switzerland and other frequented routes, in the shape of guides, horses, side-saddles, &c., and the people knew nothing of the capabilities of English women when they choose to be adventurous. Moreover, our stock of German at that time was very limited, and now that discussion and negotiation were required, our only resource was the marker of an adjoining billiard-table, and ex-waiter from Vienna, who by virtue of a little French acted as interpreter, but whose erratic visits, and disjointed and careless pieces of information, were very unsatisfactory.

'Two rather difficult Alpine passes,' says Murray, 'lead from the valley of Gastein into Carinthia,—the Malnitzer Tauern, and the Pass of Rauris.' How we scanned and discussed that epithet of 'difficult,' and the details which should explain it! The most attractive of the two paths was the second, which, crossing the mountain barrier in our front by a slant to the right, comes down by the side of the Gross Glockner, the loftiest of the Austrian Alps, to Heiligenblut, at the head of the Möllthal in Carinthia. The thirteen hours of continuous walking might have been broken into a two days' journey by sleeping at the village of Bucheben. Our intention of proceeding by this route was reluctantly abandoned under assurances of recent snow, prognostications of doubtful weather, and hints of uncertain accommodation. There remained the Malnitzer, also called the Pass of Nassfeld, which, leading directly over the mountains, would bring us in a single day to Ober Villach. Reserving two days for Gastein and its neighbourhood, we fixed upon Friday for the expedition, that we might have time to reach some pleasant spot in the southern valleys for a Sunday's rest.

Our first excursion was to Gastein. Winding gradually, and with the excellent finish of Austrian workmanship, the road ascended by the sides of green hills, and through pine woods, with the verdant valley deep on the left, till the 'Bad' disclosed itself in a series of scattered white houses, dispersed among gardens, and woods, and sheltered nooks. Where the houses were thickest a thundering cascade tumbled through their very midst, splashing its foam on roofs and balconies. The church, with an English-looking country spire, stood on one of the green mounds, and walks and seats were plentifully distributed about the recesses of the hills, which, soaring into forest-crowned summits, and higher still into jagged rocks streaked with snow, hemmed the scene closely in. It was easy to spend here some pleasant hours till the *table d'hôte* bell sounded from Straubinger's, where a vast length of board was filled, as far as we could judge, entirely by Austrians, mostly military, and generally old men, upon whom the waters are said to exercise a rejuvenating power. If so, the specimens we saw must have been in an early stage. On returning to Hof Gastein, we agreed, that notwithstanding the chance deficiency of accommodation there, and the attractions of the Bad, we did not regret our choice of quarters. The valley is more open, the outlines finer, the situation can be better commanded, and the massive old houses of the small town give it the historic air appropriate to its celebrity through Roman and Venetian times.

To climb a well-selected mountain, and see the lie of the country, was Dr. Arnold's first care in a new neighbourhood. The Gamskar Kogel (7,400 feet), which overlooks the town, offered an excellent opportunity for following his example. Thursday was devoted to the ascent, in which our wives declined to take part, having suffered severely from an attempt a few days before, when fresh from England, to reach on foot the summit of the Blassenstein behind Hallstadt. They contented themselves with fluttering their white handkerchiefs encouragingly as, led by a lad of a guide, we breasted the hill side in front of the little inn.

The mountain was like all mountains that I know of which are ordinarily accessible. First, there was a steep shoulder to surmount by zigzags, through pastures and bush; then a long slope leading to a plateau or basin, under the final peak where, sheltered in the hollow, the topmost châlet was ensconced. Beyond, a steep and shaly path, flecked with snow, wound upward to that portion of the basin-rim where the summit reared its head. A keen wind swept the ridge like a scythe, but descending a few steps under the first ledge we had perfect shelter, and leisure to survey a striking prospect. On that side, looking south, and deep in the abyss below, lay Bad Gastein. Above, stretched the magnificent array of the Noric Alps, darkened by heavy storms which filled their recesses with an awful gloom. Glaciers clung to their sides, 'plastered' up close under their peaked summits, and hanging down in tongues, from which in glistening streaks the torrents poured below. The opening where we judged our pass to lie was a caldron of white clouds, and altogether the view in that direction, however grand, was not of cheerful import for the morrow. On the other points of the compass the aspect was wholly different. To the east, the mountains of Styria, to the north those of Salzburg, to the west those of Tyrol, were clear in sunshine or careering shadow, and glorified the whole horizon. From a scene like this it would be mournful to descend to the holes and ruts of earthly existence, but that such an altitude is convenient only for the eagles, and that an hour of it lasts a lifetime. By six o'clock we had again reached our inn. A fatal accident has since occurred on this mountain. Two gentlemen and a lady, attempting to descend by a shorter cut, were stopped by precipices, over one of which the lady slipped, and was killed. There is no danger in the proper route—about four hours up, and three down.

The sun's last rays shot with a golden gleam over the valley, and we still trusted to accomplish the Malnitzer Pass on the morrow. Our hopes fell to zero as during the night an ominous wind howled over the roof, and shook our casements furiously. Morning broke with chilling flirts of rain. Yet when we met in council, at an early breakfast, some flying lights above were held to be sufficient warrant for a start. In truth we were not sorry to leave our quarters under any conditions, and the greasy billiard-marker had become simply a nuisance. At the worst, we could limit our day's journey to the ten miles which intervened before the commencement of the mule-path, and make Bochstein, at the foot of the pass, our starting-point for the morrow. So the carriage was packed, though under protest from all concerned. 'Oui,' said the ex-waiter, as we moved off, 'oui, vous aurez un goût des montagnes;' and the driver, when, seated at his side, I sought to obtain his private and friendly opinion upon the prospects of the weather, answered only with a surly monosyllable, like a vicious sneeze, which my companion translated as an emphatic '*bad.*' And bad it was to be. Soon, driving rain obscured the valley; at Gastein every roof was streaming; those under the cascade were no wetter than the rest; and as we slowly climbed into the upper basin beyond, the sweeping gusts left us no thought but shelter at the Bochstein Inn. The driver was of another mind; drawing up to the blank gable-end of a house, he declared that he had fulfilled his contract. Not a soul was visible, not a ghost of a Gast-haus; and we remonstrated with such effect that, exploding a power of ill-humour in a jerk of the reins and a cut with the whip, he started off again. Three miles farther, crossing a bridge of pine logs to a group of well-to-do peasant houses, we were set down at a small inn, where the road came to its end.

Here perforce we must spend the day, and, if the day, also the night, for which there was tolerable accommodation. Dinner is an event in the monotony of idle hours; it was served to us in a large room exterior to the inn, and balconied all round, for the use, apparently, of excursionists from Gastein. Now, the range of windows only gave prospect of the rain-drops, and rattled in the gusts; and there was but one guest besides ourselves — a picturesque figure in Tyrolean hat and feathers, broad embroidered belt, and loose breeches, too short to reach the stockings, rolled up below the knee. After a while a sketch-book slid from the stranger's pocket, and he proved to be a Viennese artist of remarkable facility in the use of the lead pencil, though in no instance had his delicate touch been applied to the delineation of mountain forms, or the 'cloud chariots' so dear to Mr. Ruskin. His subjects, with singular disregard of the majesty around, were confined to bits of detail among châlets and pine trunks. A sudden burst of thunder interrupted an inspection of his folio. Our artist welcomed the sound as a favourable omen, and within half an hour the grey veil of rain was lifted, the clouds separated and fell between the hills, and all the higher tops, including the Gamskar, upon whose summit we had been seated the day before, were seen sheeted in bright snow.

My friend and I took the opportunity to explore for some distance the Anlauf Thal, a lateral glen, once the principal line of traffic over these mountains, dating even from Roman times. That of Nassfeld, by which it has now been superseded, joins it again on the southern side. We did not reach the 'cirque' with which the Anlauf valley closes, but our walk left an ineffaceable impression of wild beauty. The slanting sun showering gold upon the wet grass, and pine-tree tops, and creamy torrents; the woods about our heads 'like cloud on cloud,' and the bare dominating peaks, composed the vivid picture.

Darkness brought us back over the white, roaring stream—that invariable accompaniment of a mountain village—to the tea-table, which our wives had busied themselves in arranging, under certain difficulties common to districts where English travellers are unknown. It was a successful transaction, and the Kellnerin, released from its unwonted requirements, could devote herself to the Vienna gentleman, who, with one patronising hand on her shoulder, and deliberately smoothing her fair hair with the other, discussed his intended supper; she, in frank innocence, looking up at his handsome face, and enumerating the dishes.

When people leave the mapped-out routes of Touristdom, they must be content to abandon also its luxuries and conveniences. We met in the morning all jaded from a bad night. A—— had spent hers upon three bony chairs, which yet she preferred to her bed; and instead of the guides and horses in waiting at the hotel door, we had to seek ours three miles away at a farmer's house. A messenger despatched to him over night, had returned with terms too exorbitant to be submitted to without remonstrance; so, leaving our wives to pack and breakfast, we brushed the morning dew through the long grass of the water-meadows to the farm—the spot our driver would have left us at the day before, which explained that mystery a little. From among his barns and wood-stacks out came the sturdy owner; his slouched hat, loose doublet, baggy black breeches, and wrinkled boots, completing a considerable personal resemblance to Oliver, the Lord Protector. And a Lord Protector he was,—of his own interests. The man was as fixed in his resolves, as he stood firm in his boots; and we could only baffle his intentions to a certain extent, by refusing to engage the horses destined for our wives farther than to the top of the col. Returning to a hurried breakfast, that, and a fresh altercation about the weight of the baggage, which ended in weighting the farmer's pockets with another gulden, delayed our departure till nine — far too late, as all col climbers know.

We started neither fresh nor lively; but the sun glinted through the clouds, and the morning air, the rapid ascent, the knowledge that we were now attacking that wall of Alps which had barred the way so long, and that, if fortune favoured, we should dip that day into remote Carinthia — all helped to brighten our faces with the brightening sun. The clammy beds, the fly-pestered breakfast, even the morose Oliver and that last gone-gulden, were forgotten.

Yet there was a dash of anxiety to flavour the adventure. The road! Of course it was not a road, only a steep and narrow track by the side of the foaming torrent; and clouds still hid all the summits; and innumerable white streaks on the hills, descending from unknown heights, had a very watery aspect. S——, whose previous Swiss experiences might have put her at ease in this kind of thing, was mounted, pannier-wise, on a large and ill-favoured beast, who, casting a sly eye behind him to select his opportunity, seemed bent upon grinding her against every projecting rock. A——, new to the scrambles of a rough mountain track, the abrupt turns and sudden depths, clung tightly to her saddle, glancing from right to left in unmistakable alarm. Of the two guides, one was loutish and careless, a mere servant of the farm, owning none of the guide's esprit; the other, a cheery old man, considered himself attached only to the baggage mule—a wonderful little fellow with thin legs, inclined to compound for carrying a heavy burden during a long day by various eccentricities, and a frequent lifting of his heels, of which we were warned to beware.

Matters smoothed with use; not so the path, which, stony and steep, crossed and recrossed the stream by narrow bridges, and was bordered by numerous mementos of frightful deaths, carefully set forth in small pictures, with name and date inscribed to bespeak the traveller's prayers. Here was a poor wretch crushed in a timber-slide; there, a man drowning in the torrent; and again another perishing in the snow. Yet, despite the tragic nature of the incidents portrayed, and our real pity for the sufferers, it was impossible to restrain a smile at the care with which the victims were depicted in clean shirts and best coats, and with their hair neatly brushed, as if they had all met their sad fate on a Sunday; while a gaily-dressed figure of the Virgin in an upper corner, looking on with a smiling countenance, and feet nestling in what were meant for clouds, but were more like muffins, by no means made the thing look graver.

Mounting in this manner for a couple of hours by rock

and stream, we entered a basin among the mountains into which several glaciers fell, none of them very imposing, but sufficient to give a dreary grandeur to the place, and a sternly isolated character to a group of huts at the further extremity of the plateau, where a few shepherds tend the herds of cattle which in summer seek these elevated meadows. This is Nassfeld, the wet field, which names the pass. Reaching the huts about an hour later, the men led to a door behind a dunghill as the usual place of halt. Within, two pedestrians were drying their socks and shoes, and warming themselves with excellent coffee—the more welcome since they had passed, they told us, through snow above. These gentlemen were Austrians who, returning from India, had landed at Trieste, and were making their way to Vienna by this remote route. Goat's cheese and bread were the only additions to the coffee, and when we included in one payment the still more humble fare of the guides, a sudden seizure and kissing of our hands expressed an unexpected gratitude in a very unexpected manner. Words were necessarily few, for the patois of the people is unintelligible to any but themselves.

But it is past noon, and the summit of the col is up in the clouds yonder; our wives mount again into their baskets, and the poor mule receives his marching orders.

A stranger might easily take a ravine to the left, and find himself 'nowhere' after an hour or two—a serious matter in these solitudes. The proper course ascends immediately upon the green hill-side, which is scored by many paths, as the individual fancy of cows, goats, herdsmen, and travellers has led them many a year. The grass soon ends in shale, where poles, leaning from the blasts of winter and pressure of snow, mark the upward way. It was steep climbing; the huts beneath were already but tiny toys, and the Vienna travellers, issuing from them, looked like pin-points on the sward. Then all was lost in cloud—cloud that was rolling in masses across the track, and boiling in a black abyss on the right, its rocky walls alternately hidden and displayed, as the awful silent billows surged and fell. Suddenly, snow glimmered through the eddying mists, and we floundered in slushy footsteps, which led to bare and glistening shale again, whence the path was still seen sweeping upward to a rock-strewn crest. It gave promise of the summit; but beyond there was a dip into a vast chasm, the bottom filled with cloud, and then another ridge, where a cross stood clear in vapoury light. That was the col, and a few minutes of rapid descent brought us to a rude block of masonry, the 'Tauern-haus,' or hospice; a solitary keeper, watching at the heavy-lintelled door, dived in as we approached to stir the embers of his fire. We had been two hours from the huts.

But from that low door-way what a prospect! The shapes and colours grew before our eyes. A far vista of a deep blue valley opened under the arching clouds, and peaks bright with sunshine stretched in long array, melting into a lovely haze. That valley pointed into the heart of Carinthia, upon whose frontier we now stood; deep at our feet, as yet unseen, lay Malnitz, its first village, and white dots in the distance marked Ober Villach, in the Möll Thal, our night's resting-place. The stone dens of the forlorn hospice had small attraction, now that sunlight shone upon our way. The horses and the sulky guide were dismissed, and the merry old man and eccentric mule prepared to accompany us to Malnitz, where we expected to find a road, and with the road a carriage. Then, down the splintery shale we went, rattling and sliding upon the slabs, and soon distancing the mule, who, prudent now, was steadying himself at the sharp corners.

There is never a more gleeful hour than the first after crossing a col; and when grassy knolls and hollows succeeded to the shale, we coursed and frolicked down them, a mad and merry party. As the shadows slanted and lengthened in the afternoon sun, and it was still down, and down, and steeper down, our spirits rather sobered; and when Malnitz was pointed out for a moment, still a speck at an immense distance, we grew graver, more silent, and slower-footed. Once, a cluster of huts touched by the last sun-ray, and backed by the intense gloom of the still-descending valley beyond, convinced us Malnitz was at hand; but, on nearer approach, the supposed village dwindled into swineherds' huts, surrounded by swinish filth; and from the brow on which they stood was visible only the long perspective of a deep-troughed valley, filled with pine woods, into which we were fain to descend, and cold shadows and grim silence fell upon us the rest of the way.

The dreariness deepened as the path left its course to cross an enormous landslip—a scar—a wound in nature's sides that had scarcely healed. The trees, still standing, but tossed and reeling in dim confusion, sent through one a shiver of insecurity. It was five o'clock, and no Malnitz yet! Soon, however, our ears were saluted by the mingled tinkling and jangling of goat and cattle-bells; the herds were coming in, and must be nearing home. Not so pleasant an indication was the state of the path, which, now shut into a narrow way by the familiar Alpine fence of pine-rails, was almost knee-deep in mud. But it was the last difficulty. At an angle of the valley, where it turned suddenly to the south, the blue smoke of the Malnitz suppers was rising above the trees; and at half past six, undemonstrative and muddy, we filed into the village, and reached the door of a humble, but clean-looking, inn. Churchill and myself had been on foot, with slight intervals, for twelve hours: S—— and A——, after riding five, had walked four. They have done better since, but were very tired then. To all, the rest was welcome—not least, doubtless, to the mule, who, when unburdened, soon had his heels in the air, and his back upon the cool grass.*

'A carriage to Ober Villach?' The tone was more than doubtful; but they could find something, it seemed, that might serve. Enjoining haste, lest we should be caught in the dark, we rested on the benches at the door, to see what Malnitz was like. The houses about were poor and scattered; but on the wooded heights above, a village here and there was shining softly in the twilight, and looking charming in the distance.

At the sound of wheels we started briskly to our feet, only to welcome two shallow, springless trays—wheel-barrows was the first suggestion. A heavy cart-horse was attached to each, at the end of long shafts, and the drivers sat dangling their legs behind their horses' tails. Seats there were none, only a little hay considerately spread at the bottom of the carts. A—— had solaced her companion, during the last hour of the walk, with the prospect of a luxurious drive from Malnitz to Villach; but the vision of a cushioned carriage was gone,—not into thin air, but hard wood! Fortunately, she was not too tired to laugh, and mounted gaily into her wheel-barrow with her husband, built up with baggage, and squatting in the hay. Nor should we have fared ill on a tolerable road; but this one was not tolerable. We were bumped down staircases of rock, tilted over projecting shelves, or

* Murray is confused in his statement of distance over this pass, calling Malnitz eight hours from Gastein, while his Itinerary makes nine and a half. The latter accords more with our experience.

pounded among heaps of stones. The so-called road was much more like the bed of a stream, which it probably was in winter time. Baggage squandered about, hay drifting into ridges, left us in cruel contact with the bare boards, and in the midst of it darkness came down upon our distressed and divided party. We of the hindmost vehicle could just discern the glimmer of A.'s straw hat in erratic movement in front, and by its jerks, and jumps, and plunges, received some warning of the jolt to come. Two hours of this took out all the fun of the thing, and reduced it to mere misery.

A distant gleam, such as might come from a hospitable inn-door bursting with light, promised speedy relief; but the leading car passed on, and was lost, hat and all, in the further darkness. The next moment we had entered the radiance of a small way-side shrine, stuck full of candles, and illuminating the faces of some score of peasants kneeling on the broken steps, and out into the road—a prayer meeting of certainly not an English type. We had scarcely recovered from the dazzle, when, deep on our right—very deep, for we were stumbling along several hundred feet above them—appeared the lights and roofs of a town, which were speedily left, as it seemed, irretrievably behind; yet soon returning upon a lower level, we began to understand our destination, and were presently jogging, as weary as you can fancy, into Ober Villach.

To those in advance had been left the final choice of inns, previously a matter of some discussion. One was passed, and another, and still the straw hat was discerned at intervals 'sounding on its dim and perilous way.' Then it disappeared, and our driver was at once bewildered in the darkness, till a figure or two, issuing from a door-way, and holding up candles, guided us into the hollow vaulted passage of the 'Post.'

Our friends were in active conversation with host and hostess. Beds, it seemed, were no difficulty; and up the broad creaking stairs we limped, aching in every bone, to a large square apartment, where six or eight beds, ranged round the walls, offered, as was supposed, ample accommodation. Our enquiry for another room, however unreasonable to the Carinthian mind, was nevertheless promptly answered by the display of a second exactly similar chamber, similarly furnished, though a shade more dingy. We were obliged to appear excessively fastidious, and take possession of both rooms, one of them fitted with a raised orchestra at the end, being evidently the scene of many a village festival. Supper was the next matter of importance: it proved a dismal failure, and, tired, if not cross, we separated for the night. To S—— and myself was allotted the dusky concert-room, where the faded effigies of drums, trumpets, and violins, looked exceedingly incongruous with repose, and the rows of beds, like those of an hospital ward, scarcely less so. S—— insisted upon a strict examination, to assure herself that no stray pedlar was under any of the coverlets, before she consented to occupy the least objectionable couch in the corner. It was an inauspicious first night in Carinthia.

A glorious morning drew me out before anybody else was stirring—a summer Sunday morning already promising heat. Seeking that central point of interest, the church, I found the churchyard crowded with people. Mass was being celebrated in the open air, in front of the principal entrance, and the banners and vestments were chequered with the shade of noble chestnut trees. The organ pealed from within, and a peasant multitude, kneeling, filled the ground, and each open gateway, and as far beyond as it was possible to witness the ceremony. A Protestant may yet look reverently on such a scene as this. But the mingled odour of incense and ancient garments was too pungent even in the open morning air; and after remaining a few minutes, I prolonged my walk beyond the village, among the softly wooded hills of the valley.

Returning at the appointed hour for breakfast, I found my friends assembled, but not in happier mood than the night before. They were discussing speedy flight, which the miserable meal on the table, and the prospect of a second night in the pedlar bedrooms, seemed to justify, if better quarters could be had within reasonable distance. We wonder now whether it was so bad after all! and are visited with some compunctions as we remember the little old landlord, very submissive and anxious, standing with a bunch of feathers at the end of a stick to disperse the cloud of flies. The alternatives offered were Spital, down the valley, where it joins the Drave, or Winklern, in its upper course; and as the poor man assured us of a Gasthaus 'sehr gut' at the latter place, some twenty miles distant, we agreed to proceed thither at once. So, instead of descending the Möll Thal, which we had entered at Ober Villach, and which would have led us directly to the Drave, we turned towards the Alpine range again, intending to reach the Drave by a short cut over the hills from Winklern to Lienz. We started as soon after breakfast as a carriage could be prepared.

I have mentioned the ancient track across these mountains, which struck up the Anlauf Thal from Bochstein. It fell in again with ours at Malnitz, and once made Ober Villach a place of great importance. Its prosperity reached its height in the middle of the fifteenth century, and a relic of those times remains in the name of its principal street. Troops of pack-horses, laden with corn, wine, brandy, vinegar, dried fruits, silks, and spiceries, then passed northwards through the town, returning with leather, wood, linen, and salt. The street where those horses were daily collected before starting is still known as the 'Samgasse,' from *sammeln*, to collect.

The road to Winklern kept along the bottom of the valley. It was thickly studded with crucifixes and pictures, all of a gloomy, some of a disgusting character, their fidelity to the details of bodily torture obscuring all that might be touching or sublime in the spectacle of human suffering. They kept our driver in full occupation, for he doffed his cap to every one. The heavy vehicle swung sleepily along through the sultry hours. Sometimes extra jolts, and a still slower pace, indicated the rough street of a village; once or twice we found ourselves suddenly in the midst of swarthy faces, and recognised Italian speech and features. Bands of labourers, we learnt, were *en route* from the south, to make good the road at various points for an expected visit of the Kaiser. Through the sun-glare little could be seen of the landscape but wooded steeps above, and a glittering stream below, or the slopes of arid débris through which it wandered.

Three or four hours of this somnolent progress, and still no Winklern. Waking up to look about us, a romantic village, 'bosomed high mid tufted trees,' appeared in sight. It occupied the corner of the valley, where it bent abruptly northwards, and conspicuous among the topmost houses was a large chateau-looking building, the beau-idéal of a country-house for its commanding, and yet sequestered situation. Nothing could be more charming than to pay a visit to the owner, had we but the pleasure of his acquaintance. The village was Winklern, 'the little corner,' that was certain; and for the inn, the driver really seemed to point to that very mansion in its midst. The notion was too extravagant; imagine, then, our surprise when, after many turnings of the steep ascent, and as many halts to rest the panting horses, we found ourselves entering the barn-surrounded court-yard of the edifice in question!

Two or three peasants drinking at the entrance, certainly gave something of an inn-door look, but quite out of character with anything of the sort was the appearance of the hostess in the porch. Tall, of a fair sweet countenance, and dressed with quaint but lady-like simplicity, she stood there to receive us. Her neatly-braided hair, and the large bunch of keys at her side, brought to mind Retsch's young mother in his 'Outlines to the Song of the Bell;' and the close-fitting caps of the batch of female servants, the ample and wainscotted staircase behind, and the dark carved presses on the landing, looked like a scene from one of his interiors. The mystery of such a Gasthaus was not immediately to be explained; but certainly here was no 'boor,' with closed inhospitable door!

Two delightful rooms, clean and cheerily furnished, were thrown open to us, the windows displaying a lovely prospect up and down the valley. Dinner, served by an elderly but assiduous kellnerin, well sustained the character of comfort which pervaded the establishment; and as we sat that evening at the open windows, what could be sweeter than to watch the purple shadows filling up the valley, blotting out the sparkling villages one by one, and creeping towards the golden uplands and crimson crags, till, when the flood of shade was full, the purple changed to grey!

Yet one more incident of this first day in Carinthia remains to be told. It had important results to ourselves, for it directed the course of several after-journeys, and gave us an object for our tours in which we hope to interest our readers. While sunshine yet lingered in the valley, and touched with silver the upper portion of a waterfall which fell, like the Staubbach, from a wall of cliffs behind the village, we had sauntered out, crossing the meadows towards the foot of the cascade. Presently, turning for a backward glance, we were surprised by a strange array of bare distorted peaks, peering over the hills to the southward. They had only become visible within the last few steps. 'Why, Churchill,' said I, 'what on earth are those?' 'Those,' said my friend, 'those!' and then, after a pause, 'those must be the Dolomites!'

Now, it has been already said that we left England with some notion of seeing the Dolomites in the course of the journey. The passages from 'Murray' which we have quoted, an outline of the Lang Kofel on one of his pages, and the mention by a friend of the Marmolata, nearly 12,000 feet in height, of which he had long desired, but never obtained, the sight, had all concurred to invest them with peculiar attraction. We knew something of their general position, extending for a considerable distance through South Tyrol, and we contemplated a detour from either Brunecken or Botzen to see them. But we did not expect to find them anywhere in Carinthia, nor that they would come into view from any part of that province. Yet, such needle-pointed, pale, and altogether weird-looking pinnacles as now appeared, soaring into the evening sky, could be none other than the wondrous Dolomites. We longed to surmount the ridge behind Winklern, which hid all but their tops, and separated the Möll Thal from the valley of the Drave, that seemed to lie at their feet. We were impatient till we could explore them, and from that moment the Dolomites seized upon us with the spell of witchery.

CHAPTER II.

FROM THE DRAVE TO THE EISACK.

What and Where the Dolomites are — The 'Great Bell' — Heiligenblut, and the Story of Briccius — The Chevalier of Winklern — The Wizards enchant us, but we arrive at Lienz — Amman takes us in Charge — More Dolomites — Tyrol road-side Inns — Brunecken — Amman's Disaster—Brixen and the Brenner road—Botzen Scenery.

In the last chapter we introduced the Dolomites, and it may now be desirable, without anticipating the fuller description, which will come in its place, to devote a paragraph or two to the general character and whereabouts of this remarkable mountain group.

The question, 'what is Dolomite?' opens up a large subject; but it is an enquiry likely to be first on the lips of those who intend to accompany us on our journeys. We will simply say at present, that it is magnesian limestone, existing in a peculiar condition, the origin of which is matter of great controversy; and that it derives its name from its discoverer, M. Dolomieu. The term, however, may be familiar to many who are nevertheless unacquainted with Dolomite mountains, for beds of it frequently occur without inducing any peculiarity in the scenery, and the fact of our Houses of Parliament being constructed of stone obtained from quarries in this rock at Bolsover in Derbyshire, has brought the name often of late before the public eye.

Yet there is but one district where dolomite so predominates as to claim the scenery for its own. There it presents features altogether remarkable, and the landscape is unlike any other landscape. That is the region with which our excursions are principally concerned, though they were extended into adjoining districts where dolomite is only a subsidiary, though a marked, geologic feature.

The Dolomite region proper, lies in the south-eastern portion of Tyrol, a little to the north-west of the Gulf of Venice. It may be described as bounded on the north by the Pusterthal; on the west by the valleys of the Eisach and Adige; on the south by a line drawn from Trent to Belluno; on the east by the valley of the Piave, and a line extended northwards to the Pusterthal. On the south and east, however, these boundaries are not strictly correct. Dolomite does not predominate quite so far south, and it does possess the landscape considerably further east than the Piave, or we should not have obtained that startling glimpse of dolomitic forms narrated in the last chapter. The kernel of dolomite scenery may be, in other words, described as within the 'quadrilateral' formed by the cities of Brixen, Trent, Belluno, and Lienz; or again, as bounded on the west by the Brenner route, and intersected on its eastern side by the Ampezzo road, which last is the only road that passes through it. Taking the length of each of its sides at about sixty miles English, the entire area may be computed at 3,600 square miles.

The loftiest and most noted mountain of the district, the Marmolata, stands nearly in the centre. North-west of it is the Lang Kofel, and to the south-east of it the Sasso di Pelmo. These are the three of greatest name, but there are several of almost equal importance distributed among the mountain blocks which are characteristic of the Dolomite region. The Hohe Schlern stands out as the most western member of the whole; the Antelao, Malcora, and Tofana majestically overshadow the Ampezzo route; and the Civita rears itself superbly above the charming lake of Alleghe, almost the only lake that adorns the Dolomites.

Now, if the reader will refer to the map, he will see that at Winklern, in Carinthia, where the last chapter left us, we were far away from the district just roughly described, and he will understand why we were quite unprepared for the sudden apparition of dolomitic mountains. We did not then know that they were to be found in isolated groups, distributed along the ranges of the Carnic and Karavanken Alps, and were, therefore, distinctly a feature in Carinthian landscape.

Into the Dolomite district itself we did not, in our present journey, penetrate at all, and in this second chapter I have only to record how we skirted its northern and western sides, and how successive glimpses of its strange scenery were afforded us, each increasing our desire to enter and explore.

But to return to Winklern. We did not yield at once to the Dolomite infatuation, of which our friends accuse us. That Sunday evening spectacle impressed us much, yet Monday morning found us leaving unclimbed the ridge which should disclose it fully, and indeed turning our backs upon it to ascend the Möll Thal, towards the main Alpine chain, which two days before, at a different point, we had crossed from Gastein. Still, there were good reasons, on this splendid day, for postponing acquaintance even with the Dolomites. At the head of the Möll Thal stands the superb Gross Glockner—the 'Great Bell'—the highest mountain of the Noric Alps, the eastern rival of Mont Blanc and Monte Rosa, and the pride of Carinthia. We might see it and return in a day.

In a pair of light single-seated phaetons, and accompanied by the landlord's son, a very intelligent lad, we went at a lively pace along a rather rough road, though little to be complained of after that of Malnitz. A week later we might have travelled more smoothly, for gangs of labourers were at work, endeavouring to tame the ruggedness of the way, and at every dangerous corner putting down heavy rails, all in preparation for the Emperor. They were Italians, such as we had seen the day before. As we passed, they stood in rows, bareheaded, on each side of the way, an attention rather distressing to our modesty; and at one spot, where the level of the road was altered, they lifted us and our vehicles bodily over the difficulty with all the good-nature in the world. Nor were the peasantry of the valley less courteous in their way—a fact which, after Goldsmith's disparaging line, we feel bound to mention.

Rounded hills composed, for some distance, the near landscape: and the principal feature was the singular Carinthian pine, which has no lateral branches,* or rather such short ones that they form only a fringe to the stem; and the appearance of the woods at a distance is almost that of a hop-garden. Neat villages and numerous waterfalls enlivened the scene, and glimpses of rocky summits on the left, rising behind the woods and pastures, gave tokens of a fine mountain range. It is that which, descending from the Noric Alps southward, here divides Carinthia from Tyrol.

The drive to Heiligenblut, at the head of the valley, occupied nearly four hours, over a distance of about sixteen miles; and not till two-thirds of this were passed could we obtain a sight of the Gross Glockner: then,

* So we believed, in accordance with Mr. Murray and other authorities at the time the above was written; but upon subsequent enquiry among the peasants, we found that the tree is no distinct variety, but owes its peculiarity to the practice of lopping the branches every five years. The object is to provide winter bedding for the cattle.

just before a steep ascent, the white cone stood out, pure and dazzling, against a dark-blue sky. A little later, and the spectacle was complete—one to which we always recur as among the most beautiful and striking in our alpine panorama. The pointed summit, as it here presents itself, perfectly answers to the ideal of a snow mountain. Towards the base it expands gracefully into that semblance of a bell which has suggested its appellation, and at its foot nestles the singular little village of Heiligenblut. This, a meagre hamlet in itself of red-brown châlets, shoving shoulders together as if for protection from the cold of winter, possesses a remarkable feature in its church, which, placed apart on a small circular terrace, or bastion, outside the village, looks, from a distance, with its high-roofed apse, narrow windows, and tall spire, like a mediæval model set out to view—such an one as a pictured saint is sometimes seen carrying under his arm, his mantle gathered up beneath it.

The shrine is celebrated for containing a phial of the holy blood, whence the village takes its name. It was brought from Constantinople more than a thousand years ago; and of course there is an accompanying legend, which I was amused to hear an honest Tyrolean repeating in the year of grace, 1862, to a passenger in the train between Augsburgh and Munich. I caught only the commencement; but a legend must surely be on its last legs when it gets upon the rail.

As collected from a more authentic source,* not very accessible to English readers, the story runs thus:—A certain Dane, of the name of Briccius, having, like many other northmen, betaken himself to the Byzantine Court, became distinguished in the service of the Emperor Leo,

* *Der Führer durch Kärnten*, von Wagner und Dr. Hartmann. Klagenfurt, 1861.

no less for valour and ability in war than for his unusually pious life. After many years, an unappeasable desire to see his native land arose in his mind; and he besought permission to return to Denmark, that he might introduce Christianity among the heathen. The request was granted, and some parting token of the personal friendship of the Emperor offered for his acceptance. This he prayed might be a few drops of that sacred blood once shed upon the cross, and now preserved as the venerated treasure of the Church of St. Sophia in Constantinople.

With difficulty he obtained the precious drops, and departed on the long journey to his home, clothed in pilgrim guise. Landed in Italy, he passed over the Julian Alps on his way to the Noric. On foot, and alone, a stormy night of snow overtook the unfortunate man in the neighbourhood of Heiligenblut; and there he met his death. Ere long, three ears of corn in flower on the spot where he lay beneath the snow betrayed the body to some peasant miners, who found a writing in his bosom explaining his name and errand. Thereupon, with all reverence, a yoke of oxen was employed to draw the body to a place of burial. On reaching the other side of the Möll, however, the beasts suddenly halted, and could be urged no farther. The intimation was obeyed, and the corpse interred upon the spot; the people appropriating the parchment and a ring.

After a few days, it was noticed that one foot of the dead body had started out of the grave-mound. On examination, under a bandage and enclosed in a deep flesh wound was found a small greenish bottle, containing a few drops of dark liquid; it was forthwith detached, and the corpse again committed to the earth. The singular circumstance reached the ears of the Archbishop of Salzburg, who, applying to the Patriarch of Constantinople, learnt the true value of the discovery. For many hundred years the little chapel originally built over the grave of Briccius remained extant, and tradition affirms that it was long the only, as it was the earliest, place of Christian worship in the neighbourhood. The present fine Gothic church dates from the year 1443, and is now the great boast of the solitary village.

So far the story, which is not without its touches of nature and suggestions of truth. The whole scene is alpine as well as mediæval. The track of the pilgrim is a likely one, for over this portion of the Alps several ancient roads are known to have crossed. The incident of perishing in the snow is too familiar to every inhabitant of these valleys; oxen are still the beasts of burden there, and the protruding foot might well occur under the violence of alpine storms, which so rapidly denude the soil. The bottle under the bandage is appropriate to the time when a precious treasure might be more safely carried by means of such a device, and its insertion in a deep flesh wound is not without parallel as an act of penance. Let the old legend live, then, and shed its gleam of light upon a distant age.

What is now to be seen is this:—On the left of the high altar is a pyramidal pillar, above forty feet in height, reaching to the roof of the church. It consists of three portions—marble, gypsum, and wood respectively. Within is a costly pyx, which protects, by means of several doors, one within another, the Holy Blood, contained in a little, broad-shaped, greenish bottle, about an inch and a half long.

Almost in the middle of the church is the descent into the crypt, which is supported by two pillars. Here is the tomb of Briccius. It is in the form of a coffin, with an altar-like elevation at the head, and supports a wooden figure representing the saint. At an earlier period this effigy must have been frequently renewed, as numberless fragments were carried away by pilgrims; at present, a trellis-work protects it from further mutilation. In the year 1724, by the authority of the Pope, the tomb was opened; it revealed the limbs of a man of middle height, and in his prime, for not a single tooth was wanting to the skull.

The grand glacier of Pasterze is not in sight from the village. Churchill reached its foot whilst I sketched this Austrian Chamounix, as it is called. We devoted but a single day to its grandeurs, and must not be detained by them here. At the time of our visit the place was known to but few English tourists; now every year adds to their number. Charnock, in his 'Guide to the Tyrol,' quotes from the stranger's book in the homely inn (which will soon flaunt into an hotel), how 'John Smith' already patronises it, and how 'Sir John and Lady'—somebody condescend to state that they 'were perfectly satisfied with the scenery.' In the last volume of the Alpine Club there is an account of an ascent of the Gross Glockner, which does not represent it as particularly difficult.

Returning to Winklern in the evening, we found our elegant hostess receiving the coppers from what might be called the ale-house bench at the door. Not the less a lady for all that, and we admired the simplicity of manners it betokened. A fortnight later she entertained the Emperor and Empress on their way from Heiligenblut to Klagenfurt. It was not, however, till the next day that all the singularity of this establishment was explained. After a cordial farewell to both master and mistress, we were slowly ascending the hill behind the house on our way to Lienz, and conning the items of a bill so exceedingly modest in amount that we almost thought ourselves bound to return to have it corrected, when a passage in Murray, which had hitherto escaped us, let in unexpected light:—'The inn at Winklern is kept by a wealthy Chevalier, whose most moderate charge of one florin per diem includes everything.' Here was an explanation! We had, in fact, been almost on the footing of guests, and were heartily vexed not to have known it sooner. All we could do now was to feel much obliged to Chevalier Aichenegg of Winklern, and to dub him henceforth *par excellence* 'The Boor of Carinthia,' who, as far as our pen can serve, must redeem his country from the imputation of the poet. Let the reader remember, however, the date of our visit before he packs his portmanteau for the residence of the Chevalier. He may be dead and gone by this time, or Sir John and his lady have frightened him out of his wits. For aught we know, the inn may now be only an inn: all its romance departed.

I hope it is understood that the hill we were now climbing was to show us the Dolomites, and then our excitement as we toiled through the woods, and approached the open pastures which form the summit, will be properly appreciated. S—— and A—— had occupied at first a small hay-cart, something like those of Malnitz; but as the track, winding amongst roots of trees and stones, was also too much like that of Malnitz, they were soon glad to join us on foot. It is but a low ridge which here separates the valley of the Möll from that of the Drave, and at the same time divides at this point Carinthia from Tyrol. Upon the summit are traces of a Roman road, the same, no doubt, tha poor Briccius trod. Murray, in his scattered and brief notices of this district, mentions 'the magnificent views of the singular Dolomite mountains on the other side of the Drave, which it commands,' and I quote the passage to justify our anticipations. Had we recollected it sooner, we should have been less surprised at what we saw on the Sunday evening. Now, as each step lifted us higher, we were on the tip-toe of expectation; nor were we disappointed. A perfect clearness of atmosphere carried the eye to the utmost limit of the horizon, which, south and south-west, was studded with peaks. The full effect, however, was not disclosed till, descending a little from the first burst of view, the valley of the Drave opened at our feet, a flat and narrow plain, in the soft beauty of distance, and, rising from it, the grand Dolomitic precipices, jagged, splintered, riven, dark in the shadow of noon, and filling the prospect like a wall. The highest eastern summits of the series, exceeding 9,000 feet in height, bear the appropriate title of the Wizard—'Unholde.' I could not sketch them then; five years afterwards, from an inferior point, and on a less favourable day, the view here given was obtained, which represents but a small portion of this striking scene, and misses that flatness of the valley which gave so much effect to the abruptly rising mountain wall beyond. This flatness is a characteristic particularly continental, for our valleys are generally basin-shaped; yet nowhere on the continent, I think, is the opposition between the horizontal and the perpendicular more finely shown than in this view from the Iselsberg.

In the sketch appended, the Drave is visible, a white line along the valley, and the thin forms of the so-called Carinthian pine are conspicuous in the middle distance.

The descent, through luxuriant orchards and by craggy paths, was charming. It was a Paradise of Pomona basking in the autumn sun. At the village of Dölsach we touched the plain, and S—— and A——, remounting the cart, were spirited away through fields of maize and bright irrigated grass towards Lienz, the first town in Tyrol, of which the towers had been for some time visible at the head of the valley. It is closed in there by mountain masses; the Drave falls into it from a ravine to the south,

LIENZ DOLOMITES.

and the Isel descends through an upland valley from the north-west: near the junction of the rivers stands the town.

Following our wives, who had vanished in dust along the high road, we had a hot walk of five miles. After crossing a picturesque bridge over the frightfully rapid Isel, and passing the gateway of the town-house, we entered the broad street, which might answer for a 'platz,' and found S—— and A—— seated on a bench outside the 'Post;' as it was not the inn we had selected, they would not compromise us by entering, and kept their seats, while all the windows filled with gazers. We were soon satisfied, however, that it would be comfortable, and its good-natured, honest landlord proved the best of fellows.

Here we had entered Tyrol, so that this visit to Carinthia had occupied but three days, and shown us only a corner of the country. We shall have much more to say of it in the sequel. Its fine scenery, secluded valleys, unsophisticated manners, and cheap quarters, no less than the Dolomites dispersed on its borders, have tempted us there during three successive years; following, in this respect, the example of that excellent judge of landscape, Sir Humphry Davy, who, as his journals show, was continually returning to this and the adjoining province of Carniola.

Of Lienz, which upon one of these occasions we visited again, it is not necessary to say more than to confirm the description of it as 'occupying one of the most charming situations in all Tyrol.' It cannot fail of this, when that situation comprises the majesty of the Dolomite mountains on the one side, the beauty of verdure-covered hills on the other, the junction of two such streams as the Isel and the Drave, and the commencement of the noble valley to which the latter gives its name; while villages and castles are sprinkled over every wood-crested height. To one of these castles, that of Gorz, commanding the town, we directed an evening stroll, and enjoyed the perfection of its prospect. It belongs to the Counts of Gorz, but is held at the present time by that well-known personage, Sir John Barleycorn—it is only a brewery! Lienz was a Roman station; a Roman road, which we afterwards explored at the point where it crosses the Carnic Alps, proceeded hence to Aquileia on the Adriatic. At the present time the town appears to contain nothing particularly remarkable. Its population is only 2,000; but it left an impression of quiet cheerfulness upon our minds which a second visit did not dispel.

Perhaps it owed some of its agreeableness to the good

landlord of the 'Post;' he took a friendly interest in our welfare, though an unfortunate lisp added greatly to the difficulties of conversation. We were discussing with him the means of reaching Botzen, and half his speech seemed to consist of the word 'Ponicken,' which was sufficiently puzzling, till a casual touch of his finger on the map showed that he was all the while speaking of Brunecken, the best place at which to divide the journey. Of course, posting was the plan which, to a postmaster, was most feasible; but he readily yielded to our preference for a Lohnkutscher, or voiturier, and recommended a neighbour of the name of Amman.

We could not meet with this man in the afternoon, but his wife promised him for the evening, and the attendance also of some French-speaking individual to assist in the arrangement. By natural consequence, when we returned from our walk we found half the town assembled at Amman's door, and the negotiation had the advantage of being carried on in at least four languages at once — German, French, Italian, and English — resulting, in due time, in Amman's engagement to convey the four 'Engländer' in two days to Botzen.

I must pass rapidly over this journey, since portions of it are retraced in later pages, and my object of introducing the Dolomites is nearly accomplished. We had received one ineffaceable impression of their grandeur, and though in the route to Botzen through the Puster Thal, and down the Brenner road, we coasted round the district that enclosed them, it is at very few points that they show themselves to advantage.

The road into the Puster Thal from Lienz ascends, at first, through the ravine by which the Drave enters upon the level valley, and here the bases of the Lienz Dolomites rise grandly, forest-clothed, on the left, though the traveller is too near, and too much below them, to see their peculiar turreted tops.

Further on, at Sillian, the valley becomes open, and might be called bleak, were it not for the bright corn crops and cheerful villages. It is in fact the watershed, crossing which we lose the Drave, and begin, a little beyond Innichen, to descend into the long valley of the Pusterthal. Here again Dolomite shapes showed themselves over the nearer hills on the south. One in particular rose, crowned with pinnacles, a most imperial presence; we named it the 'Diadem.' Still no opening in the hills occurred to satisfy our curiosity, until, at Toblach, the pass of Ampezzo broke through them, and then the gloomy gateway of precipices only excited it the more. It was the direct road, not only to Venice, always an enticing vision, but through the heart of the Dolomites. How tantalizing to leave it unexplored! Since then we have done it ample justice, and all its secrets are ours.

At Niederndorf we dined, and there the spiked forms of Dolomite, guarding the Ampezzo, still stood out to view. It must have been to these principally that Sir Humphry Davy referred in his journals of travel in 1819: '*June 20th.* Below Brunecken a magnificent chain of mountains is seen on the south, or Italian side, and accompanied my view all the way to Sillian. These mountains appear to be of granite, and excessively bold and precipitous —very like the needles in the Valley of Chamounix, and bearing almost the same relation to snow, which lay in immense masses, even at their juncture with the pine-covered hills.'

It is singular that he should have supposed them granite: Dolomite was evidently unknown to him; but he might have recognised their limestone character. Snow we did not see; but the difference between August and June might account for this.

Tyrol is a pleasant country for its roadside inns: spacious, cool, and clean, they welcome the traveller with old-fashioned hospitality. On the large upper landing, upon which the bedrooms open, they usually spread your table, if you are 'quality.' Flowers in pots adorn the wooden balconies; and the landlord's daughter will present you with pretty bouquets when you leave—a finishing touch to the little bill, which is hardly a bill at all in any sense: it is chalked on the table in items so small as to convince you these people possess every virtue under heaven. The mid-day halts of the voiturier give many pleasant experiences of this sort; and when you stop for the night, the best bedrooms, even at unlikely places, are as comfortable as need be—beautifully kept, and without any of that frowzy look so common in an English inn. The furniture is often walnut-wood; neatly framed prints are on the walls, and crimson coverlets on the beds. But the Tyrolese country inn, in its charming and kindly simplicity, will probably not long survive. It is already disappearing on the principal routes, where English tourists indulge in the 'bounce' peculiar to their nation, and shout 'Garçon' to the modest, self-respecting Kellnerin. To accommodate such tastes hotels spring up, and the real 'Garçon' is provided.

Such an inn as those I have described was the one at Niederndorf; and after a tedious and dusty afternoon drive, always descending this long Pusterthal, such another we occupied for the night at Brunecken. Here again the attraction of the Dolomites was strong upon us, for the Gader Thal, one of the great inlets to their recesses, opens on the south. In connection with Val Fassa beyond, and the lateral valley of Gröden, it is the only route given in Murray for exploring these mountains, though, as we afterwards discovered, by far the least interesting. I believe we were ungenerous enough to accuse our wives of preventing the exploration of the Gader Thal at that time, on the ground of their discontent at Ober-Villach, and the expectation of still worse accommodation in the valleys in question. In view of their late achievements, we beg to render them our humble apologies.

It was again a beautiful evening, and the views from the old Castle of Brunecken, rising steeply above the pleasant little town, which with its quaint towers abuts upon the swift river Rienz, were rich in beauty, and lustrous in the mellow light. The Valley of Taufers, joining the main valley from the north, affords a fine vista towards the central Tyrolean chain, and renders the situation commanding as well as beautiful. Remote as it is, it has its place in European history. When Charles the Fifth fled disastrously from Innsbruck, where he was so nearly surprised by Prince Maurice, his first refuge and resting-place, after crossing the Brenner, was this Castle of Brunecken, which thus became for a brief space the centre of authority for almost half the world. Was it on such an evening as this that the gouty old Emperor was carried in his litter up the castle hill? or was it by night and torchlight that they bore him groaning through the gateway?

Amman, our driver, was the politest of coachmen. His carriage was not very roomy, and his horses not very sleek; but they went at a good pace, and their master appeared along the road in the light of a gentleman conducting a party of friends. We were quite on an agreeable footing by the time we started on our second day's journey; yet I fear our company proved a snare to our good friend's conscience. We had observed that, unlike the Carinthian drivers, he took no notice of the numerous religious effigies we passed on the way; or, if he did, it was skilfully disguised under pretence of settling his hat more comfortably. We have noticed this shyness in our presence on other occasions, and always with regret: if the faith be there, it is better it should be expressed; and we should regret being thought capable of turning it into ridicule. A little incident gave us some insight into what was going on in Amman's mind. In the course of the morning one of his horses stumbled and cut his knee badly. Amman passed it off lightly, but from that moment paid marked respect to every crucifix and picture. No doubt he attributed the misfortune to his previous neglect, and felt, perhaps, that his four Protestants had brought him no good.

The frequency of these religious memorials in Tyrol produces a favourable impression as to the piety of the people; but it is a complicated question; and when they are adduced as implying a deeper religious sentiment than exists among our own Protestant population, I think we may demur. Let the traveller consider how soon he ceases to be himself affected by these representations, supposing him to have been at first considerably impressed by them, and must not this be still more the case with those who live among them?

In a village near the Stelvio, you will see a life-size figure of our Saviour under a canopy in the street. From the wounded side flows a stream of water, at which the women fill their pails all day long. That sacred symbol thus serves the purposes of a common pump! We cannot suppose that the truth intended to be taught is hereby brought nearer to daily life. It is an extreme instance; but, like the pious phrases which from some lips come so frequently and glibly that their import is clearly forgotten, it illustrates the dangers of familiarity. Still more to be borne in mind, in estimating the real value of these things, is the 'Fetish' character which so soon attaches to a sacred object. Though that figure may long have ceased to teach its lesson or to awaken emotion, its removal would no doubt be regarded as a great calamity by the village. It has become the Palladium, the mysterious guardian of the place. To sink the thought in the thing is too common to human nature everywhere.

Yet Tyrol is a religious country. A more striking circumstance than the abundance of its sacred memorials is the morning and evening litany, in which every household joins. The motley establishment of the large inns assemble thus regularly for prayers, and may be seen on their knees, men and women opposite to each other, in the common hall; and in the gloaming the deep-toned recitation is heard from under every cottage roof. At Sterzing, which, as a convenient halting-place at the foot of the Brenner, is composed almost entirely of inns, and where, on a subsequent occasion, we spent a night, not a wagoner or loiterer was left in the street by seven o'clock in the evening; and from every inn-door came a low thunder of responses. All honour to simple and pious Tyrol!

Our horse's broken knee, which delayed us a little at the next village, has delayed also our narrative. We are at last coming to the end of the Pusterthal, which, upon the whole, is not remarkable for landscape beauty, or beauty of any kind; for the women disfigure themselves by the most astonishing head-dress anywhere to be seen—more like a beehive than anything else—large woollen contrivances, appropriate rather to Esquimaux. The valley contracts to a gorge as it approaches the great Eisach Thal, into which it enters at right angles. Whenever you come to such a gorge in Tyrol, you may be sure that some scene of the famous year Nine was enacted there: so it was here, and a ruined castle across the road marks the spot of one of the severest struggles with the invading French.

Emerging from this, an open hilly space is reached. To the right is seen the deep and wooded entrance to the gorge of Mittewald, up which passes the Brenner road to Innsbruck. The white lines of an Austrian fortress—the Franzens Feste—show that it is one of the gates of Germany. Down on the left is the continuation of the same road southwards to Brixen and Botzen. This was our route. Having through the Pusterthal skirted the northern side of the Dolomite region, now, in turning southward, we were to skirt its western border. At Brixen, an old cathedral city, surrounded by vineyards and gardens, we rested for an hour or two. Below, the valley of the Eisach becomes continually grander in its features and richer in its vegetation: the whole is more or less of a ravine. After passing Klausen, a narrow street pushed close to the side of the rushing stream, the Gröden Thal, already mentioned, opens on the left, but at too great an elevation to disclose its scenery, which, as we have said, is remarkable for its Dolomites, and especially for one transcendent peak, the Lang Kofel, whose name the reader must impress upon his mind. We scrutinised every opening in that direction, but in vain: a screen of porphyry hides the Dolomites from view, and that is why ordinary tourists know so little of them.

The approach to Botzen in the evening was scarcely less than superb. There the porphyry rocks rise dark and red, yet clothed with the softest, richest foliage. Below them, vines trail over every shelf and terrace, filling the bottom of the valley. At a point where four valleys converge, and thence descend in one broad trough to

Italy, stands Botzen, distinguished by the bright green roof and red towers of its cathedral: the tinge of porphyry is upon everything, making gorgeous colour in the afternoon. Here you find symptoms of the south. Italian accents catch the ear; Italian heavily arcaded streets arrest the eye; campanile towers are set out on every knoll of the rich landscape; frescoes tint the walls; and from the roadside shrines the terrible or tragic in art is banished. Graceful Madonnas, or full-robed saints, supersede souls in agony or the horrors of the road to Calvary,* while even in the crucifixes resignation takes the place of mere physical suffering. A softness seems to prevail over both art and nature.

Yet this softness is not luxurious. Botzen may put in its claim beside Innsbruck and Salzburg for the striking character of its landscape; and I have reserved mention to the last of its most remarkable feature. From the windows of the 'Kaiser Krone,' or from beyond the bridge on the Meran road, or better still, from one of the eminences at the foot of the Mendola, you will see, looking eastward by evening light, spires and towers of Dolomite overtopping everything, and illuminated when all else is dark. It is a sight both beautiful and mysterious. They rise with such lofty independence of the surrounding scenery, are shattered into shapes so strange, cut the sky with such sharpness of outline, and gleam with so unearthly a light, that you are riveted by the spectacle. You cannot but long to explore those fastnesses, and touch the bases of those awful walls. That Val Fassa, which lies behind them, how wild and solemn it must be! What a fearful place to live in! To these imaginings the actual Val Fassa does not answer, as it will be our task

* Since this time the stations of the Calvary have been repainted, and in a coarser style.

to show, but such is the impression that glimpse of its bulwarks must produce.

Those Dolomites are the 'Rosen Garten'—the Rose Garden!—a name you would never associate with their almost ghastly aspect. The flush of sunset may, indeed, for a moment suggest it in its rosy tint; but that passes and leaves them stark and cold. The 'garden,' if there be one, lies on the further side, where the slopes of Val Fassa, at the foot of the precipices, are in their season a mass of rhododendrom bloom; but that is a secret of the vale I ought not yet to disclose, and a far more romantic origin is assigned for that singular name.

Amman drove us, not to the 'Kaiser Krone'—an excellent inn of the hotel class—but to 'Der Mondschein.' Surely the German mind must have been strangely confused when it reversed the sexes of the heavenly bodies, and called the moon a man! This 'Moonshine' is in a narrow street, and certainly possesses more character in its interior than its modern rival. On the landing between the doors of our bedrooms, a life-size figure of the Saviour on the cross, sculptured in wood and coloured, looked startling enough at dark under the gleam of a single lamp, and gave it the air of a convent cloister. But there was not conventual silence. The heavy traffic of the Brenner was continually passing through the street; wagons, with a dozen horses apiece, were arriving or departing all the night through, and diligences with their lamps—effectual disturbers of sleep.

In the morning Amman came to take leave, and begged to see the ladies, who happened to be in their rooms. To each of them, as they appeared, he dropped on one knee, and taking a hand put it to his lips with all the grace of a cavalier. It was the last touch of romance in our journey. We were now on the beaten track. The day but one after our arrival we left Botzen by the early diligence for Meran, and as we turned up the valley of the Etsch the Dolomites passed out of sight—not out of mind.

Five years elapsed before we saw them again together: and meanwhile the Alps of Piedmont, the Pyrenees, and the bleak hills of Sutherland occupied our summers. In 1858 my wife and I took the Ampezzo road, on our way from Venice to Innsbruck, and as we passed through Cadore, Cortina, and Landro, saw enough to sustain the interest in these strange mountains which had been so strongly roused. In 1860, Churchill made them the special object of a brief solitary tour, and he now takes the pen to tell how he fared.

AN EXCURSION TO VAL FASSA

In 1860

BY G. C. CHURCHILL, F.G.S.

CHAPTER III.

THE BOTZEN DOLOMITES.

Approach to Botzen — The First Dolomite — Ratzes Bath-House — The Seisser Alp and its rim of Dolomites — Hauenstein Castle and Oswald the Minnesinger — A Legend — The Porphyry Plateau in Roman and Mediæval Times — The Hay-Bath — Pass of the Duron Thal to Campitello — Village Art — The Marmolata — Excursion to the Fedaia — Vigo — The Rosengarten — View from the Ridge of Monzoni — The Volcanic Theory — The Karneid Thal, and Legend of the Karneid Schloss — Return to Botzen.

THE Dolomite district of South Tyrol is complicated in its construction, but the general direction of its main valleys is from north-east to south-west. It is penetrated by one remarkable valley from the south-west, near Trent, for nearly eighty miles. This is usually known in its upper part as the Fassa Thal, in its middle portion as the Fleims Thal, and in its lower section as the Cembra or Zimmers Thal. The river Avisio traverses its entire length, and falls into the Etsch or Adige at Lavis, a little above Trent. Nearly meeting this valley from the north is the Gader Thal, and the same point is also closely approached from the west by a short valley named the Gröden Thal. The space lying between the heads of these valleys is a mountain knot or plateau, and the routes given in Murray for visiting the scenery of the Dolomites are almost entirely concerned with this one spot and its approaches. Another valley, however, on the eastern side of the district, is quite as important for access to the Dolomites as the Fassa. Ascending from the neighbourhood of Belluno, and trending north-west, it leads at last to the base of the same mountain knot. In its lower course it is called the Val Agordo; in its upper, the Livinallongo, or from the name of its stream, the Cordevole; both portions exhibit some of the finest Dolomite scenery. Then, still more to the east, is the valley of Ampezzo, affording the only carriage road. Cortina on this route, and Botzen on that of the Brenner, are the two most convenient points of departure for the Dolomites, if the object be to cross the country, and see the finest portions of the Fassa and Agordo valleys in the shortest time. Geographically, the three valleys, the Fassa, the Agordo, and the Ampezzo, may be called the main arteries of the Dolomite system.

Connected with the above-mentioned plateau, are some of the best-known Dolomite mountains. The Hohe Schlern stands on its western border, near Botzen; the Lang Kofel, and the Sella Spitze are not far behind, and near them, to the south-east, separated only by the Val Fassa, is the Marmolata. In other parts of the Dolomite district, however, there are mountains, as we shall show, quite as deserving of a reputation.

In the season of 1860, circumstances prevented the formation of our usual travelling party, and I was the only member at liberty to proceed to the Dolomite region, which, after the long interval referred to in the last chapter, we had fixed upon as the next object of our tours. As at this time the only available information dealt principally with the western group of Dolomites, and the valleys connected with it, I naturally selected Botzen, at the foot of the Brenner, as the point of departure, and the head of the Val Fassa as my first object. Wet weather and other hindrances narrowed the visit to the short period of a few days, and I scarcely went farther than the threshold of the district. What I saw and learnt about it I will now submit to the reader.

On Wednesday, August 16, I took the train from Verona to Botzen, up that long deep trough, which, penetrating almost to the foot of the Central Alps, has admitted to a greater degree than any other inlet of the southern range the influence of Italian speech and manners. Here Longobards, and after them Venetians, from the south, have contended with Franks, Bavarians, and Germans, from the north; of which conflict of races there is still the memorial in the villages of Mezzo Lombardo (Welschmetz) and Mezzo Tedesco (Deutschmetz) posted over against each other as mutual spies at the mouth of the Val di Non, and in the presence of the figure of a Venetian general in the Cathedral of Trent. The southern end of the trough presents to the traveller, in rich and varied combination, the bosses, scars, ridges, and peaks of limestone scenery. One isolated lofty summit, near Mori, brought especially into remembrance the fine outline of the Aiguille de Varens, as seen from St. Gervais. The upper half of the great valley introduced me to the western wall of that porphyry plateau from the surface of which, as I knew, but away to the right and invisible, rose up the Dolomite peaks that formed the object of my journey. Coming nearer to Botzen, a little above Neumarkt, the eye is caught by a striking and sudden contrast between the forms of mountain and plain, in the Mittelberg, a long and narrow mountain island in the midst of the level valley, running parallel to its main direction, and rising nearly 1,000 feet above it. Whatever functions it may fulfil in the general economy of the Botzen district, it does at least serve to intensify the effect of the rich porphyry amphitheatre in which Botzen is placed.

On the evening of the following day, a walk along the porphyry slopes on the south side of the impetuous Eisach displayed the range of Dolomite peaks, some twenty miles distant, which we had seen so finely from Botzen in 1856, and brought also prominently to view the Hohe Schlern, whose nearer acquaintance I expected to make on the morrow. The effect of these bare pinnacles and walls was much enhanced by the rich grassy promontories of the porphyry plateau, each with its shining little village, which, forming the middle distance, stood out in relief against them.

After a night made sleepless by the quarter-hour clang of the cathedral bells close to my window, I was thoroughly aroused at four o'clock by the simultaneous discharge of the whole peal, and the booming of thirty-one cannon in honour of the Kaiser's birthday. Looking out of the window, Venus and other stars were shining brilliantly above the dark Dolomite line, and I hastened to join the Eilwagen, which left for Brixen punctually at five o'clock. But Brixen was not my destination; the journey in the Eilwagen terminated at Atzwang, fourteen miles from Botzen. This is a small roadside station in the heart of the gorge of the Old 'Kunter's Weg,' * with space but for road and stream, and where the steeply rising porphyry slopes on either hand are richly fringed with patches of vine, wood, pasture, corn, and orchard. It is famous for its good red wine.

Vigo, in the Fassa Thal, appeared more accessible from this direction than by the circuitous route through Neumarkt and Cavalese. The map indicates a course more direct than either—from Botzen to Vigo, up the valley of the Karneid to its origin at the foot of the Caressa Pass. But I could not learn anything in Botzen of its practica-

* The road between Botzen and Kollmann is so named, having been constructed through the gorge at the side of the Eisach by Heinrich Kunter, a citizen of Botzen, about the year 1314. Before this, and in the Roman period, the road traversed the plateau of Seiss and Castelruth, descending to the stream at the entrance of the Gröden Thal.

bility, and the alternative presented, therefore, was either that of visiting the Dolomites of the plateau, or Seisser Alp, in the first instance, and thence descending to the more southern groups, or reversing this course. I chose the former plan.

A horse being provided for my *impedimenta,* I was soon mounting the slope, breathing the crisp air, and at each turn of the ascent gaining wider and wider sweeps of view over the opposite Ritten plateau, and the villas of the wealthy burghers of Botzen. One of the villages on that side, Lengmoos, is remarkable for its earth-pyramids, consisting of red porphyry mud, with sharply angular fragments of granite and mica slate imbedded—the remains of a lateral moraine of the great Eisach Glacier, and left stranded there on its retreat at the termination of the Glacial period.

The occasional distant booming of cannon indicated that the day's festivities below were proceeding. At last the Alp plateau was reached, and in a moment the Hohe Schlern fronted me high in air, looming big, black, and solid, a thin cloud girthing its middle. This was its western face, and I had to skirt the northern side to reach a deeply lying narrow ravine, that separates its eastern precipices from the second and higher plateau of the Seisser Alp. The level summit of the Schlern itself forms the third and highest plateau of all, standing aloft and isolated, for it is connected with its nearest neighbours in the rear—the Mittagskogel and Rosszähn Berg—only by long and narrow isthmuses. Its massive and unbroken form from this point appeared to be relieved by but one isolated pinnacle at the northern end, whose roots lay hid in the dark pine forests that clung to the base of the mountain; soon, however, other pinnacles from behind their companion stood boldly out to view. A young girl, who was on her return from an errand to her Botzen home, here left me to rejoin her parents and an invalid sister, at a snug-looking cottage, which she pointed out up the slopes at the base of the Schlern. This fresh and smiling Alp must be indeed a fit place of invalid retreat from the summer heats of a town situated in a basin so hot as that of Botzen. Coasting round, I left the prettily nestled village of Seiss in the distance to the left, and entering the gorge, and winding up a steep and devious track through the thick woods, suddenly came to the edge of a small clearing, opening to my expectant view the white walls and green shutters of the little Bad and Gasthaus of Ratzes, 4,120 feet above the sea.

The establishment consists of two small buildings, united by a tiny chapel, where a friar of the Franciscan monastery of Botzen leads the devotions of the guests and household, morning and evening. A covered balcony, running along on the level of the first floor in front of this chapel, and connecting the salle with the bedrooms, is a convenient lounge for patients in wet weather. The ground-floor is principally occupied with bath-rooms, and gives forth various splashing sounds at intervals during the day. The rooms are very small and gloomy, and the bedrooms equally spare of space and of furniture. Yet the salle is cheerful. Its windows, directed to the four points of the compass, yield variety of prospect, either towards the dark fork of the gorge, sprinkled in its sheltered upper nooks of rock with snow; or at the Schlern close opposite—so close that one must crane his neck backwards to include the highest crag;—or in the two other directions, to the wooded slopes which complete the seclusion of the retreat. Two springs, one sulphurous and the other iron, issuing from the depths of the gorge, supply the healing waters, carried to their destination in the basement of the building through hollowed pine trunks. Everything about the little spot is plain, simple, and rustic, and the peasant guests—for they are mostly of that class—are equally so. A more quiet corner of the world does not exist. Here man has not yet learnt to contend with nature, and build those 'grand hotels' that surprise the traveller in the recesses of Eaux Chaudes and Eaux Bonnes. Long may the shadow of the giant Schlern fall upon nothing more artificial than this humble roof, concealed among the dark pine masses that fill the base and sides of the gorge!

I joined an early *table d'hôte* at half-past eleven, served in brown earthenware with pewter plates, in preference to waiting for a separate meal, and the remainder of the day was occupied with a stroll in the neighbourhood. Next morning promised fine weather, spite of the everlasting south wind—the great carrier of clouds. Some drying plants having been cared for, I selected the Seisser Alp, rising close above Ratzes, and immediately opposite to the Schlern, for the day's excursion. This Alp, the largest in Tyrol, at an average height of 6,000 feet above the sea, is the plateau so often mentioned as the central point of interest for the western Dolomites.

A winding track up steep pasture and corn plots, led at last to a narrow, rudely paved road, the means of access to the summit from the village of Seiss. Rough vehicles, half car, half sledge, bring down the hay from the Alp above along this road, and had worn deep rut-lines into its hard and slippery surface. Following them ploddingly for an hour, they were lost finally in the rocky edge of the Alp, and a few steps farther opened out to view its wide-reaching and undulated surface, covered with the richest grass variegated with many flowers, and dotted with numerous hay-châlets. Immediately opposite, about five miles distant to the south-east, rose up grandly out of the green rim of the Alp the Lang Kofel (nearly 10,000 feet),* and its twin brother the Platt Kogel. Their savage isolation, the sharp contrast between their lofty precipice-walls, crowned with jagged peaks and pinnacles, among which a glacier is seen suspended, and the softly swelling green slopes at their feet—giving the spectator the impression of their having been shot up from below in their present form, perfect and complete—impress the eye and fascinate the imagination. Few other peaks, even of that weird family, the Dolomite, can compare with them in this respect. Beyond these, to the left, the walls and ledges of the massive and equally isolated Sella Spitze ran back into the far distance, facing another lofty isolated mass, the Guerdenazza group; and on the right of the Lang Kofel and Platt Kogel the green ridge continued to rise westward, until it merged into the Rosszähn Berg, a line of red rocky teeth which, in turn, were lost in the long crescent curve of the Schlern plateau, now lying behind me. Beyond the green rim, to the south-east, appeared the culminating peak of the whole district, the Marmolata (11,200 feet),† with its flattish snowy dome, ending in a sheer precipice on its southern side, and running into long glacier slopes on the northern. To the north, the high grassy mound of the Puflatsch Alp, a continuation of the Seisser Alp, prevented all view beyond itself; but the whole interval between it and the Schlern to the south-west allowed the distant horizon to be visible, and the entire quadrant was fille up with the snow-fields and peaks of the Adamello, the Oertler, the Œtzthal, and the Stubay groups. To the north-east a depression in the Alp, ending in a deep ravine that carries off some of its plentiful surface-water

* 9,955 feet above the sea, according to Trinker.

† Its higher and more western peak has been lately determined to be 11,465 feet above the sea.

into the Gröden Thal, let in, as in a brilliant green setting, another equally noble view of snow-peaks. These formed part of the Noric chain. The whole day was spent in wandering over these delightful slopes, enjoying the keen fresh air, the variety of plant life, and the grandeur of the mountain forms, until dusk compelled me to slip rapidly down to the lower plateau, and seek in the depths of the woods for the little 'Bad.'

In the Speisesaal dancing was the order of the evening. The old folks were set behind the long tables all round the room, and young couples were whirling in waltzes to the music of a guitar and Jew's harp, dancing with spirit, and keeping capital time. I took a vacant corner, and watched the merriment. There was a great deal of laughing and talking, and, no doubt, a due share of flirtation. The Kellnerin enjoyed her dance with the rest, snatching a moment at intervals, to supply the courses for my supper as they were required.

The next day, as the Schlern which I wished to ascend was concealed in clouds, I resolved to explore the lines of débris near the wild gorge, cutting deeply in between the noble pinnacles already noticed. The return path led me past the ruins of an old castle—the Castle of Hauenstein—that formerly occupied a huge block of dolomite which had fallen from the mountain. Within its walls once lived a man renowned in his day as knight and Minnesinger. Entering its broken towers was like putting on the spectacles of history, and peering into the remote past of the middle ages. I never thought to experience a personal interest in any of the Minnesingers, yet here I found myself upon ground trodden by one of them year after year, and looking down on the same dark green pine woods and smiling hamlets that formed his prospect from these castle walls. The following narrative, condensed from an account of Botzen and its neighbourhood, embraces the principal events of his varied history.*

The poet Oswald von Wolkenstein was born in the year 1367, probably at Trostburg, an old castle at the entrance of the Gröden Thal, where lived his mother, Katherine von Villanders, the only daughter and heiress of Ekart II. Being the second son of his parents, he left home at an early age to put in practice that knightly romance which had been the only intellectual food of his childhood. He travelled in company of a Tyrolean troop of horse in the direction of Prussia, where the Teutonic order of knights was carrying on a constant struggle with the heathen Lithuanians and other tribes. Here he remained eight years, and won his spurs. Thence he made a journey into the Crimea, crossed the Black Sea, suffering shipwreck in its stormy waters, and escaping only by clinging to a mast. He then visited Armenia, Persia, and Asia Minor, and was even reduced for several years to serve as a ship's cook at Candia and in the neighbouring islands. Yet, when Sigismund, King of Hungary and Emperor of Germany, with whom he had made acquaintance in Prussia, lost the battle of Nicopolis, in conflict with the Turks, we find Oswald in his company, escaping with difficulty from the slaughter. Towards the year 1400 he returned home to arrange his affairs, and his father having died about this time, the brothers Michael, Oswald, and Leonhard, divided the inheritance. Michael took Trostburg and Wolkenstein (at the head of the Gröden Thal); Oswald, Hauenstein and Castelruth; and Leonhard, goods and money, with which he afterwards bought Aichach, a castle on the porphyry plateau, near the south face of the Schlern. Oswald then appointed a steward over his property, and recommenced his adventures as a volunteer in the wars of that

* 'Die Stadt Bozen und ihre Umgebungen,' von Beda Weber. Botzen, 1849.

period. He served at first under the Emperor Rupert, in Italy, in 1402, and later in Spain, Portugal, England, and in the Rhine country, distinguishing himself especially at the storming of Ceuta, on the African coast, by the Portuguese. On his return home, in the year 1410, he found Tyrol in a disturbed state. The nobility of the Etsch Thal had united together to protect their ancient privileges against the encroachments of Frederick 'of the empty pocket,' Count of Tyrol. Hitherto they had been considered his peers, and had held their possessions immediately from the Emperor, except where some special feudal tie required it to be otherwise. These encroachments gave rise to continual disputes, in which each endeavoured to enforce his rights as he best could. Oswald took the side of the nobility, became the Emperor's steward and man of business, and laboured zealously to get Tyrol out of the hands of the innovating government of the Austrian Archduke, whose deadly hatred he had incurred. The ill success of this prince at the Council of Constance appeared to the Barons of the Etsch to afford a suitable opportunity for completing their designs; but not being properly supported by the Emperor Sigismund, and unprepared for Frederick's unexpected courage and resources under the most difficult circumstances, they were at last, about the year 1426, compelled to acknowledge his superiority, and abandon their pretension to hold their fiefs immediately of the Empire. Oswald, in the contest, was twice taken prisoner, and in danger of losing his head; and it was not till the following year that the Archduke, desirous of preserving to Tyrol its poet, granted him a pardon.

These calamities, which had involved the loss of a great part of his fortune, as well as injury to his health, were connected with domestic experiences of the bitterest kind.

He had in early youth become acquainted with Sabina Jäger, of Tisens, and had fallen madly in love with her. She, beautiful and coquettish, did not, however, reciprocate the affection of the one-eyed poet. It seems that an accident at a carnival in the Castle of Trostburg had deprived him of his right eye by a shot, when only seven years old. Upon his return from a pilgrimage to Jerusalem, where he was made a Knight of the Holy Sepulchre, he found Sabina married to an old man of the name of Hausmann, living at Hall, a town in the lower valley of the Inn, upon whose death she carried on a *liaison* with Frederick at Innsbruck.

The Hauenstein property, which it will be remembered had formed part of Oswald's inheritance, was originally held of the bishops of Brixen, and later of the counts of Tyrol, but had passed from the Hauensteiners, who had died out with Leonhard von Hauenstein, in the year 1307, to the Wolkenstein family. A remnant, however, of the purchase money (6000 florins) had never been paid by the latter; and it was Sabina, the widow, who, as heiress of the Hauensteins, claimed that sum. Her enmity having thus a very substantial basis, she plotted to bring about Oswald's ruin; and enticing him into her power, gave him up to the Archduke Frederick, probably in this manner enforcing payment. This woman became therefore a source of the bitterest trouble, both in early and in maturer years. Yet he was happy in his first marriage, in 1416, with Margaretha of Schwangau; though, after she had borne him his eldest son and heir, afterwards Oswald II., and several other children, she sank into a premature grave. By his second wife, Anna of Embs, he had also several children; but he outlived her, and was left to endure a solitary and joyless old age in this Hauenstein Schloss. Dying in 1445, he was buried at Neustift, near Brixen. There still exists a collection of his poems, which include love-songs (*minnelieder*), and historical and religious pieces. The first will secure him an abiding fame among the poets of the best times of the Minnesingers. They have lately been published by Wagner, at Innsbruck, following the text of three manuscripts, one of which belongs to the Ferdinandeum in Innsbruck, another to the Imperial Library at Vienna, and the third to the present Count of Wolkenstein.

The ruins and the woods in which they stand still belong to the Counts of Wolkenstein, who are descended in a direct line from the poet.

Another interest attaches to these old walls in a ghostly legend, which the authority from whom we quote gathered from the lips of an old dame at Castelruth. This, probably, refers to a period a little later than the poet's time.

A certain knight lived at the Hauenstein Schloss, who, having bound himself to depart for the Holy Land, shut up his young wife within its walls, supplied with provisions for a year, until his promised return at the end of that time. No admission from without—no escaping from within! He then pursued his way through Hungary to Constantinople. The wife, blest with the hope of a first-born, bore her loneliness with courage, and three months later became the mother of a son. Occupied with the cares of nurture, she saw the year about to expire, and the provisions nearly at an end: but the knight came not. Day after day she watched from the tower to see whether deliverance were nigh; but in vain! Hope and strength declined together, and at last she was seen by the villagers leaning over the window-sill dead! The infant and the faithful maiden who had been the companion of her imprisonment shared her hapless fate. Shortly afterwards the knight was observed riding swiftly to the castle, agony depicted on his countenance. He unlocked the fatal door, mounted all too late to his wife's apartment, and, stricken with grief and horror, fell lifeless to the ground by the side of those whom he could not survive. The bodies were all buried in the church of Seiss, not far distant. 'Often since,' said the old dame, 'has the figure of the Frau been seen to wander from her grave to the ruins of the Schloss, and look out of her window towards Seiss, the wind throwing her loosely flowing hair across her pale countenance.'

> A novel now is nothing more
> Than an old castle and a creaking door—
> A distant hovel—
> Clanking of chains — a gallery — a light—
> Old armour — and a phantom all in white —
> And there's a novel!

This description, appropriate enough when Colman wrote, does not, fortunately, apply to the novel of our days; but, if it did, this castle ruin of Hauenstein would evidently supply all the materials enumerated.

The porphyry plateau, upon which Seiss stands, with the red sandstone derived from it that runs along its eastern border at the base of the Puflatsch and the Schlern, gives rise to a most fruitful soil. Its villages and hamlets are very numerous. Seldom in the Alps are so many flourishing human habitations crowded together in so small a space as in that which extends from the Gröden Thal on the north, to Tiers and the Tierser Thal, immediately east of Botzen, on the south. Its fertility must have been known of old, and as the Roman road before the cutting of the Kunter's Weg appears to have led over it to the foot of the Brenner, we may infer, as very probable, that its population during the Roman period also was flourishing and numerous. Several distinct facts tend to this conclusion. Some of the villages are referred by local authority to a Roman origin. Thus Seiss is derived from Susa; Völs, from Velites (Vellis, Velles), as if it had once been a settlement for *light* troops; Prösls, from Præsidium, a garrison; and Castelruth, from Castellum ruptum (Castel Rotto), the ancient name of a castle, which was itself erected upon the ruins of the original one built by the Romans. The castle of Trostburg, too, still the property of the Counts of Wolkenstein, was originally a Roman castle. Some antiquarians go further, and would see in such names as Tagusens, from Taguntum, situated close to the mouth of the Gröden Thal, and Kardaun, from Cardunum, close to Botzen, an indication of Etruscan or of Keltic origin, according to their views of the Etruscan or Keltic derivation of the Rhœtian aborigines.* At Tagusens, near Castelruth, bronze armour, with fragments of swords and lances, have been found; and at Prösls, Lares and coins, with neck and ear ornaments and armlets of Roman workmanship; some of them now preserved in the Ferdinandeum at Innsbruck. In Castelruth the present dialect still retains a common name or two—fossils of a palæozoic period—in the words *madol* for a cheese dairy, *gleir* (glis, glires) for a squirrel, and *vill* for a park or preserve laid down with grass and wood. These indications, in fact, merge into the more general one presented by the existence of a Romansch language in the neighbouring valleys of Gröden and Gader; for we may readily imagine that these flourishing Roman settlements, when attacked by the Bavarians (Bojoarii), who passed southwards through this district on

* A Roman origin may be predicated of many of the villages around Botzen, believed to be as ancient as Botzen itself. Thus in Eppan we may see Appianum; in Augia, Augusta; in Rentsch, Auronzo; in Kaltern, Caldare; in Girlan, Curilanum; in Firmian (Formigar), Formicaria; in Kampill, Campilla; in Maretsch, Murez, from Murazzo; in Ritten, Rittena; in Tirlan, Turilanum; in Pfatten, Vatina; and in Villa, the Latin Villa.

their way over the Brenner, would gradually retreat upon the high lands to the east, and into the recesses of the Gröden and Gader valleys, and there, mixing with the native Rhœtians, give rise, through subsequent isolation, to the peculiarities in language which these valleys present.

After the Roman period, Botzen and its neighbourhood became the seat of a Bavarian Margrave, under the Dukes of Bavaria; and the plateau on which Seiss and Castelruth stand fell into the hands of Bavarian Barons (Edle). Trent was then the northern boundary town of the Longobardic kingdom; and between the two rival races many a conflict was waged in the valley of the Etsch, success variously inclining to either side; but more than once the Longobards succeeded in plundering Botzen, and driving the Bavarians before them up to Klausen. No doubt the district round the Schlern participated in these alternations of fortune; and the old stories of the Heldenbuch, which allude to the 'Grüne Tan' of the dark Hauenstein woods, and describe how the little king 'Laurin the Dwarf,' encompassed and defended in his 'Rosengarten' with so much magic art, was taken prisoner by the Lombard hero, Dietrich of Bern (Verona),—the same hero who afterwards figures in another part of the Heldenbuch as the conqueror of the twelve champions of the Rosengarten of the Burgundian Princess Kriemhild, at Worms, on the Upper Rhine, and in the Nibelungen-Lied appears as a friend of Etzel, King of Hunland (Attila),—may be but the dim and flickering shadows of stirring events to which the ancient Schlern and the thence named Rosengarten Dolomites were witnesses. An old writer relates that the peasants of the Etsch were able to tell many stories of their King Laurin; but now hardly any of these traces of the past remain, except the name of 'Rosengarten,' applied to the Dolomite precipices at the head of the Tierser Thal,. which are so striking a feature in the view from Botzen,* to a part of the Schlern, and to a locality at Gratsch, near the Schloss Tirol, close to Meran.

Antiquity of an older sort, and which human records do not illustrate, has given renown to another locality on this plateau. The limestone and other beds of the Puflatsch Alp immediately overlooking Castelruth, have yielded a rich supply of minerals and fossil shells to the indefatigable search of the priest of St. Michael, a small village to the north-east of Castelruth. Herr Clara is described as a man of few words, and most diligent as a collector. With great tenacity he holds to the resolution of never parting with any object for money, or receiving a present from any person. Yet he is liberal of gifts; and if in this way he often clears out the contents of his cabinet, he is ready with bee-like industry to go again to the mountains and refill his drawers. The Innsbruck Museum possesses a fine collection of mineral treasures, of which he is the donor; and it is through his industry that the geologists of Europe were first made aware of the riches of the Seisser Alp beds, examples of which may now be seen in most of the great European collections. One of the fossil shells of the district, *Posidomya Clarai*, will hand down his name to future generations of palæontologists.

Our little Bad of Ratzes belongs to a quite modern order of things. It became known only in 1715, through the description of a Botzen physician, Anton Abmayr, and has been recommended by the Faculty of Botzen since that date. It is useful both for inflammatory diseases and those that arise from debility. But another and more primitive mode of cure is resorted to during the season in a rough châlet situated on the heights of the Schlern

* Another derivation of this name is locally given, and it is that referred to at page 45.

plateau, not far from the little Alpine chapel of St. Cyprian, and near the source of the Schlern Bach. From forty to eighty men may sometimes be seen crowded within its narrow walls, and so deeply buried in the fresh hay, that nothing but rows of heads are visible. In this moist, warm medium they continue night and day, except during the time necessary for taking food, which is supplied from a neighbouring hut. The violent perspiration thus induced is the means of cure. The hay of the Schlern is esteemed more valuable for this purpose than any other in the district, and is said to be injurious only to patients of consumptive tendency.

But to return from this long digression to my personal narrative. Next day, feeling the behaviour of the Schlern to be doubtful, I abandoned the idea of ascending to its plateau, and engaged a horse and guide for Campitello, in the upper Val Fassa, consoling myself the more readily that I hoped to revisit the district with greater leisure at command the following year. Spite of the changing clouds which mercifully played about the peaks without concealing them, I enjoyed once more the novel aspect of those isolated bergs, aground, as it were, amid the rolling green waves of the Seisser Alp. There was nothing to break or interfere with the long swelling lines, until, in breasting the grassy ridge that runs between the broad white back of the Platt Kogel on the left, and the jagged, ruinous-looking obelisks of the Rosszähne on the right, I came upon huge masses of hard olive-black rock, peeping forth here and there upon the flanks of the gully, and suggesting a comparison with the fossilised remains—skin, flesh, and all—of some mighty mammoth. The geologist, however, will tell us prosaically that they are nothing more than veins of augite porphyry, which, on this ridge, break through the volcanic ash of which the uppermost layers of the Seisser Alp are composed. And yet there is poetry even in this aspect, if we will but have patience with the crust of hard fact, and place ourselves in presence of the living forces that lie dormant beneath.

On the first slopes of the steep descent, *Salvia Horminum* (or *Horminum pyrenaicum*) grew in enormous profusion, while abundance of *Lilium Martagon* was being ruthlessly cut down by a band of mowers in full activity. To my right the bare white limestone precipices of the Falban Kogel, the northern termination of the Rosengarten Dolomites, came suddenly to view, and uniting at a narrow angle with the Rosszähne enclosed a desolate-looking corner, in which large patches of snow found shelter. From the base of the slope the Duron Thal stretched before me an almost level tract, its stream wandering at leisure, margined by plashy meadows. The Falban Kogel retired behind the green slopes, and its place was taken by bosses of dark rock of eruptive ash, which formed the southern wall of the valley to its outlet at Campitello. In these watery meadows, along with *Sedum villosum*, I gathered *Pleurogyne* (*Swertia*) *carinthiaca*, an interesting and rare form of Gentian. Right in front, and grandly filling up the gap left by the concave lines of the ridges towards the end of the Duron Thal, rose up the snowy head of the Marmolata, its base lost among the forests in the middle distance. Presently the gliding stream had changed its character: a narrow and rapid gorge lay before me, and at the foot of it was Campitello, nestled in an angle of the Val Fassa, with an outlook to the south towards Vigo, and eastwards to the head of the valley.

Campitello lies not far from the head waters of the river Avisio, which, running for upwards of seventy miles in a generally south-west direction, debouches into the valley of the Adige at Lavis, a few miles above Trent.

The place presents none of those signs of thrift and neatness visible in the German villages over the ridge to the north. It is dirty, disorderly, and has a shiftless physiognomy, like too many of those in Italy. Its height above the sea, probably 4,500 feet, may be some extenuation; still I incline to think that if the next village up the valley, Gries, with its Teutonic church and bright green bulbous spire, were Teutonic also in its people, its superior cleanliness, neatness, and prosperity would be at once apparent. This last stands out of the direct path, right under the Rodela Berg, a part of the south face of the Seisser Alp plateau, so I did not visit it.

On enquiring after supper of my landlord, Giovanni Bernard, I found his larder was a box on the stairs, containing an antiquated tongue or two, looking much more like wood than flesh. These I declined, and was fain to be content with a *mêlée* of very indifferent fare. While it was preparing I sallied out, taking a quiet stroll up the valley towards Penia, the last village in the pass leading over the shoulder of the Marmolata towards Caprile. The bottom of the valley here is nearly level, from the alluvium brought down by the numerous streams; and the Avisio, the main stream, takes to itself a wide bed, meandering among Dolomite débris, and margined by numerous clumps of alder and willow, interspersed with bushes of the tamarisk (*Myricaria germanica*) at this time in flower, and in their shade abundance of the intensely white bloom of *Silene alpestris* starred the sward. The contrasted forms of the mountains; the hatchet-like blades of the Lang Kofel bending to each other, and peeping over the ridge of the Seisser Alp; the giant bastion mass of the Pordoi portion of the Sella Spitze group, and the towering bosses of the Colatsch and other outliers of the Marmolata, combined to render this corner of the Fassa Thal exceedingly interesting. The rich green of the alluvium terraces too, upon the highest of which stands the little village of Alba, held in shadow by steep slopes of eruptive ash, and irrigated by numerous runnels of cool water, came out in strong opposition to the bare-looking burnt-up slopes on the sunny side of the valley.

Centuries of habit have accustomed the traveller to look for some manifestation of art in most Italian settlements. Campitello is not without ambition in this respect. I found my bedroom a perfect picture gallery. The ceiling had a grand ornamental centre, the colours fresh and good, and round the walls, and between the three windows, set in frames of lines of various colours, were ten scenes from nature, painted with a certain rude vigour, each with its legend underneath. One was styled 'Valle di Lauterbrunnen in Swizzera;' another, 'Campitello in mezzo giorno,' in which the Dolomites figured hugely; a third was a grand mountain scene suggestive of Chamounix, but the bed-head, too heavy to move, was in the way of the legend; a fourth, the most attractive of all, represented a wild array of Dolomite peaks with an old castle in the midst, and was labelled 'Primiero.' It put me upon enquiry, and in another year (1862) we realised all that this picture seemed to promise.

I was now in the near neighbourhood of the Marmolata, already pointed out to the reader as the culminating peak of the Dolomite district. This mountain—which might be compared in general form to one of those mahogany cases for stationery, which are to be found in most counting-houses of the present day—has its slope, a very steep one, to the north. To the south, east, and west, it is perfectly precipitous, and presents nothing but walls of bare rock. Glaciers cover the greater part of the slope, and their melting supplies the springs of the Avisio which takes its rise immediately below them. Standing in the centre of a Dolomite world, the view from the summit must be one of the most marvellous panoramas of isolated individual Rock Massives to be seen in the Alps, unclothed as on the day they first came into existence. Its height, variously estimated, but which may be taken at about 11,200 feet, raises it far above its loftiest neighbours. It stands in a line of ridge that runs from north to south through the western Dolomite district and marks the point where the divergent valleys of the Avisio and Cordevole originate.*

MARMOLATA, FROM THE SASSO DI DAMM.

The following day I botanised upon the Fedaia Pass, on the north flank of the Marmolata. The ascent commences after the last village, Penia, is passed, and I soon encountered a kind of chaos like that near Gavarnie in the Pyrenees, with fine trees growing upon many of the huge

* The view of the Marmolata inserted was obtained in 1862. The position from which it was taken is described in the 16th chapter.

blocks, and dead stems standing here and there, slanting at different angles. Beyond, the ascent was divided into a series of sudden steps, ending in a basin immediately below the summit of the col. From this spot the desolate whitened rock-slopes of the Marmolata, running steeply down below its three glaciers, were before me. The glaciers are parted from each other by lines of bosses as smooth-looking as the slopes, and the whole face suggests the idea of a remorseless and most complete removal of every sharp edge or crag. Does this indicate a past extension of the glacier? The contrast between this general smoothness and the jagged character of the Lang Kofel was remarkable. It is quite possible to conceive that the Marmolata glaciers, favoured by cloudy summers and snowy winters, might unite below in one sheet of ice, and fill the basin partly occupied by the tiny Fedaia-See, or perhaps even the upper valley of the Avisio as far as Penia. This fine pass is full of contrasts. Here nature has reserved her fairer mood for the *sunny* side; for the Alp pastures stretch in long, rich, green sheets up to the summit of the ridge of eruptive ash bounding the pass to the north, and in the Padon Spitze, attaining a height of 9,000 feet, or 2,000 feet above that of the pass itself. Nor is this all. The upper basin was a natural flower-garden, where every colour had its representatives, and even the larger blocks scattered on its surface became, through the luxuriance and variety of the plants growing upon them, miniature gardens in themselves. *Pinguicula grandiflora*, with *Pyrola uniflora*, and *Epipactis rubiginosa*, were frequent on the ascent, as also *Senecio abrotanifolius*; and, on rocks, *Achillea Clavenæ*. In the upper basin, *Sempervivum Wulfeni*, *Pedicularis verticillata*, *tuberosa*, and *fasciculata?* *Anthemis alpina*, *Pyrethrum ceratophylloides*, *Hieracium villosum*, *Senecio*

Doronicum, Chrysanthemum montanum, Oxytropis pilosa, Primula longiflora, Myosotis alpestris, with *Gentiana nivalis, tenella,* and *utriculosa,* were among the more interesting species.

The grandeur of this near view of the Marmolata is much enhanced by climbing to the summit of the ridge to the left, and so doing away with some of the foreshortening. Its snowy dome and vast bulk and height are thus much better appreciated. Rows of mowers and haymakers—men and women—were busy upon this slope, the Alpine garden quickly disappearing under their scythes. They had come from Salzburg, and complained that the last two months had been unusually wet. In the evening the inevitable lean fowl and bread, without vegetables, awaited me at Campitello.

The reader will have probably already inferred that I shirk ice-work, and am not a member of the Alpine Club; my willingness to ascend ceases with the disappearance of the last phanerogamous specimen. The snow and ice region of the Marmolata I therefore leave untouched, but it is in good hands; a late president of the Alpine Club having long ago made it his own, and we may hope some day to welcome from his pen a full description of its features.*

Taking a porter, I left Campitello the next morning for Vigo, the principal village of the upper Fassa, and about six or seven miles lower down. On this route the great objects of interest are almost out of sight. The crags and pinnacles of the famed Rosengarten Dolomites, at the foot of which Vigo lies, are hid behind the long slopes of the half-grassy, half-rocky spines that project forwards from their base. The Sella Spitze and the Marmolata disap-

* In the 5th chapter will be found an account of a recent ascent of the Marmolata by Herr Grohmann, a member of the Vienna Alpine Club.

pear, and nothing peculiar is visible but the solitary retreating masses of the Lang-Kofel and Platt Kogel. Even they are reduced to the minimum of effect, for they now exhibit neither the majesty and loftiness of their aspect from the Seisser Alp, nor their weird character as seen peeping over at Campitello. On the left, rocks formed of volcanic ash, clothed in forest, rise up steeply, continuing as far as Pozza, at the entrance to the Monzoni Thal, and completely shut out all distant view. I walked on in expectant mood, capturing a solitary specimen of *Papaver pyrenaicum*, growing in the glacier-water of the Avisio, one of the frequent illustrations of the descent of alpine plants to lower regions when favoured by the cool banks of an alp stream. Its nearest alpine habitat I met with only on the highest débris of the Monzoni ridge, about 8,000 feet above the sea. On approaching Pera, a glimpse of the Dolomite world showed itself; a long narrow ravine, with enormous masses of stony débris heaped up on each side, penetrated deeply into a distant amphitheatre of precipices of bare white rock, and allowed a momentary vision of a lofty wall rising upwards of 5,000 feet above its base, and then all was closed again to the view.

Vigo is not far from Pera, and the road now leaves the level of the river to reach it. Situated on the finest expanse of alp pasture in the upper Fassa, it possesses the elements of alpine wealth in abundance, and has a flourishing aspect. The houses are large, well built, and seem tolerably clean. There is no church in the village, but there are two, with Teutonic-looking spires, standing at some little distance—one above the village, St. Juliana, and the other, the principal one, St. Johann, below. A fine bold Dolomite bluff, belted with forest, rises on the other side of the valley from the bed of the river, and, facing the village, forms the principal feature in the near landscape. It bears the name of the Sasso di Loch. The lofty line of Dolomitic bosses and peaks that runs in this direction from the Sasso di Val Fredda and Sasso Vernale, immediately to the south of the Marmolata, terminates with this Sasso. The appellation is a frequent one in the district.

To many readers the name of this village, 'Vigo,' may possibly bring reminiscences of certain early lessons in geography. Vigo Bay, and Vigo, on the north-west coast of Spain, will rise to their remembrance, and the coincidence will soon pass from their thoughts, as it did from mine. But if I point out what I afterwards discovered, that there are at least half a dozen villages of this name in Southern Tyrol, curiosity, perhaps, will be awakened. Who or what is responsible for the frequent occurrence of this name? The family, too, is an increasing one, for is there not a Vigolo (or little Vigo) near Trent? I regret my inability, at present, to satisfy a legitimate curiosity. I can only establish the fact, and raise the question; commending the subject, however, to the author of 'Words and Places.' Three of these Vigos are in the *western* half of South Tyrol — the first being in the Val di Non, a little above Mezzo Lombardo; the second in the Val di Sarca, between Trent and Riva; and the third in the Val Rendena, to the east of the Adamello. The three others are in the *eastern* half, the most remote being in the valley of the Piave, above Pieve di Cadore; and the one nearest to our present village being in the lower Fassa, or Cembra Thal, near the point where the Avisio unites with the Adige. Then close to Trent, and a little to the west of the Lago Caldonazzo, we find Vigolo! They are all set down in Mayr's 'Karte von Tyrol.'

Antonio Rizzi's inn, at Vigo, furnishes comfortable head-quarters for excursionists, and I had intended, weather permitting, to explore the whole district from this central

J. Gilbert, del.^t Hanhart, lith.

GENERAL VIEW OF THE ROSENGARTEN GEBIRGE FROM THE SASSO DI DAMM, VAL FASSA.

point; but on the fourth day I was compelled to return to Botzen for letters, and the only excursions I now made were to the Rosengarten Gebirge, behind and above the village, and on the following day to the summit of the Monzoni ridge, on the Marmolata side of the valley.

Friday, August 25, I devoted to the Rosengarten Gebirge. The usual course is to take the path leading up to the church of St. Juliana, and then turning to the right, and crossing the streamlet that runs down past Vigo, follow the track up the side of the ravine until the upper alp is gained. Another and higher ridge has to be surmounted, and the level summit of the Sasso dei Mugoni is reached; the view is immediately in front, and comes upon you in a moment.

Imagine a gigantic amphitheatre of jagged, cleft precipices, shooting 3,000 feet above the spectator out of a depth far below him, and reaching, in the Rothewand Spitze, to the height of 10,200 feet above the sea. Let the arms of this amphitheatre stretch forwards so as to embrace nearly one half of his horizon, shutting him up to the one view of a stern, desolate, barren face, that presents itself on all sides. Let successive masses of débris descend from the base of this long line of precipices through the whole sweep of its circuit, and threaten to occupy the entire basin below, while still leaving a small patch of bright green pasture, on which a dark spot is identified as a châlet. All this imagined will still give but a very inadequate idea of the impressiveness of the scene. The surface-water of the basin finds an outlet through a gorge half choked up with débris, which, under the name of the Vajoletto Thal, runs steeply down to the main valley of the Avisio, near Pera.*

* The general view of the Rosengarten here given does not precisely answer to the description in the text. It was taken two years later from the opposite side of the valley.

But the main line of the ridge of the Rosengarten runs northwards, beyond the limits of this amphitheatre, until it merges into the Falban Kogel, already mentioned as facing the head of the Duron Thal. In the interval, the Kessel Kogel rises above the average line of the ridge, and standing at the head of a second and smaller caldron, where there is a tarn, the Antermoja See, thence derives its name. This I should have visited had weather allowed. The main line runs southwards also, until it terminates in the Kälbl Eck, where the saddle-shaped depression of the Caressa Pass, at a height of about 6,100 feet, leads out of the Fassa Thal towards Botzen.

The Dolomite 'Massif' of the Rosengarten Gebirge is one of the most complicated in the upper Fassa. But its wildernesses, caldrons, and other complexities are all on its *eastern* side. The western face of the wall runs in a simple single line, and is seen with that aspect from Botzen, awakening that feeling of awed curiosity which my friend has already described, and which is not disappointed, if the recesses just referred to are explored, though the Val Fassa itself may not answer to expectation in this respect. The rock is of the same creamy colour as that of which the Schlern and Lang-Kofel are composed, and is also like that in its cellular and crystalline characters. By the latest writer upon this district, Baron Richthofen, it is referred to two beds, both belonging to the Upper Trias. These themselves repose conformably upon a series of beds of the Lower Trias, that form the slopes on both sides of the wall, and yield the rich pastures in the midst of which Vigo and its neighbouring villages stand. Underlying the whole is the great porphyry plateau, the grand starting-point for all geologic time throughout this region. I merely glance at these facts here, and refer the reader who desires to enquire further to the summary contained in our final chapter, and to the geological map at the end of the volume.

From the elevated point at which I stood, the Lang Kofel and Platt Kogel, to the north, recovered some of their grandeur, appearing seated at the edge of the south rim of the Seisser Alp, which slopes down very steeply towards the interior of the basin of the upper Fassa. At a little distance from them, on their right, the Sella Spitze plateau stood out, as isolated from all its neighbours as the Lang-Kofel, and rearing its massive bastions, devoid of all vegetation, to a height quite sufficient to give grandeur to its vast expanse. Two great arms stretched out to the south, overlooking the village of Gries—the portals to an unknown rocky wilderness in its interior—and its summit was crowned by numerous more or less truncated cones, rising from their débris-covered bases, and flecked here and there with beds of snow.

The most prominent impression left on the mind by these Seisser Alp Dolomites was that of complete *separateness* and *isolation*, not only in relation to each other, but to the green slopes on the summits of which they are placed. Though ignorant, at this time, of Baron Richthofen's theory of their origin, and therefore with a mind unprejudiced on the subject, they seemed to me to be so little a part of the green slopes on which they rested, that, more than aught else,—they suggested the idea of icebergs of rock, which might float away and leave the country unaffected by their removal. They appeared to have no *roots* in the beds below them. This impression is assisted by the horizontal, and apparently undisturbed, lines of bedding which are here and there visible when the light falls on them at a favourable angle.* As little did they

* Sir R. Murchison observed this fact, and has recorded it in his paper on the 'Structure of the Alps,' &c., contained in the Geological Society's Journal for 1849.

look like the ruinous portions of some continuous plateau, or ridge, that had been broken up by denudation. On such a supposition there would have been left, in parts not fully exposed to the destructive action, more or less evident lines of ridge with outliers; but of these there appear no traces. An impression similar to this I have not received from any other part of the Alps. It was the first, and remained the predominant one. For some account of Baron Richthofen's theory I refer the reader to chap. 18, at the end of the volume.

Turning more to the east again, the eye rested on the lofty profile of the Marmolata, rising up beyond and above the verdant slopes of the Colpelle and Bufaure Gebirge, looking like a mountain that had been cleft down the middle, and one half of it removed. To the south were the Sasso Vernale with two glaciers in its upper basin, and the Sasso di Val Fredda; and thence the lofty Dolomite line was continued westward nearly at right angles to its former direction until it met with the Fassa Thal at the Sasso di Loch. Between this line and the mass of the Colpelle and Bufaure Gebirge, the Pozza Thal passes at a low level up to its origin in the mountains immediately to the south of the Marmolata. South of this long Dolomite wall, called the Campo Ziegelan, is the parallel valley of St. Pelegrino, which at the line of watershed, where there is a solitary church and inn, merges into another valley—the Val Falcade—that continues in the same direction, until at Cencenighe it falls into the longitudinal valley of the Cordevole, that runs southward to Belluno.

Next morning I left Vigo early with a guide, Giovanni Grazzioli, to explore the Monzoni branch of the Pozza Thal. Descending to Pera, I crossed the river to pass through Pozza, just opposite, and then entered the main lateral valley. The dew was plentiful on the crisp grass, and everything promised a hot, cloudless, still day. At the point where the Monzoni branch turns off southwards is a solitary châlet in the corner of a small pasture. We ascended to the upper story, and added our bread to some milk which an old woman boiled for us. Reaching at length the end of the valley where several large patches of snow lay in shelter, I gathered on the débris near one of them, *Geum reptans*, *Cerastium glaciale*, and *Pyrethrum alpinum*. A vigorous climb through thick Rhododendron and Vaccinium scrub then brought us to the upper basin, occupying a great sweep immediately under the summit of the ridge, and filled with long lines of loose débris diversified with patches of snow. We coasted for some distance over this débris, treading as lightly as possible, as the least encouragement set the mass in motion, and shot us down several yards below our proper course. The curvature of the amphitheatre concentrated the sun's rays, and rendered the heat intense; several small flocks of sheep appeared to be in distress from it, and I was amused at the different methods of shelter they adopted. In one of the groups they were standing close pressed against each other, so as to shut out every ray of light, and not a head but was carefully tucked under its neighbour's body. Another set had scooped out shallow hollows in the patches of snow, and lay panting in them. On one of these patches I noticed the phenomenon of *red snow*. I was detained some time in this apparently sterile region by the abundance of its botanical treasures, which lay closely sprinkled about, but their minute proportions produced no effect even upon the near landscape. Among the more interesting were, *Pedicularis asplenifolia*, *Eritrichium nanum*, *Papaver pyrenaicum*, *Primula glutinosa* and *minima*, *Androsace obtusifolia*, *Chamæjasme*, and *glacialis*, *Phyteuma pauciflorum*, *Anthemis alpina*, *Potentilla nitida*, *Soldanella pusilla, Saxifraga androsacea var. trifida,* with *S. mucoides var. atropurpurea,* and *Ranunculus glacialis.* The summit of the ridge was reached at length by a steep turn to the right.

Standing upon the highest boss in the neighbourhood, with my guide on one side, and the shepherd who had left his flock to join us on the other, I contemplated the scene from this new point of view. The circle of landscape was the same as that of yesterday, my position only in the circumference was different, and with the near view of the Marmolata substituted for that of the Rosengarten. It is from this side that the Marmolata presents the most striking contrast to the smooth glacier and rock slopes and bosses which are seen on its northern aspect. Not a particle of slope except the profile of the flattish snowy dome is visible ; all else is sheer precipice presented corner-wise to the eye, while its jagged edges retreat foreshortened to the north-west and east, until lost to view. It stood out unmistakably the dominant peak of the district.

My stand-point was about 8,800 feet above the sea, on the line of ridge of the Campo Ziegelan, which itself might be estimated at about 200 feet higher ; while the two Sassos that run in a southerly direction from the Marmolata to unite at nearly right angles with the Campo Ziegelan rise to at least 10,000 feet above the sea. Quantities are prosaic ; but they are not seldom important elements in assisting to build up the materials for a picture.

Below me extended east and west the whole length of the Pellegrino Thal, bounded on the south by a lofty porphyry ridge ; and behind it another long line of porphyry peaks ran back in the direction of Trent until out of sight. This was the south-easterly portion of the great porphyry plateau, and here were some of its highest points. Beyond these to the south rose up the isolated lofty summits of the granite Cima d'Asta (9,200 feet), an island during the Trias period, when the whole of South Tyrol was covered by the sea. In the far distance glimmered in the sun the snow-fields of the Adamello, on the boundary line between Tyrol and Lombardy.

This ridge of the Monzoni has become classic ground to the mineralogists of Europe. A mighty mass of syenite has here been upheaved, itself intersected with numerous dykes of hypersthene, through the whole series of Trias beds, including the uppermost Dolomitic bed, which forms the summit of the ridge of the Campo Ziegelan. The continuity of the upper beds of this ridge is thus completely broken, while the lower beds are exposed on the slopes of the Val Monzoni, itself a lateral valley running *across* the prevalent direction of the beds. A treasure-house of various species of minerals is thus here to be met with, and especially where the igneous rock, whether syénite or hypersthene, has come into contact with the sedimentary rocks on either hand.

The most interesting fact remains. Opposite me, to the north, rose the lofty green slopes of the Colpelle and Bufaure Gebirge, a smiling contrast to the bare Dolomitic precipices on the east and south, and rising to an equal height with my present point of view. But geology tells us of *another* contrast between these slopes and their boundary-walls. It affirms that they form a mighty mass of volcanic ash, and that their base is the ancient centre of a vast submarine volcano that poured out its materials during the middle period of the Upper Trias, before the existence of any of these Dolomite 'massives,' the Rosengarten, Lang Kofel, Sella Spitze, Cima Pasni, Marmolata, &c., which now encircle it on all sides. Of far greater antiquity than the extinct volcanos of Auvergne, we have here probably *the oldest extinct volcano in Europe.*

The outbreak of the volcanic activity in the Fassa Thal, and the subsequent formation of the Dolomite 'massives' in the immediate neighbourhood, are the two great epochs in the geologic history of the country, and the sources of all that is peculiar and attractive in its scenery. Our party visited Vigo together in 1862, and made an ascent of a part of the Colpelle Berg, an account of which will be found in its place; and I must beg to refer the reader to the chapter at the end of the volume, if he desires to possess himself of some of the details of its geology.

The day following that of my excursion to Monzoni was Sunday, and I attended a late mass at St. Johann's, at eleven—two others, one at five o'clock and one at eight, having preceded it. Notwithstanding the earlier services, the church was crowded, the men and boys standing or kneeling in the open space in front of the altar; some little urchins even sitting under the altar, while the body of the church—not a very small one—was closely packed with the old women and maidens of the population. There were several pretty faces among the latter, but only one or two with light hair and German type of physiognomy. Their taste and means were principally displayed in the ornamentation of their back combs; some were set with coloured crystals, while others preferred the milder radiance of mother-of-pearl.

Compelled to return to Botzen, I found, on questioning Rizzi, that there was a very direct route by the Caressa Pass to Botzen along the whole course of the Karneid Thal; and that, though at present only a horse-track, a road for carriages was being constructed through the depths of the porphyry gorge, from Welschenofen to the outlet of the valley into the great Brenner road. Welschenofen is about two thirds of the distance from Botzen, and the whole route may probably be about twenty-five miles.

On the Monday morning, therefore, taking Grazzioli to carry my knapsack, I set out for Botzen by the Caressa Pass. The village path, continually ascending, led circuitously round the face of more than one spur, until, on arriving at the pass on the line of watershed, I found myself midway between the ruinous-looking termination of the Rosengarten Gebirge, called the Kälbl Eck, and the more massive angle of the great crescent of the Latemar, or Lattenmar Spitzen, another Dolomitic group on the south. The pass lies in the red sandstone that rests immediately upon the porphyry plateau; and the beds of the Lower and Upper Trias emerge in regular order above one another on each side of the pass, until crowned by the bed of 'Schlern Dolomite,' so named, which, in its varied fantastic forms, is the characteristic feature of the district.

On the Botzen side of the pass the country is wide and open, gently sloping westward, and intersected with runnels of water, the primary feeders of the Karneid stream. In the far distance are the snow-fields and peaks of the Oertler and Oetzthal. Looking northwards, along the base of the Rosengarten, the country is bare, the ancient masses of forest having been cleared away; but the lower slopes of the Latemar, on the south, are still unstripped of their natural covering, which goes by the name of the 'Karer Wald;' and two lakelets, a little lower down in the same stretch of forest, bear the name of the Upper and Lower Karer See. Gradually the path descends into a hollow below the level of the plateau, the commencement of the Karneid Thal, and sinks deeper and deeper, until it takes the character of a narrow valley buried in the depths of the great porphyry plateau. It emerges at the foot of the Karneid Schloss, picturesquely situated high in air, on a promontory overlooking the Brenner route. The valley, with its broad bosses of rich red rock contrasting so vividly with the bright greens of its forest coverings, is a fine specimen of purely porphyritic scenery, and deserves to be studied, though it may not offer a single feature to recal the characteristics of the Dolomite world, from the borders of which it takes its rise. At the time of my journey, the road was not sufficiently completed to allow of my traversing the gorge, and at a mile or two below Welschenofen I was compelled to take a foot-track, passing along the slope at a considerable height above the stream, and coming out into the Eisach Thal on a level with the Schloss; but our party went by the lower or carriage route to Botzen in 1862, and I refer the reader to chapter 16 for further details of its scenery. The lakelets just mentioned possess the peculiarity of being filled with water for only a small portion of the year. Up to the middle of June their beds are covered with grass, available for pasturage. But in the latter half of this month they are in a few days submerged, and so remain until the middle of September, from which time the water gradually drains away.

It is singular how frequently the element 'Kar' appears in the nomenclature of this valley. We have the *Kar*neid Thal and Bach; *Kar*daun at its mouth, near Botzen, the ancient *Car*dunum; the *Kar*er See and Wald, and the *Car*essa Pass. In the *Käl*bl Eck it is possible that we may have a contraction of an older and fuller form, of which 'Kar' was a part. Is 'Kar' a German element, and, if so, what becomes of the asserted Celtic or Etruscan origin of Kardaun, the ancient Cardunum? Yet is not this element frequent in other parts of the Alps? We have the *Kor* Spitze in the Lavant Thal, Carinthia, and in the Gader Thal; the *Kar*avanken Alps to the south of Carinthia, and the *Kar*wendel Gebirge to the north of Innsbruck, on the Bavarian frontier.*

The Karneid Schloss is a picturesque object in the view towards the Dolomites from Botzen, and itself possesses a fine view westward, over the Botzen valley. Its history involves a link connecting it with the Wolkenstein family. The Lichtensteins, the original owners, had emigrated from Switzerland in the fourteenth century, and had received a grant of the Schloss and Seigniory from Duke Albert of Austria, to which Steinegg and Welschenofen were afterwards added. They became wealthy through the acquisition of other estates, and were made Counts of the Empire. But having joined the league formed by the barons of the Etsch against Frederic of the Empty Pocket, their castle was stormed by him, and Hans and Wilhelm von Lichtenstein fell into his hands. At this crisis, Oswald von Wolkenstein generously came forward, and, by the payment of a heavy ransom, eventually restored his friends to liberty. From this period they continued in peaceful possession until the death, in 1760, of Anton, Count of Lichtenstein, the last of his house. At a later date, both the property and seigniory were held by the city of Botzen; the castle is now, however, in possession of Anton, Knight of Goldegg, while the seigniorial jurisdiction has for some years past belonged to the Principality of Tyrol.

* Dr. Rolle treats the term as a form of the word 'Kahr,' whence Kohr or Kor Alp. He asserts that the Kor Alp of the Lavant Thal, 'at least,' derives its name from the existence of several high basins or Kahrs that are prolonged into deep ravines, radiating in different directions from the centre of the mountain. The 'Car' in Carinthia has a different origin, being Slovenic. The original form, 'Gora-tan' or 'mountain land,' was converted by the monks in the early middle ages into 'Carantanum,' which again was contracted by the Germans into 'Kärnthen,' and euphonised by the Italians into 'Carinthia.' The 'Car' in Carnia and the Carnic Alps is doubtless from the same Slovenic source. The 'Carni' would mean the 'mountaineers.'

A curious legend is attached to the Schloss. In a time of plague the family of Lichtenstein had vowed to make a pilgrimage, with presents of money and other offerings, to our Lady of Weissenstein, should they be preserved from the contagion. Weissenstein is a little place on the porphyry plateau, about seven miles south of Karneid as the crow flies, which possessed at that time a celebrated picture of the Madonna. No one in the Schloss was attacked by the malady, though great numbers in the immediate neighbourhood fell victims. But when the plague had disappeared, the Lichtensteiners, forgetting their vow, thought they might as well save the cost of pilgrimage. Suddenly the plague returned, and they were all laid low in death. On the same night the castle doors were heard to fly open, and a troop of pale horses, bearing the cloaked figures of the dead, was seen galloping towards Weissenstein. The church door there, opening of its own accord, the procession passed in, and the ghastly riders threw themselves down with a frightful clatter before the holy picture. In the morning, the monks found a heap of blackened corpses upon the floor! In this manner was the breach of faith avenged upon the perjured. It is said that a representation of this scene still exists in the church at Weissenstein.

Unfortunately, I found myself detained for a whole week at Botzen, tantalised by the fine weather which prevailed all the time. When released I returned to Vigo by way of Neumarkt and Cavalese.

Neumarkt, like many of the towns and villages in the great valley between Botzen and Trent, lies close to the foot of its bordering mountains. Its Italian name Egna, or Enna, preserves the recollection of a Roman mansion, Endide, as well as of a Schloss Enn that once existed here. Egna was built very early upon land belonging to the

Prince-Bishop of Trent. In 1222 the town had the misfortune to suffer so much from an inundation of the Etsch as to require rebuilding, and hence the present more frequently used name of Neumarkt. It is the principal outlet and inlet for traffic between the Fleims Thal and the Etsch region, and the road to Cavalese is therefore a good one. The summit of the pass is at St. Lugano about 3,700 feet above the sea, Neumarkt itself being only 770.

Cavalese is a prosperous-looking town, well placed, with a fine Italian church and campanile, and is the local centre of its section of the valley—the Fleims Thal—as Vigo is of the Fassa, the upper section of the same valley. Below the town, and across the valley, the country of the porphyry plateau extends far and wide, almost down to Trent, while above the town the Trias and Dolomite beds and scenery commence, which culminate with the Marmolata at the head of the valley. Yet here, as in Val Fassa itself, very little Dolomite scenery is visible from the main road. It will only reveal itself to explorers of the recesses of the Weisshorn, Viesena, and Latemar.

My return walk to Vigo from Neumarkt, through Cavalese, Ziano, and Predazzo, was a long one—probably forty miles; and night surprised me before I had begun the last ascent that led to my temporary home, where, on my arrival, a hospitable welcome and kind attention to the wants of a weary traveller were ready on the instant.

The next day I came across a peasant who had been accustomed for many years to accompany his master upon numerous botanising excursions throughout this region and the remainder of South Tyrol. This gentleman, Dr. Facchini, was a practising physician at Vigo, and had been dead but four years.* He had been an indefatigable

* A small Saxifrage (*S. Facchinii*), peculiar to the Dolomite district, bears his name.

collector for a very long period. According to Hausmann (see 'Flora von Tirol'), he had contributed a greater number of new species to the flora of Tyrol than any other botanist, and there were very few Alps in his own immediate neighbourhood that he had not visited. The poor old peasant was enthusiastic in praise of his late master, and I much wished that my acquaintance with Vigo had been a few years earlier in date.

It had been my intention to reach Caprile over the col of the Val Fredda, about 9,800 feet above the sea, pass thence to Cortina, and return by the Val di Zoldo, Agordo, and Primiero; but the weather was inexorable. After being detained for twenty-four hours at a small inn near the summit of the Pellegrino Thal (6,800 feet above the sea) by an incessant pour, sharing with the landlord and his wife their cold little bedroom, heaped round with sugar, meal, onions, and other odorous stores, I gave up my plans in disgust, and returned by Vigo to Botzen, and thence to England, the persistent watery skies giving me no cause to repent my abandonment of the mountains for that season.

A TOUR THROUGH
SOUTH TYROL, CARINTHIA, AND CARNIOLA
1861.

CHAPTER IV.

RATZES AND THE SEISSER ALP.

Plans and Preparations — Lake of Constance — A Cross-road to Innsbruck — The Berg Isel, and Solitary Cross — A Night in the Diligence — Morning, and the first Dolomite — Ratzes Bathhouse — A Day on the Seisser Alp — Castelruth — Ascent of the Hohe Schlern — Storm effect — The Castle of Hauenstein.

The letters of Churchill were inspiring. We also would explore those venerable woods of Schloss Hauenstein, rest under the shadow of the Schlern, and tread the breezy Seisser Alp. On our friend's return, we soon began to concert an expedition for the ensuing summer of 1861; and, as our ambitions grew, determined to comprise in our tour not only the proper region of the Dolomites, but also a large portion of the range of the south-eastern Alps. Among these, at intervals, Dolomite formations occur, and, if not Dolomitic, the scenery is similar in character, from the almost universal presence of limestone; precipice and pinnacle still the chief features of the landscape.

In arranging this latter portion of the route, our attention was drawn to two or three remarkable districts. The first was the Gail Thal in Carinthia, a long and very marked valley in the map, more so even than that of the Drave, southward and parallel to which it lies. 'Murray' was silent about it. One of the most experienced explorers of this part of the Alps, to whom we applied, had seen it only from one of its boundary ridges. So far curiosity was excited by negation, and the only affirmation that reached us was very attractive in a floral point of view—it was a rare botanical field. Then, passing the finger on the map along the chain of the Friulian Alps, it was arrested by the knotty group of the Terglou, in Carniola. Of this 'Murray' did say something, and though very brief, it was of the most tempting sort. 'Sublime,' 'magnificent,' 'superb,' were epithets sprinkled plentifully through half a dozen paragraphs. Sir Humphry Davy's 'Letters and Journals,' referring to the same district, conveyed the same impression. His visits, repeated during several years, proved that his opinion was not hastily formed, and that it was from ample observation he said, 'I know no scene more sublime than this crest of the Carnic Alps, and there are no streams more beautiful than the Save and the Isonzo.' Lastly, a mountain system remote and unvisited, but offering scenery of the highest order, was brought to our notice in the 'Transactions of the Geological Society of Vienna.' This was the Steiner Alp. Its situation as one of the final spurs of the great Alpine ranges before they sink into the plains of Hungary was a point of interest; and more attractive still, in these days of ransacked nature, was the reported difficulty of access to its caldron-like formation, and of accommodation at its single village. It may be found on a good map lying north-eastward from the Terglou group, and midway between the two great valley outlets of the Drave and the Save.

Thus our plans for this journey embraced four distinct objects: first, the Dolomite region of South Tyrol; secondly, the Gail Thal in Carinthia; thirdly, the Terglou in Carniola, with its adjacent valleys of the Isonzo and the Save; fourthly, the 'Caldron' of the Steiner Alp in Styria.

With the best maps to be obtained—Mayr's 'Tyrol'

and 'Alpenländer;' Worl's 'Tyrol,' admirably detailed for pedestrian use; Scheda's, and the government maps for Carinthia and Carniola—with these and others, through many a lamp-lit evening, we traced and pieced our devious course under coming summer skies. We were travelling all the winter and all the spring, in imagination. The journey itself occupied but a small space, in comparison with the months we were busy with it as a bright possible to be, picturing our way on the closely fretted map. Such pictures the reality is sure to displace, yet substituting others which will be permanent additions to the landscape-gallery of recollection.

We left England on Monday morning, July 22, 1861, and on Wednesday afternoon, about five o'clock, arrived at Romanshorn, on the Lake of Constance. The quiet waters welcomed our deliverance from the hot and jolting trains that in two days had brought us from Paris; and a steamer, upon whose deck we were almost the only passengers, sped swiftly with us into the midst of the smooth expanse. What a change from the perplexed web of Swiss railways, and the mob of tourists, disgorged upon platforms from trains '*en correspondance*,' and crammed, and cramming, in buffets and 'restaurations!' It is true that, after Zurich, the crowd had thinned away, till, on the homely timber-laden wharf of Romanshorn, we appeared the only pleasure-seekers left; but the din was still in our ears, rendering more grateful the calm beauty of the Boden See.

A cloud-land of mountains, Swiss and Tyrolean, circled round the head of the lake upon our right, subsiding, in front, into the rolling Bavarian hills, at the foot of which were faintly seen the towers of Lindau, just emerging from the level water-line. Towards these our boat's bows were pointed. In its wake a broad stream of rippling silver melted on the horizon into the splendours of a sky which justified the pencil of Turner in its most fantastic mood—so swept, and flecked, and broken was it by many-coloured wreaths of cloud, suffused with golden light. But now, as we neared the further shore, began that silent interchange among the mountain tops which rivets the eye. Partly swathed in evening mists, the bare or snow-streaked crests glided from behind intervening masses, stood clear a moment, and gave place to others; or suddenly, far up through a breaking cloud, shone out a glittering sheet of snow. With some we had, in former years, made loving acquaintance, and eagerly scanned the map for bearings. 'Yes, that must be Sentis, the great mountain of Appenzel, and there to the left, the Grison Hörner and Spitzen.' The mountain madness was fast seizing upon us; but we retained our sanity to enjoy coffee and rolls, neatly laid out upon a table-cloth that just shook with the engine thump, but scarcely fluttered in the balmy air.

When we next looked forward, the old walls of Lindau, girdling a small island or promontory, were well in sight; and behind them, cultivated, village-sprinkled hills. Sweeping round, our steamer made for a narrow entrance between projecting rocks, one of them guarded by a colossal lion, and in a few minutes settled to the wharf in front of an imposing hotel, whose columned portico it would have been too much of an affront for an English party to avoid. Depositing our baggage, we turned our steps without delay towards the long sea-wall, which connects the island with the mainland, to catch the last glory of a sunset such as we had not witnessed since two years before, from the Lido, at Venice. It is trite, but true, to say there is never anything like it in England; our sunsets, however beautiful, are seldom free from a haze that blurs their splendour. Here, the sky looked barred with solid, clean-cut gold, and strung with jewels, all reflected in the lake, and glowing on the far-off hills.

We lingered late in the serene air. The music of a band in some adjoining gardens came to our ears, charmingly echoed by Lindau's ancient ramparts. The pealing of vesper bells from churches and convents, near and distant, and across the water, made the air resonant with rich tones; and the passing of a train of nuns through the red gloom, each intent upon her breviary, completed the romance of this lovely evening. Poetry may indeed inhabit any spot of earth, and any form of human life; the bare common, and the 'bald street,' may possess it; but the poetry of romance requires the consecration of old-world associations and memories, and a consenting mood, both of mind and nature, such as here befel, when, reposing in the first leisure of a rapid journey, we were greeted by a scene of choice continental beauty.

Our destination was Innsbruck, but our route not a usual one. We can here only briefly indicate its course, for the sake of any who may wish to try it. Starting at five the following morning for Immenstadt, a station upon the Augsburg railway, we there bade adieu to trains for many weeks of travelling, and engaged a long-bodied waggonet to Reutte, in Tyrol. It is a cross-road by way of Sonthofen, Hintelang, at the foot of the ascent which divides Bavaria from Tyrol, and then through a magnificent defile unknown to 'Murray'—the Pass of Gacht—into the valley of the Lech, at a point a little above Reutte. The day was as bright and charming as July could make it. We were joyous at finding ourselves once again among the purple-sided mountains; delighted at their unexpected grandeur; and at Reutte, a dainty little supper under the stars, and a violin concert from a neighbouring bower, late into the soft night, sent us to bed in happiest mood for the morrow.

Early in the blue morning, ascending by the rock-perched towers of Ehrenberg—the castle which failed to stop Prince Maurice on his march to seize Charles V. at Innsbruck, we took the road to Lermoos, a three hours' drive. Here we halted for the rest of the day. From the small triangular plain in which Lermoos stands rises the lofty Zug Spitze, and the noble Mieminger Berg, the former the highest of the Bavarian Alps, here abutting close upon Tyrol. A violent storm played among the impending precipices during the afternoon, and, according to Tyrolean custom, the bells of all the villages in the small mountain-girdled plain raised their deprecating peal, in divers tones of distance, filling the thunder pauses. An expedition we had planned was baulked by the storm; but Lermoos remains a notable recollection, and is well worth a longer visit.

On the third day our departure was delayed by a great earth-fall, brought down by the storm, which had destroyed some portion of the road; but there remained only forty miles to Innsbruck, over the pass of Auf der Fern. This pass is fine with forest gloom, especially on the southern side, where the road swings down into a vast wooded gulf, at the bottom of which appears the ruin of Sigmundsberg, in the midst of a reedy lake. The postilion, locking the wheels, went blissfully to sleep as we trundled down these zig-zags, waking up, by a kind provision of nature, at all the corners. The town of Nassereit succeeds, and then a second pass of inferior height, from which we descended into the valley of the Inn.

What valley can compare with this for romantic, and yet cheerful, beauty—villages and castle towers on every knoll—woods sweeping up the slopes, and grand mountain forms above?

It was at Telfs we struck the stream, where already the volume and swiftness of its waters are astonishing. By evening-light the Martinswand, the famous precipice —such a one as the English painter, whose name it recalls, loved to introduce as a side-scene to his grand perspectives—stood forth to view, loftily bearing itself into the midst of the valley. It remained the challenging feature of the landcape till Innsbruck itself filled the scene—that queenly town, dear to all who know it, and worthy of the vale it rules!

On Saturday evening, rejoicing in a week of travel happily accomplished, just as it fell dark, and lights began to sparkle through the trees and in the rushing waters, we approached the well-known bridge, the 'Inn Bruck.' Crowds of people filled the roads, the streets, and the tree-shaded walks, thronging especially the bridge itself. Then came the dark arcaded street, with only glimmer enough to show the golden roof of that oriel window upon which the Count of the Empty Pocket spent all his money, to show that he had it to spend; and then the broad characteristic Neustadt, with its central statue of the Virgin, at this time illuminated by numerous lamps, and surrounded by kneeling peasants chanting a hymn. The stately 'Oesterreichischer Hof,' where Englishmen most do congregate, overlooks it on the right. We preferred on this occasion its opposite neighbour, 'Die Goldene Sonne,' under whose gateway we shook off our dust, and received the best welcome of the establishment.

Innsbruck on a Sunday morning looks to an Englishman very Sunday-like. All the shops are shut, and the churches crowded. From an early hour, as in all Catholic countries, the music of the mass is heard swelling from every church-door, and here the peasant voices add to its depth and fulness.

There is a low hill, the Berg Isel—'Footstool of the Mountains,' as somebody calls it, for it lies at the foot of the Brenner,—overlooking the town. The Tyrolese Rifles occupy it for their shooting-ground, and have adorned it with monuments to the memory of their comrades who fell in the wars of 1849 in Italy and Hungary, and in the last campaign of 1859. The names of the officers in gold letters are followed by those of the rank and file—a heavy list, for the late war was a murderous one for the brave Jägers. Their targets stand in long alleys through the trees, the longest ranges extending across the ravine of the Sill, which, descending from the Brenner, cuts its deep course into the plain at this point.

It is an historical site. On this spot the French invaders were three times overthrown in the great year of 1809—twice by the hero Hofer. In virtue of that noble struggle for hearth and home, Tyrol rivals the classic fame of Switzerland herself. Let us hope that Hofer will have a better fate than Tell, now consigned to the limbo of myths. Hofer's statue in the court church may perhaps do something towards attesting his life in the flesh; but who can say whether, 500 years hence, it will not have become simply the embodiment of a national idea? True there are his hat and his braces in the museum, but the addition of his breeches and boots would avail but little, I fear, under proper mythic manipulation. I must confess to a special weakness for the hero: his exploits, the story of a child's book, had seized upon a child's imagination. How well at this moment do I recall the last of the woodcut illustrations—the cloaked officer, with his sword drawn, at the head of his great-coated soldiers on the moonlit snow, to whom, before the door of the wretched hovel, his last retreat, the betrayed man calmly presents himself, saying, 'I am Hofer.' It was a poor cut, no doubt; but I have wanted to see the 'Jaufen' ever since.

Winding walks cover the Berg Isel, and several sequestered seats overlook the gorge through which the torrent rushes, deep among trees and rocks. There could be no more delicious retreat for a few quiet Sunday hours. In the distance shone the spires of the city; behind them hung the great curtain of verdant mountain. By noon, however, the whole scene was darkened; clouds of dust, as if the columns of an army were in march, rolled along the wide valley, and fell in volumes upon the fields of rye. Thunder roared from the Brenner, and a storm like that of Lermoos soon burst over the city.

The Berg Isel for the morning; but for an evening view there is another spot dear to our recollection. As you look up from Innsbruck to that wonderful mountain barrier on the north—whence, it is said, the wolves look down into the streets, and where, in honour of their Emperor, the peasants once wrote his name in miles of bonfires,—at about a third of their apparent height, occurs an unsightly scar, the result of extensive quarrying. Just below this, reached by a very steep footpath through orchards, grass, and underwood, is a narrow projecting crag, difficult to discover among the deep furrows of the hill-sides, fringed as they are by trees and bushes. But, once attained, the visitor is startled to find the small area on its summit—some twenty feet by twelve—occupied by prayer-benches, and a large crucifix, before which burns a humble lamp. It is an oratory; perhaps for the use of the quarrymen above, perhaps the object of pious care to a cottage in the ravine below. From this solitary platform, all Innsbruck, and its arrowy river, and the valley up and down, are seen at your feet. Opposite, and lifted high, are the mountains of the Brenner and the Stubay Thal;—not yet a single Dolomite: that wild group is still far away to the southward. We had discovered this spot on a Sunday evening three years before, and could not spend another Sunday at Innsbruck without visiting it again. The storm was over, and the day closing in peaceful sunshine, as we took the winding narrow road by which the stone-carts reach the quarry from the village of Hottingen, and, after some trouble, found again the lonely cross. From end to end the valley shone in yellow light, bursting from the west among clouds and snow-peaks; while, eastward, the retreating storm relieved in gloom the golden hills—a solemn and beautiful sight. But the small lamp held no flame! Was the shrine deserted? At the moment a shoeless lad emerged from below, and, staring in silence at the intruders, began to trim the little oil vessel; soon its flickering light shone among the trees, and, as darkness fell, the bleached and blood-stained figure on the cross glimmered in its beams.

Monday morning, July 29, was serenely bright. That day week had seen us leaving by the Dover train from London Bridge. To-day we were to approach the real business of the journey in the Botzen diligence. It did not start till two o'clock in the afternoon; and the delay enabled us, among other preparations, to provide a sufficient stock of current money, since no town of consequence lay in our route for many weeks. The bundles of paper gulden, and of ten-kreutzer notes, that had to be accommodated in packets and pockets, were astonishing to behold; but it is an easy form of money after all.

A diligence journey is not generally very agreeable, but this one was an exception. The weather was faultless, the dust entirely laid by the storm of the previous day, and the heat tempered by a breeze. Bright Innsbruck and its valley were long in sight, as we crept up the broad white road of the Brenner; and when we crowned the ridge, and lost them, there were ample amends in the verdant hill-sides, sprinkled with villages, and glowing in the afternoon sun; and in the vistas on each side, and onward to the snowy regions gloriously illuminated. The zigzags had lifted us into the basin of the Sill. The Patscher Kofel, on the left, showed its bare summit against the cloudless blue; and the Stubay Thal, on the right, gave a moment's glimpse of its grandeurs. But the cheerful scene around was the charm. Population suits such a valley as this. The shaven lawny slopes invite a home; the hill-sides are made for orchards; the streams are in good fellowship with saw-mills; and alpine terrors, high above, give only a few hints of their presence. So a Tyrol, like a Swiss valley, swarms with life; and comparing this crowded country with the thinly inhabited rural districts of France, one can well appreciate the petulant exclamation of the French marshal, 'Austria can stamp armies out of the ground.'

Two small towns lie in the road, Mattrey and Steinach, and at the latter they show, but not to diligence folk, the bed in which Hofer slept the night before one of his great battles of the Berg Isel. Passing these, the shouldering mountains began to purple at their bases, and evening saw the heavy vehicles climbing the last steeps of the Brenner. Above, were pine-clothed hills, delicately feathered against the sky, and dark *silhouettes* of rocky forms, edged here and there by a star: below, a small lake, and a few melancholy houses deep in shade along the bottom of the valley. Yet there was blithness in the crisp air, as the passengers, all on foot, stepped briskly on, suddenly encountering a crowd of soldiers, whose oval and olive countenances showed them to belong to the sunny clime behind them. After a wide sweep round the basin of the lake, we drew up to the solitary post-house of the summit, and there was a rush of passengers in-doors for supper. The old coach supper! Yet not like those of yore, when the guard blew his horn, and the coach-lamps flashed in the sober streets of Bedford or Northampton. Here, a low ground-floor room received the party to a rather oleaginous meal; and before it was finished a deep roar of voices, in measured recitation, issued from the vaulted hall adjoining, where the family and servants, of both sexes, were seen on their knees at evening litany. A large dog, sitting solemnly on his haunches in the midst, lifted up his mouth as we passed through, and growled at the interruption to Divine service. Whoever saw English ostlers and chambermaids at prayers, while the mail was changing horses?

Outside, several heavy-laden waggons, long and low, with huge mediæval lanterns attached to each nodding front, were preparing to descend towards Innsbruck, working their breaks by a screw behind, which required one man's constant attendance. Our conductor was taking a survey of his vehicles,—the horses, the wheels, the lamps, finally of his passengers. Then, giving the word, the wheels began to grind, the bells to jingle, and with increasing speed—sharp working of the breaks and additional locking of the wheels—we sped down the southern side of the Brenner; soon conscious of little else, amid queer English dreams, than a rocking, a lurching, a rattling and jerking, a stopping and starting, and unwonted cold, under the brazen glitter of the moon.

By daylight we should arrive at our destination, and the entrance to the Dolomite region. Let me here, therefore, say something more of our intended course, and for what purpose we had taken the Brenner route. Churchill has told how he spent four days at Ratzes, the little bath-house under the Schlern. That was to be our first resting-place, selected because of its easy access from the Botzen road, and as the best point for the ascent both of the Schlern and the Seisser Alp — that grand plateau surrounded by Dolomite peaks, over whose pastures lies the track to Campitello. This latter village, at the head of the Fassa Thal, would be our next quarters for a night or two, and then, leaving his former route, we proposed to pass by the north face of the Marmolata, over the Fedaia (whose summit only he had reached), and drop down upon Caprile, at present known only as a name upon the map. Hence, after some stay, regulated by circumstances, we should cross the mountains to Cortina, on the Ampezzo road. In this way, the principal Dolomite district would be intersected on a line running directly eastward from Botzen; and Churchill's rambles of the preceding year utilised and extended. He had then started for his adventures from the small post-house of Atzwang, fourteen miles above Botzen; and to this spot also our places were taken, the diligence being due there about 3.30, A.M. We had written from Innsbruck for a baggage-horse to be in readiness, and, for the rest, proposed that our wives should there taste, for the first time, the pleasures of pedestrianism.

Sterzing is at the Brenner foot, but we passed it in the dark and asleep, unmindful of its picturesque street of inns, and of the 'Post,' which had once been hospitable to us: so also the weird Sterzinger Moos, though who knows but that the ghostly combatants of 1797 might have been holding midnight review on that field of slaughter. At Mittewald we looked out, under a splendid midnight moon, upon the large inn that almost blocks the road. Once it was the centre of the fight, when the 'Capuchino' Spechbacher and Hofer harried and destroyed a French marshal's army for miles along this deep ravine. Then came the spick and span Austrian fortress of Franzensfeste, with its dreary lengths of wall, an incongruous object in the forest defile; and at two in the morning we entered the vacant square of a town, where, without driver or conductor, we were left for some quarter of an hour, horses and passengers all napping together. There were the footsteps of a sentinel, and the glimmer of his bayonet, and that is all the impression that any of us have of the city of Brixen! An hour later, and the dawn was breaking far above our heads, for we were descending the grand defile of the Kunter's Weg, a misty depth still below us on the left, and vines in rich abandonment trailing by the road-side. An early peasant now and then, guiding his harnessed bullocks, gave the first signs of life; the narrow street of Klausen gave more; and when we pulled up at the next post station the day was all astir. It was four o'clock; the conductor, opening the doors, announced Atzwang: the baggage was put upon a bench, the diligence rolled away, and, rather dazed and chilly, we stood at the uninviting door, waiting for the bespoken horse, and with our morning's work before us.

But it was the threshold of the Dolomites. The sky was without a vapour, and the highest villages were already sparkling in the sun. Our spirits rose with the occasion. Coffee and bread beguiled the time while the bags were thrust into sacks, which were adjusted with difficulty upon a sturdy broad-backed horse; and by five o'clock, crossing a bridge to the left-hand bank of the Eisach, we struck the steep ascent: first, through vineyards growing almost perpendicularly; then, scattered orchards and corn-patches; lastly, pine-woods—all at a similar slant. If at one moment we passed a cottage door, the next we were looking down its chimney. The track, too, was rough and narrow —more like a staircase of rude steps than a path; so that at almost every turn the labouring horse, and all the party, stopped for breath. But then at every turn the views developed in greater loveliness. The red porphyritic soil of the terraced vineyards, and small cultured plots, mingled deliciously with the bright green of grass and foliage, melting on the opposite side of the valley into more delicate tints, as recesses in the hills, each with its village campanile, opened to sight. Southward was the blue hollow in which Botzen lay, and over all was spread the mellow softness of a southern atmosphere. Judge whether our early walk was not delightful!

In about an hour and a half—'There!' cried Churchill, 'there is the Hohe Schlern!' and through and topping the trees above appeared its pale isolated peaks, rising higher and looming darker at every step; till, after we had surmounted the first shoulder of the hills, and entered upland basins of pasture and wood, it displayed itself in all its majesty, shooting up in pinnacles and walls of rock, with the morning sun behind them. Forests clothed its base; a solitary little church occupied a green mound in front; and a ruined castle hung over a ravine which fell into the valley we had left.* Altogether I do not know that a

* We have been amused to find in an illustrated work upon Tyrol, published more than thirty years ago, the letterpress of which professes to have been supplied by a companion of Hofer, the following description of the Schlern, as seen from this point: 'On the opposite side of the Eisach, the Schleren Kofel first arrests the attention, stretching towards heaven's vault in lofty preeminence its monstrous craggy summits, not unlike *various petrified rays.*' The same writer speaks of the Dolomites of the Gader Thal as '*rude and undigested nature,*' and of the upper Fassa as 'containing those singular productions of natural curiosity, called the Dolomit columns!'

The style is delightfully characteristic of what may be called the pre-Alpine period of literature.

better approach can be made to Dolomite scenery. Its splendid features break sublimely upon the sight in the noble towers of the Schlern, and it is here advantaged by a rare alliance with history and romance. You have just climbed out of the deep ravine of the Kunter's Weg, through which pours all the modern traffic of the Brenner; and now stand upon the slopes where the Roman and Mediæval road was carried, and village names speak of their Latin origin. Those forests before you are the same whose greenness is celebrated in the venerable 'Helden-Buch, the precursor of the 'Niebelungen-Lied;' and the fragment of Schloss Hauenstein, the eyrie of the one-eyed poet, Oswald the Minnesinger, will soon be seen embedded in their midst.

The two hours which yet remained were, however, rather trying to our lady pedestrians—not to say that the want of bed-rest, and the effects of cramped limbs, were felt by all. But the Schlern folk had put a wooden bench beside a gush of water from a small pipe among ferns and moss—just the place for a rest: and every backward view showed expanding prospects; and ranges of snowy alps, clear to the faintest outline, began to lift themselves into the tender sky to the west and north. Farther on, the yellow walls of a ruin peered out of the woods, and that was Hauenstein! Yet still the path turned and turned, and climbed steep after steep, through dark alleys among the pines, a roaring stream showing here and there glimpses of its foam. At last a few loungers—not tourists, and yet scarcely peasants—indicated an approach to somewhere; but it was not till within a few yards of the building itself that the humble bath-house of Ratzes came in sight, jammed close under the precipices of the Schlern to the right; while on the left rose the sides of the Seisser Alp, a thick mass of wood. The only open space was the little patch of green about the house; the only view was of the nightmare rocks overhead, the pine trunks, and the

SCHLERN, AND RATZES BATH-HOUSE.

torrent, which, hitherto more heard than seen, now appeared issuing from the dark mouth of a gorge.

It is a singular spot; and the two low white-washed buildings connected by the covered bridge-like gallery, and small intervening chapel, look rather comfortless at first sight, and do not improve upon further acquaintance. But the long journey had brought us to the first halting-place among the Dolomites, and we were not disposed to be fastidious. Several women, chatting and knitting, occupied the gallery; and several men, chatting and smoking, the shady side of the house, and an open shed upon the grass. Our appearance drew all eyes, and the Kellnerin—a very sweet-looking girl, but not the same, Churchill whispered us, who had danced so deftly while she served his dinner—quickly descended to meet us. Her voice and manner, and delicately formed figure, seemed strangely inappropriate to her calling; but her intelligence and activity as Kellnerin were invaluable. Yet, with all the good-will in the world, she could not at the first offer us a welcome, for the house was entirely full. How had we pictured to ourselves cool rooms, hot water, tubs *ad libitum*, and refreshing changes of raiment! Now, with our baggage in a heap on the ground, and the nearest village more than an hour distant, we had to discuss an imminent disarrangement of our plans. Knowing that we were out of the track of tourists, it had not occurred to us that a bath-house might nevertheless be full of patients! Under any perplexity, if you cannot sleep upon it, the next best thing is to dine upon it; and having spent, as it seemed, already half the day, although it was not yet ten o'clock, we adopted this resource. Difficulties began to disappear with the courses. The soft-voiced Kellnerin, the sharp-voiced but not ill-disposed Wirthin her mistress, and an old woman acting as grand-chamberlain, held council round the table, ending in the offer of the landlady's room—if we did not mind herself and children passing through it to a small inner apartment—and of another in the basement among the baths. By the stern rule of alternating choice, adhered to during all our journeys, Science on this occasion went below, accompanied in a cheerful spirit of martyrdom by his wife; while we of the pencil and brush settled into quarters almost as undesirable from their publicity—a defect in some degree remedied by driving nails in the walls, stretching a cord across, and suspending two or three sheets opportunely discovered in a wardrobe. The contrivance was not, however, quite to the taste of the old lady-chamberlain.

By the following night two better rooms fell to our share; but if any one thinks of Ratzes as a summer retreat, or even for a night's quarters, it should be distinctly known that it is a very rough place—far below the ordinary comforts of a country inn. The best rooms are but bare narrow chambers, with a couple of deal beds in each, blankets and counterpanes none of the cleanest, and one small window, admitting what light can be reflected under the screen of woods and rocks. Below stairs, a sloppy sound indicates hydropathy; and outside, the ear is fatigued by the unceasing rush of water, and, from earliest dawn, the clatter, the dabble, and thud, thud, of washerwomen. One large low room, with deal tables soiled and stained, forms the salle, both '*à manger*' and '*de récréation*'—the latter consisting chiefly of cards and smoking. To the cards the men sit down, with their hats on, at any hour of the day, shouting, screaming, and banging their fists upon the boards. But at seven in the morning, and at seven in the evening, all crowd into the little chapel; those that cannot enter standing on a gallery round a window which affords a peep into the interior. A friar—there are usually two or three of these cowled and sandaled personages about the establishment—officiates, and afterwards joins in a noisy meal at one long coarsely furnished table. A recess in this room offered some refuge to the more quietly disposed, and we arranged our meals at hours when the crowd had dispersed; but the general aspect was that of a workhouse, without its English discipline and cleanliness. Yet the people were good-natured and cordial. The gallery connecting the sleeping-house with that containing the 'Speisesaal' and kitchens being a favourite lounging-place for shade, view, and proximity to the chapel, it was difficult to thread one's way along it, and to acknowledge becomingly the nods, becks, smiles, and friendly words with which our passage was unfailingly saluted. Although most were of the peasant or small-proprietor class, there were two or three families from Botzen, and other places farther south, whose appearance and manners were every way agreeable; and some of the monks, one of whom was a Professor of Natural History at Botzen, were courteous and educated men. The great heat of the valley of the Adige drives its inhabitants during the summer to mountain retreats like these. A favourite resort is the Rittner Alp, rising behind Botzen on the western side of the valley of the Eisach; others avail themselves, notwithstanding the rude accommodation, of the Ratzes baths.

These are arranged on the ground-floor of the building, and present a singular appearance. The waters of two springs, one chalybeate and the other sulphureous, rising out of beds of augite porphyry, and of bituminous limestone, in the recesses of the ravine, are laid on through several damp-looking rooms, where rows of wooden coffins—literally such if appearance goes for anything—are disposed, into which the water is turned for use. A hole in the lid allows the patient's head to protrude, propped upon a board, while the rest of the body has found a watery grave. Curtains divide these social sarcophagi from each other, if desired, but they are generally withdrawn, and the members of a family or acquaintances lie in friendly communication, like the damned in Dante's fiery sepulchres, save that fire is exchanged for water, and groans and sighs for cheerful talk and laughter.

Arriving at Ratzes on Tuesday morning, July 30, we remained for nearly a week, and having plenty to do abroad, with splendid weather to do it in, discomforts within doors were not hard to bear. The principal disadvantage of the situation consists in the limited and monotonous character of the immediately surrounding walks. A few seats are scattered among the trees, but they afford no view, and though there is a torrent, there is not even the usual hand-post to a 'Wasserfall,' for the simple reason that there is no 'Wasserfall' to see. A skittle-ground is some resource for a portion of the company, but a more polite amusement is found in paddling a small boat in an almost smaller pool, black and stagnant, among the trees half an hour below the house. At about that distance, however, in another direction, the woods are left behind, and a charming prospect opens over that undulating plateau, midway between the deep valley of the Eisach and the upper platform of the Seisser Alp, which has been already referred to as a fertile and populous district, both in Roman and Mediæval times. It is still delightfully diversified by cultivation; woods, orchards, cottage homesteads, and villages are spread over its surface, and from Ratzes almost every path leads towards it. Once reached and the view extends beyond itself. On the left hand, as a lofty side-scene, rises to the sky the imposing Schlern, with the ruin of Hauenstein projecting from its wooded flanks; behind you are the steeps of the Puflatsch, and the ascent to the Seisser Alp; towards the right extend the rolling hills among which Castelruth and various hamlets nestle, backed by the distant masses of the Brenner; and in front, if you have chosen the proper hour, you will see the sun set behind the snowy ranges of the Adamello and the Oertler. Such was the view displayed to us on our first evening walk; and, returning through the dark woods, the lights of the little bath-house looked home-like after all.

I was eager to set foot on the Seisser Alp, and the following day was devoted to it. Churchill has already described his visit to this Alp, but it is so important a feature in the Western Dolomites, that I may be allowed to give my own impression as I now made my first acquaintance with its scenery. The paved pathway from Seiss to the summit passes along the western face of the Puflatsch at a considerable height above Ratzes; it can be reached by various paths from châlet to châlet on the grassy slopes, at a point about half an hour below the brow of the Alp. The paths fully exposed to the morning sun, and the paved track burning with the reflected heat of the rocks above, were so trying to S. and A., that furnished with provisions for the day, Churchill and I pressed on alone. Looking backward, the snowy range was seen greatly extended towards the north, comprising not only the Adamello and Oertler Spitze groups, but also the mountains of the Oetzthal. Every peasant pointed out the latter with promptness. Some were acquainted with the Oertler as well, but none knew anything of the Adamello, except that it was a mountain in 'Welschland,' or foreign parts. It is singular that on the same horizon an almost continuous line of mountains should be so differently known. The summit of the Seisser is reached by a gap in the rim, and looking back through this, the Schlern, which had been growing more imposing with every step, is seen filling up the space—a grand purple

J. Gilbert, del[t] Hanhart lith

THE LANGKOFEL & PLATTKOGEL, FROM THE SEISSER ALP.

mass of wall. There is still a climb, and then huge white shapes rise in front over the undulating surface, like ships at sea; a little farther, and he who wishes to behold the Dolomites has before him some of their finest specimens, circling round the green-domed Alp, which, like an inverted bowl, bears them on its sides.

The Schlern, to the south-west, forms the mighty buttress of the whole; the Ross Zähne, 'red teeth'—well named, both from form and colour—follow, stretching eastward. Then come the gigantic masses of the Platt Kogel and Lang Kofel; the first, sliced off, as by the malice of a Titan, at a single blow; the second, an array of splintered spires, ashy-tinted or pale yellow. A confusion of cindery peaks and precipices succeed, bearing northward; a green elevation of the Seisser itself hides more of them from view, as it has already hidden the Oertler and his fellows. But a sudden dip shows a portion of the Noric chain, clear, this day, with its delicate snows.

The Lang Kofel undoubtedly centres in itself the chief interest of the view. 'Murray' gives a slight outline of this mountain, as seen edgeways from the Gröden Thal. There its aspect is more remarkable, but its construction and vast proportions are better appreciated from the Seisser Alp. Yet it is vast more as a rock than a mountain. It is a citadel of the giants, walled, bastioned, battlemented, turreted, all in fit proportion; conceived in this light, it will not disappoint expectation. Churchill, for botanical purposes, pushed on to reach its base; I remained on the summit of the Seisser.

This Alp, the largest in Tyrol, is full of hills and valleys, streams, scattered brushwood, small hay-barns, and châlets; and at this season was merry with rows of haymakers, men cutting, women bundling—for the hay is all carted on their backs. Their songs and shouts filled the air; and the whole surface was diversified with colour—bright velvet green where it was mown and finished; sage-leaf where the cut hay lay; a dull green, speckled bright with flowers, where the crop was yet untouched; and yellow in the marshy bottoms. I spent a joyous day roaming from swell to swell of the noble Alp; dining on a smooth knoll, where every passing haymaker wished one 'guten appetit;' and did not turn homeward till the western sky was all a-glow. At the brink of the descent I waited for Churchill, and soon the clink of his alpenstock, and the sound of his voice in conversation with a peasant, far heard in the still air, gave notice of his coming. He had lost much time, and found little to reward him, among the entangling pine-woods at the foot of the Lang Kofel.

It was time to hurry down, but the descent seemed interminably deep and steep; and after leaving the paved track, short cuts only brought us to impossible edges, which it was necessary either to skirt or hark back from; and the woods were full of pine stumps, white faces of rock, and blacknesses of fern or moss. Ratzes seemed to have sunk miles deep since the morning; but at last we came upon S—— and A——, sitting disconsolately on a pine log under the stars, and they led us, now almost blind with staring for the path, into the radiance of the friendly Ratzes lights, which were not long in guiding us 'home.'

Thursday—of course the Schlern. No! despite the marvellous purity of the atmosphere, which promised a perfect prospect, we looked up at its aërial battlements, and—let it alone; assigning several good reasons, which would not have signified a rush had we been up and girded by four o'clock in the morning. That we were not, was a weakness; and as, during the day, the still unclouded pinnacles met our view, we felt that we were trifling with golden opportunities. The day was given to luxurious idling, yet not without a purpose, for we walked over to Castelruth, where our landlady owned an inn, the 'Red Horse,' at present in charge of our charming Kellnerin's sister. Though very hot, it was a delightful walk of four or five miles over the open. Narrow paths, rudely paved, led through grass, or round plots of arable, and sometimes under shade of the yet unstripped ash trees, from cottage to cottage, and from barn to barn, where the flails were busy. Castelruth, however, is in such a hollow that the tall spire of its church, surrounded by its clump of houses on a small hill, was a sudden apparition. The 'Red Horse' is by no means the only hostel, and as we stood at a fountain in a straggling sort of 'Platz,' a good-natured girl ran across from a rival establishment, 'The Lamme' of 'Murray,' to offer us glasses. But our credit at home was at stake; and though our friend's sister did not equal herself in good looks, she was quite as tasteful and apt; and the cool rooms of the 'Horse,' beautifully clean, and empty of guests, the dinner, and the coffee, gave us large content, and drew down odious comparisons upon Ratzes. Castelruth would certainly offer far more eligible quarters for tourists in general.

On the rocky hill below the village is a chapel to St. Kummernitz—a lady be it understood, though you might not have guessed it, for she wears a beard; but that is the miracle, and therefore quite easy of comprehension. The beard was a protection granted by heaven on account of the pertinacity of her suitors, and is said to have been entirely successful. It is still flourishing on her statue; but we preferred to rest upon, instead of climb, the ledges of rock, lizard-haunted, which lead to the shrine. The afternoon light glorified the distant Schlern, aloft over the roofs of the houses; *that* was something worth gazing at.

Also a pretty vista of a vale opened toward the east, cheerfully dotted with châlets and farms, and patched all over with bright grass plots, red arable, and yellow corn, interspersed with copse-wood—nothing particular to look at in itself; there may be many such vales. But here, at the farther end, to dignify and dominate the otherwise homely scene, uprose two or three grey wizard peaks of the inevitable Dolomite—hoary prophets of evil, or witnesses of a by-gone wrath: which you please.

We lingered too long, yet could not refrain from halting on our return, for a last view of Castelruth, backed with pine-wood hills, and over them the tossing lines of the Brenner mountains, now purple under a gathering storm, which presently lighted us through the twilight with ominous flashes. Hardly could we trace the path, and the darkness of the Ratzes woods was dark indeed. Sooner than we thought, a steady light shone through the trees, but there was something uncanny in the look—something to remind one these were the woods of old romance. A few steps further, and the flattering imp turned to a brilliant glow-worm on the bank, almost bright enough to read by. No thanks to it, but to the white 'Kühleborn' of a torrent, rushing through the forest, that we found our way to supper and our beds.

The next morning, knocked out of bed before four o'clock by a guide who would stand no more nonsense, and leaving our wives to make another night of it if they liked, we made hasty breakfast of 'cioccolata'—here, and in all these parts, a handy and comfortable beverage—and stuffing a wallet with hard-boiled eggs and bread, in which pats of butter were cunningly inserted, 'took up' the gully beyond the house, rejoicing to see the peaks of Schlern still clear in a stainless sky. It was time to do it, for over-night, on entering the Speisesaal, a rubicund dame rushed up in great excitement to inform us that she had that day accomplished the ascent on her way from Botzen, pointing to her lobster complexion in proof of the exploit, a result which, perhaps, did not encourage S—— and A—— to follow her example. It was certain, however, that our Botzen friend, whatever her hardihood, could not have accomplished the scramble which now occupied us for nearly a couple of hours—petticoats forbad. She had, indeed, avoided it by a considerable détour. Yet petticoats might not have been the difficulty, for one of the Ratzes arrivals was in the shape of a very large and solemn-looking lady, astride upon a donkey, with a result it is better not to speak of, but which she did not seem to care for, as she gravely returned our salutation. But to return; we were climbing up the steepest hill-side that pines could grow upon, with symptoms of a path sometimes—sometimes none, the principal tokens thereof being axe notches, like stiles in a Yorkshire wall, cut in the large trunks of fallen pines where they lay across the track; or, again, where, at frequent intervals, a deep funnel shooting downwards, worn by water to its backbones, showed faint footmarks across it, always glittering with wet, and often upon the ledge of an actual waterfall. These mountain woods are usually strangely silent, but here the lively notes of finches cheered the recesses, and answered to the morning sunshine.

In something under two hours sky light appeared through the trees, and we stepped again upon the Seisser Alp at one of its extreme corners. Across the deep ravine beside us stood the Schlern, sending down its walls to an unseen basement, and rising loftily above. Its real summit, now for the first time visible, was to be attained by heading the end of the ravine, and slanting up the precipitous isthmus of hill by which it is connected with the Ross

Zähne peaks. But a hospitable senner, or cheesemaker's hut, just on the edge of the alp, detained us a few minutes. An unaffected delight at seeing 'Engländer,' and the ready proffer of a bench and a milk bowl, claimed some response on our part. So we sat awhile in the black interior among the cheeses, answering the questions of the worthy folk, whom C—— amazingly impressed with the information that England was distant 'a thousand hours.' As we departed we heard the good man still repeating to his wife as they stood at the door, 'Tausend stunden!—tausend stunden!'

Crossing a rapid stream which tumbled into the ravine on our right, we ascended the hill-side, turning now towards the Schlern itself. The climbing was only tedious, and chiefly through the dwarf creeping pine scrub that haunts particularly the higher portions of the Eastern Alps, and which Berlepsch has well described; it twists and writhes, and mats its branches over large surfaces, without any appearance of separate stems. Occasionally we crossed a grassy slope, and startled into angry curiosity several heavy red-hided oxen, more like denizens of fat English counties than of altitudes like these. They were probably brought from the Italian plains for the summer, but they had learnt to climb well. Higher, we began to skirt the brink of precipices and to look down long chasms, in winter choked hundreds of feet deep in snow, and even now floored with white. Surmounting this second steep ascent, we reached a plateau, answering to the Seisser Alp below, and sloping gradually to the summit of the Schlern. It was a garden of Alpine flowers—gentians, anemones, Alpine thrift, and 'Edelweiss' enough for a score of courtships. In little more than four hours after leaving Ratzes, we stood upon the edge of those tremendous precipices which, from the bath-house, seemed to belong only to the eagles. We might have pitched a stone upon the roof of the building, a tiny toy-house, four or five thousand feet below, and our guide, selecting a fissure as a funnel for his voice, directed down it a long ululation. We watched with a telescope for some sort of telegraphic response, but nobody stirred into the blazing sunshine, and our small selves felt rather affronted. It is this great precipice which gives grandeur to the Schlern; another, so sheer and lofty, can scarcely be found out of the Dolomite district.

Of course, from every mountain top one sees a larger slice of the world than ordinary, and I am not going to walk round with a wand to the several points of the horizon. The peculiar features were: first, the nature of the summit itself, a confused mass of white rocks tumbled up in heaps, and so dazzling, as to bring the dark spectacles into use. One of these heaps, withdrawn a quarter of a mile from the actual brink, formed the summit, and from among its huge blocks three beams of wood, raised in a triangle, showed where the government surveyors had been at work. Secondly, as to the view: there was the hazy expanse southward where the hills faded into Venetia, and to west and north the snowy ranges already described, commencing with the Adamello, and circling round in numberless peaks till they ended, as we believed, in the Gross Glockner itself, far to the north-east. But, thirdly, and this is *the* sight to be seen, round the eastern half of the prospect, stood the Dolomite brethren of the Schlern, all peaks, bosses, and walls, cutting against the sky in endless diversity, from the near-at-hand Ross Zähne and Rosengarten, to the Marmolata, monarch of them all, from whose white summit of snow a wonderful precipice fell abruptly on the south. There was even a distant peep of the Sasso di Pelmo, a tower like that which Babel might have been, and which would be voted utterly inaccessible, had not Mr. Ball brought from the summit some rare plants. Of course the Platt Kogel, and Lang Kofel stood out grandly upon the rim of the Seisser, which last, twenty-five hundred feet below, lay like a tumultuous carpet, scored with the brown seams of its now empty water-courses.

We did not mean to hurry down. After dining at a slender rill among the hummocks, the guide, who had no other function, went to sleep; Churchill to prowl among rock crevices, poking out their tiny flowerets; and I did duty with my sketch-book. How still it was! While busy with pencil and brush, a nibbling at my side betrayed a fat mouse, vigorously engaged upon the greasy leather of the guide's pouch. In default of pouches, what does the creature live upon nine thousand feet in air? Its next attack was upon my boots, and though often repelled, its familiarities were as often renewed.

It was difficult to set the first foot downward from such a noble platform, but a storm brewing southward helped us to do it. By the time we reached the Seisser Alp, this same storm afforded a rare spectacle of grandeur. It was sweeping over the Mendola, and other ranges west of Botzen, and under its dark arch, and through its veil of rain, were seen shining the Oertler Spitze, and its snowy compeers, still bright in the sun—a lovely vision, as if the clouds had lifted to show a glimpse of paradise! To prolong the sight, and avoid the fatiguing gully up which we had toiled in the morning, we crossed the Seisser to its usual exit by the side of the Puflatsch, and dropped into the Ratzes woods shortly before six.

Saturday should have been cooler for the storm, but on the contrary was beyond anything sultry. It was an opportunity to visit the sloppy bath-floor. But we gentlemen drew back rather hastily at espying the jolly countenance of the Botzen lady under one of the coffin-lids, and our wives were for beating a similar retreat when they recognised her black-bearded husband *perdu* in an adjoining sarcophagus. They both invited entrance, however, in such hearty tones, that we returned in a body, and spent a quarter of an hour of needless condolence.

For us, a pleasanter retreat during the hot hours was the Hauenstein Schloss. From almost every direction its yellow fragment of a tower is seen jutting from a rock on the wooded flank of the Schlern; but we had postponed a visit till some leisure time. The wood-paths now offered grateful shade under the noonday heat, and in about half an hour we reached the ruin. A goat or two were browsing within, peering out of the gaping holes which once were windows,—perhaps profaning that where, according to the Castelruth legend, the imprisoned wife lay dead with streaming hair. The ruin is too complete, and it is difficult to invest the place with its proper atmosphere of romance. Should the reader ever find himself at Ratzes, let him reserve Hauenstein for evening shades. Then the woods around, the precipices above, the village-sprinkled slopes below, and the far dark mountains, may shed forth some of the poetry which once filled the soul of the Minnesinger, and which, earlier still, drew from the unknown author of the 'Helden Buch' his commendation of the Hauenstein 'Grüne Tan.'

CHAPTER V.

RATZES TO CORTINA.

Departure from Ratzes—Sunday on the Seisser Alp — The Herdman's Hut — The Col and the Duron Thal — Campitello — The Festa — The Fedaia — Gorge of Sottoguda — Caprile, Monte Civitá, and Lago Alleghe—Sta. Lucia, and the Pass of the Gusella—Dolomitic marvels — Descent upon Cortina.

We had intended to pass over on Saturday to Campitello, but the only procurable horse at the present hay season was one belonging to the baths, which, being employed all the week in fetching provisions from Atzwang, could only be spared on a Sunday. Nor could we well have ventured in face of the oppressive and foreboding heat that day. The expected storm came in the afternoon. For many hours it raged among the precipices of the Schlern; as night drew on, their stark shapes were photographed from instant to instant on the blackness, and illuminated crimson and blue by turns, as if for pyrotechnic display. The covered gallery was crowded with spectators during this magnificent performance, till swirls of wind and rain drove everybody into better shelter. Yet it was held to be of good promise for the morrow, and before we went to bed the hurly-burly had passed on northward, and the stars were shining in a clear sky.

Sunday morning was bright to a fault; the horse was at our disposal, and we yielded to the circumstances which seemed to compel our making use of it on that day. It was certain that Ratzes would be very gay and noisy; they were preparing for a dance in the afternoon, and we knew that the solitary hills would at least afford us some hours of congenial quiet. We should have started early, but the man who was to take charge of our baggage, first attended five o'clock mass at Seiss, and it was nearly eight before we got away. Though not dependent upon him as a guide, Churchill having crossed the col the year before, it was desirable to see him well *en route*; then man and horse took their own pace and course, and we ours.

A crowd of affectionate friends assembled in the gallery to witness our departure, and waved hats and hands, as we followed our possessions, at first swagging rather ominously on the packsaddle, up the stony wood-path. Sooth to say we were rather tired by this time of Ratzes and its inmates, including certain spiders, some six inches from toe to toe, in joint possession of the bedrooms; and it was with some feeling of relief that we climbed the peaceful hill-side. The ascent to the Seisser Alp was a steep beginning for S—— and A——; but helped by the morning coolness, and rewarded by the growing prospects, widening at every step till the violet distance was set all round with a delicate fringe of snow peaks, they kept well at it, and stepped at length upon the broad undulating surface of the Alp, now empty of its haymakers, who had all gone down to the valleys for the day. Then it was nothing but delight to stroll slowly over the rolling expanse of smooth shaven grass, and to rest in the shade of deserted châlets, breathing the pure air of six or seven thousand feet of altitude. This was our place for 'morning service.' Round half the horizon stood the splendid array of Dolomites, and northward was a clear vista to the snowy Noric chain. The whole scene, wrapped in the deepest Sabbath repose, answered to Sabbath thoughts; nothing moved but in the distance our man and horse with a chance companion—

specks upon the green Alp hills—till we finally lost them over the col.

Five hours passed in leisurely progress; then, being some way up a second steep ascent, by which we should leave the Seisser Alp at its southern corner, and cross over the ridge between the Ross Zähne on the right, and the Platt Kogel on the left, into the Duron Thal, we called a halt at a herdsman's hut, this side of the mountain being devoted to cattle.

A rest under a roof, however humble, however rude the seats and fusty the smells, is far more of a rest than under the open sky; and a meal is far more of a meal if you can add to it a bowl of milk. Here—in the dark and smoky interior, full of odd shelves, lumber, wooden utensils, pans of milk, conspicuous in their whiteness, and rows of formless objects, discovered to be cheeses—we spread out our stores. Milk was ladled plentifully into a wooden bowl, by a kindly, wrinkled old crone, who, when we were satisfied, returned to her own domestic concerns, holding long discourse in a jargon of patois with her husband, and concocting a dish of nüdeln, a kind of home-made maccaroni, which, tied in a handkerchief, was despatched by a boy up the blue mountain-side,—up into the basking sunlight there, where some member of the family was on duty with the herd. Every step or chance sound was distinct in the noonday stillness—a distant goat-bleat, or the cluck of a fowl on the door-step; and in the various corners where we had niched ourselves to rest, the effect was so lulling, that perhaps some of us almost forgot our whereabouts that Sunday afternoon, and were rather startled at the summons to step out again into the thin air of a mountain solitude.

Far above, on the sides of the Platt Kogel to the left, shone a small white chapel, marking a shorter, but much more precipitous, pass into the Duron Thal. We followed the easier path close to the Ross Zähne, and to the great walls of rock which stretch between them and the Rosengarten. These were beginning to throw afternoon shadows, while the hill-sides opposite glowed with solid colour. It was a steep climb over green bosses, where all track was lost, towards the notch in the ridge, which indicated the summit of the col ; and here occurred a first specimen of the Augite porphyry in masses of blackish and rounded rock, protruding from the grassy bases of the hills like huge elephants, very uncouth and Indian-looking. It lines the Duron Thal to a considerable extent—a total contrast both in form and colour to its tall Dolomite neighbours. At last, upon the crest, the path, again visible, dropped instantly on the other side into the long trough of the Duron valley, fenced on the south by prodigious mural precipices.

At that spot we spent a half-hour to remember; the new valley, yet untrodden, opening at our feet, and a new world of mountains, yet unexplored, peering up, one behind the other. Among them, in obvious domination, was the Marmolata itself, with its hood and robe of snow thrown back to the north, and its bare front lifted to the south. But we looked most at those we were leaving, and from which the first downward step would shut us out, to be seen no more for at least this year's journey. That glittering Noric range, which had been our charm for many hours, seemed now, as we gave it farewell, even more glorious under the declining sun than in the whiter light of morning.

A scarcely perceptible path led steeply down among bosky crags into the long and narrow valley—all grass-plot at the bottom, and all deserted of inhabitants. Grey crucifixes were scattered about, whose artistic excellence was very remarkable, as if the rude German hand had already given place to that of Italy; and a few châlets, closed and silent, bordered a bright stream, whose windings caused us some trouble, having frequently to extemporise a bridge of logs or stones. Otherwise the scene was as sweet, and the path as soft, as that of Christian's by-path meadow; while there was no chance of having, like Christian, mistaken the way. But the pastoral scene came to a sudden end, and such as Bunyan's imagination would have delighted in. The valley floor broke off abruptly into the abyss of a savage gorge, where the stream, transformed to foam, dashed madly down towards the village of Campitello, whose roofs were now visible below like small brown mats spread out upon a slope. Here we met our man and horse returning, anxious to save daylight. Enforcing upon us the number of times we must cross and recross the torrent by various crazy bridges, he parted with a hearty hand-shake all round. Evening was indeed coming up fast from the depths, and we lingered no longer: our last crumb of biscuit and last drop of cold tea bad been consumed, and we began to think of supper; yet it was nearly seven o'clock before we found ourselves among the dispersed and forlorn-looking houses of the Italian hamlet. The six hours assigned by the peasants to this pass we had extended to ten.

Churchill had retained feeling remembrance of very short commons at 'Bernard's' in 1860, and our baggage had therefore been directed to another inn, of which we had heard at Ratzes. There we found it, but the people candidly admitted they could not provide for our meals, and a glance at their beds made it equally clear they could as little furnish us with lodging. The other house looked better, but the door opened upon an ill-favoured company, shouting, smoking, drinking, and gambling; and a sulky-looking landlord sauntered out, pipe in mouth, to know what we wanted—waiting to be told rather than condescending to ask. Here was an arrival! You may picture S—— and A——, now thoroughly tired, as they peeped in at the inhospitable doors, and may imagine our compunction at having brought them to such a den. They might have been better lodged, we thought, in any of the sweet-smelling hay-barns of the Alp above. But matters soon improved. Bernard, the landlord, took his pipe from his mouth and smoothed his brow as he recognised Churchill. He even began to bestir himself after the key of the upper rooms, which fate had mislaid, and, failing in the search, energetically put a girl through a window to draw back the bolt. We ascended a staircase, beset indeed with dreadful odours, but the landing opened to an outside gallery, and was free to the evening air. It gave entrance to two rooms, gaudily painted in fresco; one of them in particular, as Churchill has already described, decorated with a series of landscapes, not exactly up to Stanfield's mark, but recognisable representations of various mountain scenes, in which some of the neighbouring Dolomites looked even more wonderful than themselves. Things were in great disorder; but the furniture was much superior to that of Ratzes, and when household stores had been disinterred, there was more notion of clean linen and toilet appurtenances than could have been expected.

Meanwhile there was a dreary interval, and the state of the larder was not encouraging. Meat there was none; but to await and hasten something in the shape of supper we descended to a gloomy ground-floor room, passing to it gingerly and swiftly through the smoking and card parties. There, established with a single candle, whose light was swallowed in the darkness of roof and floor, and only glimmered faintly on the black surfaces of ancient presses, we waited, far gone into the second hour, while sometimes a knife, sometimes a spoon, now a fork, and then a plate, arrived, as if the house were being rummaged for the remainder. The silent resignation of our wives became too appalling, and we saw that a crisis was at hand. Seizing, then, the tea-canister, Churchill and I invaded the kitchen, where desultory attempts were making to coax a fire. We demanded fresh wood, we collected all the jugs, we actually succeeded in boiling—yes, *boiling*—water in a large pan. We demented Bernard with requisitions. Then, with the steaming tea-jug, we returned into the 'presence;' a motley procession of assistants, laden with bread, butter, honey, milk, eggs, and a supply of hot water in various-sized pots, bringing up the rear. The effect was gratifying; headaches evaporated, talk began to flow; we discoursed upon the long day's solitary grandeurs, and could laugh now at our ill-omened arrival. The exploration of these valleys, which for a dark hour had trembled in the balance, so far as S—— and A—— were concerned, was restored to their thoughts as at least a possibility; and we went cheerfully to bed within the painted chambers.

Campitello is excellently situated for variety of excursion at the head of the Fassa Thal, a valley which Churchill has described in recent pages. The Fassa, I may remind the reader, is considered to afford the readiest access to Dolomite scenery; yet in itself it has little to show, and may well disappoint the traveller who simply passes through. The more remarkable mountains lie back from sight, and can only be appreciated by excursions to the right and left, while, as will presently be found, the most striking scenery, hitherto unnoticed by 'Murray,' and unsuspected, therefore, by tourists, lies altogether to the east. Campitello, however, offers the advantage of being so placed as to command not only the best portion of the Fassa valley, but the entrance to the Duron Thal on the west, and that of the Fedaia pass, skirting the precipices of the Marmolata on the east; while northward a fine pass leads into the Gröden and Gader Thals, at the back of the Lang Kofel. It is, therefore, much to be regretted that Bernard's small inn offers but one tolerable bedroom, and cannot raise either a cutlet or a potatoe for dinner. That remained the difficulty; fowls and lettuce were indeed provided for the day after our arrival, but fowls in these parts are only flaccid bags of bones, that add a feeble flavour to the soup, and then are done for. It is hopeless to construct a reasonable dinner out of any number of them. Something, however, to be called by that name was left to Bernard's inventive genius, and then, while S—— and A—— took to the shady bank of the stream—for the lovely day rivalled its predecessors, and not a cloud smirched the sky—Churchill departed to botanise towards the Marmolata, and I explored the bases of some extraordinary Dolomites overhanging Campitello, on the north.

The Marmolata is best seen from the gorge of the Duron Thal, and by far the most striking effect about Campitello is due to these crags of Dolomites, which are, in fact, portions of the Lang Kofel. Their really vast proportions are concealed by an intervening hill, but nothing can be more singular than their appearance, and in certain lights, such as sunset or moonlight, they look positively unearthly. They nod to each other like monstrous images set in a row, some more massive, some slender and spiry, or cleft so as to suggest that resemblance to sword blades which 'Murray' mentions as characteristic of certain Dolomite forms. One looks at the strange array as if they were fetish, and can hardly suppose but that in pagan times they were so regarded—perhaps are still—in a valley so remote, where ancient superstitions may lurk unsuspected. We had a good opportunity for observing the population. In the early morning a long procession was wending from village to village, saluted by all the church bells, and by puffs of blue smoke and reverberating discharges from the hill side above Campitello. Preceded by a large top-heavy crucifix

DOLOMITES OF CAMPITELLO.

and by several banners, or rather pictures stretched between lofty poles, and swaying in the gentle air, walked some hundred men, two and two, bareheaded, and reciting prayers. So far so good, but then came a distressingly bedizened Mrs. Guy Fawkes of a Madonna, seated in a chair, and with a sceptre tottering in her waxen hands. Three priests, that followed with pressed palms and down-cast eyes, only made that portion of the spectacle more painful. A train of women to match that of the men closed the procession, and continued the same monotonous recitation. As the silken pictures glanced in the sunlight and flickered among the trees, and the sound of bells, guns, and chanting voices went mingling down the valley, while the mountains looked down in ineffable calm, the incident was picturesque enough.

Whether any particular Catholic feeling was roused by the occasion I do not know, but the small boys of Campitello amused themselves afterwards with throwing stones at S—— and A—— whenever they could get a convenient shy at them; this had certainly not been provoked by any intentional acts of disrespect. But the village redeemed itself. A——, struck on the ankle, was limping to a seat, when a little girl stole softly up behind, and, taking her hand, imprinted a gentle kiss that made full amends. The friendliness of the people in general, too, inclines us to lay all the blame upon the 'naughty boys,' who probably are not more naughty at Campitello than they are all the world over. The little maiden quite won our hearts. She was overwhelmed at the notice she attracted, and escaping indoors with a small gift, could not be enticed out again, till, on our leaving the next morning, she once more darted from the doorway to bestow a farewell kiss, and a grateful goodbye with her brown eyes.

Churchill's excursion that day led him up into the high lateral valley of Contrin, lying close under the western face of the Marmolata, and terminated by the snow patches and peaks of the Campo Ziegelan. Interesting Alpine plants were the reward of a pottering search among the blocks and irregularly-heaped masses of debris lying at its head.

In the evening a stroll down the Fassa Thal showed us enticing glimpses of its descending reaches, its wooded flanks and terraces, and, high in air, of its splintered Dolomitic walls. Of these the Rosengarten are the most conspicuous; but we only saw them in profile, and must refer to Churchill's account of Vigo, which lies at their foot, and to our concluding visit in 1862, for a description of their striking features.

Our next move was to be over the Fedaia to Caprile, on the further side of the Marmolata. We had talked in England of a side-saddle of Mr. King's pattern for the use of our wives among these mountains. As the event proved, it was fortunate we did not obtain one, for we should have had frequently to reverse its destination, and carry it ourselves. We began to understand this now, and it was a matter of some anxiety whether S—— and A—— would be equal to all the walking likely to fall to their share. The Fedaia pass was reported two hours longer than that of the Duron Thal; but we trusted that, by proper management, the one expedition might be accomplished as successfully as the other.

On Tuesday morning, August 6th, we were up betimes to see the donkeys loaded—two unpromising specimens—the only substitutes to be obtained for the one horse of Ratzes. C——'s guide of the previous day—Bernard—was engaged to the summit of the col. For willingness and care, we would gladly recommend this man to any who may follow us. He has a wife and four children, and his melancholy famished countenance does not speak of prosperous circumstances. The landlord of the same name will not, after this description, be mistaken for him.

It was a grand day. In some of its features this pass is equal to any of the well-known excursions in Switzerland. Yet, at that time, it was not even named in the 'Red Book.'* After passing a considerable extent of level ground, and several villages—Gries, Canazei, and Penia—the valley,

* The last edition gives the name but no details.

narrowing always, and turning more and more towards the Marmolata, leads under the north face of that mountain, whose tremendous precipices rise upon the right in walls and buttresses of bulk enormous. The path, at first pursuing the ravine, is lifted out of it by successive rocky staircases, each a toilsome bit of climbing. Then the ravine, sinking out of sight, becomes an abyss, into which the precipices of the Marmolata plunge in gloom, and three fine glaciers, suspended on the edge of the escarpment, successively pour their streams. The two poor donkeys had to be shoved and propped and hustled, one by one, up these twisting and stony steeps; but the hillside once gained, we soon entered one of those charming verdant basins, seven or eight thousand feet above the sea, which often lie near the summit of a pass.

Here, upon the left hand slopes, sticking like flies, men and women could be discerned cutting the short grass; and in one of the huts, which make their summer shelter, dotted about the level green, we unpacked donkeys, and took our mid-day meal. This time the bowls of milk were furnished by a sturdy nut-brown lass, in a round felt hat, who watched us with laughing eyes.

On setting forth again we parted from Bernard with mutual good wishes, and losing him, soon found ourselves cast upon our own resources, since the donkey-driver, for a very good reason, as afterwards appeared, was far from communicative. For some distance it was a perfect garden of wild flowers; then, having edged round a small tarn, and climbed the further rim of the basin, we crowned the pass, and saw rise before us the new world to conquer, in peaks of wondrous grandeur, and valleys filled with blue; while on the right still soared the implacable ridges of the Marmolata, supporting its fields of snow. The sheer, hard smoothness of these scarped rocks filled one with a kind of horror only to look at them. But the greatest point of interest in the view was a summit to the south-east, a crest of pale spiry pinnacles, with light clouds partly veiling them. It rose high above an intervening mountain, and was plainly a giant of the Dolomites, though not to be easily identified. Little did we suppose we should sleep that night at its foot, and that it would rank as the chief glory of the journey.

So abrupt was the descent into the valley beneath, that the swarthy Italian faces of three ill-favoured peasants seemed issuing from the bowels of the earth as they came suddenly upon us, seated on the grassy ridge; and in descending, the donkeys seemed likely every moment to topple over—and would have done so, perhaps, had not their tails served as ropes to ease them down by. There was scarcely the vestige of a path, showing how slight was the traffic between the two systems of valleys; and we now found that our donkey-driver, although an inhabitant of Campitello, had never crossed before. Lower down we were knee-deep in heavy grass; and then winding among natural avenues of lofty pines and across flowery glades, which might well be the introduction to some enchanted region. The scenery, solemn and romantic, was just such as poets paint when they describe an approach to dreamland.

It was four o'clock, and clouds which, coming up from Italy, had gathered about the head of the Marmolata, began to sprinkle us with showers. Fortunately, after having narrowly escaped losing donkeys and all in a bog, the track became clear and firm as any footpath in English meadows. It was now trending southwards, so as to carry us under the hitherto unseen eastern face of the mountain, whose precipices impended still the more grandly as we dropped yet deeper beneath them. Arrived at the south-eastern corner, there appeared the outlet of the valley which isolates the Marmolata on the south. It ascends to the pass of Pelegrino, which C—— intended to have crossed in 1860. But at this point our path, turning sharply away from the mountain directly eastward, led into a scene of unexpected sublimity.

It was a gorge like that of Pfeffers, but grander, according to our impression—grander in its features, grander in its solitude. A torrent rushed between narrowing walls, a thousand feet in height on either side, and filled the darkness with its roar. The passage, never wider than that of an ordinary street, was fully a mile in length; and the path along it, constructed only for access to the higher pastures, was bandied from side to side on rough bridges of transverse logs, or suspended on hanging shelves, or carried lengthwise over the stream, where there was not room for both. At one such place the entire width of the chasm did not exceed twelve feet. It was like being at the bottom of the Via Mala along with the torrent there, and sharing its awful fortunes. The noise was so great that we could not hear each others' voices, but by lifted hands expressed our growing amazement. The turns were so frequent, that the donkeys in front were continually disappearing, as into some dark doorway; and when we finally emerged, the entrance was so immediately hidden, that no one would have guessed the existence of such a rift through the rocky mass.

Soon after, we entered Sottoguda, the first village on this side the Fedaia, and several hours distant from the nearest of those on the other, while still nearly two from Caprile. At the village of Rocca appeared one of those dislocations common in Alpine valleys. There was a sudden drop, some hundreds of feet, the houses occupying the craggy edge. Below, we speedily opened upon a transverse valley, running from north to south—none other, in fact, than the Val Agordo, which intersects so large a portion of Dolomite scenery—and to the south, and close at hand, beheld, to our delight, the great mountain of our mid-day wonderment. All ruddy in the sunset, its pinnacled façade rose like some stupendous cathedral in the vista of the valley, and Caprile nestled at its foot.

That view, favoured certainly at the moment by its suddenness, and by the striking effect of light, remains almost unrivalled in our Alpine experience. The mountain

MONTE CIVITA, AND CAPRILE.

is Monte Civita. We have since explored it on all sides, and for scenic effect it still holds the first place among its Dolomite brethren. Although more than ten thousand feet in height,* of which seven thousand must be actually in view as seen from this direction, it appears but a vast

* It is given at 10,441 English feet in Fuch's 'Venetianer Alpen.'

uplifted screen, so sharp and spiky are its pinnacles, so sheer its walls, so slight its buttresses!

S—— and myself were in advance, commissioned to select quarters at Caprile. But which was the inn? A low building with green shutters outside the village, and near the church — perhaps therefore patronised by the clergy — looked tolerably inviting. It was desirable, however, to explore farther before deciding; having, indeed, settled in our own minds upon a house which had taken our fancy from a distance. No one, however, would favour our wishes in this respect, but pointed to an inn in the close and dismal street, which we entirely eschewed. Back to the green shutters, then; alas! they proved the only recommendation; low dingy rooms and untidy beds sent us out again disconsolate, and as our friends had now arrived, Churchill and I undertook a more rigid comparison of merits. Threading again the narrow street, the ramshackle windows and balconies soon filled with heads and lolling elbows, as also the half-shuttered apertures of the inn aforesaid, but without a single gesture of invitation. The entrance, part cellar, part stable, looked as unpromising as the inmates. But we persevered; each flight of stairs showed improvement, and at the second story, where a young girl, after some time, answered to our calls, a suite of rooms was thrown open almost handsomely furnished in walnut wood, the walls neatly painted, and the floors quite clean; while a balcony of iron-work, bulging towards the street, displayed pots of straggling pinks and oleanders. Happy at the discovery, we hastened down stairs to instal our wives in such comfortable quarters.

But the dearth was even greater than at Campitello. Nothing was to be had but bread, eggs, and lettuces. It took some little time to ascertain the fact, since nobody here understood a word of German, and we were entirely dependent upon S—— and A——'s Italian. The landlady, however, was a worthy body; she and her daughter Ursulina, when they had overcome the first stupor of surprise, were both anxious to do their best; and though water showed the usual reluctance to boil, and there was great rushing up and down stairs before plates could be collected, or a knife a-piece put upon the table, and fearful slops ensued between pots and jugs before we could concoct our tea, a very comfortable meal was achieved at last.

Thunder had muttered all the evening among the porches of the hills; and in the middle of the night the blessed sleep was broken by the loud clangour of the church bell, followed soon after by so blinding a glare, and a crash bumping the floors up and down, that the whole village was immediately astir. Shutters banged and voices called. But without pause the bell held on, and, resounding through the midnight storm, seemed like a brave utterance of trust and hope, not a little thrilling at such an hour. A perfect spout of rain came down, but, strangely enough, not a single sound of thunder followed that last tremendous explosion. Yet it was long before everybody settled to sleep again.*

The next day, as there was nothing for dinner, we prudently left the selection of dishes to our well-intentioned hostess. Churchill had abundance of occupation with his

* It may be observed that this superstitious practice is more a means of danger than of safety. An article in 'All the Year Round' for August 1863, mentions, that 'during the night of the 14th of April 1718, four and twenty churches in one district of Brittany were struck by lightning; and M. Fontenelle remarked that they were precisely the churches in which the bells were rung to drive away the lightning, while the churches spared were precisely those in which they were not rung.' The reason assigned is the disturbance of the air in the belfry, occasioning a current which the lightning follows.

plants, and I was the only one to sally forth, retracing our steps of the previous day as far as the village of Sottoguda, for a sketch of the southern precipices of the Marmolata. To obtain a clear view of them I climbed some distance up the hill-side—a wilderness of stones and bushes. But the Marmolata was in a bad mood, darkening and thundering like a Sinai as noon came on; and when the Sottoguda steeple sent up its clear bell-tones from the depths, I took the hint, and decamped. Dinner at two justified our confidence; it was a success. The great dish was a bowl of broth, thick with peas and rice, and flavoured with some scraps of hammy substance. We almost became vegetarians on the spot. There were also, to be sure, a few small fishes, but these could only count as savoury morsels.

The weather was too unsettled that afternoon to venture far from shelter; but no prospect could be desired more imposing than that immediately at hand of the majestic Civita. It was a constant spectacle of wonder, and especially now, when for several hours a grand succession of storms played over its pallid walls, blackening them like night, or throwing their jagged lines into bright relief as they rolled behind it. But, indeed, every mountain had its separate storm that day, with which it answered its neighbours; and it became quite amusing to speculate when each cloud-invested village would feel itself sufficiently threatened to raise its bell-call. At last Caprile began its sonorous warning, and we hurried in, only just in time to escape a drenching.

Caprile, as you approach from the Fedaia, appears at the very foot of the Monte Civita ; but it is not so. The mountain is some distance lower down the valley, and a small lake, about an hour's walk from Caprile, is more immediately at its base. To this, Lago Alleghe, we repaired on Thursday morning; the cloudless sky and delicious freshness, seducing us into a day of idling on its shores. We found it a charming piece of water, decorated with its one village on a mound of green, and nobly girdled by the mighty 'Monte,' whose roots form the cup which holds it. The Civita which here bars the whole valley, rends its way round to the west by a considerable detour, descending again southward, till it issues near Belluno.

Yet it is not the Civita which has caused the lake. On the right-hand side of the valley there is a mountain, Monte Pizzo, which, near its summit, shows a bare and frightful slide of rock, stretching downwards like the nape of a neck. From this, scarcely more than ninety years ago (1771), there slid a huge bulk of the mountain—sliding, rolling, roaring, till it reached the valley, where it heaped itself across the passage of the stream; this, rising and swelling, spread into a lake, finding exit at last in a tumbling torrent over the fallen mass. It was not till afterwards, that we learnt how young was this lovely lake. Youth in this instance is not an advantage; but the traces of the convulsion would not catch an uninstructed eye. The waters look as if they had lain in that green lap for ages.

We did not care at this time to follow the valley further than the lake. What we wanted more, after feasting our eyes upon the grandeurs of the Civita, was to catch sight of the Sasso di Pelmo, that truncated cone of which a week ago Churchill and I had obtained a distant view from the summit of the Hohe-Schlern. A tantalizing unsatisfactory piece of him could be seen from the lake over a neck of hill, and Churchill determined to cross the lake for a push up to the col, where the Sasso might fairly be expected to show himself. A girl and boy, quick at calculating chances, had run all the way from Caprile to be ready with a boat; and we kept them in service all day, landing at different points to exhaust the views, while Churchill broiled up the hill. Some little way we followed him. Cottages were clustered at every turn, sometimes theatrically jutting their gable ends in front of the soaring precipices of the Civita,—pale with the sunbeams that flowed over their summits,—and now projecting their red roofs over the translucent green of the lake below.

We had sauntered back to Caprile, and almost eaten Churchill's dinner in addition to our own, before he returned. He had made discoveries in recesses of Civita unsuspected from below; and had heard of another lake or tarn, up in some impossible place there, but the Sasso had failed to show after all.

Caprile has been the starting point for more than one ascent of the Marmolata. Mr. Ball appears to have made the expedition from Campitello. There, at least, we saw the record he had left of his ascent, with the usual Alpine Club directions for finding the thermometer he had secured on the summit. That duty we quietly left to the proper persons to perform, and two years afterwards it was accomplished by an enterprising member, not of the London, but of the Vienna Alpine Club. Herr Grohman started from Caprile in July 1862, accompanied by Pellegrini, an inhabitant of Rocca, reputed the only competent guide for the Marmolata on this side. The Herr speaks of him as a man of 'inexhaustible humour,' a description which our subsequent experience enables us fully to confirm. The importance of the Marmolata in the Dolomite group will justify our epitomizing so much of Herr Grohman's narrative as will explain the character of the ascent.

They left Caprile at 1.30 A.M.; by aid of a lantern ascended the valley, threaded what he calls the 'famous' gorge of Sottoguda, whose reputation we can well support, and by five o'clock reached the empty huts of the Lobia Alp. Here his predecessor, Dr. Ruthner passed the night when making the ascent the year before. From this point they immediately commenced climbing the slopes of the Punta Serranta, the most eastern of the spurs of the Marmolata; thus avoiding the circuit by the Fedaia See. In half an hour they reached the terminal moraine of the glacier at the foot of one of its tongues of ice. Putting on 'steigeisen,' they ascended the glacier obliquely, till they struck upon a trough in its surface leading upward in a south-westerly direction. It led to a massive rock wall, reddish-brown in colour, which, beginning with the Punta Serranta, rose up in the wildest forms, sometimes in pointed peaks, sometimes broken by deep fissures, till it soared aloft in the highest peak of the Marmolata itself. At the foot of this rock wall they climbed a steep face of névé, and found themselves at last upon the rocky ridge of the mountain, which they ascended to the point reached by Dr. Ruthner the year before. The glacier they describe as enormously crevassed, some of the fissures being wide enough to have let a house down into them.

While resting by a small pool of water, not far from the eastern peak of the mountain, Grohman suddenly observed, nailed to a rock a few feet above him, a small box. This, on examination, proved to contain Mr. Ball's Alpine Club thermometer, and a roll of paper in a glass tube, with directions in English and French, left there in 1860, but evidently overlooked by Dr. Ruthner in 1861. From this discovery and Pellegrini's information, Herr Grohman drew two conclusions: first, that Mr. Ball had made the ascent from the Fassa Thal; and secondly, that this was the highest point he reached, and that, therefore, the final western peak of the Marmolata was still unclimbed. According to the recent measurements of the government survey, this peak is about 400 feet higher than that upon which Grohman stood. He carefully reconnoitred what remained to be done, but arrived at the conclusion that, with his present means, it would be dangerous to attempt it; though by a large party properly furnished with ropes and ice-hatchets, it might be accomplished. Reluctantly retracing his steps, he reached Caprile again at 7 P.M. The view appears to have been sadly marred by clouds, and our Alpine explorer does not dwell upon it, fearing to be compelled to say more of what he did not see than of what he did.

The evening of Thursday was busy with preparations for our third and last pass, which would bring us to Cortina, in the Ampezzo road. Yet the prospect of departure almost saddened us. We had taken a strong liking for our good hostess, Signora Pezzé, whose anxiety to serve us, and constant depreciation of her efforts, were quite touching. The dreary looking inn in the narrow street had become a home, which we were lucky to have found in a spot whose external advantages are so great. What with the surpassing Civita close at hand, the Marmolata, and, as we afterwards found, the Pelmo, within a day's excursion, the neighbourhood of the charming lake of Alleghe, and abundance of romantic villages scattered along the steeps, we felt that Caprile might well employ more time than we could afford at present, with so great a portion of our tour yet before us.

That afternoon S—— and A—— were invited to the private residence of the family, the identical respectable-looking building we had noticed on the first sight of Caprile. There they were introduced to Signora Pezzé's husband, and regaled with tokay and excellent coffee, gracefully served by the daughter, Ursulina. Two of the sons, they were sorrowfully told, had joined the Piedmontese army, and must therefore remain exiled from their native village; and several other young men were in the same predicament. So far had Italian sentiments penetrated into these Austrian valleys. 'We are all patriots here,' they said; but the habitual melancholy expression of poor mother Pezzé's countenance, and her frequent sighs, were fully explained. One nice lad remained; but he, too, it was whispered, was on the wing, and more trouble, we feared, was yet in store for the household. 'They all leave me!' said the father, touching his breast; and then, flinging wide his arms, 'They all leave me!'

At Campitello we had been reduced from a horse to a pair of diminutive donkeys. At Caprile we dwindled down to men, for the three forlorn bipeds who offered themselves did not look half so respectable, when transformed into beasts of burden, as even the last-named quadrupeds. We had expected to find mules here, and should have done so, but that they were all employed in bringing charcoal from the mountains. The evening before we left, a string of the laden beasts came down, stepping cleverly among the rocks and trees, rattling the loose stones, and sometimes slipping hind and front feet together on a pitch of unusual steepness. They rested at Caprile for the night, but were bound farther down the valley. The morning was the finest possible; but I must confess to being in rather sorry plight for the expedition. The second day's dinner, a repetition of the first, had entirely reconverted us from vegetarianism. Pea-soup as the *pièce de résistance* would not do, or, at least, I had reason to think so in my own case.

We left Caprile at the same end by which we had entered it, but turned immediately up a rocky path behind the church, leading towards the head of the valley. It is surprising how soon a village sinks beneath your feet as you rise on these steep-sided hills. In a few minutes we were on equal terms with the cock on the top of the steeple; in a few more, Caprile was only a cluster of roofs by the side of its wasteful stream. But as we rose, so rose Monte Civita, in presence great and wonderful, and bidding us a proud farewell.

In half an hour our men halted on a bit of level sward, and pointing to two diverging paths, left the choice to us. Supposing they would soon re-unite, we took what seemed to be the shortest, expecting only a little temporary steepness. But we soon found ourselves bearing back almost upon Caprile, on a high terrace of the mountain, and by further questioning discovered our course would lie along the very spines of the hills, crossing the highest ridge by the side of Monte Gusella, and descending upon Cortina without touching the other track, which lay in a circle to the north. It was presently apparent, however, that we had chosen well; for the path, working round to the east, displayed a yet unseen country in that direction, and in the midst of it the Pelmo! We were to be rewarded with one of the finest views of that hitherto reluctant mountain. It grew and grew in its tower-like supremacy, though Civita, still barring up the south, held well its own as a wall of shivered peaks; and it was hard to say which was the more imposing.

An hour and a half of our ladies' walking brought us to the village of Sta. Lucia, on a lofty promontory, of which the projecting corner was occupied by the church. From the low wall of its burial ground the view swept along a valley—the Fiorentina—stretching, end on, towards the menacing bulk of the Pelmo itself, thus disposed between an avenue of hills to superb advantage. It was a view to which we felt we must some day return. A few minutes only were allowed for a slight pencil outline of its features.

SASSO DI PELMO, FROM STA. LUCIA.

Yet some delay was granted for an object of greater practical importance. Our poor gaunt porters, now mopping their brows in the shade of a wall, intimated a possibility of beer at a neighbouring house; and we all trooped thither with singular alacrity. It was cool and foaming, and, if costly, how could it be otherwise at such a spot as Sta. Lucia? The man who brought, or brewed it there, must have had prophetic vision of the seven thirsty souls who should one day appear at his door. He looked gratified, as if the final cause of beer, a drink only recently introduced, were now revealed to him.

Upon leaving the village, our men disconcerted all notions of direction by turning up the wild chaos of a torrent-bed; but it was a habit of theirs to take the shortest cut. A painful toil brought us to the path again, circling round the bosky hills, rising through the upper and scanty fringes of the woods, and approaching the sweet-smelling hay-slopes above, that leaned against the blue of the sky. Cattle, under a herd-boy's care, waylaid the path where there was shade, and goats scrambled up the side to stare at us, sending down shale and earth. We began to experience that thin purity of atmosphere which attends a great elevation, and to fancy that the col was near at hand. But, crossing a burn, the path was seen ascending by its side far a-head, where it was dropping in cascades out of a distant corrie, or basin, scooped in the summits of the hills, which, though mostly rounded, were broken by frequent protrusions of white rock, like teeth from gums. At the head of the basin a huger dental mass than the rest marked Monte Gusella. The few châlets which edged the stream beside us were all closed, their occupants cutting hay on patches of green a thousand feet higher, where it seemed as if even crampons could hardly enable them to hold on. Again the guides were not content to follow the track; but, bending under their loads, took to some single foot-marks up the hill to the right, so steep that the leading man was always gone over into the sky, and his companions half in air.

S—— and A—— were almost beat. They had never yet had so many hours of relentless climbing—nearly six since leaving Caprile. The hollow which enclosed us denied the exhilaration of a prospect. The summit of the col seemed at a hopeless distance; and as we here touched again the stream, now in the sparkle of its early course, with one consent we cast off burdens, squandered ourselves down upon the turf, and putting the bottles of tea into the water to cool, spread out our meagre dinner. Yet we did not envy that day the gayest pic-nic in England. We were within hearing of the marmot's whistle, and the rush of the eagle's wing! An hour's rest was so entirely restorative, that the remaining slopes, now lying at an easy inclination, were taken at cheerful speed. Nor was it long before points and crests soaring up on the western horizon gave notice that our toil was about to be rewarded. A mountain flank had hidden them till now; but there they all were, peak after peak, that we little thought to have seen again, and the noble Marmolata in their midst bearing his wealth of snows, for we looked now full upon his icy bosom, and could estimate as never before his wilderness of summit. Even the Schlern, we fancied, was visible from this point among a sea of tossing lines stretching round far to the north.

But while stopping to observe the new aspect of the Marmolata, a shout from above gave notice of something more. Churchill was standing there beside a cross, marking the crest of the ridge, and looking down upon the most extraordinary prospect we had yet beheld. The entire course of the descent was seen at a glance down a broad and lengthened trough, the sides of it showing an amazing variety of rocky shapes, fantastic, desolate, and grand, and beyond it, filling up to the horizon, range above range of bare broken-walled mountains, some of them in form and size as majestic as any in the Dolomite district—Monte Tofana to the left, the Croda Malcora directly opposite, and southward the snow-capped obelisk of the Antelao. Mr. Ruskin affirms that overhanging, or even perpendicular precipices, though often represented, are not really found in nature. We agreed that here there were plenty of both sorts, and the aptness of A——'s remark was at once appreciated when she compared the scene before us to one of Gustave Doré's marvellous groupings of peak and precipice in his illustrations to the

'Wandering Jew.'* The broadening afternoon shadows brought out the most surprising effects, and the strange spectacle bound us to the spot. Nowhere are some of the peculiarities of Dolomite landscape more strikingly displayed; but I must stipulate for a similar effect of light if anyone wishes to verify the description.

The long gully beneath seemed entirely empty of inhabitants. A dark pine forest filled its lower reaches, and beyond this we could discern its distant outlet into the Ampezzo valley. There, in blue mist, was traced the white thread of road upon which we had travelled three years before *en route* from Venice to Innsbruck, and which would now finish our pedestrianism. Cortina itself was out of sight to the left, and remembering that some hours of walking lay between us and it, we shook off our trance of admiration, and started at an accelerated pace. This was easy down the rolling slopes. Full of glee, we spread over them at large among the interlacing tracks, partly cattle, partly water-worn. As we descended, the most curious resemblances to architectural forms came out on either side—on the left particularly. There Monte Gusella guarded the head of the pass, and its eastern end towered like a castle-keep, lofty and impregnable. Next to it a mountain, likewise presented endways to the descent, took the likeness of an apse to some enormous cathedral; and lower still, we were in doubt for a time whether a wooded ridge were not really crowned by the ruined walls of an abbey, till their real magnitude became indisputable.

Our men now pointed to some long low sheds, surrounded with mud and manure, on one of the grassy platforms, and, though not a tempting spot, we turned

* His magnificent illustrations to the 'Inferno' were not then published; many of them are thoroughly Dolomitic in character.

aside for the chance of milk. Two unsavoury-looking fellows gave us rather grudging access to a very dirty interior, black with smoke as well as darkness, and heaped with tubs and vessels. The only seats they offered were the round pieces of wood, with a single leg stuck in the middle, upon which they balance themselves for milking; but by turning up a few pine stumps, and a tub or two, we contrived more practicable seats. Then came a liberal enough outpouring of the creamy fluid into bowls—whose thick rims developed an art of drinking—with a pailful of water, to modify the libations of those who wished it. When it came to payment, kreutzers were for the first time somewhat doubtfully regarded, and we added twopences to the amount till the younger man, amidst the laughter of the company, punched the elder in the ribs as an unconscionable rascal for pocketing so much money. So far as I was concerned, it had been excellently bestowed; having been unwell all day, and afflicted with grievous thirst, something like a quart of milk and water here effected a perfect cure.

Soon after leaving the cattle-sheds we fell into the woods. The trees were huge dark cones, standing thick and tall like cypresses, with solemn avenues between. The gloom and silence were oppressive, but there was peculiar grandeur in the effect. Again occurred the resemblance to Doré's designs, for above the funereal tops gleamed pale spires of Dolomite, in ghastly concord; and below, the roots of destroyed trees contorted themselves into every dragon semblance. These old roots are quite a feature in the wild scenery. White with age, and partially blackened by fire, they look as uncanny as may be, and perhaps have aided by their appearance the peasant superstition, which reckons it of evil omen to stumble over them in the dark. Here they gave a very

Salvator Rosa aspect to many a craggy corner, where the light struck faintly down. If, according to some critics, Salvator is not like nature, nature, in these instances, was very like Salvator.

For an hour or more we were threading these melancholy groves, and descending so rapidly that we flattered ourselves we should issue at once upon the Ampezzo valley. But we came out upon a shoulder, or table-land, of open pasture, still far above Cortina, which, with a string of glittering villages and farms, gave an air of unwonted cheerfulness to the broad expanse of valley below, still full of light from end to end. It was a charming sight; a genuine piece of bright industrious Tyrol—German Tyrol; not a bad change after the week of savage gorges and dishevelled Italian hamlets. Perhaps nothing marked the difference more than the presence here of farms, or at least of comfortable well-to-do houses, scattered about the green mounds in peaceful security. Within the Italian-speaking frontier, with higher elements of scenery, there is a frequent lack of cheerfulness, partly owing to the absence of such honest-looking homesteads. Houses are huddled together in sombre villages; and the surroundings want the German neatness. Yet here the view was not all greenery. Opposite to us, hemming in the verdure, rose the stark precipices of the Croda Malcora; and many a desolate peak was set round the evening sky, reminding us of the regions we had dropped from.

The smooth slopes helped us quickly down. We were soon among the hay-châlets, and their substantial many-galleried houses. Foot-paths on the grass merged into fenced and stony horse-tracks, and everything betokened the inevitable road, still a level streak below. Cortina was spread along it, a place of perhaps five hundred inhabitants, its tall church tower set stately in its midst. Half in doubt whether to turn towards the southern end, and seek the small but comfortable 'Stella d'Oro,' or at the northern to betake ourselves to the more roomy 'Aquila Nera,' the point was settled for us by an adroit damsel, who, accosting us as strangers, and charging herself immediately with all the lighter articles she could lay hands on, took it for granted we were bound for the latter hostel, and, with abundance of small talk, undertook to show the way. Triumphantly she marched at the head of our cavalcade through the village plaza, gave directions right and left as she entered the inn doors, summoned the landlady, snatched at a bunch of keys, ushered us upstairs into airy, handsome rooms, and revealed herself as the happy Kellerin of the establishment, who knew she had done the right thing for us, whether we knew it or not.

It was a very different reception from that at Ratzes, Campitello, or even Caprile. The broad floors were spotless; beds and furniture dainty in their cleanliness; flowers adorned the landing-place, and pictures of rare merit the walls! Hot water and towels came as a matter of course, and with them suggestions of a savoury supper. Certainly we were gipsies no longer. A little regret mingled with our return to decent life from the fortnight of pic-nics, and we were rather shy at first of postillions and post-carriages; but plentiful ablutions were an undeniable luxury, hot meat was voted an excellent institution, and tea looked itself once more, served in cups and saucers instead of tumblers.

CHAPTER VI.

FROM THE AMPEZZO TO THE GAIL THAL.

Cortina—The Castle of Peutelstein—The Höllen Thal and its Apparitions—Descent into the Pusterthal—The Source of the Drave—Lienz again—Amman's 'Turn Out'—Ober Drauberg—First Sight of the Gail Thal.

THE arrival at Cortina marked the termination of a distinct portion of our tour. We had crossed, on foot, from the Brenner road to that of the Ampezzo; traversed three passes of remarkable beauty; and seen the hitherto most noted of the Dolomite mountains; for the Hohe Schlern, Lang Kofel, Marmolata, and Sasso di Pelmo, have all a place in the 'Handbook,' and each a reputation to sustain. They amply fulfilled our expectations, while Monte Civita, which we felt to be something like a discovery, was in our opinion unrivalled in its grandeur.

Though the Dolomite character was everywhere prevalent, yet there was much variety. Each of the passes left an impression of its own. That of the Seisser Alp, open and cheerful, as well as noble in its features; the Fedaia, grand, solemn, romantic; the Gusella, wild and strange. There was as much difference, too, in the three halting places. Ratzes, secluded in its woods, German and jovial in its people; Campitello, sweltering in sunlight, meagre in entertainment, disorderly—in a word, Italian; Caprile, Italian in a better sense, hospitable, despite an empty larder, and comfortable, though in a narrow street. But all varieties of circumstance and landscape blended into one happy recollection of a fortnight's splendid weather, amidst surpassing scenery.

Cortina is recommended in 'Murray' as convenient head-quarters for the Dolomites. After what we had seen, we were disposed at first to underrate its advantages. Perhaps we felt ill at ease upon a high road, and were loth to believe in scenery that might be looked at from a carriage window. Perhaps we were a little surfeited with grandeurs, poor mortals that we were, and wanted a change—in that condition, when, according to Mr. Ruskin, you should turn away from Mont Blanc, and study a daisy! At any rate we persuaded ourselves that we had seen the principal features of the Cortina Dolomites, as we descended

CORTINA.

from the Gusella; and were more powerfully attracted eastward by the unknown and distant Gail Thal, the Terglou, and the Steiner Alp. So we left Cortina the morning after our arrival, and regretted it all the rest of the journey.

Indeed, the more we thought about it, the more Cortina rose in our estimation. Excellent quarters, and a fine, open cheerful valley to begin with. And then, what mountains! That obelisk-shaped Antelao, at the southern end, how grandly he lifted himself ten thousand feet or so into the sky! And the Croda Malcora, impending over the town on the east, and said to display somewhere the finest precipice scenery in Europe—though too jealous of the honours of Monte Civita, to admit all that—yet we ought to have verified the fact by an excursion along his flanks. And there was the Tofana, to the north-west, a snow-capped and weird-looking mass, in some aspects almost reminding one of the Matterhorn, and reckoning no less than ten thousand feet like the others. These three mighty ones, why were they not in the sketch-book? More than all, there was the Pelmo! He must show himself down the valley there to the west, if the map be true, and Churchill demanded of me whether I had not seen this noted mountain in passing through the Ampezzo, three years ago. My answer was confused and unsatisfactory. I had no map I pleaded, and puzzling over my recollections, could get no further than 'there certainly was something very big there, and perhaps it was the Pelmo.' The severity of C——'s countenance indicated his opinion of me, but he dropped the subject, perhaps not quite at ease in his own conscience, since the early departure from Cortina was mainly his doing. It was evidently imperative to return another year, if we presumed to describe the Dolomites.

Cortina is the last town in Tyrol on this route. The province of Venetia commences a little beyond the next village, southwards. Judging from the inns, the place might almost be called Italian at one end, and German at the other. At the Stella d'Oro in 1858, they spoke only Italian, at the Aquila Nera, German, and the Teutonic style of things prevailed; though the name of the family to whom it belongs would not lead one to expect this. Travellers cannot fail to notice some vigorous designs in fresco upon the outside walls; they are by the same hand as the pictures within doors, Ghedina's, a son of the landlord, and one of the most eminent of the Venetian painters of the present day. We afterwards saw more of his works, admirable for delicacy of feeling and thoroughness of workmanship, even if spent upon the portraits of homely faces. A younger brother is also a skilful artist, but I must say more about them when I speak of a visit to their studios the following year. Though resident in Venice, they spend the heats of summer in their native valley.

Cortina looks larger than it is, for the buildings are spread spaciously about. Several are official, for the administration of the Ampezzo district; and many of them inns, accommodating a busy traffic in timber and flour between Italy and Tyrol. The tower of the church, a recent erection by a Vienna architect, is a handsome campanile, separate from the edifice, after the Italian manner, and so helps to mark the place as a border town.

As we were anxious to push on to the Gail Thal, the next object of our excursions, and for that reason had neglected the claims of Cortina, it was rather inconsistent to take only a single stage the day we left it, and arriving before noon on Saturday at the solitary post-house of Landro, to remain there till Monday morning. But travellers have fancies sometimes. I had been rather captivated with this desolate spot, during an hour's repair to the carriage in 1858, and Churchill had views of his own to carry out. It lies about three hours' drive northward of Cortina. The road, first ascending to the head of the Ampezzo valley, suddenly strikes back again upon the right hand hill, and ascends by zigzags towards the ruined castle of Peutelstein, which, perched upon a narrow promontory, commands the pass, and was once the northernmost outpost of Venetian territory. While the carriage took its slow way up, Churchill and I climbed the castle hill, and sheltering from the wind in the disembowelled towers, surveyed the landscape, of which doubtless many a man-at-arms has in his time become sufficiently weary. To the south stretches the Ampezzo valley; round every other point of the compass rise the fear-inspiring Dolomites. The grandest of these, as seen from this spot, is perhaps Monte Tofana to the west; but eastward, whither the road now turns, appear the scarcely less striking masses of the Cristall Köpfe. Mrs. Ratcliffe might well have adapted one of her romances to these wind-whistling walls, built up sheer from the precipice on three sides, and over the dull roar of a cataract. He that kept this castle against both fleshly and ghostly foes through days of storm and nights of darkness, must have been a captain of stout heart. Siege and battle it certainly more than once encountered: the Emperor Maximilian finally wrested it from the Venetians, and so gained command of the Ampezzo valley.

The real grandeur of its situation is, however, not appreciated unless the traveller takes a path, that we discovered on a subsequent visit, and the description of which I here anticipate. Coming from Cortina, this path strikes off to the right, before crossing the deep ravine which isolates the Castle-rock on that side. It ascends along the sloping side of the frightful-looking gorge, and is safe, though narrow. Opposite, the rock rises to a pinnacle, crowned by the feeble-looking wall of the castle—feeble compared with the massive buttresses of naked rock. Beneath is a dizzy depth, where the torrent is seen twirling in coils of black and white. The terror of the scene rises to its height where a crazy bridge crosses the gulf, and suspends you in the midst; the path then climbs through a pine wood to the road, which it reaches half a mile or so beyond the castle. The passage through this chasm—which, it is true, I saw by evening light, and therefore at its most impressive time—would almost compensate for the loss of the view from the castle itself; but both may be secured, as the path cuts across a considerable angle of the road—let alone its zigzags—and is always used by the country people. No one, however, pointed it out to us on two occasions when we passed this way. The tourist must take the matter into his own hands, for the *voiturier*, or postillion, will not help him.

From the summit of the pass the road descends towards the small lake, or tarn, of Landro, the Düren See, as it is named. Here, on the right, the 'Cristall' mountain continually developes forms of great sublimity, with glimpses of glaciers in its hollows; and on the left hand, two singular features attract attention. First, not long after leaving Peutelstein, a hole in a mountain-side, near the summit, through which you strangely see the sky. And next, a lofty blood-stained Dolomite—blood-stained, for its precipitous front is streaked as with the red drip of a mighty sacrifice—some veritable hecatomb—slaughtered there ages agone. It fitly introduces you to the gloom and dreariness of the 'Höllenthal'—the hell valley—in which Landro is situated. Here, after passing the sheet of dull green water, the Düren See, we pulled up at the post-house, itself a comfortable-looking building, with a small railed-in garden, and a diminutive chapel, not much bigger than a pigeon-house, over the way. Though the situation is solitary enough, the place looks busy. There is not only a brewhouse, but a flour-mill, and wagons are always halting or starting, or baiting their teams before they take the last steeps of the ascent. But, once out of the road, and you are in a waste of loose stones and pine scrub; and in a few paces the houses sink into a roof or two, shouldering together for company, and you are alone in the valley bottom, absolutely closed in by the mountain monsters—monsters as much in shape as in size. Monte Cristallo,

DÜREN SEE AND MONTE CRISTALLO.

shooting up in towers between its glaciers, is the dominating object,—the red Mount of sacrifice is only seen from the upper end of the valley. Not far from the post-house, however, through a gorge opening eastward, there is an apparition of three splintered spires, the Drei Zinnen (three battlements), than which, in the way of mountains, I know nothing stranger.

The lake, with its dry salty shores, might have been the site of Sodom. Two streams flow into it, but none flow out, and there is fearful suspicion of hidden gulfs. The trees, the grass, the mosses, seem all blasted and unwholesome; and in the sides of the hill, cracks and chasms, dipping strata and slanting pine-trunks, look as if all might some day go into depths below. Landslips have, indeed, at different times, destroyed the road which once skirted the opposite margin of the lake.

That evening we saw the sharp peaks of the Drei Zinnen burn in the sunset as we looked through the dark portals of the gorge; we saw the Cristallo turn ghastly cold as the light went down; we saw the lake turn blacker than night, and the stars shine as never before, so vividly, the milky-way streaming overhead like a bright aurora; and we went to bed feeling that we had chosen a prison for our Sunday.

As much as could be seen of the sky the next day was so pure and lovely, that it was an absolute grief to have left cheerful Cortina, or not to have reached the stately valley of the Drave. No sunshine could sweeten the grim forms around; and cold shadows fell early over the dreary patch of level, and the sullen lake.

Churchill took a long walk up the eastern gorge, and touched the base of the Drei Zinnen. He found a pleasant path, at first along the border of steep woods and of the stream, until a track turned off through an opening southwards, in the direction of Auronzo. Farther on it disappeared altogether, having been washed down into the stream, and progress was only possible by the stream-bed, though this was sometimes entirely clogged with enormous boulders. Toiling on, with a very limited view in any direction, he reached the termination of the valley in a small semicircular basin, out of which a series of zigzags led into one much higher, tenanted by some sixty or seventy bulls, feeding together in perfect stillness. Neither dog nor man was there to companion them, and they appeared at first rather disposed to resent the intrusion of a stranger. Crossing this upper basin in a southerly direction, a track led up to a stony, hummocky plateau, to the base of the Drei Zinnen, now appearing to consist of five great masses rising precipitously from the plateau, and standing in a barren talus of their own débris—themselves so white, and the débris so fine, as to suggest the idea of sugar-loaves set in a heap of flour.

The rest of us spent most of the day on a narrow ledge, one of the highest we could reach, whence a small peep of the Pusterthal and the far-off Norics, soft in a hazy glory, was like a glimpse a prisoner might obtain by climbing up to the bars of his cell.

Still, the Post House itself was far from forlorn. The rooms were thoroughly comfortable, with good portraits by Ghedina on the walls. He was a friend there, and the people of the house showed us some pencil sketches of their children, which were really exquisite. The mother was fair and lady-like; the husband a brisk little miller, honest and kind. On the Monday morning when we started for Lienz, he took upon himself to pack all the baggage, and to his own detriment as post-master insisted that one horse was quite sufficient for our light vehicle the first stage—all down hill. But that we were eager to look round the corner at the sunny world again, we should have been quite sorry to part from the worthy folks at Landro. As it was, we were glad to find ourselves swinging down the long reaches of road which lead through a deep ravine from the lofty basin of the Höllenthal—it is some 5,000 feet above the sea—into the broad Pusterthal. This—one of the great longitudinal valleys of Tyrol, ranking next after that of the Inn—runs westward for some eighty miles from the point we entered it, joining the Eisach and the Brenner route a little above Brixen. We traversed its entire length during that journey of 1856 which gave us our first sight of the Dolomites; now we were to turn east instead of west, ascending to gain the head waters of the Drave, and our old quarters at Lienz.

The lower portion of the Ampezzo road passes through extensive woods, and by the side of the infant Rienz, afterwards the stream of the Pusterthal. While still in the gorge the sun, beginning to glisten through the trees fringing the summit of the enormous precipices to our right, displayed to perfection the phenomenon described and explained by Professor Tyndal in his work on the 'Glaciers of the Alps.' The trees, wherever the sun's rays struck them at the proper angle, were transfigured into shapes of light, the entire form perfectly retained, but brilliant as frosted silver. The rocks rise to a great height on both sides of the gorge, narrowing the view forward; then the road skirts the small lake of Toblach; and when the Pusterthal is fairly opened, the Noric mountains having sunk out of sight to the north, the scenery is rather tame, only that villages jut out on every side, and crops are bright to the edge of the woods. But these again, as you proceed eastward, begin to show the peculiar Carinthian character; the pines, with their short lateral branches — little better than hop-poles at a distance—giving a monotonous and bristly air to the landscape. The compensations consist in the few peeps of Dolomites on the southern side, especially of the Drei Schuster Spitzen near Innichen, a mountain which, on our first journey, we had christened the 'Diadem,' from its crown of airy towers, but now found to bear the plebeian designation of the 'Cobblers.' At this time the impression it had formerly made was scarcely borne out, which we attributed to having seen so many giants of the Dolomites, that the edge of our admiration was blunted.

A third visit, however, two years afterwards, when, not content with the view from the road, we explored the valley at its base, entirely restored its supremacy. It is indeed one of the mightiest members of the group, and its soaring summit, as seen from Innichen, may well challenge very respectful attention. The latest authority gives its height at 10,350 feet.

THE DREI SCHUSTER, SEXTEN THAL.

But, apart from scenery, there are sufficient sources of interest in this somewhat bleak portion of the Pusterthal. It is bleak because, at this point, it is nothing less than the watershed between the Adriatic and Black Seas: on its eastern side, shortly above Innichen, the Drave begins to ripple towards the Danube, and you feel that you have entered another geographical area. Mr. Inglis, one of the earliest tourists in the Tyrol—so early, that when he first saw its distant mountains from a church tower in Munich, he enquired what they were—Mr. Inglis took the trouble to visit the source of this river, about two hours' walk from Innichen. He describes it as 'wild without being imposing, a lake about half a mile across,* lying among the outposts of the mountains, but not at any great height, nor surrounded with any very striking features. The lake has many tiny feeders, and the Drave issues from it in a stream, across which one can hop without difficulty.' Yet the sight seems to have impressed him, for it leads to a chapter of lucubrations upon the sources of rivers in general—the result of a reverie suggested on the spot. Not a word, however, about the Dolomites; one might have supposed them to have shot upward to the sky since he visited the country. Sir Humphry Davy was keener-sighted, though he mistook them for granite.

There is yet another reason why the traveller should not resign himself to napping as he descends this road. At Innichen the valley leading up to the Drei Schuster—the Sexten Thal—is masked from sight by a long, low, wooded hill, which also hides from view all but the upper portion of the Schuster itself. You may chafe as we did to be deprived of what might prove a striking opening to a wild Dolomitic region; but that low hill once held a Roman city! and if the Drei Schuster has not sufficiently impressed you with its own commanding presence, look at it again with the thought that it was the familiar guardian, or perhaps evil genius, of Aguntium. The selection of the site is easy to understand. Close to the midway watershed it would command from end to end the whole valley of the Pusterthal, and in addition would occupy the entrance to one of the easiest passes across the main Carnic chain. We have since crossed that

* We strongly suspect that Inglis must have mistaken the Toblacher See, which lies on the other side of the watershed, for the source of the Drave.

way by the Sexten Thal, and over the low col, to the Italian district of Comelico, communicating on the east by Sappada and Rigolato with the Tagliamento and Friuli, and therefore in Roman times with the great port of Aquileia; and on the west with the Piave country and Belluno. On the grassy pine-covered hill, obscure mounds and depressions are the only vouchers for the assertions of antiquaries.

Yet Innichen itself may be a relic of the former importance of the site. This village, otherwise not at all remarkable, possesses a fine Minster church of the thirteenth century; close by is the large parish church, and in the outskirts a Franciscan monastery. The ecclesiastical importance must have followed the military: no other reason for it can readily be found. The stately and grave interior of the Minster puts to shame that of the adjoining parish church, which affects flamboyant classic, and flaunts all manner of abominations. A curious picture in the Minster vestibule represents the renewal or extension of the Charter of the Chapter in the last century, by the prince-bishop of Brixen, who, in ruffles and powdered wig, looks neither prince nor bishop, but reminds one of that mixture of feudalism and coxcombry to which the French Revolution put an end—an end of which the inscription below is significant, for you read therein the ominous name of Napoleon. That remodeller of Europe put his finger upon this obscure spot in the map, and drew the frontier of Illyria across the watershed, ordaining also that the Sexten Thal should be included within its limits.

It was not till the later visit referred to, that we became acquainted with these, and other points of interest about Innichen. At present it was the Drei Schuster alone that drew our attention as we rolled by, white with dust, and baked in the sun, lamenting the green Alps aloft we had so lately trod. Sillian was the first stage; Mittewald, where we dined, the second.

Before reaching Mittewald, the Lienz Dolomites begin to show themselves finely in profile, and the opening to the Gail Thal is passed. A rough horse-track leads to it, which would have served us, but there were difficulties in the way of entering the valley at this extremity; letters, too, a fortnight old were waiting for us at Lienz, so we passed on thither, intending to cross over to the Gail by a more practicable road lower down. The scenery rapidly gains in character after leaving Mittewald; the valley narrows, and woods sweep up the closing hills. One of the death pictures by the side of the way represented a wolf standing in a contemplative attitude over a man; the beast, we may suppose, had, some unlucky day, descended from the woods. They usually tell you that both bears and wolves come over in the spring, either from Croatia or Hungary, and perhaps the visits of these animals may have some connection with the large dogs with which every inn is furnished: a huge lion-like fellow winked at us with one red eye all dinner-time at Mittewald. The narrowing valley soon becomes a gorge. It is one of those historical spots of which Tyrol is full, for here, in the famous year Nine, a French general came to grief in attempting to force his way. Seven hundred of his men were shot dead; the Tyrolese, up among the crags, were too good marksmen to merely wing their men.

Here, too, the Drave had found a voice, as it rushed through the Lienzer Klause. The road clings to the left-hand cliffs, and on the opposite side rise the lofty forest-clothed Dolomites of Lienz. Suddenly is disclosed the noble far-sweeping valley—the true Drave Thal, at the head of which Lienz is situated. It was an intensely hot afternoon as we entered its straggling streets, driving up to the Post, of whose honest, perspiry, and 'complimentary' landlord we had particular recollection. He met us perspiring and complimenting, as usual, and nothing altered in the lapse of years. Unluckily, the postmaster-general of the district was on his rounds, and, having engaged the best rooms, we were fain to be content with the prospect of the stable-yard. Just then the sun did not shine there, and that was enough; yet at night we lay in a bath, afflicted with every noise and smell pertaining to stables; and at four in the morning a merry round of threshing from an adjoining floor shook us from uneasy slumbers.

Everybody remarked upon the heat, so perhaps it is not peculiar to Lienz. The beautiful valley, both on this and the following day, was filled with a hazy glare; but on the evening of our arrival its repose was delicious, surveyed in the orange glow of twilight from the vantage ground of a small hill. There is much of the fine character of the valley of the Inn, due to the breadth, the numerous villages, the castles, the woods, and the superb mountain forms, which on the south rear their Dolomite walls with grand abruptness from the level floor of the valley. Northward, though there are purple abysses lifted up on high, and peeps of the Noric snows in a few places, the valley is generally bounded by rolling orchard-covered hills, rising into Carinthian woodland. The Drave itself is not much seen—it hugs the southern precipices, and does not pass through Lienz. It is the Isel, descending from the Teffereggen Thal, and joining the Drave just below, that rushes with amazing vehemence, like the Inn at Innspruck, through the town.

A little shopping at Lienz was not very satisfactory. The landlord, anxious to introduce us to the best shops in the place, led the way to certain dark-looking cellars, where coarse goods of every kind were huddled together. 'Compliment,' said he, as he doffed his hat at each cellar door, and the politeness was reciprocated within. Paper was of antiquated size and texture; raisins, so useful to munch with dry bread on the hills, were no bigger than currants; and tea was 12*s.* per pound. We were more successful in a call upon Amman, our gentlemanly driver of five years before. The good man was probably in siesta, and bustled out, putting on his coat, bewildered at the unwonted crowd about his door; yet he was not long in recognising his four 'Engländer,' and was happy to undertake our conveyance to the Gail Thal.

Five miles down the valley, a little off the road, is the village of Dölsach, nestled at the foot of the ridge which divides the Drave from the Möll Thal, and at the point where the rough track strikes off to Winklern, and Heiligenblut. We arranged a day's excursion to the summit of the col, where, on our former journey, we had been so impressed with the view of the Drave Valley and its Dolomites. As far as Dölsach we took one of those easy four-wheels common in the country, wherein two sit comfortably on the deep seat behind, and other two, if necessary, upon the apron, dangling their legs behind the horse's tail. When it came to walking—for above Dölsach that is the needs must—the heat inclined us to be content with reaching a few cottages about two-thirds up the ascent. The inmates, unasked, brought out milk and flowers, and gathered round to see our sketches, and to identify the mountains, but especially their own portraits transferred to the sketch-book of A——. The self-consciousness of 'Thomas,' and 'John,' and 'Anna,' during the sittings, and the glee of the spectators, were abundantly amusing. It was a happy morning with a happy folk—they looked so, and why not?—on their grassy orchard slopes, with the blue vale beneath, cleft by the white stream of the Drave, and across it the uplifted grandeurs of the Wizard, woods wreathed about its base like the shadows of clouds.

The clean little inn of Dölsach gave us an excellent dinner, and then we ought to have gone home, but I coveted a remembrance of the red-steepled church, seen from the heights above through a vista of pines, with the brilliant yellow sunlight streaming along the valley beyond; and thereby we came to trouble. We should have heeded low-rolling thunders far in the west. When at last we started for the five miles' walk in the 'cool,' the head of the Lienz valley was swallowed up in blackness, upon which lightning played incessantly. Soon it was darting, now on this side, now on that, as if searching out objects of vengeance on the hills; and each mountain form was successively blotted out by sheets of rain. There was nothing for it but to walk into the storm, which, on its part, advanced to meet us. Not a particle of shelter was to be found between us and Lienz, as the villages lie off the road, and the hay-sheds were all fastened. Not a creature was to be seen abroad, and the long stretches of sodden road looked dismal enough, though glittering under the flashes with the same varying colours we had noticed at Ratzes—now crimson and now blue. We were nearly at the entrance of Lienz before we obtained shelter in a small cottage; it was yet an hour before the storm, still clinging to the hills, had passed down the valley; and quite dark before, in sorry plight, we gained the inn, passing to our rooms through the post-inspector's supper-party on the landing. As we afterwards heard a ludicrous attempt at 'God save the Queen,' followed by much laughter, I suppose we were an incident to their evening.

Amman and his vehicle were ready at nine the next morning, when the usual splendid sky reappeared overhead, and a sun as hot as ever. We had not jogged far out of Lienz before we were visited with that consciousness, occasionally so perplexing, of having at some previous time been placed in precisely duplicate circumstances. The explanation in this case was not difficult. In this same carriage we had been packed five years before. The same Amman was sitting on the same seat; his jacket, a little tighter, was the same faded check with which we had grown familiar as we jogged to Brixen; and we verily believed the same horses were pulling at the same traces. He confessed to the identity of both carriage and horses; we did not press the matter of the jacket; but equipage, party, and all, being thus reproduced, might just have wakened from a long nap to pursue the interrupted journey. With what enviable monotony must the years roll by in Lienz!

This time, however, our faces were set eastward instead of westward, and in a couple of hours we had crossed the frontier from Tyrol into Carinthia, through which latter province the Drave holds most of its way. Being the direct route for Klagenfurt, the capital, we enquired after Görgey, the celebrated Hungarian General, who, after surrendering his army to the Russians in 1849, was allowed by the Austrian Government to reside in the neighbourhood of that city. 'Ah,' said Amman, rather quickly, 'a traitor to his country! Yes, I have seen him; he once came to Lienz, but no one would even lift his hat to him.' At Caprile we had found Italian sympathies. Here was a significant indication that Hungary possessed some well-wishers.

At Ober Drauberg, after dinner, Amman made his politest bow, but, whether through the progress of ideas, or that it was the middle of a street, omitted the knightly obeisance by which he had formerly distinguished himself. He consigned us to a postillion, and a pair of stouter horses than his own, for the ascent by a country road out of the Drave Thal and the descent into that of the Gail. We bade Amman good-bye, for perhaps another five years. In the mutation of all things, will he have arrived at as much as new buttons when we see him again?

The steep and bad road by which we were now lifted out of the valley was only tolerable that sultry afternoon, as it was shaded by thick woods. Churchill and I, with the postillion, panted up without our coats. Farther on, heavy timbers protected the edge from a deep ravine, full of trees; and in about two hours we reached green glades, whence a soft prospect opened to view the long-desired Gail Thal. Do you ask what we wanted there? Turn, then, to the map; see the long valley, marked but partially with a road, and learn that no tourist's steps have ever reached it! Do you not understand the yearning which seizes upon the traveller's soul when he hears of such a valley—remote, unvisited? If you do not, you will fail to appreciate our feelings as we crossed the dividing ridge that afternoon and through the openings in the oak glades saw the vale at last—no stern, inaccessible seclusion, however; simply a rich and smiling expanse, with houses and churches. Then it was hidden for a time, till the road pitched suddenly down upon it, where a tidy village sheltered under the hill. A comfortable-looking inn threw open to the evening air the closed shutters of its two best guest-chambers for our reception; and, as fine organ tones were wafted in with the breezes from a large church opposite, it was difficult to believe that Kötschach—that was its name—was really a village of the unknown valley of the Gail.

Mauthen is marked in capitals in the map as the town

of importance hereabouts; but our postillion would only recognise Kötschach; and a stroll across the valley that evening to the former place showed us a decayed village, once of note, when the now deserted pass of Santa Croce, which from this spot crosses the Carnic Alps, was in use, but which has fallen with the fortunes of the road. It was here the Counts of Görz, the owners of almost all the Gail Thal, levied toll—'mauth'—upon all travellers, and the name remains to tell its former history. From a pilgrim-chapel on a height above Mauthen there is a good view of the Gail Thal—a long soft vista between wooded hills, crowned by a few isolated and distant ashy-grey pinnacles of rock. We half suspected that nobody came here, because there was nothing to come for. Before the week was out we had rectified that hasty judgment.

CHAPTER VII.

THE GAIL THAL.

Auf der Plecken and its hearty Dame—The 'Römischer Weg'—The Polinik and Kollin Kofel—Kötschach and the Festa—The Upper Gail—Hermagor—The Wulfenia—The Gîtsch Thal and a chatty Driver—The Weissensee—The crazy Boat—Bewilderment—Approach to Tarvis—Austrian Alpine Roads—What we have done, and what we are going to do.

FROM the first moment of our descent into the Gail Thal we had been attracted by an opening into the hills behind Mauthen, in the direction of the Santa Croce pass. The track itself is interesting as an old Roman road. Part of it we had already traversed in coming from Lienz—then Leontium—and it continued its course southwards over the opposite range to the port of Aquileia on the Adriatic. Once it was the most frequented way over these alps; but when commerce deserted Aquileia, it deserted the road also. Tradition still speaks of Julius Cæsar having crossed this way, and no doubt poor Briccius limped along it with his bandaged foot. Beside the historic interest, however, there was the promise of striking scenery. On the eastern side of the gap, just mentioned, rose a sharp conical mountain — the Polinik — of whose botanic treasures Churchill had note in his pocket-book. On the western side huge bare bosses of Dolomitic rock peered up behind the nearer hills, and were identified as part of the Kollin Kofel, or Monte Cogliano. Between the two the pass must lie, and somewhere up there would be Auf der

Plecken, half inn, half farmhouse, formerly the Hospice of Santa Croce. It was the very spot for an ascent of the Polinik, and a peep at the Friulian mountains—also, let us hope, for a little fresh air: the stifling heat of these valleys was taking all nerve out of us.

So, wakened at five the next morning by obstreperous bells, and a fine swell of the organ from the church over the way, where processions of peasants were already arriving for some great festa of the valley, we packed a couple of knapsacks, and despatched S—— and A—— by a rough cart, while we followed on foot. Crossing the flat valley, a third of whose width was occupied by the destructive Gail, and ascending by the little Pilgrim Chapel we had visited the evening before, the track, just wide enough for a single pair of wheels, became very steep and stony as it climbed the sides of a profoundly deep chasm. Have we not talked of chasms and ravines till the reader is tired of hearing of them? Well, here was a novel feature in a forest of the noblest beech trees, shading the path for miles with their mossy arms. Their huge boles glimmered in the depths below, and stood in columned majesty on the heights above. Villages, or even châlets, except at one spot, there were none; and we now, for the first time, recognised Sclavonic as the language of the few peasants we met.

In about three hours we stepped upon the open grass. Here the Polinik was on our left; in front, a rocky wood-covered barrier, through which there tumbled a hidden stream; and to the right an open valley, which bore away, till abruptly closed in by the giant buttresses of the Kollin Kofel—all naked, treeless rock. This valley—the Valentiner Thal—was tenanted only by a cluster of cattle-sheds, ranged, as customary on the Italian side of the Alps, in terraces one above another, the cattle themselves at this hour, as the telescope discovered, browsing in large herds against the sky upon high and steep slopes, which it was a marvel they could reach. Up the barrier before us was our course, by a path of rattling stones, shaded by trees, and occasionally wet with the rills that gushed from the rocks. Surmounting this ascent, a verdant hollow appeared, holding in its bosom a large and singular building, with farmhouse appurtenances—the Hospice of Auf der Plecken. Here the beeches and chestnuts for the most part ceased, and only sparse woods of pine hung about the hills, as was natural to an altitude of more than 4,000 feet: the solitude and breezy coolness were just what we wanted.

A very hearty dame, full of hospitable bustle, received us at the door, especially gleeful when she found we were English—the first she had ever seen. In the excitement of the occasion, every instant gave excuse for a peal of ringing laughter—now at the discovery that we were uselessly puzzling each other with Italian, she being a native of Villach, and therefore of German stock; now at the loops in S—— and A——'s dresses, which had thwarted her well-meant efforts to brush them straight; now at her meagre bill of fare. When did she not laugh? Of course, in ten minutes we were the best of friends. A large stone hall ran through the house, and above, a corridor answering to it. The windows were everywhere defended by iron lattice-work of elaborate pattern, and old portraits in oil lined the walls; for the place, our hostess told us, had belonged to a 'high family.' Even the bed-rooms were full of engravings—some of them English prints of the last century, such as the 'Nightmare' of Fuseli, and others. Three of these chambers were fitted up very comfortably; but the rest, evidently of the old Hospice type, were narrow, and crowded with beds, appropriate to the time when travellers were expected to lie pretty close, and did not mind it on winter nights.

We had arrived at noon, and enquiries about dinner at once betrayed that dearth of meat which is characteristic of the Italian frontier; nevertheless, a fair repast was provided with no unreasonable delay. Soup, with the necks and gizzards of a couple of fowls, to be fished for therein; a pudding, very good; and the remaining odd bits of fowl browned with bread-crumbs—that was all: it was of no use suggesting either a salad, potatoes, or rice. In such a dinner one learns to be chary of morsels, and to be rigidly just in their apportionment. It is too serious if one's neighbour's plate shows an extra claw. Tea-time, too, is a hungry occasion. Here, fortunately, there were eggs in plenty, but no egg-cups; and observe, it requires some dexterity to butter your bread with one hand while you hold your egg with the other.

These few privations, however, did not prevent our spending here three very pleasant days, during which we pretty well explored the paths; and Churchill ascended the Polinik, whose speciality was well known at the Hospice. No less a person than the late King of Saxony, a devoted botanist, had once been tempted here by its proximity, and the floral treasures of the district.

A ruined building, once the much-sought chapel of 'Maria Schnee,' stood a little beyond the house; and beside it the track of the old road passed on with many windings up the green hill-sides into the sloping woods, and so along a narrow terrace cut in the mountain-flank to the summit of the pass.* Here stern walls of rock, closing and retreating for about half a mile, present the aspect rather of a Pyrenean port than of an Alpine col,

* About 4,600 feet above the sea.

and approached in either direction have a striking effect. Twice we took our evening walk through this tempting portal into Venetia, but the only prospect forward was into gulfs of wood, among rounded and solitary hills, dreaming in that hazy beauty which is characteristic of the Italian lake districts. There is no traffic except that of light and narrow carts, carrying a score of sawn planks a-piece; and the road admits only one of these at a time. Nor do they cross the summit southward. Their loads are deposited at the top of the pass, in charge of the owner of a solitary hut, and are afterwards taken away by a similar set of carts on the Italian side. They are all in the employment of a Trieste company, who have contracted for the timber of the neighbouring mountains, and keep the road in sufficient repair for their purposes.

On the south side of the pass the road is carried, in some places, on wooden brackets round the faces of precipices, and across the deep scores of torrents. Both props and flooring are here and there decayed, and through various holes, into which the foot might easily slip, the blue depths below are visible. Two hours farther, and Timau, the first village, called also Tischlwang, is reached, whose population, with that of three hamlets in neighbouring valleys westward, speak a dialect of German so peculiar as to require the services of a native-born priest; no other could make himself understood. A Carinthian writer conjectures that their origin dates back to the period of the first movements of the German tribes towards Italy. A careful collection of their vocabulary by a competent hand, might recover some new and interesting forms of Old German.

How the original Roman road was engineered on the

south side of the pass it would be interesting to determine with exactness. That it came through the gap above, is certain from the nature of the ridge, even without the testimony of two weathered Latin inscriptions upon the rocks. It did not, however, turn, as the present road does, to the left, and across the precipitous faces just mentioned, for traces of it are still discernible on the right, immediately after leaving the jaws of the pass. Here it slopes downward for some distance, and then, apparently returning upon itself, rises to some three hundred feet above its first point of issue. This very singular arrangement seems to have puzzled some explorers, but can easily be explained, if, instead of being parts of one road, the two portions belong to two roads, the result of an alteration of level at some period. That both are Roman is evident from undoubted marks of antiquity. The deep ruts, four inches wide, are there as the ancient chariots left them, wherever the solid blocks of stone remain. And more than this; of the two inscriptions referred to, one belongs to the lower, and the other to the upper, reach of road.

Of these inscriptions, the first—the lower—is the more curious. For centuries it has been claimed as offering conclusive proof that the road over this pass was constructed, or made practicable for vehicles, by Julius Cæsar himself. Yet of all the various transcriptions, of which a dozen might be quoted, no two are exactly alike; and the last transcriber—a writer in a Carinthian journal, who visited the spot in 1855, and whose copy Churchill took the trouble to verify—does not find the name of Cæsar at all. Most of the others, beginning with one in the fifteenth century, profess to have distinctly seen 'C. Julius Cæsar, viam hanc rot F.' (rotabilem fecit).

The entire inscription, as given by the writer in the journal, runs thus:—

RESPECTV . ET . H . S.
N R . ICHNI . . VECP .
GAL . LI R . . . SERV
. . . .
. . ALPIN . . .
PER . . . . .
RICLITA . . . . . . VN
TAM . . . ST .
SEXTO . . . .

Yet, that Julius Cæsar did construct the road, and even held it of great importance in his operations, is probable from evidence which has been educed, with care and fulness, by the latest historian of Carinthia, Von Ankershofen. It is certain that three of Cæsar's legions had their winter quarters near Aquileia, and named after him two places, Forum Julii and Julium Carnicum, both in the direct line between Aquileia and the Plecken Alp. The second of the two is still known as Zuglio, a village between Paluzza and Tolmezzo; and the Gail Thal itself is said to be none other than the old Vallis Julia.*

The first inscription is at, perhaps, fifty yards from the mouth of the pass, on a smoothed face of rock, obscured by bushes, and three or four feet above the surface of the paved road.

The second inscription is found on a similar, but much larger, face of rock, at the upper bend of road, and about six feet above it. It is thus given by the latest transcriber :—

* Paulus Diaconus, the Lombard historian, speaks of this valley under the name of 'Zellia;' and it is remarkable that one of the names of the Kollin Kofel is 'Der Grosse Zellon,' while its neighbour, eastward, overlooking the pass, is called 'Der Kleine Zellon.'

IS CETERISQVE DIB . .
MO . . . SOLEMNE VOTVM DI . . .
HERMIAS SVSCEPTOR OPERIS AETERNI
TITVLVM IM . MEM MONTEM ALPINUM
INGENTEM LITTERIS INSCRIPSIT QVOT
SA . PE INVIVM COMIANTIVM PERICLITAN
POPVLO AD PONTEM TRANSITVM NON
PLACVIT CVRAE ET ATTIO BRAETIANO
Q. ORVM VIRO ORNATO VIAM NOV .
DEMONSTRANTE HERMIA . MVLT . NI
MIS FIDES OPERISQVE PAR . TVS VNA
NIMES OMNES HANC VIAM EXPLICVIT . .

If the 'Viam Nov' in the ninth line be correct, it is decisive as to an alteration of road at a later date than that of the first inscription. It may have been carried at this higher level to avoid the fall of rocks which are thickly strewn in the interval between its upper and lower course. There is a third inscription, near Timau, for a copy of which we are indebted to Ankershofen :—

MVNTPICENTIAD . D. AVGGVE
N. N. HOCITER VBI HOMINES ET
ANIMALIA CVM PERICVLO
COMMEABANT APERTVM EST
CVRANTE APINTO TRAM.
MATTO CVR . . R . PAV . A .
D . D . D NNN . VALENTINIANO
ET VALENTE. AVGG. IIII. CO . .

These inscriptions, particularly the last, show that then, as now, Alpine roads were frequently a prey to the elements ; and illustrate also the care bestowed from time to time on this one by the Imperial government, from

Cæsar to Valentinian. The stages upon it from Aquileia to Loncium (Lienz) are given in the 'Antonine Itinerary.'

Each evening that we returned after dark by the gate of the pass from the Venetian to the Carinthian side, the lights of the hospice were seen sparkling cheerily below, as soon as the passage was cleared. A hospitable welcome was always ready—the salle in bright illumination, a white cloth laid for tea, and muslin curtains drawn over the windows. They had clearly an eye for comfort, and tea was here no conventional term; we had actually discovered enough for two makings in a small paper tray, among some curiosities preserved by our hostess. The precious store had been left by some Villach visitor of peculiar tastes, and, our own stock being nearly exhausted, was cheerfully surrendered to our use; to witness the concoction of the beverage was reward enough. This was the hour when the good lady was most at leisure for conversation; and Frau Claus soon showed herself a person of intelligence, as well as of the most abundant goodnature. She had supplied herself with a tolerable store of books for winter reading, while her maidens spun, and her own fingers were busy with the knitting needles. In this occupation her industry was marvellous. She showed us, among other results, a complete set of ornamental bed-furniture; and as for stockings, she was a good daughter of her mother, who presented her on her marriage day with a hundred and fifty pairs, knitted with her own hands. The whole family remain at the hospice till immediately before Christmas, when they descend in sledges to Mauthen, leaving two or three men to attend to the cattle, and receive chance wayfarers, for the pass is in use throughout the year. At the beginning of March, just before the greatest fall of snow, they return, and have then been sometimes shut up for several weeks. The Frau was related to the original owner of the property, which now belongs to herself and her husband. It pastures a large number of cattle, which in summer is increased by flocks and herds from Italy, paying a rent of one zwanziger per head per month.

Frau Claus's most interesting communications, however, referred to the customs of her neighbours, the Slovenes, who are the principal inhabitants of the middle and lower Gail Thal. When the labours of summer are over, come games and weddings—the latter invariably in the winter. Among the games is the 'Kufenstechen,' supposed to be of great antiquity. A barrel of beer is set up, and horsemen, riding at full speed, thrust at it as they dash by with sharp-pointed poles: he who first succeeds in staving in the barrel receives, as prize, a wreath and a measure of wine. The feat requires great strength, as well as skill. Their dances also are peculiar. The 'Hohe Tanz,' a very violent and saltatory affair, in which only the unmarried take part, rivals, in Slovenic antiquity, the game of the 'Kufenstechen.' It is commenced by the women alone, who, from time to time, and after certain tantalising delays, condescend to select their partners from among the waiting crowd of men. The Slovenic bride always wears black, with a white veil, and a wreath of flowers. After the wedding, her parents are presented by the bridegroom with wine in which to wash their hands; and as she approaches her husband's house, several children, each with a piece of cake, are despatched to run through every room, propitiating good luck thereby in the shape of a large family, and plenty for them. Stranger still, before the bride sets foot on the threshold, a hen, intended to represent the Holy Spirit, is made to fly over her head into the house!

Our lively hostess had frequently participated in these

ceremonies. Her early years had been passed among the Slovenes, and she was of a very social disposition. Generally, the Slovenes live very much to themselves in retired districts, and seem to be viewed with some distaste by their German neighbours, who, annoyed apparently at the Slovenic speech, rather testily assert they could talk 'Deutsch' well enough, if they liked.

Frau Claus had much to enquire about England, and took great amusement in an English lesson. She was a quick pupil; but 'How do you do?' 'Good night,' and a few other examples, soon sent her off in fits of laughter to repeat them to the rest of the establishment. Yet the merry dame had her troubles, and the lack of suitable fare for her guests was one.* Her spirits, and ours also, were somewhat depressed at the unsatisfactory nature of the second day's dinner. But the next morning she announced with glee the arrival of fresh meat, for which, it was suspected, her husband had been despatched to the Gail Thal the night before, after the good man had finished his hard day's work on the hay slopes. Haymaking, in addition to the ordinary tending of the cattle, was the great occupation just now. Many servants, male and female, came in to supper every night in the ample kitchen, and there, in the gloaming, 'kneeling on their knees,' recited their evening litany before going to bed. Since leaving German Tyrol we had lost this pious practice; but it well accorded with the patriarchal simplicity and seclusion of this mountain farm.

The ascent of the Pollinik, nearly 8,000 feet above the sea, scarcely repaid the labour, as the plants were burnt up by heat; but the view from the summit displayed

* We are bound to mention that on a subsequent visit of C—— and A—— (1863), extending over eleven days, the meat provided was abundant and good.

nearly the whole course of the Gail, the picturesque and numerous forms of the Lienz Dolomites, and the peaks of their opposite and far more lofty neighbour, Monte Cogliano (the Kollin), with a small glacier running down from them almost to the edge of its magnificent precipice.* The summit of the Pollinik is a narrow edge, a few feet long, and less than a foot wide, crowning a cap of Dolomite Gerölle or debris.

A small lake lies over the head of the Valentiner Thal, called the Wolayer See, nestled at the roots of the north-west face of the Kollin Kofel at a great elevation; this we ought to have visited; but no one could be spared as guide, or to carry provisions for the long day requisite. We therefore penetrated only so far up the uninhabited valley of the Valentiner as to disclose a grand view of the Kollin Kofel, rising like an enormous Egyptian Pylon at the furthest end. Its summit, broken into a succession of cones, and the sheer flatness of its walled sides, give it a most peculiar appearance. A woodland terrace path, dark with beech umbrage, leads into the Valentiner Thal from Auf der Plecken; its principal use must be to reach the cattle-sheds, or to give access to the woodmen, two or three of whom, speaking only Slovenic, we encountered, hacking wastefully at noble trees. Much reckless de-

* Monte Paralba, on the south side of the Gail Thal, 8,812 English feet, has hitherto been considered the highest of the Carnic Alps. On the 22nd of September 1862, however, Edmund Von Mojsisovics ascended the Kollin Spitze, and, as the mean of three barometer observations, made its height 8,467 Vienna feet, or thirty feet less than the Paralba; while the two Keller Spitzen, part of the Kollin Massive, standing a little to the west, which he found he could not climb, he estimated at 500 feet higher, or 9,000 Vienna feet—9,333 English, which is only 37 feet less than the Terglou!

The glacier lies at a height of more than 6,000 feet above the sea, below the three peaks of the Kollin Massive, and shut in on the east and west by high precipitous ridges, running northward to the Valentiner Thal.

struction of this kind seemed to be going on all through the valley, as ashes and burnt stumps testified.

KOLLIN KOFEL.

To some readers it may be interesting to know that my friend Churchill, during his last visit to the hospice, found specimens of a fern, which, on comparison in England with fronds from North America, proved to belong to *Woodsia glabella*, a plant hitherto supposed to be absent from Europe, and only to be met with in Arctic North America. It had, however, been very recently detected in small quantity in the Sexten Thal and Brags Thal—two lateral valleys of the Puster Thal, in Tyrol.

On the last evening of our stay—Saturday—we strolled a short distance up the side of the Pollinik, for a general survey of Auf der Plecken. Into its verdant basin the moon presently began to pour her rays, contesting with the crimson glow of sunset; while from every rocky steep, far up to where the eye could scarcely distinguish the atomies, resounded the calls of the herdsmen collecting the sheep, goats, and cattle, to be folded for the night. It was a pretty sight to watch them dropping from impossible heights—trickling like comfits poured out of a bag down their accustomed narrow paths to where, on some green ledge or recess in the woods, the sleeping-sheds were placed, tier above tier. It was almost dusk before all were gathered; and then how still it was! On all sides above the drapery of wood rose, interspersed with open alp, cones, bosses, turret walls of rock, pale among the stars. Below, in the dark hollow, the hospice lights answered to those serener ones above, and centred in themselves the sole human interest of the scene.

We had purposely avoided returning to Kötschach that evening, knowing that the only Sunday quiet to be found in these countries is out of doors, and that the walk down the beech-shaded ravine, taken leisurely, would afford the best opportunity for it. I think our departure relieved our good friend from culminating anxieties as to another day's dinner; and we delighted her much by leaving our names and addresses at full length in a book intended for the purpose, but which was nearly blank. Her final

English lesson—an exercise in their pronunciation—ended, as usual, in an explosion of laughter. A boy accompanied us to carry our few belongings, and for a visit to the lower world of the valley—the only world to him. He had adopted shoes and ragged stockings for the occasion; but they proved too incommodious, and were presently disposed with infinite care behind some fronds of fern, to be reclaimed on his return.

They had spoken of a festa in the valley, in honour of the Emperor's birthday; but we did not realise its possible inconvenience till, clear of the ravine, we stood upon the last rocky and pine-covered steep which overhangs the Gail. There, with Mauthen at the foot of the green slopes beneath us, and Kötschach opposite on the further side of the stream, the clangour of bells first broke upon our ears, and glimpses of flags and of moving crowds shimmered in the hot sunlight among the trees in the distance. Descending to the valley, we were soon in the midst of them. All the peasantry of the Gail Thal seemed to be there, from their number, and as Kötschach possesses the largest church, so it may have been. Church, and churchyard too, must have been full that day; and as we approached the inn, every window and door appeared stuffed with heads or backs. To our great relief, however, the keys of our rooms were safe at the sturdy waist of the Kellnerin; our darkened chambers were empty and cool; and dinner was soon provided in a style far beyond the means of poor Auf der Plecken. Yet, as soon as the sun hung low, we were glad to escape into the woody uplands above the village, where, as the noise of the merriment faintly floated from below, the festa, separated from its accompaniments, could be pleasantly idealised, and the far-stretching valley also, as it lay bathed in softening light. It was the place and hour to decide a question: Should we, on the morrow, ascend or descend the Gail Thal?

The upper Gail, called also the Lessach Thal, bearing away to the right as we now looked down from the northern slope of the valley, forms about a third of its entire length, and is traversed only by a rough horse-track. It is divided from the middle Gail, commencing at Kötschach, by one of those barriers of rock and wood which so often separate the 'Ober' from the 'Unter' in Alpine valleys. Sta. Maria Lukau is its principal village, and, judging from the map and the information we could collect, the mountains on both sides are lofty and picturesque. Those we had seen from Lienz, magnificent in their mural precipices, must abut upon it from the north; and Monti Antola, Paralba, and others, if they are worthy brethren of the Pollinik and Kollin Kofel, with which they stand in line, must furnish some grand scenery on the south. It was tempting; yet, on the whole, having important districts—those of the Terglou and the Steiner Alp—yet to explore, and an attraction, still to be mentioned, in the lower Gail Thal; having also devoted so much time to Auf der Plecken, we elected to abandon—to the reader, if he chooses—the untrod region of the upper Gail. Yet, if anyone be minded to achieve the honours of exploration, let him lose no time, or he may chance to find that we have repaired our neglect—perhaps encounter there our veritable selves: in the latter event, we hereby invite him to supper; or rather, to that 'pot-luck' which, in these parts, is a serious contingency.

Thus arranging our plans, evening drew on—that beautiful time, in these southern climates, when colours deepen into hues so wonderful, and all the poetry of the landscape is breathed out into the air, and conversation dies into reverie. It was late when we descended to the inn, which was still a noisy place, so many people preferring to enjoy the moonlight, and to bandy their harsh gutturals in interminable discussion, close under our windows. Sleep for several hours was impossible, for if any pause occurred, the watchman filled it, chanting his verse, or the implacable church clock seized the opportunity to strike the quarters.

On Monday morning, the first cloud we had seen for many days barred the Pollinik, and spread in a fleecy veil over the hollow of Auf der Plecken; but it was still bright and hot as we left Kötschach, turning eastward down the lengthening and widening valley. Our vehicles were two light little wicker 'wagen,' of true Carinthian type; in which, as in the ever-memorable Malnitz drive, our baggage, ourselves, and a quantity of hay, were speedily shaken up together in a formless heap, and powdered with pitiless dust.

Our destination was Hermagor, about twenty-two miles below Kötschach. The whole of this portion of the Gail Thal is richly wooded in great slopes and terraces up the sides, while the bottom is either rank and marshy, or stony, as the river wastes and wanders from side to side, compelling the road to avoid it by skirting the foot of the northern hills. The slopes are, in fact, extensive fans of débris that have been shot out from what are, in the summer season, dry gullies, running down from the northern ridge. In more than one instance they projected nearly across the valley, and pushed the Gail close up to the foot of the opposite, or southern, hills. Churches, usually perched upon the ridges of these fans, were both few and small, with grey shingle-covered spires, after the manner of Essex; but the resemblance to anything English ceased with the spire, for all, and even road-side shrines, had enormous open porches, sometimes as large as the building itself—evidently a provision against heat. The dress of the women, too, looked like labour under a sweltering sun, the neat felt hat and clean stockings of the mountain peasant girl giving place to a red handkerchief bound across swarthy brows, and to naked brown legs, the petticoats reaching only to the knee.

During the greater part of the day the sharp-pointed Pollinik was the principal feature, wherever the turns of the road invited a backward view up the valley; but a striking-looking mountain, occupying the opposite side of the Gail, gradually took possession of the prospect in front. It proved to be the Gartner Kogel, of which we shall have much to say. We knew nothing of it yet, and little suspected the interest it would presently excite.

After sheltering for an hour or two from the mid-day heat in a small village inn, we reached Hermagor, picturesquely situated at the entrance of the Gitsch Thal, about four o'clock. We were charmed with its quaint and sequestered look, as we turned into its single street of clean large-eaved houses, where with some difficulty we hit upon an inn, 'Zum Mohren,'—also a shop,—just opposite the church. Two small, but quite elegantly-furnished rooms, opened on each side of the upstairs landing, and a funny old woman, assisted by an active lad, took us briskly in hand, promising a speedy dinner. The failure was in the speediness, and perhaps in the pudding, which, immediately following the soup, we took the liberty of postponing till the next course had been served. Alas! in the interval its goodly and delicate proportions had collapsed to the bottom of the dish; and the old lady who, expecting congratulations on her triumph, had timed a flying visit from the kitchen for the moment when its excellence should have been demonstrated, was loud and dramatic in her lamentations over our perversity.

In the balmy evening we sauntered up the Gitsch Thal.

A solitary chapel on a rising ground, hard by a quaint-looking building, whose conical-roofed towers spoke of some ancient lordship of these parts, soon tempted us out of the road, and across open fields of corn and maize, as much for the point of view which would be afforded, as from curiosity respecting the antique edifices that occupied the spot. We found that the castle was now a farm; its moat, and gateway, and crazy gates, guarding only the wains and stalls of the farmyard, and the old walls so hidden among sheds and bushes, that there was less to be seen near than at a distance.* The adjacent church, with bare whitewashed walls, stood upon a small patch of turf open to the fields, and offering a charming prospect. Below lay Hermagor, shrouded in trees; the broad Gail Thal beyond was shut off by pine-covered hills, stretching in long line down the valley behind the town; but askance, to the east, the eye passed down through the opening of the Gitsch Thal, and was arrested by a magnificent mountain mass—pale red, yellow, and purple, seamed and scarred, and burning in the sunlight. This was the Dobratsch, the great bulwark marking the junction of the Gail valley with that of the Drave, and which, opposite the pass of the Predil, southward, occupies a most conspicuous position. Its huge bulk was repeatedly in sight for nearly a fortnight afterwards. Westward of our point of view were the soft glades of the Gitsch Thal, sinking into evening shadow.

The landlord or *principale*, as in the odd mixture of languages in these parts they called him, had not been at home on our arrival, but appeared on our return to the inn. At the first casual question addressed to him, 'Ah,'

* Two years afterwards gateway, walls, and moat were gone—not the only sign that the spirit of innovation had seized upon Hermagor. One of the neighbouring Bauers, for no personal reason that we could find, had inscribed 'Neu America' upon his fence.

said he, 'you come for the *Wulfenia.*' Now this was what we *had* come for; and it is what any stranger visiting Hermagor does come for, such stranger being pretty certainly some roving botanist, whom the fame of the *Wulfenia* has drawn to that remote spot. Now I must not anticipate what the proper authority will have to say about this unique plant. I will merely premise, by way of indicating the kind of interest which attaches to it, and to account for the prominence it took in our after arrangements, that it possesses no other known habitat on the surface of the globe, than a particular mountain in this neighbourhood,—the same in fact whose striking contour had challenged our attention as we descended the valley. It was discovered in 1779, by the botanist whose name it bears, Baron Wulf of Klagenfurt, on the northern slope of the Gartner, and the King of Saxony found also a locality for it upon the western spur of the same mountain; but that it should be confined to this one mountain is the more extraordinary, since there it flourishes in the greatest abundance, ruthlessly usurping in some places all the soil to itself, and, unlike Alpine plants in general, is of large size. How is its strange isolation to be accounted for? Is it the relic of a flora which geologic changes have destroyed, and which this mountain top, islanded in the surrounding ruin, has alone preserved? I must leave Churchill to tell us all he can about it, and of his successive visits to its mountain fortress.

'You come for the *Wulfenia,*' said the landlord, 'you will not find it in flower but in seed;' and so our botanist's hopes were frustrated, as frequently of late, by the unusual heat of the summer of '61. He engaged a guide, however, for the morrow, and the rest of us arranged an excursion which had formed a secondary object in coming to Hermagor. This was a visit to the Weissen See, a long and narrow lake in the hilly district between the valleys of the Gail and the Drave; and accessible either from Greifenberg in the latter, or through the Gitsch Thal from the former. 'Murray' has a short paragraph about it, *à propos* of his description of the Drave scenery; for, as I have mentioned, he leaves the Gail untouched, and we almost felt it a condescension to return into the domain of the 'Red book.'

The morning's drive to the head of the Gitsch Thal, some two hours, was through remarkably agreeable scenery, cheerful with farms, fields, and timber-shaded lanes; the hill sides above, clothed with woods, a village here and there niched up between them. The driver, as is usual with such supernumeraries, had been a soldier, and was full of his Italian experiences in '48, of the cities he had 'occupied,' and of his general, Radetsky. He had not seen English before. 'Not in Venice?' we exclaimed, which he had just described as 'sehr lustig.' 'In Venice? ah, yes, and there one sees Turks also,' an association we did not take to be very complimentary. The chatty fellow rattled on with his tongue, and his wheels, till we reached Weissbriach, the last village in the valley. Here he proposed leaving the carriage, as there was no inn at the lake; and ordering dinner for five o'clock we started on foot with our loquacious driver for guide, over the woody ridge which shuts in the Weissen See on the south.

It opened pleasantly to sight, a sequestered piece of water, as we crossed the summit, marked by a small shrine, and descended over rough heathery ground, very Scotch like, and then through lush hay meadows to its reedy borders. These meadows were full of those singular racks —sometimes single, and stretching like walls across a valley; sometimes double, and roofed over like an open barn—which abound through Carinthia and Carniola, and quite affect the appearance of the landscape. They are used during only about eight weeks in the year for drying the different crops. We struck the lake near its upper extremity. Some distance lower down, a long, low, wooden bridge crossed at a narrow part to a cluster of houses, almost sufficient to compose a village; indeed the peasant habitations, clean and comfortable, and in cheerful contiguity, were sprinkled all along that opposite shore, open to the sunny south. A few boats and rafts laden with hay, were paddling over the glittering waters, and the people were busy with their autumn gatherings.

The simplicity and completeness of the picture, as a rural spectacle—the suggestion of Arcadian peace—formed its attraction. The pastures on the one side, the orchards on the other; the soft woodlands above, the softer lake below, with its gliding boats and fringe of white homesteads, breathed gentle poetry, and gave an idyllic charm to a scene destitute of any marked feature, either of grandeur or beauty.

We bargained with a good-natured, but rather reluctant peasant, to put us down the lake as far as time allowed; and dismissed our talkative companion to wait for us at Weissbriach. But the boat, which we had not previously examined, proved to be simply a straight-sided, flat-bottomed packing-case, or open coffin, very narrow, and of course without seats, which were improvised with a loose board or two, put across from rim to rim. My two companions having scarcely room to sit side by side, adjusted themselves with difficulty, and with an expression of countenance which did not bode a happy voyage; and when we pushed into the poppling water, which a sudden breeze had ruffled, and the peasant boatman sitting in a helpless way at the hinder end, for it could not be called the stern, rocked the frail bark with each stroke of a wretched little paddle—dipped Otaheite fashion, first on one side and then on the other—their alarm rendered it advisable to bring the expedition to a speedy end, and instead of continuing down the lake, we landed as soon as might be on the opposite shore. There a shady lane dodged among houses and orchards, but arriving at the bridge, we recrossed the lake and walked for two or three miles along its grassy margin. That side was open and tenantless, though valuable as pasture; and at various convenient points small wooden jetties were constructed, where the raft of each proprietor lay moored, some of them big enough to hold a haystack, which indeed we more than once saw moving bodily over the water.

We obtained no particular view, except of a solitary waterfall tumbling behind the roofs of some cottages on the other side; and, towards the lower end of the lake, of a more precipitous closing in of the hills, that seemed to preclude space for further habitations, and to justify Murray's remark that the finest scenery, if the less cheerful, is to be found in that direction. He speaks, moreover, of the walk down the Stockenboyer Thal, beyond, as very agreeable, notwithstanding numerous iron forges; but that it takes three hours from the extremity of the lake to reach the only inn. The valley eventually enters the Drave Thal, near Paternion. From the spot we reached, the Staffberg, the highest mountain of the vicinity, might have been visible but for unwonted clouds that began to hang about the sky, and which, though not immediately threatening, portended a change in the hitherto brilliant weather.

Striking a different path from that by which we had descended from the col, we remounted the hill, turning frequently for pleasant views of the stretch of water, and its quiet habitations. One almost longed to return for good to that peaceful shore, to paddle one's own haystack, thresh one's own corn, pick one's own pears and walnuts, and so pass life, with no other mutations than those of the seasons, and no other incidents than those that befal a few homely hearths. What a dream it is! I suppose that in every such scene we fancy we detect a corner of the old Paradise, left, like the *Wulfenia*, astray in the world; and truly it is a relic of things which the steam-horse is everywhere fast trampling under foot.

Returning into the Gitsch Thal, we dived through the woods by stony footpaths that crossed from angle to angle of the road; and finally down a steep slope of grass, almost slippery enough for a glissade, into the village of Weissbriach, whose open green spaces, large spreading trees, and cottages plotted about under their shade, almost transported us to rural England,—perhaps because the Weissen See had put us into a sentimental mood. It was late for dinner, and we walked briskly on to reach the inn. Ere long we spied its humble doorway, with our vehicle, as we had left it, drawn up under the eaves. Yet a chilly feeling of strangeness grew upon us as we approached. The vehicle, like the 'deacon's gig,' looked as if it had run through another cycle of existence since the morning. The house—yes, there were doors and windows, as we remembered them, but the neat parlour that had been ours—was now full of men and full of smoke! The landlord—he gazed at us with a stolid countenance. Why the man is moon-struck, or else we are! We ventured on a question:—'Ja,' was the reply, 'that is the "wagen" from Hermagor.' Curious! but was it *our* wagen? We scrutinised the crazy thing for some decisive mark. The lining—was it yellow? 'No—red;' 'no,—certainly blue:' each colour had its advocate. At last the handle of the break settled the matter; ours, we agreed, had none. 'Is there another inn?' we asked. 'Ja,' said the man, and pointed back the way we had come. More puzzling still! Yet back we went, and truly found another hostel, though undoubtedly on the wrong side of the road—unless there were two roads, to settle which point we made desperate incursion upon the back premises, retreating the next moment, baffled and confounded. A dreadful suspicion now entered our minds that we had somehow come down the wrong hill, into the wrong village, perhaps into the wrong valley. 'What is the name of this place?' I asked, with my heart in my mouth. 'Weissbriach.' 'And are there only two inns?' 'Only two; this and that other.' One began to feel the horrible bewilderment of a dream, when things are like and not like, and you are yourself and somebody else at the same time, and every thing becomes another thing. Walking faster and faster, followed by S—— and A——, now manifesting mutiny and utter distrust, which they might well do, seeing I had lost confidence in myself, I pushed on right through the village into open country again, where the prospect seemed hopeless enough. Fortunately at this moment, a passer-by threw sudden light upon the matter. Another inn, some quarter of a mile further, lay hidden among the trees; and at the next turn the whole mystery was explained. We had passed this space unheeded in the morning, and had forgotten the relation of the village to the inn. There it now stood, just as it should be—carriage, and driver, and landlord, and chamber, restored in the twinkling of an eye to their right friendly and most welcome aspect.

Under a lovely evening sky we enjoyed a delightful drive back to Hermagor. The hill-slopes on the left, shone in the western glow. Lorenzen, nestling among them, is the only village of importance after Weissbriach, and a path leading from it over to the Weissen See would pleasantly vary a pedestrian excursion. But a glimpse down the valley, and through its opening upon the Gail Thal, riveted for the moment all our attention. Sublime, cloud-piercing peaks stood suddenly revealed there in unexpected grandeur, and white, either with snow or with the pale tints of Dolomite. They could be no other than the great Terglou group of Carniolan mountains, guarding the head waters of the Save and the Isonzo, where the next portion of our journey lay. It was but a glimpse, and they were gone. Then, as we approached Hermagor, the Dobratsch, which, the evening before, we had seen gloriously illuminated in opal tints, due both to the lustre of the atmosphere, and to the delicacy of its rock-colouring, again stood nobly out to view, though only as a silhouette of grey.

Of course our driver could not be expected to sympathise with evening reveries; and besides, he wanted to introduce his mother and family to our notice, who were keeping watch for our return on the balcony of their house—a respectable peasant abode. It was evident that his good fortune in having conducted us would be a distinction for the household. The mother looked proud and gratified, and every lad and lass was round-eyed and smiling. These attentions withdrew us from the poetry of nature to that of life; and presently entering the cheerful little town at that foot pace which, as in a royal progress, is considered the proper thing in a street, we encountered similar demonstrations of respectful admiration from doors and windows. We were happy to find Churchill just arrived from his *Wulfenia* expedition. Discussing our respective adventures, we made a cheerful tea-party—that is to say, when the usual difficulties, aggravated on this occasion by the perverse ingenuity of the old Kellnerin, had been overcome. Always great in her ideas, and always wrong, the old lady, observing that hot water was a considerable item in our requirements, hit upon the notable expedient of a soup tureen, which, steaming with greasy water, was put upon the table. In this we were expected to concoct our tea, dispensing it with a ladle!

Over the tea-table we learnt from Churchill that his route had led him, in the first instance, directly southwards across the Gail, through the village of Möderndorf, and a scattered pine-wood growing upon the river alluvium, to the foot of the Gartner Kogel. The ascent, mostly through woods of beech and pine, commenced at a point where the Garnitz Bach, rising in the Berg of the same name to the south of the peaks of the Gartner Kogel, issues out of a deep and narrow 'Graben' to join the waters of the main stream. Presently, at the edge of a precipice overlooking the more open part of the ravine, appeared a little chapel, dedicated to St. Urban, into which the guide entered and muttered a few words of invocation. From this point the track skirted the edge of the 'Graben'—a ruinous, desolate-looking depth, in which the torrent of the Garnitz raved. Directly opposite, the bare crags of the many-peaked Gartner rose precipitously to the height of 7,200 feet, scored in the intervals between the peaks with long lines of débris. Compelled to follow the edges of the Graben, the track was very circuitous, but finally an alp, or spur, was reached at the foot of the actual peaks, occupied by a few miserable Senn hütte, and known as the Kühwege Alp. Mainly on the north slopes of this alp was the *Wulfenia* found; at first singly, but further on in large masses, partly in the shade of pine trees, and partly in the open. Thousands of stems rose up within a comparatively small area, and scores of colonies in twos and threes—often of young plants—were scattered sporadically around over a much wider space. The habit of the plant would probably remind the unbotanical observer of a *Foxglove*; it is about eighteen inches high, provided with a rosette of large scalloped leaves of a lettuce-like form, and a stem all but bare of leaves, crowned with a spike of deep purple-blue flowers, all turning one way. Certainly, when in flower, the mass of colour must be visible at a great distance—like that girdle of gentians which Mr. Ruskin describes as having vividly attracted his eye from a distance of several miles, near Landeck, in North Tyrol. The German name of the plant is 'Hundzunge,' or 'Houndstongue,' no doubt from the shape of the leaf. The height of the locality above the sea-level is probably not far short of 6,000 feet. At that time Churchill did not visit the opposite and, as it proved, more interesting side of the mountain.

Hermagor, or more properly, St. Hermagor, may be considered as the ecclesiastical centre of the Gail Thal. Although this little town, and a few neighbouring places, are occupied by Germans, the whole of the remainder of the lower Gail is inhabited by Slovenes, as the names of the villages testify. These are given both in German and Sclavonic on the boards, which, according to an excellent Austrian custom, are placed at the principal entrance of every village. The following may serve as a specimen of this system of double designation, although it belongs, not to the Gail Thal, but to the neighbouring valley of the Save:—

DORF WURZEN
BEZIRK KRONAU
Vas Podkoren
Okraj Krainska Gora.

The dialect is one of the branches of the South Sclavic stock.

Some authorities are of opinion that these Slovenes are part of the Sclavonic vanguard that led Attila's Hunnish battalions over the Carnic Alps into Italy, and have been settled here since that epoch. Be this as it may, Hermagor is named from the saint and apostle Hermagoras, the first Christian Bishop of Aquileia, and said to have been appointed to that office by St. Mark. The Slovenes call him Sveta Michor, or Mihor; and the people of that race in the Gail Thal attribute to him their conversion to the Christian faith—at a date far earlier, therefore, than the rest of Carinthia. This fact is easily explained from the connection of the valley with the great Roman road, and thus with Aquileia, at that time the most important city of Northern Italy.

This valley, remote as it seems from the volcanic region of Italy, has yet suffered from earthquake. On January 25, 1348, an earthquake destroyed part of Villach, overthrew many castles at the mouth of the valley, and brought down a mighty mass of the Dobratsch from its south-west side, burying several villages and hamlets, and stopping the course of the Gail. From this a great lake was formed, drowning out villages which had escaped the previous destruction. In the course of years the river worked out for itself a new bed through the masses of ruin, and drained the lake, but the borders are still visible; and it is worthy of notice that this is the only part of the valley below Kötschach where the Gail is confined between high banks. The district still retains its desolate character, and is full of hillocks and irregular plots of ground. Not a village or house stands upon it. Other traces of the catastrophe come to light occasionally. In the neighbouring parish of St. Leonhard, the ruins of a chapel have been discovered, with colours still fresh on the walls; and within, some prostrate skeletons.

On Wednesday, August 21, we left Hermagor in two cars, as usual; but instead of the flood of sunlight, an ominous roofing of cloud possessed the sky, and we called dolefully to mind, that at the end of our day's journey—a small mining village at the foot of the Predil Pass—we should have approached one of the wettest districts in Europe. On the southern side of the mountain barrier on our right, lay Tolmezzo and Udine, and over them the clouds, driving up from the Adriatic—forced as into a funnel, and denied outlet by the barrier just mentioned—settle in heavy masses, and pour down their streams. While yet in the Gail Thal we were on the northern, and safer, face of these mountains.

On leaving Hermagor, a large pine wood, closely planted, and confined to a tongue of rising ground, is seen occupying, like an island, the centre of the valley, extending down it for two or three miles. This is 'Kaiserlicher,' or a preserve of the Emperor, the forests on the hills on either side being owned by Prince Porzia, who resides in Milan, but possesses large estates in Carinthia and Tyrol, including the *Wulfenia* mountain itself. Perhaps this preserve may date back to the time when the valley, on the dying out of the Counts of Görz, about A.D. 1500, fell to Austria. According to tradition, the Emperor Maximilian frequently visited the Castle of Aichelburg, situated immediately to the north towards Paternion, and then, probably, this wood was used for the chase of the boar. No boars, however, are seen there now; nothing more rare than hares and foxes constitute its inhabitants; and yet no one, we were told, was allowed to disturb its dark recesses. Behind it—yet little suspected by any passing traveller—are three Slovenic villages; hidden from sight and cut off from the traffic of the valley, they suit the shy Slovenic character. After clearing the wood, a small lake shows itself, filling the centre of the basin in this branch of the valley; it forms with the noble Dobratsch behind it, as seen from the western end, or with the Gartner Kogel in a similar position, when viewed from the eastern extremity—a very picturesque scene. The lake furnishes a peculiar and notably ugly kind of crayfish, which, at Hermagor, we were assured was a delicacy.

The valley now widened considerably, and put on a very foreign aspect. It appears thinly inhabited; and the road, as if conscious of danger from the broadening stream, which seems to threaten inundations upon the marshy flats about it, clings, as above Hermagor, to the woody foot of the left-hand hills, twisting up and down, and in and out, among sequestered villages, where frequently, on the steep above, a ruined castle juts into view. Those castle towers, and the hearts within them, must once have shaken at the sound of Turkish artillery, for here the horse-tailed hosts swept and ravaged before their great defeat at Villach, a few miles lower down. It was new to us to associate the Turban and the Crescent with a landscape, and here they seemed strangely out of place.

At Emersdorf, where we halted for an hour, we had hoped to see the Dobratsch towering grandly overhead, but were too near, and too much enclosed in woods. A better chance was afforded as we soon after bore across the valley to its southern side, passing the river by a long wooden bridge, unprotected by the friendly roof you find in Switzerland, the value of which we appreciated, as a violent wind nearly cleared everything out of our vehicles. Here the Dobratsch would have been a grand object, but that its precipices were only seen rising from the plain to disappear above under a dark curtain of cloud. On the northern side of the Gail we had travelled along a tolerably good country road. Here, after passing through Feistritz, we entered a stony track, scarcely to be called a road at all.

All this time we had been eagerly scanning the southern hills for that opening leading up to Tarvis which should disclose the Predil pass, where, if Fortune would but favour, we might expect to see something of that grand Terglou group, or at least of its nearest member, the Mangert, which we knew to lie in that direction. Slowly, but promisingly, the hills unfolded, and dark masses peered up behind; but in a few moments a veil fell thick before them, and we had scarcely regained our labouring vehicles (for we were all on foot), and scarcely unrolled our long disused wraps, before rain dashed in our faces; and we learnt once more what a wetting was. By good hap, we had nearly cleared the tortuous and rugged lane, and were soon upon a broad highway—no other than the great road from Villach—or rather we may say from Vienna itself—which here enters the Carnic chain of mountains, and dividing at Tarvis, descends upon Trieste and Venice by the respective passes of the Predil and Pontebba. The greater portion of this road has been lately reconstructed; broad and beautiful in its bridges, earthworks, and parapets, as Imperial Austria takes care that a new road shall be. The works on the Carinthian side appear, however, to be suspended, the railway to Trieste having probably rendered it of less importance as a means of communication with Italy than formerly, though it never rivalled the Brenner in this respect.

It may be well to give a brief enumeration of these Austrian Alpine roads. The Stelvio is the most westerly of them; its only value was the military access to

Lombardy which it afforded. That province being lost, it is perhaps an inconvenience rather than a benefit; and at one time it was thought the Austrian government would abandon it to the speedy destruction of the winter storms. The next in order is the Brenner, an ancient and useful road, both from its low elevation and the districts which it connects on either side of the Alpine ridge. Innspruck and the valley of the Inn; Trent and the valley of the Adige, have always been of great importance; and in recent times, the direct communication with the Quadrilateral which this pass affords has still more enhanced its value. Then comes the Ampezzo; but this can scarcely be considered more than a local road, as it does not cross the main Noric chain, and is only subsidiary to the roads which lie right and left of it. The Pontebba and Predil uniting at Tarvis, form the fourth and fifth of these lines of communication. Beyond them are, sixthly, the pass of the Loibl, penetrating the Karavanken chain (a continuation of the Carnic Alps), directly to the south of Klagenfurt, and so by Laibach, reaching Trieste. And seventhly, the pass over the Steiner Alp, a portion of the same chain, leading by Kappel up the Vellach Thal, and down the Kanker Thal on the other side, to Krainburg. This very steep pass has, since the opening of the Loibl, fallen much out of use, and consequently out of repair, as we verified in an excursion presently to be related. Lastly, far to the east is the railway route, the only complete one between the capital and Italy. This has little to do with anything Alpine, except at the Sömmering, on the borders of Styria and Austria Proper. It avoids the mighty barrier by sweeping round its eastern extremity, and then slanting down upon Trieste. The greatest distance between any two of these roads is that between the

Brenner and the Pontebba, excluding the Ampezzo for the reason mentioned. This may be roughly estimated at about one hundred miles. It contains the Dolomite district, and to the absence of great intersecting routes may no doubt be ascribed much of the seclusion in which it has hitherto lain. With the principal Roman track over these Eastern Alps—that from Aquileia to Lienz—we have already made the reader acquainted.

When we had fairly gained the smooth incline of this Tarvis road, the rain storm moderated enough to show that the pass was now open before us. Precipices frowned in preternatural gloom among the clouds, and one fine conical bulk—the Königsberg, planted in the centre of the opening—stood conspicuous, now gathering round him the revolving masses, and now flinging them from his bare sides. Notwithstanding, too, the unfavourable weather, we began to notice in the nearer landscape some of those features which rendered this neighbourhood so favourite a resort of Sir Humphry Davy. The Schlitza Bach, coming from the foot of the Predil, breaks into the Gail Thal through an immense gully, whose sides lie in slopes and terraces. These, carpeted with verdure, and adorned with village spires, justified Sir Humphry's frequent comparison to park scenery in England. Had but the afternoon sun at this time poured its rays over these slopes, what a lawny richness might have been displayed! Now, we could only see them under scudding rags of vapour. Further on, the banks, escarped to secure the safety of the road, were curiously laced over diagonally with wands of willow, already sprouting, so as to form, in time, a thick bushy covering, whose roots would sustain the crumbling soil. Suddenly, we struck down a narrow lane by the side of the embankments and arches which bore the great route onward, and found ourselves in the small town of Tarvis, or more strictly 'unter' Tarvis, where the Pontebba valley turns off to the right, the ascent to Weissenfels commences on the left, and that to the Predil pass immediately in front.

Now, again, it was a steady pour, and the long spouts formed a succession of douches to be carefully steered through as we navigated the street. In at a dark archway—dark, but dry—and we are welcomed to the bosom of the fusty old post-house of Tarvis. 'A bad inn,' said a friendly letter from the only traveller we could hear of who had passed this way. 'Of course you won't sleep at Tarvis!' So the inn at Tarvis had been long in our black books. But the inn at Tarvis was now a friend in need. The landlady might be fat, the staircase dirty, the dogs abundant, but it was shelter; and if the landlady were not prepossessing, the Kellnerin was. The dear creature! how promptly she bundled off our soaked wraps to the kitchen fire! how quickly drew out a table in the only feasible bedroom, too gloomy to display much more than the dusky forms of beds in three of the corners; and in the briefest space served up a meal! Truly, while this swash of rain lasted in the narrow street outside, we might be thankful and content.

Let us take the opportunity, while we loll upon our elbows, for a little geographical exposition. We had just turned out of the Gail Thal—the southernmost of the three great valleys of Western Carinthia, and the second principal object of our journey—having traced it from Kötschach through about two-thirds of its length, to nearly its exit in the more important valley of the Drave. Its upper course, as already explained, we had left unexplored; and though no very striking scenery occurs along its lower portions, we had been rewarded for the expedition, on the whole, by becoming acquainted with two or three interesting localities, and by ascertaining what this secluded valley really was. Its isolation may be ascribed partly to its great length—some eighty miles, necessitating a three days' journey—partly to its being virtually a *cul de sac*, the passage through it at the upper end being too rough and difficult for wheels to traverse; and partly to the greater population and importance of the Drave Thal itself. To this, however, it stands in the relation of chord to the arc; for while the Drave winds about northward from Sillian by Lienz, Greifenberg, Spital, and so to Villach; the Gail valley, commencing near Sillian, takes a singularly straight course direct to Villach.

The most interesting portions to us were, first, the 'Römischer Weg,' or old Roman pass, breaking through the hills southward at Mauthen, with the remarkable Pollinik on one side, and the Dolomitic Kollin Kofel on the other—offering, besides, so pleasant a spot for a few days' halt as the Hospice Farm of 'Auf der Plecken;' and, secondly, the picturesque neighbourhood of Hermagor, with that notable botanical curiosity, the habitat of the *Wulfenia*, on the slopes of the Gartner. A pilgrimage to that secret spot of nature's wonder-working is well worth the trouble, and we all regretted that we had left Churchill to undertake the ascent alone; while he was full of hope that, the following year, he should be able to describe the appearance of this strange alp, when covered with the bloom of its cherished flower.

Below Hermagor, the valley acquires an air of grandeur from its breadth, its woods, its loftier rocky barriers, the distant and impressive apparition of the Carniola Mountains, or Julian Alps; and, above all, from the noble Dobratsch, baring its scarred front to the southern sun, or purple under its burden of clouds.

After this retrospective glance let us now look forward. We are about to explore a new district, which at its very entrance had great promise in its aspect. 'Murray,' who had been no help to us in the Gail Thal, now came again into requisition, but his notices were meagre; it was the attraction of Sir Humphry Davy's name, and the enthusiasm of his descriptions, that had brought us here. Generally, the country may be described as the site of the head waters of the Save and the Isonzo; both breaking away from the neighbourhood of Tarvis. The one rising near Wurzen, some three hours to the eastward of Tarvis, over the pass of Weissenfels, takes a long course by Krainburg and Laibach, and so on into Croatia, till it reaches the Danube. The other, the Isonzo, rising south of Tarvis, over the Predil Pass, pursues a southward and comparatively brief course through the principality of Görz, till it enters the Adriatic near Trieste. The angle between the two rivers is occupied by the great Carniolan group, of which the Terglou is the dominating peak; while the Mangert, nearer the point of the angle, is scarcely less imposing, and has this geographical importance, that it forms the corner-stone of the three provinces, Carinthia, Carniola, and Görz.

The scenery of both the Save and the Isonzo derives its grandeur from this mountain range, usually known as the Julian Alps, viewed on the right hand as you descend the Save, and on the left as you pass down the Isonzo; though the latter is more entangled in its recesses than the former. Upon the mixture of beauty and majesty with which these valleys are thus gifted, Sir Humphry is never tired of expatiating. 'I know no scene more sublime than this crest of the Carnic Alps, and there are no streams more beautiful than the Save and the Isonzo. I think this valley (the Save) from Laibach to Wurzen the most beautiful in Europe.' And to Wurzen the philosopher, with his white hat lined with green, and unfailing fishing-rod, came no less than six successive years, sadly seeking health too fatally impaired. 'To my old haunt Wurzen,' is one of his latest entries, 'which is sublime in the majesty of Alpine grandeur.'

No wonder that on the threshold of this scenery we regarded ourselves as approaching one of the most interesting portions of our journey. No wonder that the descending rain, which here barred our progress, filled us with doleful apprehensions. Of the two valleys, we proposed taking the Isonzo first, at least as far as Flitsch, where we intended to remain for some days. It was possible that there we should find it practicable to cross the mountains to the Wocheiner See, and so by the beautiful lake of Veldes reach the Save and Wurzen; but it was more probable that we should find it expedient to return over the Predil to Tarvis, and approach the Save at its source over the ridge of Weissenfels.

CHAPTER VIII.

THE ISONZO.

The Königsberg—Rain, Night, and Soldiers at Raibl—Amelie sits for her Portrait—Raibl Mines and Raibl Lake—The Mangert—The Fort and the Lion—The Predil Pass—Desolation—The old Fort and its Siege—Flitsch—The Stony Valley—The Curé of Sotcha—The Prestelinik and its Wilderness—The brave old Guide—Character of the Isonzo.

After the digression at the close of the last chapter, let us return to the dull inn chamber, whence through iron-latticed windows we watched the endless rain-drops. If this down-pour should continue, must we not sleep at Tarvis despite all warnings? The question was under discussion when the watery din without slackened upon our ears; and as evening was now drawing on, we gave instant order to 'einspannen.' To relieve the tired horses in the expected ascent, as well as to protect S—— and A—— from weather, we packed them off singly in each vehicle, and followed ourselves on foot; the distance to Raibl, where the same authority that had decided against Tarvis advised us of a tolerable country inn, being only about five miles. Not far from the town we met a party of jägers, returning with empty game-bags from some cloud-enveloped height above; but the clouds by this time were lifting, and the rain ceasing, so that, arrived near the foot of the Königsberg, where the valley splits into two, descending from each side of this isolated mountain, there was a fine glimpse up the right-hand branch to the snow-streaked and glistening precipices of the Wischberg, a considerable mountain of these parts. The road here crossed the stream to ascend the left-hand valley, opposite the now wooded flanks of the Königsberg. That mountain bears this royal title because Alboin, when he was advancing, at the call of Narses, with his Lombards from Pannonia into Italy, is said by the historian Paulus Diaconus to have ascended it for a view of the Italian plains, or more likely the better to guide his army through these defiles. The road continued a gentle ascent; on the right, across the Schlitza, was the 'Berg'; on the left a steep commingling of rock and wood, rising till lost to sight in clouds. At about an hour from Tarvis we entered a small basin-like expanse, bare and torn by the waters of the stream, and saw at the farther end the roofs of the few houses of Raibl.

One of the larger houses was apparently the inn, but it showed nothing of our party. Instead of them was a group of soldiers, looking forlorn and chilly in their blue tights and grey cloaks, hung loosely over their shoulders. No landlord came out to greet us, and we had learnt to understand what that meant. With some difficulty we got the curt answer that the inn was full—to wit, with soldiers; that two ladies had been there, but had gone away again, a jerk of the thumb pointing where. We had cleared the village, vainly looking for another inn, before a small 'wirthshaus' showed itself nearly under the spout of a waterfall. Still nothing of S—— and A——, nor of vehicles, nor drivers, till one of them, a surly fellow, who when necessity compelled could produce some dozen words of German, sauntered from a shed to say that the 'damen' had gone back into the village. Back went we by a different road; and at last, when the game of hide and seek was becoming serious, descried our unhappy wives at the door of the larger inn in earnest conversation with the officer in command of the detachment which, to our misfortune, was in occupation of the place. A——, exercising all her powers of persuasiveness, was explaining our dilemma to the lieutenant, and soliciting his good offices with these crusty Sclavonians; he, clasping his cap devotedly to his breast, and balancing on his toes, stood the picture of gallantry, but assuring his interlocutor that we must either, as he believed, return to Tarvis, or obtain horses for Flitsch over the Predil. These he would do his best to procure. It would be a tedious drive of four hours in darkness and rain, which was now recommencing; but as S—— and A—— pronounced absolutely against the 'wirthshaus' under the hill, on the score of a wicked-looking old crone—so they called her—and the one wretched little room she had shown them, we acquiesced in the arrangement.

After half an hour spent in the lieutenant's quarters, to which he had kindly invited us, his messenger returned reporting total failure; no one would lend a horse for the Predil that night. So the other horn of the dilemma was to be tried; and with many thanks to our military friend, we betook ourselves through the puddles to the little hostel, where our men received the proposition of returning to Tarvis so unfavourably, that we were fain to fall upon the third horn in this case presented to us, and requested to inspect the condemned cell above stairs. But instead of the old crone, who sat glowering like a witch in the corner, a handsome young fellow, her son, now sprang up with a light. Throwing open on the floor above, a narrow chamber with two small beds, and no other furniture, 'They are clean,' said he, 'and they are all we have—except this one,' leading back to the large roughly-paved landing, where a pallet stood against the wall, beside a heap of old saddles, boots, and nondescript garments—two or three chickens, winking at the sudden light, on a shelf above. The small room, seen under better auspices, was now voted snug, but it would only hold two; opportunely the spirit of fun seized upon A——, and she and her husband undertook to spend the night along with the chuckies.

Fortunately, at the moment, a good genius appeared. The Commissary of the detachment occupied with his wife the only decent room in the inn, and the latter now came forward offering to vacate their apartment in C—— and A——'s favour. That was gratefully declined; and then the wife, a sweet-looking creature, but with a melancholy on her brow which made us think at first that the Herr might not be all he should be, devoted herself to do the best she could for us, soothing the old landlady while she ransacked her stores, and adding everything she could think of from her own. So, before long, we were all tolerably tucked in under the rough sheets in our several domiciles; thankful for a roof as we heard the rain rattling upon its shingles. If C—— and A—— felt any insecurity from the absence of a door, they were compensated by the presence of the dog of the establishment, as usual an enormous fellow, who, taking up his quarters for the night at the top of the stairs, guarded their slumbers so effectually, that it seemed doubtful whether he would see fit to allow of their rising from them in the morning.

They were awakened by 'the cock that crowed in the morn' from the shelf above. We were all up pretty early, but the plashing rain was the only sound out of doors; and people clattered about on the stone floors within, in that depressed and desultory manner so indicative of a wet day. Yet Fortune was not obdurate, and her first relentings appeared in the shape of an excellent breakfast. The best coffee, best bread, and best butter for many a day, were served on a clean cloth below stairs; while the old crone, not nearly so ugly now by daylight, and in presence of her good deeds, brought her stool and her knitting to see us enjoy it, screaming to her maidens for fresh supplies at any symptom of deficiency; subjecting us, it is true, to a very close scrutiny with her sharp eyes, and putting in pointed personal remarks from time to time which did credit to her shrewdness. Presently the Commissary's wife stole in, and as time seemed likely to be heavy on our hands, we persuaded her to sit for her portrait. Unfortunately the conversation did not take a lively turn. She confided to us her husband's scanty pay—four shillings per week—which, though she eked it out by working for the soldiers, compelled rigid economies; neither coffee nor meat could be afforded: and they had lived so differently! she as an upper servant in Vienna, he as clerk to a factory in the Voralberg, belonging to an Englishman. As she spoke, tears swelled to her eyes, her lip quivered, and the portrait-painting for a time did not prosper. It was scarcely concluded, when a sun-gleam shot suddenly into the room, and then we remembered that while listening to poor Amelie's story the sound of rain had for some time ceased. Hastening to the door we beheld the Königsberg glistening in a watery light, and bare peaks piercing the cloud-wreaths in all directions.

Raibl is a mining village, and this corner of the Königsberg appeared scarred with mining débris, which, with smelting-houses and official establishments, spoil the view of the mountains on this side. The mines of lead and zinc, which have been in existence for hundreds of years, are worked in dolomite of the Muschelkalk Formation, and at present extend to a height of 900 feet above, and a depth of 480 feet below the valley level. Raibl is remarkable, too, in a geological point of view. Certain beds occur here, the highest members of the Trias formation, which contain numerous and interesting fossils, and take their name from this village as the 'Raibl' beds. They are met with along the Southern Alps as far west as the Italian Lake district, and their equivalent beds are recognised also in the limestone zone on the north side of the central Alps.

Owing to this valley being quite open to the north, and closed in by lofty precipices on the south, its warm season is but a fleeting one. The snow begins to melt only at the end of May, and appears on the ground again at the beginning of September. As a consequence, the dwarf pine, *Pinus Mughus*, the Knieholz of the Germans, that usually appears on the mountain slopes at an elevation of six or seven thousand feet, here descends to the bottom of the valley. Raibl is the proper point from which to ascend the Mangert, whence a view can be obtained of the Italian plain and the Adriatic. One mile above the village is a small lake through which the Schlitza flows, descending from a valley to the westward. The road of the Predil ascends by the side of this lake, though at a considerable height, and finally turns sharply to the east by zigzags over the ridge which here divides Carinthia from Görz. It keeps this course for two or three miles, till it touches the flanks of the towering Mangert, standing on the frontier of Carniola; then plunging down a tremendous abyss to the southward, it reaches, through a succession of gorges, the valley of the Isonzo, a little above Flitsch. This forms the pass of the Predil, and now that the clouds were clearing, we had every hope that its fine scenery would be displayed to advantage.

Horses had been bespoken early, but seemed as difficult to obtain in the morning as on the evening before. It was between ten and eleven before one horse and a particularly small pony made their appearance; the latter attached to a diminutive contrivance like a London costermonger's fruit-tray, intended for the baggage; while the horse, harnessed to one of the usual light four-wheels, was destined for the ladies, who preferred, however, to accompany us on foot up the long steeps of the ascent. The poor Commissary's wife, whose face had been brightened into smiles by a trifling gift which we hoped would stand her in coffee for some time to come, and the old crone, now transformed into a grandmotherly body with whom we were almost affectionate, were full of help and counsel. The young man, our chamberlain of the night before, took us under convoy himself, and we left Raibl with a materially improved opinion both of the place and people.

It was not long before we looked down upon the Raibl Lake, lying at a great depth upon our right; it is excellent fishing water, and of a green so brilliant round its shallow shores that it looked as if set in malachite. The side we were mounting fell abruptly, all rock and wood, to the water; and about two-thirds down, a narrow covered gallery was pointed out, creeping round from crag to crag, provided for winter use, when the road above is impassable from snow, or when in spring dangerous from avalanches. A small fort occupying the ridge, a little on the south side, and commanding the Predil, renders it important to keep communication open at all seasons. We learnt, however, from Amelie that this is sometimes impossible. It had been part of her husband's duty to provide the fort with bread, and on one occasion the snow lay so deep, that he was prevented for a whole week from taking up the usual supply, and the garrison was all but starved out.

As we rose higher, the upper valley of the Schlitza—solitary and pine-wooded—was seen descending from the west, and skirting the north base of the Wischberg. Behind us, the isolated Königsberg lifted himself to his full height, 6,450 feet; and above the ridge which we were now attaining, peaks and faces of rock shot upward among the still entangled clouds. But the moment the ridge was gained a fresh scene opened, and the Raibl country was lost. In great grandeur the Mangert, 9,026 feet, now stood displayed, or so much of him under the sun-illumined vapours as was sufficient to impress us thoroughly with his dignity. The characteristic contour of this mountain, like the rest of the Carniolan or Terglou range, is that of a bare bulk of rock, rising, not so much into peaks, as into bosses at the summit. The true form is better seen from the northern, or Weissenfels side, where it appears as a length of wall—here viewed end on. In the middle distance, upon a ledge, the only passage for the road, was placed the fort just mentioned. To support its garrison our lieutenant and his detachment were quartered below in Raibl; and we found piles of timber, ready cut for stockades, on both sides of the road under the walls, showing recent care for its defence.

Conspicuous also beneath the ramparts was a fine bas-relief of a dying lion, cast in bronze; it lay, pierced to the heart by a spear, though still with outstretched paws guarding the imperial shield. This was another of the frequent tokens in these Eastern Alps of desperate conflicts with the French invaders. On the face of the monument, cut in gilt letters, appeared the inscription following:—

ZUR ERINNERUNG AN DEN HELDENTOD
DES K.K. INGENIEUR HAUPTMANNS
JOHANN HERMANN
VON HERMANNSDORF
AM XVIII. MAI, MDCCCIX.
UND DER MIT IHM GEFALLENEN
KAMPFGENOSSEN
KAISER FERDINAND.*

Of such conflicts this pass has been more than once the scene. In 1797 Massena forced the Pontebba, and defeated the Archduke Charles at Tarvis, while a French detachment under Serrurier, advancing up the Predil, carried the fort by assault, and captured or dispersed a large body of Austrians retreating by this route with artillery and stores from the Tagliamento to join the Archduke. Napoleon himself soon after transferred his head-quarters to Tarvis for a night or two, on his way to Klagenfurt, driving the Austrians before him through Carinthia, and beyond it into Styria, till the peace signed at Leoben in the Mur Thal arrested his progress.

In 1809 the contest was of a different character, and the peasants of Tyrol were the chief actors. It appears, however, that the custody of this pass was committed to regular troops under the engineer officer to whom the inscription refers. Macdonald from Italy and Marmont from Dalmatia, were then advancing to support Napoleon in the campaign which ended with the battle of Wagram; and it was probably two of Macdonald's corps, numbering 6,000 men each, that simultaneously attacked the fort of Malborghet, on the Pontebba, and that of the Predil,

* 'To the memory of the heroic death of Johann Hermann, of Hermannsdorf, K.K. Captain of Engineers, and of his comrades in fight, who fell with him on the 18th of May, 1809. (This monument is erected by) the Emperor Ferdinand.'

which then stood considerably lower down the pass. Hermann and his people died bravely in its defence, and the garrison on the Pontebba perished heroically in the same manner.

Below the present fort, opened that wonderful abyss of which I have spoken. The road, commanded by the cannon above, was carried in a long sweep round the rim and sides, to a corner where its further course was lost to sight, and the small hamlet and church of Ober Preth jutted out into blue mist. At the bottom, far, far beneath, appeared Unter Preth. How the road should achieve the descent to it was a marvel, or, having reached it, in what direction it would seek an exit; for opposite, and barring all progress southward, rose one of the most stupendous rocky walls that had ever met our eyes. Tier above tier it rose, crowned by a long serrated summit, and circling round eastward as if to attach itself to the Mangert on our left, whose height it almost equalled. It bears the name of the Sebnik.

It was a pity I could not record in my sketch-book either the view of the Mangert from the ridge, or this descent upon Unter Preth; but for the first, ever since the misadventure of Messrs. Brown, Jones, and Robinson on their foreign tour, one has been shy of sketching landscapes with an Austrian fortress in the foreground; and for the second, as S—— and A——, trotting down in their car, had already disappeared round the distant corner, it was necessary to follow without delay. Soon after leaving the fort, a fine cascade dashes from above, and, passing under the road, disappears into the gulf. A couple of miles farther, at Ober Preth, if one had launched into the air, one might have dropped pretty directly down upon Unter Preth, some two thousand feet below; and, indeed, by a very precipitous path, a pedestrian may, if he choose, accomplish something like that feat. The road effects the same descent by a long stretch round the corner, and back again, in full view all the way of the prodigious buttresses of the Sebnik. By the time we reached the bottom, the proper exit of the pass disclosed itself at the western end of the rock-wall, which seemed indeed as if it had once extended right across, like an enormous dam, connecting itself with a similar mass of mural limestone stretching away to the west: there was but a rift between the two. The real construction, however, of this tremendous barrier it was difficult to make out.

There is a small inn at Unter Preth. The incident of our halt there was—not dinner, which they could not give us—but a terrible affair between the dog of Unter Preth and him of Raibl, who had condescended to accompany us on the express condition, which no one was inclined to dispute, of reposing himself at full length on the seat of the carriage whenever it was vacant. It required half the village to separate these two champions. Such contests are frequent along the roads, for the inn dogs cannot, it seems, learn the proper courtesies towards the travelling public of their own 'persuasion.' The afternoon was now so bright that S—— and A—— preferred joining us in the walk, of about six miles all down hill, to Flitsch, and the baggage went on without us.

The scenery was peculiar in its barren grandeur. The sides of the mountains, where not precipice, were little else than avalanches of stones, interspersed with stunted beech scrub, burnt already into autumn tints, and, when touched by the sun, gleaming like smouldering fire. This district is said to be excused from the ordinary taxes on account of the poverty of the soil; and the only patch capable of cultivation that we saw, was a strip of grass by the side of the stream, which threw itself, foaming, amongst the whitened rocks at the bottom of the glen. The fall of rocks is a cause of great and frequent destruction in these parts. We presently came to a spot where, down an opposite gully, an astonishing mass had recently come down, destroying the bed of the ravine for perhaps a mile, damming up the stream of the valley by a Titanic weir, and dashing huge blocks, like mere splashes of mud, up the opposite slope; had it been a few yards lower, the road would have been crushed under the catapult discharge. What a sight and sound it must have been! Yet the source of the mischief seemed but a hand-breadth scar on the distant precipice. It is all very well on a fine afternoon like this, when everything is tipped with silver and gold, and the powers are at peace, to stand in a row, as we did, admiring the magnificent devastation; but I suspect that in spring, when the peril is greatest, the traveller is not disposed to be contemplative, but hurries through the defile, and is apt to flinch and turn pale at any sudden thunderous sound among the scarred tops.

Farther on, the valley narrows to a gorge, and the river is madder than ever with the torment of the rocks. Then its roar sinks into a dull distant sound; and when you look for it, there is nothing but a chasm, which narrows to a rift, almost concealed by bushes. Here a bridge is thrown across, and as you lean over the parapet, you see at a shuddering depth—only a moving blackness! The remains of the old fort stand on a mound by the side of this fearful chasm, which cuts off all approach in that direction, while on the other side, a precipice rises in a perpendicular face of rock which nothing could get down. The unmilitary mind does not therefore readily comprehend how the fort could be taken by six, or sixty thousand French. Brave Hermann fell in a final sally, sword in hand; one fancies he might have waited for them to come to him. The details of the attack, however, somewhat explain the matter.

It was on the evening of May 15, 1809, that the head of the enemy's column pushed up the defile, and sought protection from the fire of the fort by quickly throwing up earthworks. A violent cannonade compelled them to retire; but in the night, they completed the works that had been commenced, and early the next morning opened fire against the fort, yet without result. Each attempt, also, to establish themselves nearer was a failure, and brought destruction upon the troops engaged.

In these circumstances negotiation was resorted to; but nothing could shake the devotion of Hermann, whose invariable answer was 'No surrender.' Another plan was tried. The fort of Malborghet on the Pontebba had already fallen, and some of the prisoners taken there were sent into the garrison, that, learning the fate of their comrades, and that the country behind was already in the hands of the enemy, their constancy might fail them. The reply of Hermann was decisive. 'The defence of this fort is committed to me. I do not fear death, and will die on the field of honour.'

The French then prepared for storming, and amidst beating of drums, and fierce shouts, desperate assaults were made upon the place; but the cannon and small arms of the defenders still mowed the assailants down, and the enemy began to doubt the possibility of success. Suddenly a flame burst forth within the defences, welcomed with loud shouts by the French. Four companies of voltigeurs had with infinite difficulty climbed the precipitous height behind the fort, and thence flung hoops of blazing pitch upon the wooden buildings that sheltered the garrison. In a moment they were in flames; the fire spread with frightful rapidity, and the vigour of the assaults was redoubled. Hermann in extremity of despair exclaimed to his men, '‘Let us go out, comrades; the enemy shall not get us into his power alive.’ All then threw themselves with a wild irregular rush upon the thickest ranks of the French. In a few minutes Hermann fell bleeding from many wounds, and with him perished also most of the brave defenders of the Predil.

So it was that impossible-looking wall of rock above which was after all their ruin. We looked with awe upon the savage spot that seventy years ago was wrapt in sulphurous smoke, and rang with the tumult of the fight. If any poor wretches went down that blue-black depth it was a fearful fate. The Austrians have now, as will have been seen, removed the defences some five miles farther back from the entrance of the gorge, to the summit of the pass, doubtless to the greater inconvenience of an invader, and advantage to themselves.

Beyond the fort, the road, which is cut in the face of the precipice, enters a short tunnel; and near this, in the rock, is a tablet, surrounded by heraldic devices, and inscribed with the name and titles of an illustrious, ‘well-born,’ and now certainly well-dead, individual, who, in mediæval times, first constructed here a place of strength. Soon afterwards, opening out to the right, is seen the small plain of Flitsch, encompassed by the wildest mountain forms. Yet, at first sight, in contrast with the defile, it looks cheerfully open, and the few strips of vineyards, and patches of grain, and green grass are refreshing after the barrenness. Flitsch is about two miles from the mouth of the pass, and is rather pleasantly surrounded by trees and open fields; but as we walked in, it was easy to see we had passed into an Italian province. Vines straggled over broken walls, or hung on decayed trellises;

houses had that forlorn tatterdemalion air which only hot sunlight can enliven; the roofs were flat, and covered with the round tile, and in the midst was something vaguely intended for a plaza.

Here was a good-sized inn, which we concluded to be our destination; the more so, that the Raibl vehicle, with our huge canine acquaintance stretched in sublime repose upon the seat, was drawn up at the door. Arriving without the usual premonitory sounds of whips and wheels, we had to invade the kitchen to announce ourselves, which produced amazing flutter in the establishment, but no satisfactory admission that this was 'Leschnegg's;' from which we gathered that it probably was *not* 'Leschnegg's.' The supposition was presently confirmed by an Italian gentleman just arrived from Trieste upon his annual shooting excursion among the Flitsch mountains, who kindly offered to show us the way to our inn, about a quarter of a mile farther, at the southern end of the town. This had a quieter and more rural look than the other, though we are bound to say that, according to our informant, there was not much choice between them. Our rooms were separated from the rest of the house by a chamber, half lumber-room, half granary, and being approached by an outside gallery, were free from certain prevailing odours; while the view from their windows, over gardens, and meadows, swept the valley up and down on its softer eastern side, where a 'chorus' of mountains stood in multitude to hail the rising, and salute the setting sun.

At Flitsch, the first two questions on our lips were—Where is the Isonzo? and where is the Terglou?—the one the river, the other the mountain. The river flows into the plain of Flitsch, at its eastern corner, from an almost undistinguishable gap in the hills, and delves for itself so deep a course, that from the town, or passing along the high road, no one would suspect its existence. The Terglou has no immediate connection with Flitsch, but being the highest of the neighbouring Carniolan range, and in the direction of the Upper Isonzo, one naturally expects to find it a commanding object. This also disappoints expectation; that mountain led us a long dance before he would show at all, and on this side kept himself at a very haughty distance.

When we rose on Friday morning, August 23rd, all traces of bad weather had disappeared, and the sky was the bluest of blues. Our object for the day was to explore the upper valley of the Isonzo, with a hope also of reaching a point whence the Terglou would be visible. It could only be done on foot. We hired a guide; but as there was a prospect of fish and potatoes at the village of Sotscha, did not burden him with a provision basket. Crossing the plain to the village of Coritenza—all which part of the walk, both from the near verdure and the surrounding girdle of mountains, was very pleasing—we entered the gorge of the Isonzo. We shall not soon forget that stony desert—two deserts set up on end, with the weary water struggling between them. The mountains showed nothing but their teeth, and faces of white horror, while not a village or a house, for two hours of walking, cheered the way. Death pictures were positively the only signs of life, and became so frightfully numerous, that one might suppose the inhabitants had been all killed off; the accidents being pretty equally divided between falling from rocks, and falling under them. Ominous scars defaced all the precipices above; and below, tons upon tons of limestone-blocks lay in heaps, the path constantly climbing over some fresh descended mass. I, for one, should decline the office of daily postman for this district: fortunately, the Upper Isonzo can do without one.

The small church of Sotscha was in sight over the mounds of débris for some time before we reached the scattered village. Our guide, a silent individual, indicated the 'public,' but shook his head at the suggestion of there being anything to eat there, and led on to the curé's, close to the church, and to the only tree of any proportions in the neighbourhood. The curé himself, a portly man with regular good-natured features, was standing before his door, clad in a long greeny-brown coat almost down to his heels, and stiff black boots up to his knees. Our uncommunicative guide opened his lips at last, and we were amused to hear him introduce us as 'four people who could speak nothing and understand nothing.' 'So,' said the priest, 'how are we to get on then?' His German, however, was very different from the strange conglomeration of sounds that had occasionally issued from our man of Flitsch, and C—— and A—— soon found they could get on very well. The good parson presently bustled in and returned with something like curd, bread, and a bottle of startlingly acid wine; but the question of dinner for later in the day he entertained with a reflective sort of smile, and a gentle nodding of the head, which looked dubious, to say the least of it. Yet we were not unhopeful; and after further enquiries about the Terglou, of which he suggested we might sooner obtain a view by climbing the unpromising hill sides, we left, engaging to return at four o'clock.

From the aspect described, it may readily be supposed that the hills *were* unpromising—of anything but toil. The curé confirmed our impressions of their fatal character; the most frequent accidents occurring, he said, to his people when carrying down the bundles of 'wild hay,' or beech scrub, along the narrow ledges which supply the only foot-hold. I think we understood that the greater proportion of deaths arose from some form of alpine peril. Several mementos that we saw represented drowning in the stream; and the artists had almost always chosen to heighten the effect by introducing chamois in a state of extreme agitation, perched singly upon the tops of the peaks at regular distances, and in various affecting attitudes, which unfortunately only looked very comic. Our guide had evidently never been on the hill side before, and grunted his disapprobation at each successive steep. We soon left S—— and A—— to rest under a bush, and clambered vigorously with the hope of gaining our object, but only attained a projecting bluff where farther advance was cut off, and any view of the Terglou as well, by a soaring precipice. This attempt lost us the opportunity of exploring the valley itself to a point an hour below its highest village of Trenta, where an opening extending to the foot of the Terglou is said to display 'a scene of singular magnificence and beauty.' Murray, who gives this information, speaks of the rest of the valley to Flitsch as 'very dreary,' and this we had sufficiently verified. It is from the village of Sotscha that a pass of nine hours leads, by the 'Scala' over desolate scenery, to the gloomy Wochein See, south of the Terglou; this was one of our destined points sooner or later, and by taking this pass we might obtain a second opportunity of pushing to the head of the Isonzo valley. If not, there was still the chance of crossing into it from Wurzen by the pass of Kronau.

It was time to think of the curé, and we duly presented ourselves, with expectant appetites, soon after the appointed hour. The good man had shaved since the morning, and cleaned his long boots; he seated us at the table, and then withdrew his chair a little distance, on declaration that he had himself dined earlier. The housekeeper was evidently very busy within. At her first appearance he started up to bring in the dishes, and insisted during the meal upon acting the part of garçon, notwithstanding all our remonstrances. Soup, a savoury omelet, turnips, and potatoes—cold, in thin slices, and steeped in vinegar—and a capital pudding were the courses; then a pause, and we pushed our chairs from the table to intimate we had dined to our full satisfaction. But our host, while maintaining a lively conversation, still turned a furtive eye from time to time towards the kitchen door; at last it opened, and jumping from his seat, he bore in a smoking dish of trout, plumped it triumphantly on the table, and stepping back a pace or two with a peal of hearty laughter, stood rubbing his hands in glee; while the little old housekeeper flitted from side to side behind his bulky figure, with a countenance brimful of gratified pride. We set to again as if we had not dined at all.

But the countenance of our entertainer was not always so radiant; on the contrary, we were struck with its frequent relapse into a very melancholy expression, which, when alone, we feared might be habitual. The solitary and dreary scene in which his lot was cast might be the sufficient explanation, especially as several years of his life had been passed at Trieste—a far more congenial residence for a man of his information. Before ascertaining this, we had been rather surprised at some of his questions; 'were we Catholics,' was not an unusual one; but the further enquiry, whether we were Anglicans or Puritans, showed more knowledge of English Protestantism than we should have expected in this remote spot. When he afterwards asked after 'that eminent Anglican Bishop, Pheelipota,' we did not at the moment recognise, Philpots, and were a little puzzled as to who Archbishop 'Veesiman' could be, till we recollected, Wiseman. What with dinner, and conversation, we almost forgot our long walk back to Flitsch, which our kind host admitted it was getting rather late for. We put into his hand nearly double what the price at one of the inns of the country would have been, and did not forget the little housekeeper in the kitchen. Both stood at the door with cordial adieus, and friendly urgings to accept the offer of beds for a night, if we determined to cross the mountains to the Wochein See, in which case it would be better to start at three o'clock in the morning. As it happened, we did not do so, and probably have seen the last of the good priest of Sotscha as, in front of his humble parsonage, he watched us disappear down the rugged pathway.

The red sunset-glow can bring beauty into even such a scene as this. The effect was like draping bare walls with crimson; and for living creatures there were now the fish, which quite blackened the green pools with their multitude, and explained the resources of the curé. The guide, too, had now found his tongue, though not much to our edification. He pitied our deficiencies, and explained that *he* was master of six languages—German, Italian, Krainerisch or Slovenic, Piedmontese, Bohemian, and Hungarian—a wide range of accomplishments, that threw light, we thought, upon his special unintelligibleness. It is probable that each sentence contained something of all six. The valley soon retook all its gloom, deepening every minute; the water was either a blackness, or a whiteness, hurrying on below; the rocks glimmered grey and cold, and the path seemed to consist of nothing but heaps of sharp-cornered stones. It was quite dark when we reached Coritenza, and from thence to Flitsch the pleasant walk of the morning was transformed into a groping and a stumbling up and down grassy hills, or through narrow paths. The result of the day was, that we had acquired a new idea of desolation—and that we had dined with the curé of Sotscha.

Half a mile from Flitsch, and away from the road, stands a lonely church or chapel, with two or three trees about it to redeem its nakedness, and to give shade, if you seek that spot as a point of view. For this it is well-adapted; thence you may watch the groups of peasantry trooping along the numerous footpaths on the open plain, or lift your eyes to the mountains circling round. The entrance to the pass of Chiusa di Pless, where the old fort stands, though out of sight, is the most picturesque direction for the eye. The mountains rise there with remarkable abruptness, and conical form, some of the lower ones covered with brushwood. Amongst them is a tall isolated boss, with a single patch of green in the thick wood near the seemingly inaccessible summit, which, sloping to the south, commands the whole valley. What a place for a hermit, we said, if he could but get there! Presently applying the telescope to the spot, there truly was the hut in the corner of the plot of green! If anyone wishes to be in the world, and out of it, at the same time, he could not be better suited. Near this is another tall isolated hill, of a very sugar-loaf character, called the Sau Kopf, the terminal of the narrow ridge bounding the upper Isonzo to the north. It is a very counterpart of the Pain de Sucre of Courmayeur, and that of Gavarnie, in the Pyrenees.

But now look westwards. I have said nothing about that yet, though it is by far the most characteristic side of the Flitsch scenery. *There*, is a range of the most arid-looking mountains you have ever seen, embossed with rock protuberances of the strangest shapes—ridges, spines, horns, all of the hardest and severest character; while not a single stream, cascade, or runlet flashes light or life upon the savage scene. As we first approached Flitsch this was a dark rampart, whose battlements and towers cut sharp against the evening sky. In the daytime it was a mass of grey distorted forms.

There lay our next day's work, at least for Churchill and myself. One of those mountains was a great object of attraction to the former; and when I said that two questions were on our lips when we arrived at Flitsch, I forgot the third—'Where is the Prestelinik?' Yet it is only a question for an insatiable botanist to ask; no one else would seek it up there in its fastnesses of snow, and of course S—— and A—— declined to do so. A far different guide from the other was provided for this excursion—Anton Mitscherlich—no waster or inn-yard supernumerary, but a cheery-faced, though wizened and brown old man—a man of the mountains, full of stories of his gallant life as soldier and chamois hunter. We had not yet given up enquiring for the Terglou, and as we ascended the sloping base of the mountain—part meadow, part stony débris, and part wood—we asked how soon it would be visible. 'Not till we get above that,' said the old man, pointing to the highest of the ridges in sight; 'four hours from here.' As this was unexpected as well as unwelcome information, we began to cross-question our companion upon the point. He stopped, turned sharp round upon us, and repeated his statement with emphatic distinctness. 'Now, believe me,' he added, placing his open hand upon his breast, '*for I know*.' Then, striking his staff into the ground, he turned quickly to the hill again, exclaiming, 'Onward! onward! we have no time for this.' There was something grand in the 'I know.' We apologised, professed our perfect confidence in him, and felt that our noble old guide was a born leader of men.

Something like a ravine, or rather trough, broke through the wall of precipices, and towards this we crossed the lower slopes. At the edge of the ravine was a scrambling and indistinct path, composed principally of single foot-holes, among roots of trees and rock ledges : anywhere else a stream would have been tumbling down beside us, but here it was utter silence ; and we began to understand that these mountains were *waterless.* Think of Switzerland resounding with torrents, or of the Pyrenees gushing with bright streams, or of the soddened hills of Scotland, and you will appreciate the extraordinary contrast.

The sun from the east beat full upon us (delays from various causes had put our start much later than it should have been), and we rained perspiration in the toil of hand and foot climbing. 'Water soon,' said the old guide askance, and looking down upon us. Presently he stopped at the foot of the precipice we were skirting, and stooping, pointed to a small cleft, holding about a breakfast-cup of water, as you might in the hollow of your two hands. 'There is never more, and never less,' said he, 'and you will find no more till you reach the snow.' This modicum ! It was almost more expressive of scarcity than if there had been none at all. One or two peasants were resting there, and the grass and rocks were worn with feet, showing that, like an oasis in the desert, it was a place of resort. Two hours up the ascent and you reach the rim of the gully, out of which there should naturally shoot a cascade. Here, looking downward on one hand to the valley, through the crags and wood of the ravine, and upward on the other to the sky, through a wilderness of stones, stood a miserable hut, and goat-sheds, trampled all about with miry manure. Notwithstanding the assurances that had been given, we could hardly believe but that some spring supplied this habitation, and ventured to suggest as much. 'Bring them what you drink,' said our old hunter; and a bowl of a yellow warm liquid was produced—goat's whey—so unpalatable that we could scarcely touch it, though urged repeatedly with 'Drink, drink; it is wholesome.' In this hovel a distinguished English botanist, two years before, had spent a night for the sake of a long day on the Prestelinik. It was now so late in the season that Churchill expected to do little more than make himself acquainted with the site.

Above this spot grew only a few lätschen—that low, twisted matting of pine peculiar to the upper alpine region; herbage was confined to tufts, growing in interstices or upon ledges; and higher still, it was a vast desolation of stones, or rather blocks, poured down from the ashy-pale peaks and precipices around. Here *my* object was attained, and I sat down to sketch the wild and soundless scene. Churchill and his guide, speedily reduced to pin-points, alone broke the deathly silence as they toiled up the enormous motionless stream of stone, white and sweeping as a glacier, which descended from a hidden source between two peaks; beyond which again, and among glimpses of snow, appeared the grey, and florally hopeless-looking form of the Prestelinik. Such an upturned wilderness as this is more striking than the corresponding scenes of ice and snow. The latter smoothes over all form, and the roundness, combined with the glaring whiteness, destroys distance as well as variety of feature; while again, there is no such silence as in these waterless solitudes. The glacier groans and murmurs in its sleep, and the rocks about it on a summer day are streaming; here, nothing moves. I puzzled my way down again alone, reaching Flitsch after an absence of six hours, and had time enough to secure a general view of the whole mountain mass from the plain, before a storm, which had long been brooding, enveloped all the tops. Evening and the tempest came down together, and we should have been more anxious for our friend than we were, had it not been for confidence in the old guide. About eight o'clock the two returned, drenched, but safe.

I learnt from Churchill the following particulars of his expedition after parting from me:—

Following the course of the wide deep gully, that rose steeply up to a distant sky-line, and was filled at its lower end with huge blocks as if tumbled pell-mell out of a quarry, they got upon a succession of small snow-fields, where the footing was much easier and progress more rapid. The last patches of herbage, with little cushions of *Silene acaulis*, were left behind with the blocks. Beyond was barrenness, hardly negatived by the isolated appearance of a few small alpine plants, such as *Thlaspi rotundifolium*, *Papaver alpinum*, *Arabis cœrulea*, &c. Arrived close upon the sky-line, a sharp turn to the left, along narrow ledges, brought them to the ridge that runs from the base of the Prestelinik proper, over the plateau towards the Flitsch valley. Here the Terglou first showed itself. A steep rock-climb led from this point to the summit.

The Prestelinik rises out of the western precipitous edge of the great plateau to which it belongs. The eye follows the descending lines of the edge until they are lost at a tremendous depth in the shades of the Raccolano Thal, a continuation by a sudden turn, and with an opposite slope, of that where Raibl is placed. The vast wilderness of the plateau—miles long—is tilted so as to present the long slope towards Flitsch; and looking diagonally across it, they saw, standing prominently out of the corners, the near neighbours of the Prestelinik, Monte Cernjala, or the Confin Spitz, the Rombon, Monte Canino, and Monte Baba. Opposite, and to the south-east, rose up a similar wilderness plateau. But the centre of interest was the majestic mass of the Terglou—twenty miles distant as the crow flies—a clear thousand feet higher than his neighbours, looking like a king of men surrounded by his court. All the multitudinous ashy-pale peaks of the zone of mountain-land lying between the parallel lines of the Wurzen Save and the Isonzo were distinctly in view; but a diligent examination of the map was required to trace out their interlacing lines, and with the guide's assistance to identify them. Mitscherlich seemed quite at home in this wilderness, and pointed out places where gemsen (chamois) had been shot last season, when he was upon this plateau with a son of Count Radetsky, and a friend of his from Vienna. The mackintosh cup being filled with snow, in default of water, and drenched with wine, prosperity to the Prestelinik and its inhabitants, if any, was toasted, and the toilsome descent commenced. Whether snow varies in gastronomic quality under different circumstances, we cannot say. Our guide of to-day quite approved of its incorporation with wine; while, in the Pyrenees, the attempt to swallow a morsel was strongly deprecated, as tending to produce colic, or, as the Bearnais guide expressively put it, 'L'hiver dans le ventre!'

To give an idea of the labour involved in clambering over these heaps of sterile stones, we may state that Mitscherlich estimated the ascent from Flitsch at seven hours, which is an unusually long time, distance only considered.

It may be interesting to the reader to add to our own record of the characteristics of this 'Flitscher Gebirge' that of an Austrian geologist, given in his report upon the geology of the Isonzo district, and to be found in the

Journal of the Vienna Geological Society. The clefts and the funnels spoken of were also seen by Churchill. Herr Stur says—'It is a fearfully desolate plateau, whose parallel can hardly anywhere be met with in the Alps. I went from Flitsch to the Wratna Vrh * (whose precipices immediately overlook the hut we passed on the ascent), and the surmounting of its steep, almost precipitous, wall of 5,000 feet in height, before the high alpine plateau of the Wratna Vrh is attained, costs not a little exertion. Thence I turned my steps in a northerly direction, to Monte Cernjala. Upon the plateau itself the climber meets with,—here, fearful gulfs—there, gaping clefts, that but seldom can be overleapt, and require a circuit. Sometimes he finds himself separated by a deep and extensive funnel-shaped depression from a pleasant, easy-looking, level tract, holding out hopes of better progress; but no sooner has he laboriously got across, or round it, than a few steps of advance reveals a similar, or some new obstacle. The irregular clefts, down which the eye cannot see far, can only be estimated, as to depth, by the long-continuing sound of stones thrown in for the purpose. The funnels, too, often covered over with a thin snow crust, forming a deceitful and dangerous bridge, have to be tested with stones, that, breaking through and rolling, reveal the depth underneath. These, and similar obstacles, so added to my labour, that instead of the two hours which, under ordinary circumstances, would have been sufficient for my return from the Cernjala to the Rombon, five hours and a half were occupied in constant movement—clambering, jumping, working round, ascending, and descending.'

The Isonzo had certainly, so far, given no indication of

* The Slovenic synonyme for the German 'Berg.'

that beauty which caused Sir Humphry Davy to rank its stream as one of the most beautiful in Europe. Its interest in this upper part of its course—there is always interest where there is character—was quite of another sort. At the extreme southern end of the plain of Flitsch, however, there was a sudden turn, and a hint of soft tints and shapes, which might well be the commencement of a lovely region. Tolmein is the first stage, in whose castle Dante was for a time a guest; and next to that is Görz, the seat of the archbishopric and capital of the small province of that name, squeezed in between Venetia on the west, and Carniola on the east, and descending southward to the near neighbourhood of Trieste. The whole province is almost comprised within the valley of the Isonzo, and it does not appear that Sir Humphry Davy saw more than the lower portions of it above Görz. He makes no mention of the Predil; and if he had become acquainted with the neighbourhood of Flitsch, its wildness would have probably led him to modify his description of the river scenery as a whole.

Yet, even Flitsch had beauties for those who sought them. Sunday—which, to our comfort, was here a quiet day, so that we could either remain within doors undisturbed, or stroll into the fields without passing through the racket of a fair—gave us the opportunity of noticing several pleasant paths, and green sequestered nooks, and villages, both by the side of the Isonzo, where it wandered in its deep course out of sight from the level of the plain, and also among the spurs of those arid hills which look all so hopeless and forbidding. Here from their cavernous sides gush forth the long hidden waters, and many a busy mill and cluster of cottage roofs enliven the glens and hollows which open unexpectedly to the view of the pedestrian.

CHAPTER IX.

THE UPPER SAVE.

Return over the Predil—Sir Humphry Davy's 'Haunt' at Wurzen—Pufitsch's Inn at Kronau—Views above Wurzen—The Lakes of Weissenfels—A Pilgrimage, Mountain and Sledge Practice—Peculiar Scenery of the Upper Save—Lengenfeld and the Terglou—A Day upon the Prisinig—The Campanula Zoysii—Flocks descending from the Mountains.

IN consideration of the greater importance, as a whole, of the valley of the Save, we did not pursue the Isonzo farther ; and agreed also that with the former it would be better to begin at the beginning—its source near Wurzen. So, on Monday morning, packed in one long shallow tray, the luggage forming the seats, we left Flitsch to retrace the pass of Predil. The horses were excellent, and a brilliant sky filled us with that joyousness which morning sunshine alone can give. The broad mid-day light is not however suited to scenery so bare as that of the Predil. These stony-faced mountains require the breadths of evening shadow, and the glow of evening colour to bring out their gloomy grandeur. But the Sebnik even at noon, standing as it does with its back to the south, looked an awful bulk as we slowly climbed from Unter to Ober Preth. The Mangert, on the other hand, as seen again from the fortress, was dwarfed under the remorseless glare, and did not recover itself, in our estimation, till we saw it on its more imposing northern side. We had not time to stop at Raibl, but the old Wirthin, disturbed in her cabbage garden by the sound of wheels, telegraphed a greeting as we passed, by every gesture she could command. Perhaps, if Amelie had been visible we should have spared a moment. The Tarvis people seemed equally glad to see us; strangers who disappear over the Predil seldom I suppose return, and they looked upon our reappearance and demand for a second dinner as a special compliment. The dull old inn really warmed up into cordial welcome; or, perhaps, it was only that the good-natured Kellnerin lit up every dark corner with her smiles.

Early in the afternoon we were ascending the country road which leads out of Tarvis eastward, up a succession of green and wooded hills, to the small town of Weissenfels, where is a foundry, and the stream from the lakes or tarns of Weissenfels at the foot of the Mangert, comes rushing down a wooded hollow. Soon after this the summit of the ridge is gained, and a fine view of the Mangert appears on the right, with a perspective of peaks stretching onward, evidently the southern boundary of a considerable valley, into which, after a space of open country, you find yourself descending. This is the Save Thal. We were all eagerness for the first impression. Would it answer to the visions we had formed? This we could feel, that there was fresh and cheerful beauty in the open pastures of the valley itself; that the soft and wooded hills on the north gave it a comfortable air; and that there was something very imposing in the ranges of limestone precipice and tower which guarded it on the south. We passed through the village of Ratschach, and then by the side of a small and shallow lake with the grass and rushes sloping gently into the water; no other than the source of the Save. A shed or two for the use of sportsmen marked it as a resort of wild fowl. At present the people were raking the hay out of the very ripples.

A little farther appeared a clump of trees, upon a hill pushed into the valley from the left-hand side, and among the trees were some houses and a spire. It was Wurzen—'my old haunt, Wurzen,' as the thought-worn philosopher, in whose steps we were treading, so lovingly called it. During one of his visits he amused himself with composing a romance: 'The Last of the Donoghues.' Surely it must have been during a spell of bad weather! We were wondering whether we should be able to identify and obtain the rooms he occupied, when our cogitations were disturbed by the appearance of a tall and civilised-looking stranger, with a white felt hat of tourist shape, and altogether a very tourist air. A figure like that we had not seen for weeks. Was this one of our dear countrymen already in possession of Wurzen and the Save? We lifted our hats tentatively; the response was hardly English, yet not decisive of the point. At the village, a rural-looking inn was pointed out, a little way up the hill-side, among several scattered houses dropped along the tree-shaded road. We drew slowly to the door, and learnt from a stout landlady that her rooms were indeed occupied—she had but two—by a gentlemen from Vienna. He was no 'Englander,' but, like an Englander, came every year for the fishing.

It was a great disappointment to be denied admission to the 'favourite haunt.' It looked clean and comfortable, and its position upon the road which branches off here, and crosses the hills to Villach, gave it a commanding view down the valley. It commended itself as a sequestered retreat, and the white-curtained windows above looked very cosy. 'Could we sleep anywhere in the village?' The landlady, hitherto provokingly unconcerned, relaxed so far in our favour as to send round to two or three houses, and we dispersed ourselves up divers old staircases, discovering a room here, and a room there, full of lumber or garden stores, and not at all inviting for the week's sojourn we proposed. We returned to the inn, a group had gathered there, and 'Kronau' and 'Pufitsch' were on every lip,—the former, a village we could see about two miles down the valley; the latter, a personage who made provision there for strangers.

It was a pleasant drive, and the valley began to exercise its charm, especially as, on approaching Kronau, we found it occupying the entrance to a magnificent defile on the south, whence a stream came sweeping in a broad water-washed course; the first accession to the hitherto feeble Save, which it raised at once to the dignity of a river. Through the village we went, inquiring for Herr Pufitsch, till, after passing the tin-plated church spire, a handful of shavings suspended from a lath indicated an inn, while a brightly coloured picture of various articles of drapery, stuck at the side of the door, explained that it was also a shop. Two young people had, in fact, just set up in business with a baby in arms—and very little else. Our arrival was an alarming incident. There was commotion in the house; a woman ran up stairs, and a man ran down, and the *haus knecht*, or Jack-of-all-trades—he was certainly both carpenter and ostler—stood at the door and stared; at last Herr Pufitsch himself, a pale-faced young man, pushed his way to the front, and doffing his cap awaited our explanations. Two rooms newly furnished, and therefore clean, were at our service above stairs, though various extraneous articles had first to be removed; the young Herr working with a will, but with very little notion of the result desired.

To give time for these arrangements, we strolled back that evening through the fields to Wurzen; a green and woodland walk. We said to ourselves that the Save would do. Turn southward, and all was grandeur; northward, and it was soft and lovely. The air was fresh and Alpine, the cottages white and clean. Kronau, though small, possessed good-sized houses, and had a brisk and tidy air; doing credit to Carniola within whose frontiers we now were. After dark, one solitary light beamed in the quiet street,—it burned there both day and night before a shrine of the Virgin. Though we had lost Wurzen, we soon reconciled ourselves to Kronau, splendid weather making up for many deficiencies in poor Pufitsch's establishment.

Sir Humphry Davy, usually came to Wurzen by the road from Villach. It crosses the hills that soon become a lofty mountain range, the Karavanken Alps, separating the valley of the Save from its neighbour the Drave. He thus describes one of his arrivals:—

'The views from Villach along this high mountain road are very glorious. The road is through forests of beech trees and spruce firs; the mountains on the Italian side occasionally crested with snow. But in descending (*i.e.* down to Wurzen) these mountains open on the view in their greatness. They present the noblest forms calcareous rocks can assume, and a great variety of colours. They rise above beautiful green valleys and high wooded mountains breasted with snow, and presenting their inaccessible summits to half the sky.'

We devoted our first morning to testing this description. From Wurzen the road ascends by zig-zags till it reaches a rather bare valley which crosses the ridge. It is on the northern, or Villach side, that the woods of beech occur; through these the road, by many windings, reaches, in the first instance, the valley of the Gail, but passes immediately out of it into that of the Drave. Here necessarily our old friend the Dobratsch is the principal object; as soon as the edge of the descent on that side is reached, the continuous range of yellow-red precipices are fully displayed, and the small white pilgrimage chapel on the summit can be discerned.* But the road is so immediately sunk among trees and gorges that it is difficult to obtain an outlook over the two noble valleys beneath. Returning towards the Save, occurs the scene of Sir Humphry's description. We are bound to admit that on the present occasion we were disappointed, but it must have been owing to unfavourable conditions of some sort: partly that it was blinding mid-day, partly that we had weakened the impression by frequent observation as we came along; partly, perhaps, that sensitiveness to any scenery was dulled for a time. That our present appreciation was not the correct one, may be gathered from the fact that in the following year C—— and A—— coming this way from Villach, and opening therefore upon the prospect as Sir Humphry did, were quite as much struck with its grandeur; and considered this the finest possible introduction to the mountains of the Save.

On the present occasion the view from the hill above Wurzen, a sort of open down, and displaying a fine stretch of the valley, checked our incipient murmuring; and in the evening we were enchanted with the prospect commanded by a small green plateau on the steep Alp-side opposite Kronau. Those 'inaccessible summits occupying half the sky,' were immediately in front, vanishing on either hand in a vast perspective; while the setting sun was streaming crimson from the west along the entire length of valley, a gorgeous sight.

Our second excursion was to the small lakes at the foot of the Mangert, the favourite and principal resort of our philosopher. A rough, but handy, vehicle carried us through Wurzen to Ratschach. Then, on foot, we followed

* An ascent of this mountain two years after is described in our 17th chapter.

a cart-track to the left, more or less marked, through pastures and woods, till we entered the glen which has been already described as descending to Weissenfels. Turning in the opposite direction, the enormous walls of the Mangert, flecked and wreathed with snow, rise up sublimely before you. You seem penetrating to their very base. Suddenly the torrent at your side has ceased its roar, and you find in its stead a silent lake deep among the trees. Farther, and a second lake is seen, still so

VIEW OF THE MANGERT.

embosomed and rock-guarded that it is difficult to reach its shore, a very solitary strand, and then you have the grandeur all to yourself—an expanse of water, vivid as emerald and smooth as a mirror, but for the circles of rising fish ; beyond it receding woods, and above them the sheer impending mass of the Mangert, casting its mighty image into the water at your feet, as itself soars into the sky.

Here the great Chemist spent long and lonely days; lighting a fire on that patch of shore from the dead wood provided by winter storms, and cooking the fish he caught. On his first visit he says: 'I have seldom viewed a scene of more savage and peculiar wildness;' perhaps there is too much of surrounding wood to answer precisely to that description; but the trees and brushwood add greatly to the sense of seclusion. Rising thick behind, and hiding the lower lake and all below, they screen the spot from intrusion, and shut you up to the one spectacle of the gleaming water, and the vast quarry-like precipice of mountain. It is a spot that would have suited the author of 'Vathek;' we know it suited the author of 'Consolations,' and that it soothed the last days of a philosopher. How many threads of subtle speculation were spun in that busy mind as he sat on these lichened rocks! How often, with sudden inspiration, would his genius flash light upon some secret of nature, as he brooded in the silence of this, one of her choicest solitudes! And again, how many an hour was passed of sad despondency under the fatal disease that pursued him, even to this far retreat! Such a scene one might have stumbled on and thought it grand, but its association with this bright intelligence and suffering frame, has bestowed a consecration beyond the power of nature's utmost necromancy.

A passage exists here, by the side of the Mangert, to the pass of Predil, a very fine excursion. C—— explored for some distance by the base of the mountain, while I sketched the view from the upper lake. He overtook us on our return, while still in the romantic and roaring gorge which descends from the silent basin of the lakes towards the little world of life at Weissenfels, and the greater one of Tarvis, for the stream, thrown westward instead of eastward, turns aside from the near source of the Save, and finally enters the Gail. It seemed a rather long walk back to Ratschach, though probably not more than four miles, but we had taken the excursion without a guide, and had to pick out the path. Returning from Ratschach to Kronau we passed again the pool of the Save, and watched for the occurrence of the 'Sorgente Sava,' circular bubbling holes in the water, which seem to have attracted Davy's particular attention; but we saw none that we could attribute to any other cause than fish or insects.

That day we had been pilgrims to a shrine of nature and of science; the next we made a pilgrimage in a more literal sense to a 'holy mountain'—the Luschari Berg—beyond Tarvis, in Carinthia, almost on the borders of Friuli. On our excursion to Weissenfels, its conical shape, with a minute white speck upon its narrow summit, the pilgrimage church, rose in the distance. The place was very noted in all these parts, and Pufitsch strongly recommended the expedition for the wonderful view. So the one horse of Kronau was put to the pole (they always drive here in that lop-sided manner) and the one old driver tucked his wisp of straw under him for a seat, and away we went on Thursday morning, back again over the Weissenfels road, and so down to Tarvis, and up on the other side, and through Upper Tarvis on the great road, away towards the Pontebba pass. The driver made a feeble attempt to deposit us at the inn of Ober Tarvis; this we resisted, but noted that both the inn and the people had a comfortable look which might remove, another time, the objection to Tarvis on the score of accommodation. Five miles farther is Saifnitz, immediately at the foot of the mountain; before reaching it, a footpath for the use of pilgrims coming in this direction strikes off on the left, and there the figure of an angel with silvered wings, on the top of a small column, stands by way of finger-post, with outstretched arm pointing the way to the sacred hill. It was more convenient for us to disregard the angelic invitation.

There are several inns at Saifnitz, which must make great gain of godliness, as also numerous booths in a ravine, about half a mile from the town, where the real steepness commences. Here are all sorts of provision for the flesh, which is apt to arrive, whether on the ascent or descent, tired and thirsty, and in need of shade. For the last, interlaced boughs of trees forming a rough thatch, and supported on posts, shelter rows of benches for some distance on each side the path. It was rather a vacant hour when we passed, and we had each been fortified already by a glass of tokay at Saifnitz. In the course of the climb, however, we met several parties of returning pilgrims, some of them respectable-looking women, in quite other than peasant dress—one in white muslin, and with a parasol—yet all walking barefoot and carrying their shoes. These we expected would soon be found, a merry company, in the booths below. The path, though unrelentingly steep, was broad and worn, and, for at least the first half of the ascent, was carefully and variously *watched*—by blind men at set distances, by very old women judiciously interspersed, and by flying patrols of children, each and all with the inevitable extended palm—that itching palm—and the endless plaint. Such a gigantic begging system was too much for us; and besides, was it not necessary to put in a Protestant caveat against 'good works?' So we looked stern rebuke, for which the blind men, at any rate, were not much the worse, and left the almsgiving to the genuine pilgrim.

It is called three hours to the summit. The greater part of the distance is up an interminable gully, which shuts out all prospect except that immediately behind, and this consists only of dull grey hills. At last the open alp is gained, where the path ascends, terrace-like, round the conical summit of the Berg. Then the view begins to open, and the church and a few buildings are seen above. These consist of a house for the priests, another for travellers and sick pilgrims, and a cluster of booths, not like those below for refreshment, but for the sale of rosaries, trinkets, and votive offerings,—all mere tinsely rubbish as regarded their material value, unless some of the rosaries of polished stones be excepted. Here, again, we were too late for the fair; the mass of pilgrims for the day had completed their task, though one poor fellow, an elderly peasant, was still a quarter of a mile below, toiling on his knees up the gravelly path. He was moving very slowly, with a jerk and a pause, and a haul upon his staff, as he thrust forward each wounded knee. An hour afterwards we saw him prostrate on his face before the altar in the church. It was a spectacle of contrition; a visible acknowledgment of a deep-felt need; we believed he might have been taught a better way of crucifying the flesh, and a nearer approach to a still holier altar; yet we looked with sympathy and reverence upon this expression of God-given aspirations, which had found no other channel.

The church was built in 1360 upon the spot where, according to tradition, the shepherds found a carved wooden image of the Madonna among the juniper bushes. The other buildings are of later origin; all occupying a hollow just below the actual summit. In the church, a small edifice, there was nothing but mean and tawdry decoration, and to us no element of sanctity except the soul-trouble of that figure stretched upon the floor; while the faint smell of incense, and the sickly odour of a recent assemblage, inclined us to seek with small delay the pure air and noble prospect of the mountain top. There, under the infinite arch, were spread majestically round, some of the great things of God, which it was worth a pilgrimage to behold. We stood upon a space hardly large enough for a dozen people, and were immediately joined by two priests, who, like panorama men, began to designate the features of the view. One was a young man, for the residence attached to the church is a sort of seminary, though resorted to only in the summer; the other, a man of middle age, had that open, honest, simple-hearted expression, characteristic of mountain men, whether priests, guides, or hunters.

And here, as this good man stands beside us, let us say our word for these Catholic clergy of the mountains. We could not admire the rites they administered, nor their connivance at peasant superstitions, but we could often much admire the men themselves. They were, as a class, hard-working and conscientious, often, like the Curé of Sotscha, intelligent and well informed; and, as far as we had intercourse with them, courteous and hospitable. Theirs is no pampered lot; they have to face weather and danger, like their peasant parishioners, and do it bravely. When they come across Protestant leanings in their people, as they sometimes do, no doubt the professional man is touched to the quick, and they are no more charitable than the professional man generally is, when his particular function is in danger. Their natural weapon is then the anathema, and that is an ugly weapon, wounding the hand that wields it. A curse generally clings the most fatally to him by whom it is uttered. The priest, from the nature of his calling, is more exposed to this danger than other men; and if the *odium theologicum* is a hateful hate, it is yet the more excusable in proportion to the profounder importance, and to the soul-moving character of the matters with which it deals. It was not our part to probe this sore place, and we saw only the better—the genial—side, of the clerical character in these remote valleys.

Our two friends, upon this peak of prospect, were thoroughly enthusiastic about the 'Aussicht;' and it was truly a noble view. Eastward, the eye was led down the valley of the Save, with its long line of Carniolan peaks, following in succession from the near mass of the Mangert. Of course, the Terglou was not visible—that respectable mountain was fast becoming a joke; here he hides behind the Mangert. Westward, there was the furrow of the Pontebba Pass to the angle where it turns off toward Italy; and beyond it a rather dim confusion of Friulian mountains. Northward, appeared the white cones of the snowy Norics, distant, but set sharply, like a rim of frosted silver, upon the horizon—among them the Gross Glockner. Too distant for grandeur, these only possessed the interest always attaching to the pure snow. Southward, was the most striking scene. There, stood the magnificently jagged peaks of the Wischberg, rising out of the unfathomable depths—a group of giants! We were near enough to their wild inaccessible summits to realise all their fearfulness. Such a scene strikes awe with the sense of power it presses upon the mind—power, not in action, but in absolute repose, which is perhaps the more impressive of the two. It is force congealed and dormant. Here we looked and questioned long, for each of these monsters has a name, and the name invests with personality and in some sort informs with soul. Adam set an example which all his sons have followed, and that not merely for convenience of memory. There is a far deeper significance in the necessity. We claim and elevate into our own spiritual region the thing we have *named*. It is the baptism which mind bestows upon matter.

The priests were busy with their staves, pointing and naming for an hour. These great presences of nature were their friends of morning, noon, and eve. 'Oh,' said they, 'the sunrise! Oh, what magnificence!' and they spread out their arms towards the sweep of the horizon, as if they would embrace the glorious spectacle.

We were half inclined to yield to their persuasions, and spend the night in the pilgrim's house, though the accommodation was of the roughest, in order to secure the burst of morning upon the scene; but it would have cost too much disarrangement of our plans. After, therefore, painting the features of the view carefully upon our brain-tablets,—it was too extensive for the poor efforts of the pencil,—we descended, after the manner of men, to dinner at the small refreshment house, where, considering the labour of bringing up every article of provision, it was very tolerably served.

Then came the question of getting down again. We might do it on foot of course, but that would take two or three hours, and besides, that was not 'à la mode.' For all who can pay for it there is a peculiar contrivance of descent which, sooth to say, had been one of the attractions of the mountain, though, whether or no to avail ourselves of it, was matter of much discussion. Standing about the house were two or three men with long spikes attached to their shoes, and leaning against the walls appeared certain light wooden frames with long handles; these are sledges (Schlitten), and, to do the mountain properly, you should go down it, like a streak of lightning, on one of them. It looked a queer and nervous operation; the sledge marks were visible down the steep crest for some distance, and then pitched round a corner into unknown space. There were, moreover, but two men available just then, so that our party must be divided. S—— and A—— were, however, willing to try, and all the little colony of the hill assembled to see them packed. The priests assured us of their safety, and that they would reach the bottom in twenty minutes; one portly old fellow, with a trombone of a voice, was not only emphatic in his assurances, but, putting a hand on the shoulder of each of the men preparing to descend, warned them to take special care of the two English ladies. Yet you should have seen them as they were tilted over the edge! A small pillow tied on each sledge formed the seat; two crooked pegs were all there was to hold by; the feet were pressed against the runners. For precaution, a string gathered in all habiliments lest they should catch against the rocks. The men, putting themselves between the handles in front, and leaning well backward, struck their spikes into the ground—in a minute they were beyond shouting distance—in a minute more, were shooting round the shoulder of the hill, and, whether for better or for worse, our wives were gone!

As we could not know the result till we had reached the bottom ourselves, we made hurried adieus to the friendly priests, and set off at our best speed down the path we had ascended, reaching Saifnitz in an hour and half. We met two or three sledges coming up, carried on their driver's backs, but could not learn the fate of those in which we were interested. At the door of the inn, however, we spied them, propped against the wall; and within doors were S—— and A——, hardly yet knowing, it seemed, whether they stood on their heads or their heels. They described their unwonted flight as a short agony,—which it must be also for the sledgemen themselves, who were streaming with perspiration and looked much exhausted. The men either ran with the sledges, guiding them round the many turns that occurred, and pulling them lightly over obstacles; or, when the descent favoured, suddenly seating themselves in front of each occupant, left the sledge to its own momentum; then down went driver and sledge, and lady and all, at a velocity which took away the breath. If a check occurred, or the ground varied, the spiked feet were struck out in a moment; but what with speed, shaking, and fright, poor S—— and A—— were aching all over; and though glad to have acquired an experience, were not inclined to repeat the experiment.

Naturally, more tokay followed this exploit, and before we left, in marched the portly priest with a long and strong alpenstock in hand. He had descended from his perch to see how we all fared. Shouting and laughing, and shaking hands many times over, he poured out his congratulations, requiring us, moreover, to renew again and again our praises of the view from his favourite Berg. 'Nothing like it in Switzerland,' he exclaimed, 'nothing like it, eh!' Then, turning to the innkeeper, he roared out: 'Here are Russians, Bavarians, French, English, and Turks, all coming to the Luschari-Berg—all the world is coming—nothing like it in Switzerland, nothing like it, I say!' We were the first English, I fancy, who had made the pilgrimage within the historic period, and our advent was a sensation. It was rather amusing, however, to find ourselves again associated with Turks.

The drive of three hours through the limpid atmosphere was one of those pleasures which only a southern climate can bestow. The absolute purity of every tint, and the definiteness, and yet delicacy, of every form, are astonishing; while the smooth softness of the air you breathe is a positive physical delight. It was twilight as we climbed the last hill above Weissenfels, and entered upon our valley. The stars were out as we passed the pool of the Save; troops of them danced in its waters, and the long line of dark peaks vandyked the dark sky. A little later, and the gleam across the road of the shrine lamp at Kronau, told us we were home again.

There is this peculiarity about the scenery of the upper, or, as it is often called, the Wurzen Save, that the grand limestone range on the south, while, as a line of peaks, it almost everywhere gives token of its presence, is at successive intervals displayed suddenly and magnificently to view by short lateral valleys. It is as if the mass of debris, which encumbers the base of the lofty chain, and forms the immediate hill-side as seen from the valley, had been at intervals scooped away, so as to reveal the bare masonry of that stupendous wall. The suddenness with which each of these rock glimpses breaks upon the eye greatly adds to the effect. You pass down between rounded and wooded hills, and in a moment the wood and the hill have disappeared on your right, and you look into the depths of a vast amphitheatre—tier upon tier of pale, pitiless rock—'occupying half the sky,' to quote Davy's expressive phrase. The first of these openings runs up to the high wall connecting the Mangert with the Predil Kogel; the second brings to view the Mittags Kogel; the third is filled by the Mangert, and holds the lakes of Weissenfels; the fourth occurs near Ratschach, and displays the Sebnik and Traunik; the fifth, near Wurzen, breaks a way up to the Moistroka; the sixth, at Kronau, brings the Prisinig to view; a seventh, a little lower down, is very characteristic of this scenery; it shows the bare masses of the Spik and the Kukowa; and the eighth, at Lengenfeld, has the honour and glory of unveiling the Terglou itself.

Lengenfeld was destined for our next excursion. Nothing could exceed the beauty of the weather all the time we were in this Save country, and we rattled down the valley under the purest of skiey canopies. The scenery was richer and more gracious every mile—always excepting the burst of savage grandeur at Mitteberg, where the bare, blistered, snow-streaked Spik stood sternly in the gap. Approaching Lengenfeld, a village out of the road on the left, sprawling up the hill, and encompassed by rich greenery, a broad vista opened southwards—too broad and too deep to answer to the abrupt breaks I have described; and instead of being filled by the bulk of the Terglou, as we had hoped, that mountain was retired among a wilderness of inferior peaks—dignified, but very tantalising, behaviour, and far from bearing out that passage in Murray which speaks of 'the rugged precipices of this magnificent mountain terminating the view.' Dismiss that vision of the Terglou, and you will probably not be disappointed, for it is a beautiful and varied scene.

The busy village of Moistrana occupies the bottom of the valley, and is surrounded by orchards, gardens, bright green pastures, mills, and a foundry; and, where the lane turns off to it from the high road, stands, of all things, a direction-post to a waterfall! It was a dreadful tourist symptom; and we had been so long accustomed to find out our waterfalls for ourselves, that we were inclined to resent the indignity of being shown one. The fact was, we had now trenched upon the excursion grounds of the gay lake of Veldes, several miles below; and a panting gentleman in spectacles, following his fat dame in a cart down the stony track, soon corroborated it. Churchill and his wife, however, were not to be daunted, either by the heat, which was now fierce upon the shadeless path, or by the possibility of stumbling upon a pic-nic They did not find their three hours' walk ill repaid. The way thither was pleasantly and agreeably varied. A considerable body of water, taking into account the dryness of the season and the character of the district, fell over a broad ledge of rock that projected, for a mile or more, along the face of the northern wall of the valley, and plunged into a deep basin excavated in the enormous heaps of debris below. Climbing up the debris to a level with the fall, they found a deep and lofty cavern behind it; and, from the point where they stood, a small and perfect circle of rainbow played over the spray at their feet, contrasting charmingly with the rich dark-brown of the wet rocks, studded in every chink and crevice with lovely ferns, and the graceful foliage of *Astrantia carniolica.*

SHRINE AND RACK NEAR LENGENFELD.

As for S—— and myself, we wandered towards an ancient church, but found the shade of some walnut trees upon greensward so welcome, that I was easily persuaded my proper function was to sketch a field shrine which stood handy in the sunlight. It was a quaint conical-roofed thing, with niches on its four sides, in each of which, faint blotches of colour indicated that a frescoed saint was waxing dim. Beside it, stretched one of the long Carniolan racks, empty as yet of its stores of beans and barley; and behind, the rocky outline of the Lengenfeld side of the valley rose white in the hot sunlight.

We had arranged for dinner at a small inn at Lengenfeld, where the mistress, when meat was mentioned, reminded us, with grave surprise, that it was Friday; as soon, however, as she understood the rights and privileges of English heretics in that particular, she was willing to do her best, and succeeded excellently. There is one neat whitewashed bedchamber, and we conceived that a quiet couple might find this pretty village very pleasant quarters for a summer.

Again there was the jog-trot home in the delicious twilight. There is a primitive country inn at that end of Kronau, bearing for sign a picture of the disciples and the 'Stranger' at the door of Emmaus, with the inscription, 'Abide with us, for the day is far spent.' It seemed always appropriate in the dusk of evening, and suitable to the homely simplicity of the house. We have since frequently met with this inscription on houses of entertainment. Ours was more pretentious, though it boasted only a bunch of shavings. Under them, far into starlight, sat a group of smokers, who would rise and salute as we approached, Pufitsch holding a candle overhead, appearing from within to escort us upstairs—not to a comfortable salle, however, but to a dreary open landing, where the dirty cloth of the previous meal, and of many before that, was spread upon an extempore deal table. Among divers relics with which it was sure to be strewed, was the one lump of butter, daily diminishing, and now hacked to almost its last fragment. There was no prospect of a fresh supply; and though we pitied young Mrs.

Pufitsch in her troubles, between baby upstairs, and pot-boiling below, we could not admire her domestic management.

Yet we must hold to Kronau a little longer. Saturday was to be a great day—a day devoted to an excursion which C—— and myself must take alone. I have mentioned the opening behind Kronau, a winding, solemn-looking gorge, with a broad white bed, partly stream and partly stones. Davy appreciated this grand portal. 'Took a ride at six,' he says, 'to the opening of the glen below, where another stream joins the Save—a glorious valley!' It leads to the recesses of the Prisinig; and from its upper end there strikes a path over the Julian range into the valley of the Isonzo, though far above the village of our hospitable Curé of Sotscha. Somebody has told Mr. Murray enough about it to lead him to say that 'the scenery is of the boldest character.' Morning and evening we had looked up this gorge, reserving it for a last and crowning expedition.

Morning air and morning light, with peaks ahead to reflect its glow; stout alpenstocks, a well-filled wallet, a lithe bright-eyed guide, and an inspiring sense of adventure—what elements of earthly happiness! For two hours we kept to the broad bed of the torrent; then, in company with a party of *sennen*, or cheese-makers, bound to fetch cheeses from the Isonzo, whom we had overtaken, we mounted for two more hours steep slopes of grass, or threaded a difficult upward path through pine forests, having always on our left the amazing walls and terraces of bare rock that build up the Prisinig. As we mounted higher, and higher still, the ledges where the chamois feed, or retire for their noonday siesta, were exposed to view; but the sunshine streaming across prevented our guide from picking any of them out, though he was certain they would be there; and, as he confessed to having shot as many as seventy-six,—that is to say, committed so many acts of poaching,—he might be considered a man of experience. After leaving the torrent, that want of water, which afflicts the Isonzo mountains, began to show itself; and we found all the cheese-makers, who were a little in advance, flung down in every attitude of repose beside a rill—the only symptom of a stream on the whole mountain-side.

From the summit of the pass we diverged to the left, towards the shoulder of the Prisinig, upon which we intended to mount as high as possible, and thence survey the course of the Isonzo. To have descended to the deep valley would have been useless fatigue. On this side an enormous geröll descends from the sheer precipices of the Prisinig. That term is applied in the Alps to those vast slopes of stones—not pebbles, but angular fragments, from the size of those of a macadamized road to that of a chest of drawers,—which shoot downward from a mountain side, in a line of mathematical straightness, often for several thousand feet. Among these mountains the geröll is a remarkable feature, and here was one of the completest specimens. For two hours we crossed it diagonally, continually bearing upward, and attained at length a bluff of rock with a little soil and heather, which gave us all we wanted. It commanded a perfect view of the head of the Isonzo valley, which curls round upon itself in a most singular manner, like the end of a shepherd's crook; its sides being also of remarkable depth and steepness. Trenta, its highest village, occupies the point where it begins to bend, and was so immediately at our feet, that a dislodged fragment might have almost bounded down upon its church roof, which yet was so far below, as to be but a speck among the other little roof specks. The wonderfully precipitous sides of the mountains at the back of the Terglou ranged eastward, like successive buttresses; and to the west were the like towering buttress masses of the Sebnik and Mangert. To have ascended higher, we must have attacked the summit precipices of the Prisinig, and turned our backs upon this view; so we emptied the wallet and dined, while eagles sailed slowly by beneath, on balanced wings.

Churchill spent all the time that could be spared among these arid crags, and found his reward. It was in crossing the geröll that, after lagging for some time among its hopeless-looking blocks, where to my eye, at least, no green thing grew, he quietly remarked on rejoining me, 'I have found it at last.' The prize was a very tiny floweret, the *Campanula Zoysii,* peculiar to Carniola and South Styria, not more than three inches long, with a slender leafy stem rising out of a rosette of leaves, and crowned by a pale-blue, narrow, tube-like flower, bearded at its mouth, very different from any other European *Campanula.* To discover more specimens was an object; and by close and continued search, several others were added to the vasculum; but in recrossing the geröll, which had afforded the first discovery, it seemed as if the only individual had been already captured.

Instead of retracing the path of the morning, we took a rather difficult but directer course, much closer to the Prisinig; and our guide, continually approaching every vantage spot, searched long, but vainly, the ledges of the stupendous walls above, for some sign of chamois, uttering repeatedly a peculiar whistle in imitation of that by which the chamois sentinels are supposed to spread the alarm; but nothing stirred. It was amusing to witness the abstracted absorption of his gaze and the dilation of his eye, as he stood, without the movement of a limb, watching as a cat would a bird. To him the great prize of life was game. It was astonishing to be told that up the craggy and tangled steeps which we were now descending—using often the elastic branches of the lätschen by which to let ourselves down—a bear, in the spring, had carried or dragged the carcass of an ox which he had killed below. These creatures, and wolves also, wander over from Croatia, especially in the early part of the year, and are tracked and killed by the villagers of the Save. We slaked our thirst at the water issuing from a snow-bed. Some of the finest precipice effects are to be seen about here, not only among those of the Prisinig, but in a vast amphitheatre of rock which joins it on the north, full into which we looked on our descent, its grandeur heightened by illumination from the western sky, above the black tops of the pine forest.

As the red-tinted gloom of evening fell around us, we descended from the woods upon the green border of the wide and wasteful torrent. Here, sounds which had for some time filled the air were explained; a large flock of sheep and goats were dribbling down the opposite mountain side, and following the course of the stream to Kronau. It was the last day of August, and their summer sojourn on the alpine pastures was ended. Three shepherds, wearing large bunches of dark-blue monkshood in their hats, and one fine dog, who seemed to consider driving no part of his business, accompanied them. It was by voice and gesture only that the flock were guided, spreading loosely for more than a mile, and jingling their many-toned bells. The sheep, content with an occasional nibble, pursued their way in a peaceful frame of mind; but the goats, with which they were intermixed, betrayed their restless and inquisitive temper by bleatings, and excursions across the stream, whence it required many wheedling calls from the shepherds to lure them back. Both sheep and goats, however, were mightily tempted by our pockets, and licked our hands for the expected salt. When Kronau came in sight, the hillocks round were seen covered with people, and, availing themselves of an open space, the shepherds—significant sight—'separated the sheep from the goats.' Then, marshalling the former into a compact mass of white woolly backs, the principal shepherd marched at their head, with quick military step, through the town, proud to bring his charge safely home, and welcomed by every voice.

S—— and A—— had met us outside Kronau. It was several weeks since we had received any letters, and during our absence a batch of them had arrived. The grave faces of our wives prepared us in measure for the sad tidings they bore. The remainder of the journey was shortened, and robbed of its gleeful joyousness; but we must not allow our pages to be darkened with the shadow which then fell upon ourselves.

The following day, a serene and lovely Sunday, it was as if nature had surrounded us with her most soothing influences; and, as at Flitsch, there was welcome quiet in the village, though a large number of the valley peasantry were assembled round the church. The women wore generally a broad band of black velvet over a white cap, which had rather a picturesque effect; and the men, almost universally, black boots up to the knee, somewhat in the fashion of Frederick the Great. There was a prevalence of blue eyes in the population, with an open and pleasant countenance, which gave a favourable impression of the peasantry of this portion of the Save. Even in this cheerful valley many fatal accidents were depicted on the memorial tablets. One, which had occurred by night, at the bridge near Kronau, when the stream was in flood, had sadly perplexed the artist, who was only equal to daylight effects. To get over the difficulty, he put torches into the hands of all the bystanders, and that was considered to sufficiently indicate darkness!

That evening, S—— and myself, following a steep path up a hill on the north side of the valley, two or three miles below Kronau, and marked by a small white shrine which always shone like a star in the setting sun, reached a spot, which—upon that occasion, for the beauty beneath our feet and above our heads, earth and sky all radiant in rainbow hues—is almost unparalleled in our recollection. The Luschari Berg was enveloped in the golden haze of the west, whence the rays streamed down the Save valley, illuminating every farm and village, every forest-crowned hill, and every bare peak, till the lovely view faded into a mist of dolphin colours in the extreme east. 'Yes,' we said, ravished with the sight, 'it *is* the loveliest valley in Europe.'

CHAPTER X.

THE LAKE OF VELDES AND THE WOCHEIN SAVE.

The 'Gem of Carniola'—Feistritz and the Wochein—We invade the Terglou—Petran's Illness and our Defeat—A Vision of the Steiner Alp—Ascent of the Terglou by Capt. Holsmay—The Terglou Wilderness and the Julian Alps—Sclavonic Mass Music—Radmannsdorf and Sir Humphry—Krainberg.

ON Monday morning, Pufitsch, arrayed in a smart blue coat, intimated his intention of complimenting our ladies by driving them himself to Veldes; taking his seat in the same old vehicle, and behind the same old horse, that by this time seemed almost our own. Churchill and myself were consigned to a surly fellow in a straw-stuffed waggonet, but with a capital horse; Pufitsch led in good style, and we went at great speed down the valley. Again of course through Lengenfeld, and then on to Assling, the scenery dismissing the open Alpine look which characterises it at Kronau, and breaking into richer, more romantic forms. At Assling, larger houses decked the green knolls, nobler trees clustered about them, and iron forges sent up the sound of the tilt-hammer from deep umbrageous hollows.

After Assling, we left the valley by a side road to the south, climbing steeply up through woods, and, when the height was gained, entered beautiful glades studded with fine trees in English park-like fashion, with here and there a village, and more than one gentleman's house, a most rare sight in these countries, and very grateful to our rock-wearied eyes. And so, through many twistings and turnings of narrow lanes, shaded by oaks, beeches, Spanish chestnuts, and walnuts, with peeps of church spires and glimpses of castle turrets upon rocky heights—we descended at last with a sudden sweep round the base of a precipitous hill, crowned by mediæval towers, upon the charming little lake of Veldes—the gem of Carniola. That it was a gay pleasure-place was clear at once from the two handsome hotels and two or three elegant villas, which, with gardens, boat-houses, and pavilions, lined the near border of the lake.

After six weeks' association with peasants and publicans, and the dilapidation consequent upon so much rough travelling, we felt rather shy of the groups of ladies and gentlemen, who curiously lifted their eyeglasses as we passed their al-fresco dinner table; and when we were shown into handsome apartments were at first hardly more at ease than Caffres in a drawingroom. There was an immediate overhauling of bags for almost-forgotten habiliments which should, in some measure, restore the fitness of things. Of the two hotels, we chose Petran's, 'Stadt Triest,' the oldest, nearest to the end of the lake, and, I believe, the best. It commands a lovely view.

No river flows out of this little perfection of a lake; its clear green waters are fed by a small branch of the Wochein Save, probably supplying not more than enough to balance the evaporation. The Wochein Save seems, indeed, to have originally given rise to the lake, and at one time to have continued its course through its basin to a junction with the Wurzen Save, by a ravine now half filled up, instead of turning, as it does, suddenly to the right, and at last joining its brother Save at a much lower point—Radmannsdorf. Across the lake, just opposite the hotels, is the picturesque castle of the Bishop of Brixen, on the summit of an abrupt rock draped with wood; and at the further extremity of the lake, a graceful, wooded islet, bearing a white campaniled church, approached by flights of steps from the lapping water, offers a miniature representation of St. Giulio on the Lake of Orta. A village or two, in their original homely simplicity, lie along the banks, and in every direction, except that of the Save valley, forest-covered hills enclose the scene. The one break in

LAKE OF VELDES AND BISHOP OF BRIXEN'S SCHLOSS.

their circuit is filled by the noble, hazy mass of the Stou, an outlier of the Loibl Pass. Over the hills on the south and west are seen mountains of varied contour; and crowning all, westward, the high bare ranges of the Terglou; yet, as at Lengenfeld, not with predominating grandeur; that does not occur till you are far down the Save valley, or at least have reached Radmannsdorf. The mountain is still as perverse as ever.

Rough country boats—square, broad-bottomed things,

large enough for a family dinner party, and mostly furnished with awnings—are sculled about the lake by women; the usual voyage being to a pretty village and rural inn at the upper extremity, and round the ecclesiastical island. We walked to this village, a distance of about two miles, and, in one of these boats, returned by starlight,—past the shadowy islet and under the dark precipices of the castle. The season was growing late for visitors. They are principally from Laibach, and we could not hear of any English tourist. An English family had indeed spent the summer there, but they were formerly resident in the neighbourhood, and now lived, we were told, in a castle in Styria. The name was so unlike an English one that we scarcely believed the story at first, but afterwards found it to be true.

Veldes may be said to occupy the fork between the two rivers—the Wochein and the Wurzen Save, which unite below it to form the proper Save. Churchill and I had thought of leaving our wives for a couple of days at the hotel, while we explored the Wochein valley, visiting the gloomy lake which bears that name, and, if possible, reaching the base of the indomitable Terglou. S—— and A——, however, preferred taking the chance of a tolerable inn at Feistritz, five miles short of the Wochein See, to being left behind.

We started for this excursion the next day after our arrival, and enjoyed an afternoon drive of twenty miles up the Wochein valley, which surpassed our expectations. Fine picturesque crags guard the entrance; and though, for the most part, it is a confined ravine, we do not agree with Murray's depreciating account. The Wochein Save speeds through it, a shallow but broad and brilliant stream, the vivid green of its waters being quite remarkable; and there are some charming open grassy spaces, full of pastoral beauty. An inconvenience to the traveller arises from the trains of black charcoal carts, which, at many a pretty turn of road or river, come like a smutch upon the landscape, as well as block up the way.

Feistritz itself, fifteen miles from Veldes, lies well in an open basin; the mountains which enclose it have a fine sweep in them, and are mantled in black pine forest with a sombre grandeur. At a point north-westward of Feistritz they sink sufficiently to display some of the lower ranges of the Terglou, if not the mountain itself. Clouds prevented our certain identification of the fact. The inn is through the village, by the side of a bright stream, and beyond it the valley stretches with unfenced fields, encroaching woods, or orchard-surrounded villages, towards a recess in the hills, which, as we approached in the afternoon, was filled with hazy light. Before we reached it the light was gone, succeeded by dull gloom, and presently was spread before us a sheet of water, rolling short waves on a very solitary strand, and in the midst of a solemn monotony of desolation. A single boat was crossing from the farther shore, which was veiled in dun shades; and two or three men, waiting for its coming, were dangling their legs over the lower wall of a churchyard. The church itself, the only building in sight, increased, by its dreary isolation, the sense of solitude. This lake, in all respects a contrast to that of Veldes, is the Wochein See, and the church is that of St. Johann.

As we looked towards the dark hills beyond, we congratulated ourselves that we had not crossed them, as we once intended, to reach this spot from the Isonzo, and could well believe the Curé of Sotcha's assurances as to their sterile and desolate character. The source of the Wochein Save is amongst them, five miles beyond the lake; there it issues from the rock in a cascade, which the Veldes visitors think worth an excursion. Our greater interest lay in another direction—northward—where a wild valley broke direct for the Terglou, his frowning mass being actually visible there for a few minutes among tumultuous clouds.

At present, having dismissed our cars at the lake, we had before us the evening walk of five miles back to Feistritz. When you wish to be in full accord with nature—and evening is the very time—touch mother earth with your feet, tread the springy turf, or the wayward path; linger here, to catch the glimmer of the stream, and there, to mark the purple peaks against the dull evening red; pause to listen to the murmur of sounds, from the distant goat-bell to the near whistling of the grasshopper, and turn your cheek, from time to time, to the soft fluctuating air. We enjoyed all this, and more; and then, as night came down, and the mountain shapes were muffled in mist, and the road lost itself in darkness, and a distant light, which, might be Feistritz, twinkled, and was gone, we began to think of England and English homes, upon which as in far off Carniola, the same summer dusk was settling, and the same stars were peeping.

Feistritz affords the nearest sleeping-place to the base of the Terglou, and even then he lies some twenty miles back in his wilderness of rocks. On Wednesday morning, having engaged a car to convey us to Mittersdorf, about ten miles, Churchill and I started with the idea of penetrating this area of desolation as far as time allowed. A footpath to Mittersdorf passes over the depression in the hills immediately opposite Feistritz, and greatly reduces the distance; we drove round only to save our legs. Having repassed the end of the Wochein See, we turned away from it through the village of Althammer into the

Mittersdorf valley, running nearly parallel to that of Feistritz. This took us beyond the entrance of that wild gorge, rending its way up to the Terglou, that we had wished to explore. The fact was, our guide—a tall, dark-haired, interesting-looking fellow, bearing the name of Petran, a common one in this district, and whose soft low-toned voice was also distinctively 'Windisch'—would by no means agree to it. He supposed our intention was to reach, if not to ascend, the Terglou, and knew *that* to be a hopeless route. Our object, which was only to obtain an effective view of the mountain, would, as it turned out, have been better served if we had taken the gorge in question, by a herd-path which twists itself up the barren heights to the left.

Petran's path turned up the hill just before reaching the church of Mittersdorf. The bell was sounding as we arrived, and the driver and he, suddenly jumping from the vehicle, threw themselves on their knees in the road, two or three peasants in the churchyard did the same; and a priest, bearing something in his hands, and attended by the sexton, appeared at the church-door. It was the Host, about to be carried to some dying person. A peasant was waiting with a cart to receive the priest and his charge; but there was something incongruous, if not grotesque, in the circumstance, that the sacred guardian of this most sacred mystery was troubled with toothache, his face hung woefully awry, bandaged up and poulticed. It was an incident for the sarcastic, yet pitying, humour of Carlyle.

Here we were six hours from the foot of the Terglou. The path, a steep one, through brushes and scrub, showed the Mittersdorf valley below, in great variety of beauty, for the wildness is all above. We had not mounted far before Petran, who had rested sooner than guides are wont to do, confessed to being unwell. Brandy he spat from him in great disgust; a draught of cold water was the remedy he longed for; but as usual, no sound of water disturbed the silence of these hills; the only chance of it was at a village about two hours up the ascent. There, our surprise was great to find the sole supply to be derived from kegs, which are daily filled and brought down from a spring, an hour farther up the mountain. Petran took a long pull at the bunghole of a keg, and seemed revived, but when we reached the spring itself, lay down, acknowledging that he was quite ill, and could go no farther. All this time, the conviction had been growing upon us that, apart from this misfortune, we should be baulked of the Terglou; for the higher we rose upon the stony steeps, the more was reared across our view in front, a mighty barrier—the Drassberg—which, it was evident, we must either ascend or pass round. At the spring, where two or three wretched hovels go by the name of Končza, we found ourselves in a deep hollow, into which, in front, the debris of this mountain fell. The path (if path it could be called) lay up the debris, and across the precipitous face above, promising so much toil and delay that, deprived of our guide, we gave up the thought of attempting it; and, at Petran's recommendation, determined to try the slopes and crags to our left, whence he thought the Terglou might be visible. After a hard climb and scramble among rocks and rhododendrons, we gained a singular ridge, just wide enough for a goat-path, and no more. It commanded a wonderful prospect—but no Terglou! The bulk of the Drassberg hid every atom of him.

The ridge we occupied, extending a considerable distance, formed one side of the deep gorge I have spoken of; so deep was it, and so narrow, that it looked but a blue fissure beneath us. Across it lay a fearsome region, a confusion of the most ruthless-looking precipices, peaks, white wastes, and dismal abysses, which clouds were darkening and disclosing by turns. In the direction from which we had come lay, deep among the mountains, the still waters of the Wochein See. The bright side of the prospect was towards the Save to the north-east, a vast and softly-coloured scene. In the midst of it, about fifty miles distant, rose an object of the greatest interest to us; for days past we had been looking for it—anything which should answer to the great mountain group—the Steiner Alp, to which the last week of our journey had always been devoted. Now, and for the first time, it stood revealed—a nobly rearing, gigantic form, wreathed with light clouds, and gleaming with the delicate tints of bare and distant rock. It was the Grintouz, the westernmost outlier of the Steiner, and the loftiest; the corner-stone of Carinthia, Carniola, and of Styria, and the guardian of perhaps the most secluded valley in Europe.

We were consoled by this sight for the loss of the Terglou; and, after an hour's enjoyment of the view from our narrow perch, scrambled down again to our guide, whom rest, coolness, and water had greatly restored. He had, in the course of the summer, achieved the ascent of the Terglou in company with the English gentleman whose family had been staying at Veldes, and a young friend of his; and showed us a pocket-knife, of Sheffield make, given as a memorial of the exploit, which he valued highly. The party slept at a hut named Belpole, 'white-field,' expressive of the stony waste amidst which it is placed. This is 5,430 feet above the sea; and at the immediate base of the mountain. Four hours, as we understood, took them thence to the summit; but it is represented as an ascent of much difficulty, and some danger. The first recorded ascent is that of Captain Bosio in 1822, when engaged in a trigometrical survey, who appears to have experienced, in ample measure, both the difficulty and the danger, losing a guide by lightning, and compelled in the utmost peril to spend a night upon the summit.

Another Austrian officer—Captain Holsmay—was more fortunate, and has given, in the recent volume of the Vienna Alpine Club, a narrative of his ascent, made, not from the Wochein, but from the Save Thal side, his starting-point being Lengenfeld. For such of our readers, who, not being Alpine professionals, are not likely to see the volume, we may extract some details of the adventure.

Captain Holsmay and his party left Moistrana, near Lengenfeld, at 4 P.M., and at about 9, having lost themselves for an hour in the dark among huge blocks, reached the upper Kerma Alp, nearly corresponding in height to the Belpole hut on the opposite side. Here they remained till 5·30 A.M., when they started for the ascent. An hour brought them to the top of the saddle connecting the Drassberg with the Terglou, at the height of 6,330 feet. From this a difficult path descends to Belpole. Descending for half an hour in a northerly direction, along the inner side of the saddle, they arrived at the actual base of the Terglou 'massif.' Here Holsmay found himself at the foot of the most colossal slope of geröll he had ever seen, which it cost much labour to ascend by short zigzags. At the summit of this slope rose a precipice sixty feet high, which, running round the crest of the mountain, seemed to bar all further progress. Fortunately, a single cleft three or four feet wide, was found, and up this with much difficulty the party forced their way. Captain Bosio, who on his ill-fated attempt, first climbed this cleft, calls it not without reason, 'Das Thor des Terglou.'

The Terglou 'Thor' was passed by nine, and they rested for a few minutes, as at this point the special dangers of the ascent commence. Everything superfluous, even the alpenstock was left behind, for the hands had now enough to do to help the feet. The Dachstein limestone, of which the Terglou mass consists, is much weathered, and full of cracks, so that the firmness of every projection must be carefully tested before trusting to it either hand or foot; and there is this further inconvenience, that the weathering has left the edges of rock as sharp as a knife. Captain Holsmay had not climbed far before his gloves were in tatters, and his fingers cut all over. In half an hour he reached the peak of the little Terglou, 8,820 feet above the sea.

He now descended to the saddle that connects the lesser with the greater Terglou, pursuing it in a north-west direction. It is broad at first, but narrows gradually till it requires the greatest caution, for precipices drop on both sides, and at last for the distance of ten feet or so the width is not more than eight inches. This portion the captain prudently took astraddle. Arrived thus at the base of the final peak, the ascent resolved itself into a strenuous scramble up narrow clefts, alternating with abrupt faces of rock, where foot or hand-hold seemed denied. This was the most exhausting part of the whole, and required frequent rests. On the top of this final wall, a sloping ridge conducted the climbers, in about thirty paces, to the summit of the highest peak, 9,370 feet above the sea, which they reached at 10 A.M.

During the ascent they suffered much from want of water. Snow was the only resource, their wine having been accidentally left behind. The highest spring is only half an hour above the Kerma Alp, and they were therefore eight hours without sufficiently slaking their thirst. The peak, much weathered, and covered with rocks, stretches from south-south-east to north-north-west, with a length of about thirty yards, and a breadth of but five or six. Two wooden posts with other fragments lay there, the remains of the pyramid erected by Captain Bosio. The horizon was not clear, or Venice itself would have been seen; but a part of the Adriatic, and the serpentine courses of the rivers along the Venetian plains were visible.

At 11 A.M. they commenced the descent backward, on all fours. At 12 they passed through the Terglou Thor. At 1·30 the hut of the Kerma Alp was reached, and resting there an hour they got back to Lengenfeld at 6·30. P.M.

From this account it is clear that the Terglou is a redoubtable mountain, and Churchill shall now add a few particulars respecting the Terglou district, which will explain some of the peculiarities we have dwelt upon.

The Terglou is the culminating peak of four short rocky ridges, running in a north-east and south-west direction, parallel to each other, and allowing room only for narrow, deep, and debris-strewn valleys between them. They occupy, orographically, a singular position as the transition district and meeting-ground of three different systems—the system of *longitudinal valleys and ridges*, which are dominant to the north and east; that of the *irregular and broken district* of Venetian Carnia, with *isolated peaks* scattered through it, on the west; and finally, the system of *peakless plateaus*, without regular valleys, and full of funnel-shaped depressions, caverns, and subterranean rivers, to the south and south-east. The country therefore exhibits great variety in its relief. A lofty line of elevation nearly parallel with the line of the Karavanken Alps forming the northern boundary of the Wurzen Save runs across these four ridges, almost at right angles, connecting them with each other. The whole constitutes the Julian Alps, their highest peaks, such as the Terglou, Razor Spitze, Prisinig, Sebnik, and

Mangert, occurring nearly at the points of junction of the four ridges with this main ridge. The cross ridge determines, too, the line of watershed from which streams flow down the intervals between the four ridges. On the northern aspect, they fall into the longitudinal valley of the Wurzen Save; and on the southern, give rise to the Isonzo and its affluents. Hence, also, the numerous short valleys, which open out into the valley of the Wurzen Save, and originate the peculiarities of its scenery, which all occur on its southern side. On the Isonzo side the contrast to the Save landscape is very marked. Two of these short ridges, for example, are at last united and lost in that vast plateau behind Flitsch, in which it is difficult to say whether the 'ridge' characteristic, or the 'plateau,' predominates. Both are there in great perfection. The fourth, and loftiest ridge, containing the Terglou, terminates to the south-west in a lofty plateau—the Krn—where peaks stand at the angles, and overlook a desolate depression, which constitutes its interior. Here the 'ridge' element is absent. Then, pushed up against this Terglou ridge, and its terminal plateau of the Krn, is a vast plateau of triangular form, with a base line running nearly east and west for twenty-five miles, and with sides of twenty miles in length. Its area would probably comprise about 200 square miles; its rocky irregular surface everywhere slopes towards the interior, and the Wochein See occupies the point of greatest depression, still nearly 2,000 feet above the sea level. The whole interval between the level of the Wochein See, and the summit pyramid of the Terglou, consists of one enormous bed of 'Dachstein limestone' of the Lias formation.

The reader will thus note that the position of the Terglou is very central, not only in relation to its own ridge, but to the whole district in which it stands. If the traveller endeavours to see it by standing on the cross ridge, there is sure to be some peak of this ridge, or of the four parallel ridges in the way; and the valleys are too deep and narrow to afford a glimpse of aught beyond their immediate boundary walls; it can only be seen by penetrating to its foot; by climbing such outposts as the Mangert or the Prestelenik, that out-top everything; or, by getting quite outside the district, and viewing it from a distance, the culminating point of a grand whole, as seen from Radmannsdorf.

The pass of the Predil, uniting Raibl and Flitsch, is taken over a depression in the first of these four parallel ridges; and by the Flitscher Klause through a much deeper depression or rather cutting in the second ridge. Finally, the Saukopf, that fine sugar-loaf peak mentioned at page 231, which stands immediately opposite Flitsch to the NE, is the termination in that direction of the third ridge.

It took us three hours to return to Mittersdorf; no doubt heightened by contrast, the valley struck us, even more than in the morning, as extremely beautiful. The last portion of the descent into it is very steep; I happened to be in front, Churchill following at a little distance, Petran, who still suffered, last of all. In turning a sharp corner of the path, among dwarf oaks, I stood transfixed. 'Churchill!' exclaimed I, 'look here!' 'What is it?' cried he, 'snakes?' It was well this reached no ears but mine. Before me were our two wives, seated demurely, with their needlework, under a tree. We had no notion but that they were ten miles away at Feistritz, where we had left them in the morning. They had taken advantage of the vehicle returning in the afternoon to come so far to meet us, and had climbed the hill a little way to surprise us more effectually. The addition to our party, however agreeable, was a little embarrassing. Petran was too ill to walk, so he and the driver were accommodated in some way behind the horse's tail; S. and A. took the proper, and only legitimate, seat; Churchill and myself a second one of hay, rigged up behind them. This, however, when we began to jog down the rough lane, quickly dissolved into nothing at all, and we two unlucky pedestrians were reduced to lying at the bottom, like calves in a cart, with legs sticking out on each side—of course under much kind commiseration from the ladies in front, which neither softened the jolts, nor prevented toes and heels from catching against trees, rocks, and cottage walls, as we passed along. Yet we cannot deny that the twilight drive home was a pleasant one—once again past the solitary Wochein See, and by the banks of the young Save,—once again past the end of that vista which brings to view the obstinate Terglou—once again to the rural inn at Feistritz, where, in a snug little back parlour, they good-naturedly did all they could to assist in the concoction of tea.

The next morning we returned down the narrow valley to Veldes, looking as lovely as ever, and dined—yes, dined, after that leisurely, orderly, civilized fashion, which alone can be called dining. But then instead of a garden-seat in the shade, and the 'Gazzetta di Venezia'—our restless habits being too strong for us,—we ascended the castle rock, peeped into the apartments of the bishop and his chaplains, looked into the private chapel, and strolled round the little plot of garden, fenced by a low wall from the brink of the precipice. What a view for the clerical gentlemen—when once they have got there—into the lake, over the mountains, and down the great valley of the distant Save, lost in quivering heat! At the foot of the rock is a small village; the schoolmaster is the post-master as well as organist to the church, and, while waiting a few minutes in his room, A—— turned over and tried a few pages of a Slovenic mass. She was so pleased with the rich, plaintive, and peculiar character of the composition, that as we were not likely to visit Laibach, where the composer lived, she struck a bargain with the schoolmaster for the possession of his rather tattered copy; and now those sweet strains serve to remind us sometimes of our days of Carniolan travel.

That afternoon we left Veldes for Krainberg, an old town four or five hours' drive down the Save. At about a third of the distance is Radmannsdorf, very picturesquely situated; it is not, however, on the present post route: the valley of the Save is here of great width, and the chief road for traffic keeps along its northern side. Sir Humphry Davy, whose track we were still following, thus speaks of his approach to Radmannsdorf in returning from one of his earliest visits to Wurzen: 'Left the post-road at Assling. The plain between the two chains of mountains is elevated, on the side where it meets the Carinthian mountains, above the valley of the Save, and is rich in pasture, with clumps or hedgerows of trees, walnuts, ash, elm, chestnut, lime, and beech. It is like an English nobleman's park with an intermixture of corn, clover, and maize. There is a fine cliff to the right, topped by a picturesque castle,* and one range of broken hills, and four distinct ranges of mountains—the last, the bare and snowy Terglou. Through the valley the Sava winds, and the meeting of the two waters, the one bright blue, the other sea-green, is distinctly visible. The lowest hills have the same vegetation as the plain; the next range, oak and beech; the third, pines; the fourth, pines and bare rock; the fifth, without any appearance of vegetation—cliffs of

* It is that of Veldes. Sir Humphry at that time had not seen the lake, with which he was afterwards much enchanted. Our own impression of the scenery just described by him is given at p. 265.

marble or masses of snow. By the sides, or upon the bases of the hills are seen beautiful villages with white spires rising amidst trees. Man seems here capable of enjoying life, animated nature is gay, and inanimate nature beautiful and sublime.'

To this no less accurate, than charming description, the one phrase, 'man seems here capable of enjoying life,' imparts a tinge of melancholy; the philosopher must have breathed a sigh, as his pen traced the words. He, the bright ornament of the choicest London society, the possessor of an European reputation, must come to distant Carniola before he can find a spot where 'man seems capable of enjoying life.' There is a touching, though a trite moral in the words. How would the Carniolan peasant endorse the supposition? I have mentioned their low-toned voices, and the pathos of their Sclavonic chants. A writer,* who knows them well, describes their temperament as 'melancholy, compared with the German and Italian, yet shy and diffident rather than uncharitable or ungenerous.' In figure, too, they are tall, slender, with dark hair and a sallow complexion. I am afraid the bright gifts of nature are rather thrown away upon these people, if gladness and happiness be their proper result. But the reader must have noticed how, in this Carniolan landscape, a stern and dreary desolation lurks behind every fair scene; how frequently the bare skeleton protrudes through the flesh! How nature, while she laughs in the valleys, sits in haggard silence on the hills. Severity, therefore, rather than beauty, seems the characteristic feature of the landscape; scenes as beautiful, perhaps, may be found elsewhere—seldom such traits of sombre grandeur. It is with this latter element in their scenery, that the

* A. Paton, 'Danube and the Adriatic,' vol. i. p. 412.

Windisch character seems most to harmonise. Their national temperament finds its key-note here ; and perhaps the beauty of their valleys reminds them only that the bright threads of life are shot upon so dark a texture. Nay, this is the very effect that appears to have been produced upon our philosopher himself. To his own mind the point of his sentence lay doubtless in the 'seems capable;' there was capacity, there were the conditions—but was the result attained after all ?

From Radmannsdorf, as I have already intimated, the Terglou was seen at last in that attitude of majesty which became him. Now he towered towards the sky, and ruled the subject landscape. Here, for the first time his three-headedness was apparent, though it might be better described as a head and two shoulders. The four ranges referred to by Davy were distinctly delineated, and with the richness of the two lowest, the utter bareness of the Terglou masses was finely contrasted. Yet the Save valley itself must not be conceived as a soft and smiling scene of verdure ; it is rather a plain, cut up into deep ravines, and sunken spaces, where villages and fields lie hidden along with the stream ; the road passing up and down among them with many painful hills, deep in true continental dust. Heavy wagons toiled along them, and a costume was prevalent among the men, about the ugliest that can be imagined. I think I remember it in an old book of costumes, on the page headed 'Windisch,' its principal peculiarity being breeches quite open at the knee, from which loose dingy-coloured drawers descend, and are stuffed into squat open-mouthed boots. It is utterly unpicturesque, and has a most slovenly appearance. Whenever we were traversing the upper plateaus of the plain of the Save, their comparative bareness was compensated by the view to the right and left of the bordering mountains, gracefully wooded, sweeping up into isolated cones, and each surmounted by a white church, or monastery;—a landscape, entirely unlike anything English, and radiant in those soft atmospheric tints, which our climate never bestows.

It was longer than we expected before the towers of Krainberg became visible through the dust we raised on the now high road of traffic. We were approaching the district where the Austrian troops lie massed ready for action either in Hungary on the one hand, or Italy on the other; and the villages, were occupied by soldiery, which made us nervous for our night quarters. Another source of uneasiness on the same score, was the information that the bishop of the diocese was at the time holding a visitation at Krainberg. 'Avoid the Post,' said the guide-book. So we passed through the town, and descended a steep hill to the bridge, according to its further directions —only to find the inn there quite full. 'It is the bishop that has filled the town,' we mildly suggested to the stout old landlady, who had been emphatically demonstrating the lack of accommodation. 'Bishop,' said she, with a toss of her head and a tone of amazing contempt, 'we don't care for bishops here!' So we reascended the hill and went humbly to crave admission at the Post itself. There we found not only rooms decent enough, but a young hostess, positively charming, and evidently much younger than Mr. Murray. The change of administration in itself promised well, and so it proved. We fared better there than for many a long day, always excepting Veldes, so that travellers need by no means 'avoid the Post' in future.

Krainberg looks an old town, as far as we could judge by dusk and starlight, and it stands picturesquely on the high bank of the river. We were not to pursue the Save farther. Below the town, the valley widens still more, and takes quite the character of a plain, till it reaches Laibach, about twenty-five miles distant. Our course lay at right angles to the Save, up the country road turning northward, which has been already mentioned as the seventh of the Austrian alpine passes. It is the least known, and the least traversed, of any; a fact which on the morrow we could well understand. It leads across the Karavanken Alps, and along the western face of that mountain group, which we had generalised under the name of the Steiner Alp, and within whose recesses lay the mysterious 'Caldron'—mysterious we might well call it, since nobody of whom we enquired as we came along knew anything about it. Yes, there was one, the son of the old crone at Raibl. He had not seen it, but aptly described the district as a natural fortress, and mentioned the baths of Vellach, not far from Kappel, in Carinthia, as a spot whence it might be scaled. With this exception, every one had professed ignorance of the place. To discover such a spot as Vellach we had long been wishful, as it would save the long circuit, otherwise necessary, by Laibach; Cilli; and thence, by a long day's journey—if it could be done in a day—up the narrowing funnel of the valley, which finally penetrates into the heart of the Steiner.

Even at Krainberg, and at the Post, information was scarce; but then the landlord confessed to having been not long a resident. Still, the continued negatives to our enquiries, even on the threshold of the district itself, concurred, with what little we knew, to throw a very tempting obscurity over this final object of our journey.

CHAPTER XI.

THE CALDRON OF THE STEINER ALP.

The Oistriza Spitze—The 'Caldron' described by Lipold—Departure from Krainberg and Ascent of the Kankerthal—The Hill of the Seeberg—A Giant in the Twilight—Mrs. Popp and Kappel—The Sulzbach Woman—St. Leonhard—Firs of the Caldron—The Widow's Inn—Early Visitors—The Waterfall and the Bauer—The Grenadier and his Comrades—Are we Christians?—The 'Needle's Eye'—Laufen,—The Grenadier makes a Night of it—The Drive to Cilli—Railway Retrospections.

THE railway from Vienna to Trieste crosses the river Drave at Marburg, and about half way between that place and Laibach, the capital of Carniola, passes the town of Cilli. 'Here,' says 'Murray,' 'the Oistriza Spitze, 7,704 feet high, near Sulzbach, a mountain situated between Styria, Carniola, and Carinthia, on whose top rests perpetual snow, is seen in a westerly direction.' No further information is given respecting this remote and final member of the snow-covered Alps, or of the country at its foot. It is to this outlying mountain district that we now ask the reader to accompany us—regretting, however, that we can afford him but a passing glance, as it was all we had ourselves, of a singular region.

The passage above quoted, although quite sufficient to attract the notice of any mountain enthusiast, had not been our sole inducement to explore the neighbourhood of the Oistriza. We had other, more detailed, and more stimulating information, derived from the 'Transactions of the Geological Society of Vienna, for 1856.' A paper in that volume thus describes the visit of Herr Lipold to this district, which he approached from the side of Cilli:—

'On the triple boundary of Carinthia, Carniola, and Styria, the limestone Alps rise up into a mighty mountain "massif" (Gebirgstock), which in each province takes a different name: in Carinthia, that of the Vellacher Kotschna; in Carniola, that of the Steiner Alp; in Styria, that of the Sulzbacher Alp. The group reaches its greatest height, of 8,625 feet, in the Grintouz. Although the Vellacher Kotschna belongs to the finest portion of the Carinthian limestone range, and the Steiner Alp has an imposing aspect seen from the Carniolan plain, the Sulzbacher Alp excels them both in beauty of form and in grandeur, when approached through the valley of Sulzbach.

'The village of Sulzbach, 2,145 English feet above the Adriatic, lies in a mountain caldron, traversed by the river Sann; and can only be reached, either by passing, near Leutschdorf, through a rock chink—the so-called "Needle eye"—only three feet wide, and many fathoms above the bed of the stream, forming the entrance to a very narrow gorge; or by mountain passes from Carinthia and Carniola. Of these, the pass leading into the Caldron from the Wistra Thal, in Carinthia, is 4,252 feet; that from Koprein, on the north, 4,414 feet; that from Kappel, 4,458 feet; that from Bad Vellach, 4,416 feet; and finally, that from Stein, on the Carniolan side, 6,197 feet, above the sea. The Caldron is shut in on every side by high mountain peaks, of which the Raducha, on the NE., rises to the height of 6,720 feet; the Oushova, on the N., to 6,300 feet; the Merslagora, on the W., to above 7,300 feet; and the Oistriza, on the SE., to 7,701 feet. Beyond Sulzbach, another narrow gorge, rich in picturesque rock scenery, leads upward still. At the end of an hour the traveller is surprised by its sudden expansion, and finds himself in the finest part of this valley, so varied in natural beauty. This is the Logar Thal, about five miles long, and half a mile broad, 2,500 feet above the sea, stretching from north to south, and hemmed in east, west, and south by lofty precipices. The contrast between the level valley, and these mountain masses is extraordinary; for while the valley, rendered cheerful by its scattered farm-houses, shows luxuriant vegetation, and by the alternation of arable, meadow, and wood, produces a friendly impression; the grey limestone masses around are fearful in the abruptness with which they rise more than 5,000 feet above, partly in precipitous walls, partly in a countless variety of peaks and pinnacles, among which the Oistriza, Skaria, Skuta, Szinka, and Mersla, are the more prominent. Numerous waterfalls throw themselves over these precipices: that of the Plessnig above the farmhouse of that name, remarkable through its similarity to the Schleier fall at Nassfeld, near Gastein; and the Szinka, in the uppermost corner of the valley, from its height and volume of water. The Szinka fall, 1,000 feet high, is also to be noted as the special source of the Sann, although its waters, almost as soon as they reach the valley, lose themselves in the earth, and only come to light close to the "Logar" farm-house, yet in such strength as to drive a saw-mill.

'The colossal mountain "massif" which thus encloses the sources of the Sann, and whose almost inaccessible peaks still shelter numerous chamois, while their deep gullies serve as a refuge for bears, presents much variety in a geological point of view. The eruption of plutonic rocks, such as diorite, porphyry, and basalt, especially at Leutschdorf, has brought about great disturbance in the bedding of the sedimentary rocks, and has led to the great upheaval of the latter above the sea level. Most of the Sulzbach

Alps are composed of members of the Carboniferous and Trias formations—that is to say, of Gailthal limestone and schists, and of Werfen, Guttenstein, and Hallstadt beds. Only on the highest ridges are the Dachstein beds of the Lower Lias to be seen. Newer formations are nowhere present.'

There was here, as the reader will allow, enough to excite much curiosity about the Caldron of the Steiner Alp. At Krainberg we were as far to the south-west of it as Cilli is to the south-east; and were about, therefore, to attack the 'natural fortress' from the opposite side to that from which Herr Lipold gained access. We asked for a vehicle of some sort to the Baths of Vellach. Much consultation, and shaking of heads ensued. A man who was sent for to furnish information, reported that two heavy passes, which an ordinary carriage could not possibly surmount, barred the way; and that light country cars could alone be used. We were well accustomed to these, but saw there must be something unusual in prospect when the blacksmith came to attach to each of those intended for us a double set of slippers.

On leaving Krainberg—Friday morning, September 6—an extensive view presented itself over the whole valley of the Save; for the town stands, as I have mentioned, on the edge of the ravine in which the river flows, and the road keeps along the elevated plain. The long ranges of mountains on either hand stretched into hazy distance; those to the north, for which we were bound, being much the more lofty. They constituted part of that range already frequently referred to—the Karavanken Alps,—which forms the southern boundary of Carinthia, and separates the Drave country from that of the Save. At this time we had not visited Klagenfurt, and were unacquainted with the marked importance of the Karavanken in its landscape; and though familiar with that portion of them which lines the upper Save on the north, their inferiority there to the opposite Julian Alps deprived them of the attention they deserved. Farther to the east they are more imposing: the Stou was a fine object from the Lake of Veldes; the Loibl Pass crossing them lower down is noted for its scenery; and here there rose before us the partially-veiled form of the Grintouz, a truly noble spectacle. This mountain answers on the western side of the Steiner group, to the Oistriza on the eastern; and the Caldron itself belongs to the Karavanken. To the south of us there was no such mountain mass as the Grintouz. The Terglou is the last dominating object on that side of the Save, and was now but faintly, though still grandly, defined in the distance.

It was refreshing, even after so short an experience of a dusty and traffic-worn road, to find ourselves on a hard-bottomed country track, bordered with meadows, and bearing right away across the broad valley to the blue mountain foot. Where it should find entrance there was long undiscovered; but at the end of an hour we were received once more to the bosom of the hills, shut up within a deep and green recess, flowers yet wet with morning dew fringing the untravelled road, rocks glistening above in clear light, or dark below with the umbrage of thick woods, and a pure stream leaping along the bottom, laving roots and stones, and flinging hither and thither lapfuls of watery pearls. To our taste all this verdurous Alpine beauty was delightful. We were ascending the Kankerthal, which here penetrates the Karavanken, and in about two and a half hours from Krainberg, reached the village of Kanker, which is, however, little more than the inn of that name. From the moment of entering the mountains the road was remarkably solitary.

From Kanker, the Grintouz, which we had lost after crossing the plain, was again visible, and now overhead,—impending and mysterious, in a robe of cloud. The road wound steeply up close at the base, compelling the temporary use of a 'vorspan,' this being the first of the 'bergs' or passes of which we had been warned. An upper valley, long and narrow, succeeded, hemmed in between the spurs of the Storsitsch on the left, and those of the Grintouz on the right. Here we frequently passed iron-works deep among trees; most, if not all, of them out of use, so that neither smoke nor noise disturbed the rich seclusion. A curious feature common to these sequestered foundries was the figure of a saint surmounting the top of each blackened chimney. Cassock and mitre looked rather ruefully begrimed, but in England the holy personages would have been black as sweeps. The effigies, constructed apparently of sheet iron, had once been gaily painted.

From this long valley, another lift introduced us by mid-day to Ober Seeland, a beautiful hollow, green and sparkling, where two or three villages sat pleasantly about the meadows, and the Grintouz towered magnificently above. With our entrance upon this basin-like expanse we had also entered Carinthia; yet the principal mountain barrier was still in front, the streams still ran southward to the Save, and, looking forward, a yellow perpendicular streak upon the dense, forest-covered hill, which for some time we took for a water-course or a timber-slide, turned out to be the road by which that barrier must be surmounted. At the foot of it our drivers drew up for a long halt, at a house which looked more of a farm than an inn.

This open valley, holding, as in the scoop of a hand, a wealth of rural life aloft among the glorious mountains, was so charming, that it was a great disappointment to find the inn affording scarcely possible quarters for a lengthened stay, should we ever return to it. And, besides, no one spoke anything but dreadful Sclavonic—all k's and z's. Our drivers themselves knew scarcely a word of German, and it was with difficulty we got anything to eat, the people being all, as it seemed to us, excessively stupid. Ah! but nature smiled, and made amends right lovingly to her votaries, spreading around, her brightest carpet of soft-bladed grass, draping the hills with her richest tapestry of woods; and if she reared above them awful walls of verdureless rock, it was surely to shut off this favoured spot from the great world without, and keep it ever fresh and fair. From the Grintouz, now standing to the south, a range of the hardest precipices circled round upon the east, connecting his detached bulk with the mass of the Steiner group.

After a couple of hours' delay the two horses were yoked to one of the light cars; two tawny bullocks from the farm—immense but innocent-looking creatures—were attached to the other, and the ascent began. In the hot afternoon, and with this ample draught power, we thought we might allow ourselves to be pulled up any hill; but a few minutes' experience of the perpendicular gutter, called a road, turned us out upon our feet, as well to relieve the straining beasts of our weight, as ourselves from the sensation of being dragged at their tails head downwards. We can all aver we never saw such a hill in our lives. The bare notion of a travelling carriage getting either up or down it is a joke, only to be appreciated, however, on the spot. It was a *succession* of steeps; at each supposed crowning of the hill we were at the foot of another just as steep. The whole goes by the name of the Seeberg.

At last upon the summit! It is a meeting-place, more frequently, I suspect, than not, among the clouds, for whatever traffic is upon the pass. A few sheds, and a cottage or two, men and horses resting themselves—that was all we found there; and for view—woods—woods—woods—sloping downward out of sight, and scattering thinly above, upon the sides of conical hills, which hid most of the rocky and snow-streaked mountains. The bullocks were unyoked, all the slippers, chains, and breaks adjusted, and we seated ourselves for the descent. But to see the horses sliding down upon their haunches, and to feel the carriages slipping sideways, till they were sometimes almost hind-part foremost, was worse than before; and we were quickly out again. It had seemed as if there would be never a top to the hill we had climbed; there might be never a bottom to that we were descending. Knees ached with the continued strain; and the carriages above, scraping down in an absurdly helpless manner, reminded us of their difficulties, by dislodged stones rolling at our heels, or sudden sounds that seemed to say the crash had come at last. There is an end to everything, and so, in time, there was an end to the hill, its desperate pitches subsiding into a deep and narrow valley, thick with trees. There was scarcely a sign of habitation, and we began to consider where the Vellach Bad could be, at which, according to every computation, we ought before now to have arrived.

Still the drivers jogged silently on. We had long given up attempting to extract from their Sclavonic minds any serviceable information, and were becoming dull with the monotony of scene and movement, when a curious object started to view. Upon a face of rock which seemed to bar the road, there suddenly appeared a gigantic figure, rising above the trees, and illumined by the reflected glow of evening. Now, giants of old time were not favourable to travellers. Fortunately, in this case, the giant was a saint—no other than honest St. Christopher, bearing 'the child' upon his brawny shoulders, and preparing, with his oak sapling, to ford the stream which here flowed so appropriately at his feet. He had been evidently freshly painted or retouched, and shone bright with colour. We had often met with the saint on church walls—for the legend, as it deserves, is a favourite one in these lands of streams and forests—but never had we encountered the good fellow in a veritable solitude like this, and on a spot that might have been the actual scene of his strange adventure. In the darker shades of evening, or fitfully irradiated by moonbeams, the unexpected apparition might prove not a little startling to a lonely wayfarer.

Not far beyond, where the valley lay a little more open, the double towers of a church in the distance gave promise of a town, and we presently entered a considerable street. The drivers nearly cleared the houses again, before they stopped in front of a low but fair-looking inn, with a strong granary smell, and passage and staircase white with flour. A Mrs. Popp was the proprietor—a pleasant, matronly body. She gave us two good-sized rooms, and seemed to have liberal notions respecting supper. I think it was the next day before we accidentally discovered that we were not at Vellach, but at Kappel! The former—a cluster of rough bathing-houses, shut up and forlorn, and nearly hidden by trees—we had passed unnoticed, about five miles back on our route. The men had good reason, certainly, for not setting us down there, though that was the bargain, as far as we knew. Most likely they had all along intended to take us to Kappel, leaving our benighted selves to talk about Vellach as much as we pleased.*

Rather than sup in the dignified seclusion of a bedroom, we descended to the Speise Saal below. It was small, smoky, and many ways disagreeable. The evening habitués—the priest, the doctor, the lawyer, as they might be, and a few others, all boon companions—were noisy, and rather rudely curious; but we had our advantage in presently obtaining information from the only one among them who, even here, knew anything of the Caldron, and its village of Sulzbach. It was satisfactory to learn that there was now a small inn at the village. Herr Lipold could only lodge at the curé's. Also, that as the people were in the habit of coming over to Kappel on a Saturday to supply themselves with various necessary articles, we might, this being Friday, avail ourselves on the morrow of their returning parties to carry our baggage and show the way. 'And mind,' said our informant, 'to take with you as much meat as you are likely to want during your stay: it's a strange spot.' 'Are there still bears in the mountains?' we enquired. 'You are not likely to meet with any,' was the reply. 'Not likely!' S—— and A—— would have preferred a more decided negative.

In the morning some of the Sulzbach people were hunted up—three men and a woman—the latter a bonny

* A few figures illustrating the different levels on our route from Krainberg may interest some readers. Krainberg is 1,200 feet, the church of Ober Seeland 3,026 feet, and the summit of the Seeberg Pass 4,100 feet above the sea. On the northern or Carinthian slope, Bad Vellach, which lies immediately at the foot of the Seeberg, is 2,831 feet, Kappel 1,794, and Völkermarkt 1,526 feet above the sea. Völkermarkt occupies the same relative position on the Drave as Krainberg on the Save. It follows from these data that the difference of level between the plains of the Drave and Save amounts to more than 300 feet.

creature worth all the others. Dressed in a short blue petticoat, a red handkerchief crossed over her bosom, white sleeves, and a round, broad-brimmed waggoner's hat, she stood laughing at the solemn looks of the men, as they lifted and pondered over the weightier articles of our baggage. Thrusting at last the heaviest into her own creel, and raising it and herself together, with no other aid than her own stout stick she started gaily alone for the march, beckoning S—— and A—— to follow. Burden and all, she stooped to kiss a child or two in the street, and to distribute handfuls of 'sweeties' among her favourites as she passed along.

Churchill and I were obliged to wait the pleasure of the slower-minded peasants, and while kicking our heels before the door were accosted by a tall priest, whose black cassock showed his fine figure to advantage, while his handsome features were set off by a military gold-laced cap—a phenomenon explained by the fact that he was an army chaplain on furlough. He had been much puzzled by seeing our ladies and the Sulzbach woman trudging off alone for the mountain. Our appearance somewhat relieved his mind of the difficulty, and still more the discovery that we were English. We almost expected to be again associated with Turks; but he only complimented us all upon our 'strong legs,' and predicted long life for such adventurous walkers.

We left Kappel by the same end that we had entered it, but soon turned off to the left. Kappel is a pleasant little town, set among woodland hills, where, however, blue wreaths of smoke, high up against the sky, show that the charcoal-burners are at work. The valley is an offshoot from that of the Drave, and, from the rough nature of the Seeberg pass, must be practically almost a *cul de sac.* Völkermarkt is the point on the Drave from which the Kappel road strikes off, and a post-cart, offering but two seats besides that of the driver, goes to Kappel and back every day. The Gross Obir, a mountain of great fame among the Austrian botanists, and a fine object from the neighbourhood of Klagenfurt, rises from a lateral valley to the west of the town, to which it must be of much importance, on account of the extensive lead mines near its summit. Botany was now over for the season, but the Gross Obir brought Churchill here the following year in time to avail himself of its treasures.* The mines and plants of the Obir, the rude baths of Vellach, and perhaps a little traffic over the Seeberg, are probably the sole inducements which bring people to Kappel.

We had walked an hour, after leaving the road, up a charcoal-cart track, and through picturesque clefts of rock, down which a stream tumbled, before overtaking our wives and the Sulzbach woman, all resting under a tree. The latter was in lively flirtation with a charcoal-burner, Sclavonic appearing to afford as much facility for that kind of thing as any other form of human speech. For a parting pleasantry the charcoal man clapped his two black hands on each side of the lady's face. It was very promptly resented upon his ears, and the march delayed till the offended cheeks had been well scrubbed in the stream. All around was very solitary—nothing but bush or tracts of pine stumps, where the axe had been, or belts of fir wood, which the axe had spared. Upon the stream we had passed occasionally a small mill, scarcely bigger than a sentry-box, but thumping busily; now, upon the hill-sides, the only objects were a quaint shrine or two, placed where an open space of grass invited rest. Near one of these, a plentiful display of blackberries revived

* See A——'s letters.

the schoolboy delights of an English lane, and supplied the want of water on these hot and thirsty steeps. In three hours we had nearly topped the hills, and were walking in pleasant air along their ascending ridges, where, sheltered by a sloping pine forest above, and clustered upon a smiling plot of green, appeared the hamlet of St. Leonhard.

A chapel dedicated to the saint occupied a grassy mound, and there the whole party—eight in all—sat down to rest and enjoy the milk, cheese, and bread which the dame of a neighbouring cottage was not long in supplying. The view from this elevated spot, though not remarkable, was interesting. The open country towards Klagenfurt was visible over the hills to the north-west, and south of that stretched, in long perspective, the numerous peaks of the Koschutta Gebirge, a portion of the Karavanken in near neighbourhood of the Loibl Pass. Eastward, and close at hand, was a lofty rocky ridge—the Oushova; and this was the most attractive portion of the prospect, since that mountain forms one of the outworks of the Steiner group, while, from the appearance of the forest above, we judged that a view into the Caldron itself could not be far distant. A rusty chain, supported on hooks, was carried round the walls of the chapel. All the explanation we could get was, that this was St. Leonhard's; and the chain, probably, bore reference to his martyrdom. Unfortunately, in carelessly handling the chain at a corner out of sight from the village, it broke under my sacrilegious touch, and dropped to the ground. I was sincerely sorry, but trusted that if either the saint or the Evil One had anything to say about it, the wandering Protestant would be held alone responsible.

Above St. Leonhard's, we were soon among the tall

stems of the pines, and, before long, nearing the crest of the long-defiant hill. The view came in a moment. The trees thinned away; there was an open space of heather and fern, and then, as if carved out of purple clouds, the Caldron lay at our feet. It was one of those scenes which memory can reproduce at will; nay, sometimes, when least expected, it flashes into sight, as if its colours, dissolved into the substance of the brain, required but a breath to bring them out clear upon the retina. I see it now; but if you wish to possess a similar picture, there is nothing for it but to climb the heights of St. Leonhard, and look for yourself into the great Caldron of Sulzbach.

The valley, after penetrating from the east for many miles as a wonderfully deep and narrow gorge into the centre of a mass of limestone mountains, breaks finally in their midst into three heads, all turning southward, parallel to each other, separated by spiny ridges, and all included within the 'Caldron.' The first leads to the base of the Oistriza, the second to the Skuta Vrh, the third to the Merslagora Vrh. The Grintouz stands beyond these outworks of the great citadel. The middle branch is the true head of the valley, and contains the source of the Sann.

From our station on the heights of St. Leonhard, we looked directly down upon, and along, the second and third of these vast troughs or hollows, out of which the mountains rose with a wave-like sweep, rearing crest above crest, and soaring their highest, eastward in the Oistriza, westward in the Grintouz. The singularity and grandeur of the view consisted in the complete command of the bifurcated valley, and the horse-shoe rim of mountains, seen not too near for oneness of impression, not too far off for detail. The mountain-sides were, for the most part, thickly wooded, and the thin smoke-wreaths of the charcoal fires, floating upwards into the noontide atmosphere, bestowed that final touch of grace which Turner introduced so well upon his sunlighted distances. It was a grief, however, to observe the result in many bare strips and spaces where lately there was unbroken forest. The Oistriza, the most prominent of the mountain masses, of course disdained all covering for his iron shoulders, except a slight vesture of snow. In him there was all that rigid mural aspect to which Dolomite had so long accustomed us. One other mighty object must be mentioned to complete the idea of the Caldron. This was the Raducha, a vast spiny ridge projecting from that on which we stood, and blocking up all view eastward. It is the principal object from the village of Sulzbach itself, and the last lofty mass of the Karavanken Alps.

Not a single village graced this scene, extensive as it was—only here and there a farm-house, so far as we could make out specks of white among clumps of trees. Sulzbach, deep at our feet, lay concealed in the throat of the valley. The waterfall, mentioned by Lipold as the source of the Sann, was known to all our people, and visible even here to their keen mountain sight. Our good peasantess took great but fruitless pains to point it out at the valley-head.

From this spot,—no doubt the true point of view for the Caldron, and where, at the first step downward, we passed from Carinthia into Styria,—we descended at a rapid pace by precipitous wood-paths, and an alp fully as steep, towards a small chapel on the brow, named 'Heiligengeist,' for use of a few houses on the slopes. These habitations, farms rather than châlets, indicated a more substantial class of peasantry than is usual among mountains. Even from the brow nothing of Sulzbach could be seen—nothing but a blue depth. Over the edge we went, scrambling down the steepest of bosky paths, which twisted and dropped from bluff to bluff; and still from each craggy brink we craned over in vain for a sight of Sulzbach. The hill-sides opposite closed in nearer and nearer, and the grip between sunk deeper. The bottom, reached at length, was just the stream, and a slip of meadow here and there, where the stern crags allowed; and half a mile or so below, Sulzbach showed itself at last, a village of a few decent-sized houses, where a sudden opening broke away northwards and let in light and air.

The inn—a house which had only taken that name to itself within the last two or three years—was kept by a buxom widow, who, folding her arms, looked at us with an amused expression of countenance, as much as to say, 'Travellers! the idea!' and who, when told we might stay a few days, received the information with a shrug and a pout, that made us feel we had taken an absurd liberty. True, we had brought some meat with us; but there was the trouble of cooking it, don't you see? which we had certainly not considered. One small room, with three beds in very disorderly condition, and one large room with none, and furnished only with a fixed bench round the walls, tables, and large boxes, were the only accommodation; and we should have fared ill with the impassible landlady had not our porteress, notwithstanding her eight hours of heavy toil over the hill, set herself briskly to work to improvise beds for the great room, and rummage all the stores. German was at as great a discount as ever; but we had by this time constructed a brief Sclavonic vocabulary, which enabled us to make known the simplest of our wants.

At this comfortless inn we had to spend an afternoon of storm and rain. The Grintouz had been the only angry spot in the grand prospect of the morning, and now he flung upon the valley the tempest he had gathered; while we four unlucky strangers from the west sat ruefully together in the great room, till the darkness of storm was succeeded by the darkness of night, and an evil-looking face, painted on a clock-case, whose eyes at every tick turned in their whites from side to side, lost its ugly fascination in the gloom. Churchill's bed, on the lid of a large box, was under this mechanical demon; its tick-a-tack might mix with his dreams, but it rolled its eyes quite ineffectually over his night's slumbers.

Next morning we were breakfasting under the villainous optics, when the village street, and the house below, began to fill with people. It was a bright Sunday morning, and there were all the signs of a *festa*—that plague of all Sundays. Presently the door opened, and two tall handsome fellows, in embroidered jackets, black velveteen breeches, and long Carniolan boots, strode into the room, and upsetting Churchill's improvised couch, proceeded to open the box, and extract various articles of attire. The original purpose was to change their shirts, but, looking over their shoulders at S—— and A——, they faltered in mid process, held perplexed conference in whispers, and finally compounded the matter by putting on the clean shirt over the dirty one—not a very comfortable arrangement for a hot gala-day. It was clearly better to absent ourselves, and a prepossessing young fellow—who, having served in the Austrian army, could speak a little German—undertook to show us the way to the waterfall. So we told our singular hostess that she would not see us again till evening; and as group after group of holiday-dressed people met us in our walk up the valley, we were glad to think we should find quietness in the remote recesses of the glen.

Till we reached the point where the valley branched off

to the Oistriza, it was the narrow ravine I have described; then it became smiling meadow bottom, diversified by woods, which had slipped into it, as it were, from the heights above. A bauer's, or small farmer's, cottage could provide us, we were told, with bread and coffee; but we continued our stroll, and found but one other habitation in all the further stretch of valley. This was a respectable farm-house, with one of those large ornamental trellis-work barns attached, of which the sketch below is a specimen. These erections give a quaint richness to Styrian landscape; and here the cluster of rural buildings set upon a level plot of shaven grass, whence the woods rose skyward, backed by the great Oistriza, whose ledges of snow glittered in the sun, formed a perfect picture of a secluded homestead.

STYRIAN BARN.

Beyond, wood followed wood, and the circling walls which closed in the valley showed their stern fronts. The waterfall was amongst them; and after we had spent some time upon a felled tree-trunk, enjoying the stillness of the day and scene, Churchill and I went on with the guide to search it out among the foliaged crags. We had for some time suspected a flaw somewhere in the glowing narrative of our Vienna geologist. The small quantity of water in the tangled stream-bed we were pursuing confirmed our suspicions; and when at last we spied a thread of water dribbling down the rocks, and were assured it was the great cascade of the valley, we turned back in disgust. Either these people don't know what a torrent is, and so think much of their one waterfall, or the unusually dry season had robbed it of its proper proportions. Herr Lipold's account leads one to suppose the latter. Having spoken so warmly of the view of the Caldron from its rim, we can afford to admit this disappointment in its waterfall.

The bauer, proprietor of Plessnig, the last farm of the valley, was a young man of very pleasant aspect; we met him returning early and 'doucely' from the *fête*. The peasant owning the cottage, where on our return we thought to refresh ourselves with coffee and a loaf, answered more to our English notion of a 'bauer,' that is to say a *boor*. He assailed us with violent execrations as we approached. They were, of course, entirely unintelligible to us, and the weight both of attack and defence fell upon our companion, who responded vigorously. He was accused of having left a gate unfastened, by which certain pigs had obtained entrance to the potato plot; the intention was simply to make us pay for somebody else's carelessness. Our ignorance of Sclavonic was a great convenience, but there was no mistaking the tone of the vocables flung after us by the entire family as we passed on. It was the only instance we encountered of that rudeness which Sir H. Davy experienced upon one occasion from the peasantry of the adjoining district; * from which, as will be told, a learned Professor suffered on his search after the *Wulfenia*; and of which, doubtless, Goldsmith had some feeling recollection. The man was evidently a well-known churl, for the story repeated to every group we met, was received with much merriment. The mention of several peasant groups may seem inconsistent with the paucity of habitations spoken of; but there was something of a hamlet at the point of junction with the main valley, and there might be farms out of sight in its farther branch.

We had ordered an early supper—or late dinner—at the inn, hoping that by that time the company would have dispersed, and our guide hastened on to Sulzbach to help in its preparation, knowing well perhaps what was likely to be going on there. The place was in truth filled by a noisy crowd, of which the inn was the centre, and the great room, our sole refectory, and the Churchills' sleeping chamber, cleared of all their possessions, was given up to riotous dancing. It was impossible to enter, and, though tired and hungry, our only resource was to wander and wait among the trees outside the village till, by the efforts of our guide and the good-natured portress, who, to our comfort, had again turned up, the revellers could be dislodged.

But we had not done with them then; anybody who could speak a little German felt bound to introduce himself, each volunteering as an excuse some little fact of his history. This, had seen an Englishman once in Venice; the other, had been wounded in Hungary in the war of 1849. Our principal visitor was a ci devant grenadier—

* Sir H. Davy was assaulted and roughly handled for having crossed some meadows. He complained to the authorities, who promptly interfered, and inflicted a fine upon the commune.

oh, that grenadier! twenty times he rapped his broad chest, repeating 'Grenadier, grenadier,' as if we had not sufficiently apprehended the fact; and twenty times over extolled his general, Radetzky,—'Father of his soldiers, father of his soldiers,' till his fuddled voice almost broke into sobs. Then drawing his stool closer, he would confide to us the fact that the landlady was very rich, 'a widow, very rich, and only two children!' We believe, indeed, that this circumstance accounted in measure for the throng of men about the house; they were half of them suitors. They came rushing up one after another to hand a plate, or bring a chair, in ludicrous competition; more than one informing us in stage whispers, when the lady's back was turned, what a catch she was.

Dinner over, we hoped for quiet. Few minutes, however, elapsed before the grenadier again presented his person, on plea of arranging for the porterage, by himself and two or three others, of our baggage on the morrow—for we had made up our minds to go. With infinite trouble the terms and the time were settled, and our friend descended. A few minutes more, and another stalwart fellow entered, announced himself as comrade of the grenadier, and engaged in our service; thereupon proceeding to an elaborate recapitulation of the terms, followed by an interval of profound meditation upon the same; after which, taking up his hat, he departed. Then a third heavy footstep was heard upon the stairs, a third knock at the door, and a third tall figure darkened the threshold. His errand was the same; and the conference proceeded through the like slow stages of explanation, reflection, and exit. Surely it is all right now! No, behold the grenadier again, there is still a difficulty; and at last it turns out that one o'clock after mid-day had been mistaken for one o'clock after midnight, and they naturally thought daylight would be preferable over the rough paths.

That matter explained, we were left alone for rather a longer interval than usual, when a rush upon the stairs sounded as if all the suitors were coming in at once—and so they were; the grenadier, of course, at the head of his company. 'Here,' cried he, 'here is a great bird of the mountains, very big, very scarce, trapped only today, very good to eat; what will you give for it?' Now it is not usual to purchase one's provisions in this fashion when staying at an inn, but it seemed to be expected here; and our stock of meat had proved so unsatisfactory that we were glad to make any addition to our stores. So we paid a gulden for a fine specimen of a female capercailzie, and very good we found it next day at an early meal.

Our best course now, we thought, was to lock our doors and go to bed, trusting that the noise below would subside as the night advanced. Not at all! 'Penelope's suitors' were making a night of it—or the porters were celebrating with their friends their novel engagement. Song succeeded song, cheers, shouts, and thumping of tables; and though one and another were heard stumbling off in the darkness from time to time, their wild *jodels* dying away in the distance, enough remained to keep it up—and without doubt the grenadier, whose stentorian voice was always in the ascendant—till morning light disturbed the revel, and the last half-dozen topers trooped out to the water-trough to souse their faces. After such a night, during which we above stairs had lain without a wink of sleep, we rather expected to find the grenadier and his friends in not the best condition for their work; but their ablutions had put them all to rights, and they would have shouldered their creels, and marched off with our baggage directly after breakfast, had they not been seen and stopped.

We had determined to go, principally because the distance to Cilli, where we should take the railway for Vienna, was rather too far to accomplish in a single day. There were in fact twelve or fourteen miles of rough walking through the long neck of this singular valley, before we should reach, at Laufen, a road upon which wheels could run, and then there would still remain some forty miles to Cilli. So we agreed to take the chance of night quarters at Laufen, and not to start till the afternoon of the day, employing the time to obtain a sketch or two. The great Raducha looked magnificent to the eastward, and from the opening below Sulzbach, a vista of farm-sprinkled slopes was closed grandly by the Oushova.

I was sketching the first of these scenes, and soon, as usual, surrounded by a group of men, women, and children, all squandering on the grass, when the schoolmaster of the village good-naturedly advanced with an umbrella to shade me from the sun. Presently an animated discussion arose among the company—its purport of course all unknown to me, till, amidst a sudden silence, the schoolmaster addressed me in German with the question: 'Do you believe in Christ?' 'You mean,' said I, 'do we in England believe in Christ?' He nodded. Asserting as emphatically as I could that we were Christians like themselves, I added, by way of confirmation—and with uncovered head suiting the action to the word—that in England it was our custom in church to bow at the name of Christ. This information renewed the discussion, but I trust they will have a little better opinion in future of the faith of Protestants.

By one o'clock, having picked the bones of our bird, we were ready for the march, and our three fellows—they preferred not to have a fourth, and their broad backs seemed equal to anything—led off in line, jolly companions every one. It was a charming afternoon; but as it was to be our last walk a mingled feeling took possession of us. There was something of regret at saying good-bye to the mountains and their rough folk; and something of the pleasure of going home, though that was yet a long way off, and our course lay still in an opposite direction. The only exit from the Caldron was through the long gully pointing eastward, unless we returned as we came, by climbing over its rim.

A foot-bridge, with a queer little wooden saint shrined in the middle, leads out of Sulzbach, then the path skirts the stream along pleasant slips of green for some distance, always with the mighty Raducha frontwise, or endways, on the left. The narrow entrance of the third fork of the valley is soon passed on the right, leading to the Oistriza; it is one which, with that at the furthest extremity of the Sulzbach system turning towards the Merslagora, we should certainly explore should we ever find ourselves in this labyrinth again. The labyrinthine character is due to the exceeding narrowness and very tortuous course of the valley bottom, and we soon realised, far more than we had yet done, the isolated position of the Caldron, as the path was squeezed through gorge after gorge, where for a moment all passage seemed denied. Here there was no longer a green margin to the water, but the path climbed painfully up the precipitous sides and round craggy corners. One such spot, and nearly the last, is that referred to by Lipold, and is certainly very remarkable. Narrow ledges and rough staircases support the track till it penetrates the rock through a mere cleft—'The Needle's Eye,' as it is called. Our porters, with their bulging loads, successively quite filled the gap, and seemed to thread the 'eye' with difficulty. Looking back after a few yards, no trace of an entrance could be discovered. This sealed-up opening, and the chasm passages beyond it, well sustain the character of seclusion which belongs to the Sulzbach valleys.

But the ups and downs did not agree with the grenadier, who 'larded the lean earth' as he went along, and was inclined to be rather crusty at having to foot it on so hot an afternoon. In about three hours, it should perhaps be only two of good walking, we reached the first village—almost the first house—after leaving Sulzbach. There had indeed been room for none before, but here an expansion of the valley left space for Leutschdorf, where our three troopers stooped under the lintel of a wine-shop door, and slipping off their loads intimated they should rest and refresh. At this point the valley changed both its character and its course. It had been rounding the end of the Raducha, among the roots of which it had been struggling and working southwards hitherto, and now turned with a freer channel to the north-east. We left our men to come after us as they pleased, and kept on at a steady pace among rounded and sparsely-covered hills, with the Raducha constantly in view behind us, and the crest of the Oistriza just showing to the west. We had in fact at last emerged from the recesses of the Steiner mountains, and their giant shapes were beginning to show 'en bloc.'

But the windings of the stream, and the closing hills, and the failing light, soon deprived us of this view, and the walk became a plod amidst a sameness of umbery tints—sometimes by the water, sometimes on a stony hill-side, sometimes through a wood. It was nearly seven, and entirely dusk, before we entered Laufen, a village sprinkled over a tree-shaded plateau, and whose inn we found with difficulty.

We took heart at the sight of a comfortable, capable-looking old lady, inclined to bestir herself, and showing us, when she had found her keys, two clean and decent rooms. Yet appearances were deceptive. We ventured to urge an early supper, as our bird at twelve o'clock had proved remarkably light of digestion; but the delays and mismanagement of everything were dismal. The meal came in driblets; we had finished the fish before the bread appeared, and the bread before the butter, and all before the coffee, of which last poor S—— and A——, after their fourteen miles' walk, were sorely in need.

And then, the grenadier was in the kitchen! too surely we recognised that ponderous voice. He and the others had clattered in about an hour after us, had received their pay and largess, and we hoped by this time were fairly tired out. But the fun was beginning: Laufen had assembled to welcome Sulzbach. The grenadier was great that night; some Laufen hero was there to match him, and he rose in glory as the clock went round. It will be long remembered by them—and by us. Churchill was for making desperate incursion upon the company with an appeal to the sacredness of the night-cap; but who could hope to stay victory in its tide of conquest? who the flow of those mighty bumpers? So we turned and grinned upon our pillows, and discussed our sorrows through the wainscot. In the morning, to add insult to injury, the cost of the entertainment appeared footed to the bill, whereat our wrath rose so high that the landlady discreetly withdrew the offensive item.

They were all gone by morning light, and though we have no wish to encounter the Sulzbach men again, we often wonder how the wooing has fared. To this hour we are divided in opinion as to 'Penelope's' final choice. If she be wise, the little woman will eschew the grenadier. Our sympathies go with the quiet fellow who accompanied us to the waterfall, and who was certainly far the most handy and assiduous about the house.

Some hours passed before horses and a vehicle could be hunted up; it was a straw-seated waggonet, and took some time to prepare. Meanwhile we were rather sorrowfully occupied in packing away our mountain paraphernalia, and in trimming up town habiliments. A stroll about the village showed it to be pleasantly situated, and possessing an unusual feature in a large open green, studded with fine old oaks, under whose shade the cottage doors were invitingly sheltered. A pilgrimage-looking church shone white upon a hill, and in the distance to the west rose the rocky barrier of the Caldron—one huge stony mass in particular, the Raducha, representing in this direction the last bulwark of the Alps; eastward now, lay the plains of Hungary, and then—the Carpathians.

With two heavy farm-horses we started for Cilli about eleven o'clock. At the leisurely pace they took, it was seven at night before we reached it,—all down a widening valley, expanding till it was almost a plain, and a cluster of dark peaks on the backward horizon alone remained of the mountain world. The day was pleasant, with a fresh autumn feel in the air. Gardens, gay with dahlias and China-asters, orchards laden with plums, corn plots with the harvest all gathered, low hills covered with wood, crowned with small white churches by the dozen, and stretching into bazy, sunshiny distance on either hand; a river flowing broadly in the centre, and bearing innumerable timber-logs, to be formed lower down into rafts for the navigation of the Save and Danube;—such was this Styrian landscape. This was to be our last drive, as the previous afternoon had seen our last walk, and we chatted over all our Dolomite adventures.

By five o'clock the valley had become quite a plain, an

expanse of Indian corn, though still bordered by hills.* Villages thickened, and twice or thrice a tract of blackened timbers showed that one had been destroyed by fire. Then a long low cloud of dust marked a high road in the distance, and chateaux, in a sort of dishevelled grandeur, lifted their turrets here and there. Suddenly, we were in the broad road itself, not more interesting than that of Barnet in times of yore; but unlike that of Barnet, for where an avenue turned off to a mansion, a great golden crucifix was fixed, the rich man's testimony to his religion; while farther on, three lofty statues, in marble, of sainted ecclesiastics, marked the limit of his estate, and shone far over the landscape. Soldiers were seen lounging about the inns and villages, an unpleasant suggestion of crowded quarters at Cilli, which appeared at last in the distance, glimmering over trees and backed by castle ruins on a hill. And there—there are the long low lines of the rail! Oh, how different in their mathematical rigidity from the soaring, sweeping, tossing, broken lines of mountain and hill, and the trembling lines of lake and stream, that had been our delight so long!

The town is a market for the Hungarian vine-growers, and looked a busy place. At this point the Sann takes its course southwards, by a narrow and sinuous valley, through the belt of hills already mentioned, to join the Save; and the railway follows the same course, afterwards accompanying all the windings of the Save until it emerges into a second little plain at Laibach. The best inn took no notice of our arrival, and we had to ferret

* Triangular in shape, it is bounded on the south by a range of hills running west as far as the town of Stein—Sclavonicè, Kamnik, from Kamen, a stone or rock—from which the Feistritz Thal leads up directly northwards to the southern roots of the Grintouz, Skuta, and Oistriza. Hence the name of 'Steiner Alp,' given to this group of mountains as seen from the south.

out somebody to give us the expected answer that it was full. They all seem to resent an application for rooms if they happen to be occupied. People were watching us from a neighbouring hotel, so we drove there; but they took care to vanish in the interim. A third inn was equally unaccommodating; but a fourth met our enquiries with a ready assent. It was comfortable, but dear, which we found to be characteristic of Styria, compared with its neighbouring provinces. After two sleepless nights, it was rather trying to rise at three for the train from Trieste, which, after all, was two hours behind its time.

It came; and, seated in the carriage, we knew that all was over—all the romance—all the adventure—all the freedom—all the wildness, the grandeur, the beauty! We shot through tunnels, and flitted by stations; but our thoughts were busy with the vanished Dolomites, with our days at Ratzes, and our discoveries at Caprile; with the now far distant Marmolata, Pelmo, and Civita; with the mysteries of the Gail Thal, the wilderness of the Isonzo, the beauty and sublimity of the Save, the loveliness of Veldes, and last, not least, the seclusion of the Steiner Caldron. Yet the passage of the Sömmering recalled us to a present scene of wonder. The circling flight of the rail round those mountain shoulders, and over those stupendous depths, is perhaps the most astonishing exploit that ever railway accomplished. Once upon the northern side of that last of the Alpine ranges, and a thick veil of rain blotted them all from view. Wet and forlorn, we entered Vienna. Two days later, Churchill and his wife left direct for England, where S—— and myself, by the more circuitous route of Prague and Dresden, arrived a week later. There, settled for the winter at our respective firesides, we disappear for a time from these pages of summer travel.

TOUR THROUGH

CARINTHIA, FRIULI, AND THE VENETIAN ALPS.

1862.

CHAPTER XII.

A——'S LETTERS.

Introductory—Grätz to the Lavanthal—Wolfsberg—Ascent of the Kor Spitze—Kappel and the Gross Obir—Klagenfurt—Legend of the Dragon—The Zollfeld and its History—The Wörther and Ossiacher Lakes—Bleiberg—Hermagor and the Wulfenia—Professor Vulpius's Adventure—Klagenfurt again, and the Satnitz Plateau—Wurzen and Raibl.

If the reader has accompanied us faithfully to the close of the preceding chapter, we may hope he will not be disinclined to hear a little more about the Dolomites. We have yet to open some of their recesses; we can yet lead him to pastures new. Nor perhaps will he decline to revisit with us, in this summer of 1862, one or two favourite spots of our last year's ramble.

But first, we commit the pen to another hand. Churchill, anxious to secure the fleeting flowerets of the Alpine world before another summer's sun, or the mower's scythe, had laid them low, left England with his wife a month earlier than ourselves, appointing a rendezvous for the 2nd of August, at Ober Tarvis, in Carinthia. With all the speed of rail, they were to reach Vienna, and thence Grätz in Styria. Then, across country, and over a mountain pass, they would enter Carinthia near the head of the Lavanthal—a region rich in botanical interest. Kappel, where they looked for a kindly welcome from Mrs. Popp, would be their next halting-place —not for the sake, however, of revisiting the Caldron, where the grenadier kept guard, but of ascending the Gross Obir, and of exploring afterwards, if time served, the mountains of the Loibl. Finally, and as a crowning object of their journey, there was the *Wulfenia*, which, this time, was to be caught alive in its rocky fastness, and consigned to the honourable captivity of the botanical folio. This would of course take them to Hermagor once more, in the near neighbourhood of our rendezvous.

Of their movements and adventures, A—— was to keep us informed; and as their journey took them where English tourists never go—for even at Klagenfurt, the capital, they found themselves to be *raræ aves*—we have thought that some extracts from her letters may prove as interesting to others, as they were to us at home—waiting eagerly for the hour to strike which should set us free to speed over the Continent, and join our friends for a few more days in the Dolomite region.

Wolfsberg: July 3, 1862.

Dear S——,We left Vienna for Grätz by the night train, for though sorry to pass the Sömmering in the dark, we were anxious to make up for lost time. Arriving at six in the morning, we were provided with a comfortable breakfast in the station, and at ten left for Köflach, two hours' distance, on a branch line of rail, and a very charming ride in the direction of the western mountains. All round Grätz bright little churches are perched on the heights, just as we observed them last year about Krainberg and Cilli. Köflach, you should know, is situated in the north-east corner of Carinthia, far away, therefore, from that part of it with which last year we made acquaintance; it possesses beds of lignite, or brown coal, which have led to the construction of the line.

At Köflach there was a neat but diminutive stellwagen, carrying only four persons, on the point of starting for Wolfsberg, the chief town in the Lavanthal, our destina tion. The stellwagen is in correspondence with the trains, but as it only travels twice a week, we were very fortunate to meet with it, and to find two places vacant. There is a steep ascent up the mountain ridge—the Kor Alpe—which shuts in the Lavanthal, and having the opportunity of walking, the search for flowers began. An orchid with a fragrance like vanilla was new to me, but we welcomed the sight of many an old acquaintance, and our botanising overcame the shyness of one of our new companions, a worthy countryman, who had previously kept at a respectful distance. He became quite interested in the pursuit. Our other fellow-traveller was of a very different grade; indeed as it afterwards appeared, something of a 'Grand Seigneur.' He commenced acquaintance by courteously presenting me with a rose, then, launching out in French, he poured forth abundance of talk, himself the hero always, as might be expected of a man with so many decorations. He had been visiting the Duchesse de Berri, and had much to say of the Duc de Chambord's recent levées at Lucerne. Of course he was a thorough legitimist, and we could sympathise little with his views upon Italian liberty, or his antique politics in general; nor, however amusing, much more in the staple of his conversation, which was society, good dinners, and good wines. Travelling in a stellwagen upon a mountain road seemed to be an unusual incident to this fine gentleman, and when we came to the extremely steep descent he threw himself back with a groan, committed himself to 'destiny' and the 'cocher,' and announced that he was 'not accustomed to travel down precipices!' Neither of us had any other choice than the inn of the stellwagen at Wolfsberg, and as our tastes were so different, a few days of further intimacy were quite enough. Fortunately, a 'grave matter' decided at last his departure for Klagenfurt. The dinner one day was not satisfactory! He gave me a bouquet at parting, as a souvenir, and asked C—— for an exchange of cards, from which we discovered him to be Le Commandeur Chevalier, &c. He is taking 'les eaux' for his ailments, or he would not be found 'en ces lieux sauvages.'

Our inn at Wolfsberg is rough, but not uncomfortable, for the people are attentive, and the living is good, always excepting the chicoraceous coffee. 'Il Signor,' however, declares that 'La Petite,' as he calls the hostess, is the only good thing here. She and her husband, young and comely people with a baby, remind us of the Kronau establishment, but are much superior to our friends there in point of equipment. The street is narrow at our part, and full of soldiers, a regiment 800 strong being quartered in the town. They are mostly quite young, and some of them so fond of beguiling their time with practice on the flute, that they begin their tootling at day-break close under our windows.

Fortunately they afford us sometimes better music than that, for yesterday, just as a thunderstorm was ceasing, their band struck up a grand, solemn march upon occasion of a soldier's funeral, which was as fine as anything of the kind I have ever heard. All this by day; and at night a nightingale pours out her notes from the garden below.

Our first day was occupied by a stroll to the Alp or Alm, as the country people call it. The path ascends behind a very fine modern Schloss, which looks down the valley upon the distant range of the Karavanken right and left of Kappel. Several of them showed outlines which reminded us of our old Dolomite friends. The scenery, however, of the valley itself is quite different; the mountains, of gneiss and mica slate, are broad, rounded, undulating and grassy, very little rock being anywhere to be seen. The slopes are, indeed, richly interspersed with woods and cornfields, but there is too little character to furnish subjects for the sketch-book.

The following day, taking the return stellwagen at four in the morning, we retraced our previous journey four hours up the mountain towards Köflach, tempted by the profusion of flowers we had noticed. Alighting at a favourable spot we ate our second breakfast in the shade, and then botanised luxuriously down the pass again, with the sun behind us, and a crisp breeze blowing in our faces. A wayside Gasthaus gave us lunch, and a carriage ordered from Wolfsberg brought us back there in the evening. Upon this pass there is an iron smelting establishment, and perched upon the edge of a romantic rock above it is the Schloss Waldenstein. A Schloss should always have a story; and this is not without one. In the tower is a small room known as the 'Cornet's Chamber.' Here a certain unlucky cornet, Peter Eckard von Peckern, was starved to death through the jealousy of the then owner of the castle, Philip von Dornbach. On the wall of the little room a hardly legible inscription, scratched by a nail, is to be seen:—

O Richter, richte recht!
Du bist Herr, und ich dein Knecht!
Wie du wirst richten mich
Wird Gott einst richten dich.

1669. Peter Eckard V. Peckern, Cornet.

Now for an excursion of much more importance than either of those I have mentioned; nothing less than an ascent of the Kor Spitze, 7,200 feet, which involved our sleeping upon the mountain. It lies some distance to the south-west of Wolfsberg opposite to St. Andrä, the next town down the valley. I must acknowledge that the prospect of spending the night in a hut at about two hours from the summit, was not very agreeable to me, having in recollection certain horrible dens into which we have sometimes peeped in similar situations ; but I made up my mind to it whatever it might be. The entire ascent is reckoned at from seven to nine hours. I astonished the Wirthin on the previous night by personally superintending a brew of tea stronger than any she had ever seen, which was bottled for use. Further provisioning the expedition with loaves of bread, chocolate, portable soup, hard-boiled eggs, cheese, raisins, biscuits and wine, we started—well provided, you will say—and accompanied by a guide, at two in the afternoon, July the 5th.

From the town we ascended by stony narrow paths behind the Schloss, and then up steep gullies in the midst of pine woods, filled with bilberries, with *Cytisus nigricans*, *Genista sagittalis*, in rich masses of yellow bloom, and many other plants. Higher still, the pines rose majestically, reminding us of that solemn forest through which with you we descended to Cortina. Here, however, some were white and weird with lichen, and at their feet, conspicuous for beauty and splendid growth, was a profusion of the white Veratrum.

We reached the open, and the hut, about seven, and you may imagine my relief to find a tidy little wooden erection fresh and clean. It had been built only last year. The young woman to whom the guide explained our wishes had a remarkably handsome face, so delicate and refined in outline, that she might have been a cultivated Englishwoman. It is a characteristic you will remember to have observed before in Carinthia—as also a brusque independent manner and speech, which quite destroy the resemblance. There was a small interior room from that we entered, with a bed of hay in the corner, which we were free to appropriate. A place upstairs had already been assigned to an expected party from Wolfsberg; for we now learnt that since the erection of the hut, the expedition to see the sun rise from the summit of the Kor had been a favourite diversion with the young Wolfsbergers.

While the guide boiled water for the chocolate, we sauntered on the alp, enjoying the exquisite mingling of evening glow with the increasing moonlight. Soon after eight, the cows appeared, slowly moving down from above, and nearly all of them milk-white, softly shining on the turf. It was more interesting to watch them, than to survey the landscape, which, from this point, is not panoramic. The Kor Spitze itself blots out everything to the south, and the Lavanthal is out of sight below; but the rolling country occupying the broad back of the Kor ridge, and retreating into the far distance northward towards Styria, looked pleasant and gracious in the slanting light. With night came chill, and the warmth of the stove in the hut was as welcome as the repast, which—thanks to *chocolate à la crême* and our mountain appetites—was delicious. A man and boy, their peaked hats ornamented with the Alpine rose, had now filled up the number of the household, and darkness having settled down, it began to be surmised that the expected party had lost their way. The man, therefore, issued forth with his horn, and sounded it long and loud, to which, at last, from the still woods below, there came distant answering shouts—a signal for us to disappear into the little chamber at the back. We had scarcely done so, when a noisy party—three young men, and one young woman, in the height of jollity and glee—burst into the hut, and filled its narrow space.

We had disposed ourselves in the hay, and carefully

deposited our belongings upon a form, when, to our consternation, the door was thrown open, bringing us under close observation of the company; and the hostess entering, seized the bench, upsetting in a moment the provision-basket, and everything else. With a loud laugh, she did what she could in replacement, and then, raising what seemed almost all the floor at once, in the shape of a vast trap-door, disclosed beneath, an awful void, into which she descended with her light. Her object was to draw, from two large casks, what we supposed to be beer, but discovered afterwards to be red wine kept on hand for the supply of the neighbouring shepherds. This was not the only incursion upon our slumbers, for we unfortunately occupied the store-room, and stores and cellar had to be frequently visited for the supply of our noisy neighbours. Left in darkness at last, we tried to sleep. The crevices between the wooden planks of the outside walls were filled with moss, through which we were, nevertheless, quite conscious of the night-air; but no moss closed the cavities in the wall separating the two rooms, and the riot of the new comers could be almost as well seen as heard. In fact it was soon apparent that they did not mean us to sleep. They laughed, stamped, sang uproariously, and kept up all the racket in their power, till after midnight, when, retreating upstairs, they started an artificial snoring, all for the benefit of the 'Engländer,' as we plainly enough heard them say. But for this, the soft hay bed would have been comfortable enough—far more so, indeed, than those we had left below, which, in the chevalier's opinion, were stuffed with corks.

At three, our guide entered the room to announce the approach of dawn. I should say that he had done what he could the previous evening to guard the door, establishing himself like a watch-dog on the threshold.

In half-an-hour we were upon the grassy slopes which lead to the summit of the mountain, composed of a few bare rocks. G—— had laid out the minimum thermometer, and expected to find a low register; but it marked 50° Fahrenheit. The wind as we turned out was fresh, the sky quite clear, and Venus shone brilliantly. Yet the east and west were beginning to contrast in tint, though there was not light enough to see the green of the rhododendron scrub at our feet. These bushes were so heavy with dew, that my skirts were soaked; and upon reaching the top, which was involved in mist driven rapidly by the wind, I was glad of the travelling rug pinned round me in addition to the cloak. The sun had then risen, but of course was of little use to us. Early as it was, two gentlemen were already on the summit, one of whom enquired of G—— whether he had found any specimens of the 'speik,' a plant so characteristic of this mountain, as well as of the neighbouring Sau Alpe, as to obtain for both the name of the 'Speik kogel.' He had been unable to discover any. 'Why, there are thousands!' answered G——, pointing immediately to four plants at the speaker's foot. As the view was so much obscured, we also betook ourselves to what we could see at our feet, and this was nearly as varied a carpet as on the flowery pass of the Fedaia. The Speik (*Valeriana celtica*) is a very small plant, formerly exported in great quantities, as an article of commerce, to Venice and thence to the East, where its fragrance was valued for baths. You will be familiar with it as 'Spikenard.'

We continued botanising downwards till we reached a sort of 'corrie,' where, sitting down by a spring, we took our second breakfast. About seven, the mist having cleared, we re-ascended for the view.

The interest of this centred in the limestone peaks of that Karavanken range to the south, which we were soon to visit. Stretching up from them, and forming the western boundary of our valley, rose the Sau Alpe with long soft slopes and a broad back, like its more lofty companion, the Kor upon which we stood. Over the Sau Alpe, to the north-west, the Gross Glockner ought to have been seen, but only a few black peaks stood out among masses of cloud. In the distant plain, Klagenfurt was barely visible; but the occasional booming of cannon throughout the day marked its whereabouts. The Kor and the Sau are, you see, the two great mountain features of the Lavanthal, and they afford the opportunity for a very interesting eastern custom which is not met with in any other part of Carinthia. On Easter-eve piles of wood, which have been placed at intervals stretching from the bottom of the valley to the summit of the mountains on either hand, are simultaneously lighted to welcome the approach of the Redemption morn. It must be a stirring spectacle—the flickering of these scattered lights visible through the whole extent of the Lavanthal—seeming like a reflection on earth of the starry sky above, a token for a few hours of the coming reconciliation of both!

We reached our hut again at twelve, and Wolfsberg at four, much pleased with our successful and very pleasant excursion. To morrow we leave for the Karavanken Alps, and shall touch at Kappel upon our last year's route. Hitherto, according to our usual fortune, the mountains have shown us only their sunny aspect.

Yours, &c.

Kappel: July 9, 1862.

DEAR S—, Wolfsberg and the Lavanthal had attractions that we feel the more sensible of now we have left them, and our thoughts frequently recur to that luxuriant valley, well called the 'Paradise of Carinthia.' One of the charms of our stay there, was the singing of birds, which, as we have previously visited the mountains in the silent months, was quite a new pleasure. Our guide upon the Kor Alpe imitated the various notes admirably, and drew after us a number of the deceived little warblers. The cuckoos we were surprised to find as vocal as with us in May.

At 5 A.M. on a grey unpromising morning, we took the diligence for Völkermarkt in the Drave Thal. The road does not follow the rich and pleasant expanse of the Lavanthal to its exit, but turning aside at St. Andrä crosses the Griffenberg and passes through the village of Griffen clustered round a lofty isolated rock. Völkermarkt is one of the six largest towns in Carinthia, and stands on a high diluvial terrace that overhangs the Drave. At this point the great high road from Klagenfurt, not itself situated on the Drave, touches the river, and accompanies it on its eastern course out of Carinthia into Styria, and so on to Marburg, where it reaches the Vienna and Trieste Railway.

Arriving at Völkermarkt at ten, we engaged places in a small country 'wagen' which plies daily with the post-bag between that place and Kappel, starting at half past one. It was covered in with canvas, but soon after we set off, such a heavy storm came on that the rain penetrated the thin roofing and we were glad of an umbrella and all our wraps. A short distance out of the town a peasant girl, half-drowned, looked so piteously at the little wagen, that the young driver made room for her at his side and presently became so engrossed in flirtation that the horse was left to take what pace it chose. The love passages on the part of the gentleman commenced with efforts for the possession of the damsel's ring, proceeded to an exchange of hats, and finally reached the interesting climax of the transference of his cigar from his own lips to hers. Of course, from our little den behind the lovers we could see nothing of the country, but at five the sun shone out and we got the curtains withdrawn. Then we peered out upon patches of snow on the ground about us, and upon mountains showing hoary, one of them, the Gross Obir, which G—— intends to ascend, being the most prominent and striking.

We were entering Kappel at half-past six, and looked out eagerly for the old inn. Frau Popp herself, standing in front of her Gasthaus, was the first indication of the permanence of the former state of things. She recognised us immediately, and having a lively recollection of her hospitable supper of last year, we were in no doubt of a similar one to greet our arrival. We were doomed to disappointment, and during all our stay the fare has been very meagre. Wolfsberg was a land of plenty in comparison. In other respects, too, there are signs of deterioration. The salle we thought so comfortable, is now dirty and dreary; one of the walls looks positively as if it had been daubed with blacking. Swallows have built in the doorways and lobbies; you enter your room and see swallows comfortably nested just over-head! The place seems going down, and the good Popp appears to know it. Our chamber is the large passage bedroom. That within, is occupied by Herr somebody, with his wife and child, who pass backwards and forwards at all times with perfect nonchalance.

The Gross Obir, famous among Carinthian botanists for its floral treasures, was the attraction that induced us to revisit Kappel; and the first day after our arrival the weather would have been perfect for the ascent, but G—— was too ill with a feverish cold to do more than stroll about with me. We obtained a fine view of the Grintouz and its neighbouring Dolomites over the Seeland ridge to the south, and in the evening came upon traces of fortifications in the gorge just below Kappel, which, it seems, were erected in 1740 against the Turks, who threatened an attack from Carniola. G—— was now better, and the brilliance of the full moon as we returned determined us to engage the guide for the Obir on the morrow.

It was half-past six before we were fairly off, and a dull grey sky looked ominous, but the guide, with an abundance of 'nixes' assured us it was 'all nothing,' the wind being in the right quarter; and we were fain to put faith in him, though with lingering distrust. The ascent was by the side of a stream in the valley opening from the west, till, near a village called Ebriach, we turned upwards to the right, entering woods of beeches, pines, and larches. As we climbed, the Oushova, Raducha, and then the whole range of the 'Caldron' mountains came fairly into view behind us, their bare precipices of many thousand feet seamed with snow. I cannot say we felt tempted to renew our acquaintance with that singular spot. Mrs. Popp informs us that the Sulzbach landlady is still surrounded by her crowd of suitors, and the dreadful grenadier is no doubt, therefore, still in attendance. Other fine peaks of similar character were appearing in the west, but the Obir showed a head grim and black above his pine-covered outliers, and thunder was already growling in the dark clouds behind him. Still our cheery young guide bated nothing of his confidence, and on we went up the steep zigzags of the highest woods. Suddenly volumes of mist rolled down upon us, and then rain fell heavily. We stopped for counsel; but the guide declaring that a miner's hut or Knappen-Haus was but an hour distant, and not far from the summit, we advanced once more, only to encounter the increased violence of the storm, thunder, lightning, and hail being incessant. We were fairly beaten, and could do nothing but wait in the partial shelter of the trees until a lull in the tempest allowed us to descend, as we best might, the steep zigzags, which were now rivers of mud. The guide took my hand, and, by a variety of glissades, we reached at length the main track, and thus, toiling under the weight of saturated garments, trudged into Kappel about one o'clock. We wanted everything that was hot and comfortable; but, on mounting the stairs, it seemed as if the storm had done its worst within as well as without. Madame Popp had taken advantage of our absence to deluge her floors, and three maidens were at that moment in the midst of the flood, directing its course. Fortunately, in the inner room, vacated this morning by our neighbours, the waters had subsided; and there we took refuge, deriving some satisfaction in the midst of our troubles from the contemplation of hundreds of drowned fleas!

Saturday.—After the discomfiture of yesterday we confined ourselves to-day to an excursion up the valley, about six miles, to Bad Vellach, the same which we passed rapidly on our descent from the Seeland Ridge last year. This is a Sclavonic country, and the name is derived from the Sclavonic word *biela, white*, an epithet applied to the stream. The mineral springs are four in number, arising out of carboniferous limestone, and are designated by Roman numerals. Only one is used for bathing, the rest being reserved for drinking. The temperature is very moderate, not more than 48° Fahrenheit, and the water contains much carbonic acid gas, with sulphate and chloride of soda. They are resorted to for a great variety of diseases, but are little more than a cluster of sheds upon a green slope among the trees. The road, as you will remember, is beautiful, winding among picturesque rocks on either hand, and we had now an opportunity of examining the St. Christopher, whose gigantic figure occupies the smoothed face of rock so startlingly by the side of the stream, and seems, as you return from Vellach, almost to bar the road. The lower portion of the scaffolding employed by the artist is still left standing in the water.

On Sunday, from very early in the morning, the peasants were coming down from all the hamlets round in gay holiday dress. Preparations had been making in Kappel the night before; the women sweeping and watering each their own bit of street till the whole place had a holiday air. The early mass was crammed, and a kneeling crowd was gathered round each entrance. During sermon we could just see the preacher from a distance. The women in general wore snowy white handkerchiefs bordered with lace, hanging down from under their straw hats, and another handkerchief of bright colours covering the shoulders. A white chemise sleeve reached a little below the elbow, and the skirt was of some strong contrasting colour. Flowers were stuck in their hats, and there were few of the men whose hats were not similarly adorned, either with flowers or feathers. The inn that day was so full of people, drinking bowls of soup and smoking, that we were early driven out of it, and taking refuge on the hills, reached a great height upon an alp just opposite the Obir. There we sat down upon grass newly mown, and as soft as velvet, to enjoy a magnificent view. The Obir in front crowned the series of ridges which ran up towards him both from right and left. Southward the Sulzbach Alps impending over the 'Caldron' showed a jagged line of bare precipices, with little fields of snow lighting up their deep recesses; and to the north we looked out upon the great plain of the Drave, broken by folds of hill, Klagenfurt occupying the dim distance. The sublimity of the mountains and the loveliness of the plain, flecked by the shadows of light changeful clouds, were equally attractive; while the utter solitude that surrounded us—for all the peasants were gone below for the Sunday—made the scene exceedingly impressive. It was late before we reached Kappel, having lost our way in the woods and got on the wrong side of the stream. The place was still full of people; and later yet, when we sauntered down the street, groups of friends were chatting and plenty of couples flirting under the stars. Peeping in at a window, which had attracted us with sounds of music, we found a dance just concluded, and the fatigued partners regaling themselves with beer.

* * * * * * *

The Gross Obir has been done at last. It was Monday, and I was so tired with the walk on Sunday, that I was obliged to leave G—— to make the ascent alone. The day was perfect; and starting at six, G—— and his guide reached the summit in four hours, and then spent five in botanising, with great success. He would gladly have remained the night at the Knappen Haus had it been so arranged; and on the second day have explored the western side of the mountain, which, a chasseur told us, was remarkably rich in plants, returning in that way to Kappel. The excursion is quite feasible, and I could easily have accompanied him, as there is one tolerable room at the Kappen Haus, which is a large place, with accommodation for thirty miners and a superintendent. Lead and zinc are the metals worked; and G—— observed that the Austrian mining code, suspended in the superintendent's office, was printed in both German and Sclavonic. The great feature of the view from the summit was the entire range of the Sulzbach group to the south-east. To the south, through the deep cleft of the Kanker Thal, a part of the Laibach and Save country was visible, and to the north, the plain of the Drave, the silver band of the river winding in the far distance from almost as high as Villach, behind which towered the bulky mass of our old friend the Dobratsch, with the mountain valley of Bleiberg in its rear. On a clear day the Gross Glockner can be seen, but there was too much haze on this occasion. The double character of the Karavanken Alps appears very distinctly from this point; the northern Ridge, of which the Gross Obir itself is part, running exactly east and west, while the higher and more southern range, including the Sulzbach group, takes a great sweep to the south, and only comes back to the more northern line at the south-east corner of Carinthia.

My solitary day in G——'s absence went slowly. I had thought to be very industrious, but employment grew wearisome, and I felt like a prisoner. About four the idea struck me of meeting him on his return, and opening my door I was startled by the sight of a prostrate figure on the bed in the passage-room. 'Pardon' was muttered as I tiptoed past, and Frau Popp afterwards informed me that some officials had arrived at the inn that morning, and this was 'der Baron' taking his siesta. The sun was blazing outside, and under my umbrella I went down the road till I found I had missed the turning, and began to fear I might have missed my husband too. 'Which is the way to the Gross Obir?' I asked of a passing peasant. The man stared with surprise, waved his hand with a short 'hinauf,' and then added something in which I distinguished 'nit für frauen.' The absurdity of a lonely lady asking the way to such a mountain as that, and at that time of day, struck me forcibly enough, but I could not explain my particular intention, and I dare say the circumstance is still a puzzle to the good man. The scorching sun and shadeless road, and the uncertainty after all of meeting G——, determined me to return; and I had again to disturb the baron's slumbers—this time with a 'pardon' on my part, as I gained the shelter of my room. G—— returned between six and seven, after a glorious day, whose results compensated him for the time lost in waiting for the opportunity, and allowed him to dispense with one or two other projected ascents. On Wednesday we bade good-bye to Kappel, and shall preserve a more vivid recollection of its pleasures and kindnesses, than of its indisputable discomforts.

Klagenfurt: July 16, 1862.

'DEAR E—, Before this letter reaches England, S—— will be, I hope, on her way to join us; I address it, therefore, to you, who follow us, I know, closely on the map, and understand the intention of our wanderings.

'We left Kappel in the early morning by the same little post wagen that brought us there, returning on the same road to Völkermarkt. But how different it appeared under a bright sky! The Gross Obir overlooked our route all the way down to the great plain of the Drave, changing his aspect as we proceeded, and only growing grander by distance. At about two-thirds down the valley we passed through a pretty little village called Eberndorf, situated in gently-broken scenery, and then our little wagen drove under the massive archways and dashed across the deserted courtyard of a large pile of buildings, dating from the eleventh century, and once in possession of Augustine monks. Those walls and a wide moat were constructed by them as a protection against that Turkish invasion of which so many memorials remain in this country. We reached

Völkermarkt between nine and ten, and took the diligence at twelve for Klagenfurt. Through the dusty plain and under a blazing sun we jogged on in the sleepy afternoon at the rate of four miles an hour. The view to the south as the sun's rays began to slant was a fairy land for variety and intricacy of mountain form ; ridge behind ridge, all softened into the most tender outlines and delicate tones of colour, reminding us in some degree of the grand view of the Terglou Alps from Radmannsdorf. The whole range of the Karavanken was displaying to our farewell its highest ideal of loveliness, set off, too, to great effect by the long line of isolated cliff that formed the middle distance. This is the edge of the Satnitz plateau, which, covered with wood and pasture, runs east and west for miles like an island on the green level of the Carinthian plain, and separating it from the Drave, which flows to the southward, at the base of the Karavanken chain. The structure, situation, and inhabitants of this plateau are all peculiar, the latter being entirely Slovenes. We must confess to having lost the approach to Klagenfurt, for the heat and the slow motion sent us off to sleep at last, like the rest of our fellow-passengers. I can, however, make up for the omitted description by relating a few particulars respecting the situation and history of this capital of Carinthia, which G—— has picked up from various sources.

You will see on the map, near Klagenfurt, a lake called the Wörther See. The plain of Klagenfurt stretches from this lake fifteen miles eastward, to the point where the Drave emerges from behind the Satnitz plateau. Its width is about half that distance, and the city is situated about three miles from the See, which appears to be the remains of a much larger lake that in prehistoric times filled the whole of the basin.

The plain, covered to a great depth with diluvium, is

watered by three rivers, the Glan and Gurk in the east, and the Glanfurt in the south, running at the foot of the tertiary plateau. Being nearly fifteen hundred feet above the sea and between two great chains of mountains, it is liable to sudden alternations of temperature, and the Wörther See is frozen over in winter, affording to the Klagenfurters the favourite amusement of skating. The city itself is considered healthy, and its rate of mortality compares favourably with any other in the empire.

Certain remains testify to the site of at least a Roman villa where Klagenfurt now stands, but all that civilisation vanished in the migrations of barbarous tribes, and the land became a wilderness till the Slovenic and after them the German, race began to settle in the valleys; the latter, in course of time, under the Carantanian Dukes of Karnberg, subjugating the previously independent Slovenes. At that period—so tells the legend—the district between the Glan and the Gurk was impassable forest and morass, enveloped in cloud and mist, tenanted not only by the boar and urus, but by some monster whose cries and roarings were heard even when storms were at their loudest. No one venturing into this dreadful region ever returned; and the Duke, after vainly commanding his bravest followers to attempt the adventure, at last offered the entire country between the two rivers to whomsoever should succeed in destroying its frightful inhabitant. The serfs with this promise, and the additional incitement of freedom, hit upon a plan that proved successful. They fastened a fat bullock to a stake, having first attached a strong barbed iron to the animal. Its bellowing filled the air, and presently attracted from a distance the attention of the dragon. A horrible-looking beast, winged and scaly, was seen rushing from the forest, its claws clutched at the bullock, and its jaws opened to devour it. Then, the crooked iron, being buried deep in the roof of the monster's mouth, the serfs sprang from their hiding-place, belabouring him with their iron-headed clubs till he was dispatched. Where this combat took place a peaceful village was planted, the Duke built a protecting Schloss, and, in course of time, village and Schloss became Klagenfurt, the plough of the farmer invading in all directions the once dragon-haunted wilderness.

The Schloss is gone, but tradition still points out the 'Golden Goose' in the 'Old-square' as its site—the centre of ancient Klagenfurt—and in the 'New-square' is a great greeny-bronze figure of a dragon (*Lindwurm*)

THE DRAGON OF KLAGENFURT.

opening its mouth upon a man with a club, in memory of the dragon conflict. It was erected in 1590 upon a mass of stone brought from the Kreutzberg, near the lake. Some people, I should tell you, prefer another explanation of the origin of Klagenfurt, derived from its etymology. They suppose that the town gradually clustered round some difficult 'ford' of those times when so much of the country was a morass; portions of it still remain in that state.*

West of the dragon monument is a statue of Maria Theresa, with the Hungarian crown on her head. This, the work of Balthasar Moll of Vienna, a pupil of the famous Donner, was erected in memory of a visit of the Empress in 1765. And for another historical monument, I may mention an obelisk on the 'Cardinal' square, commemorating the peace of Presburg in 1809, placed there by the Cardinal Prince of Salm, the Mæcenas of his country. The material was brought all the way from the Untersberg near Salzburg. This is the Cardinal, it may interest our Alpine friends to know, to whose benevolence was due the construction of the Salmshütte, now in ruins, 9,000 feet above the sea, on the side of the Gross Glockner. The Carinthian House of Assembly, marked by two towers, dates from 1591. It contains a fine room decorated from floor to ceiling with the arms and shields of the Carinthian nobility, while upon the ceiling is represented the homage to the Emperor Charles VI., painted by a Carinthian artist. Two other paintings in the same hall depict the old mode of homage to the Dukes of Carinthia.

You will now be able to appreciate something of the interest with which we sallied out on the evening of our arrival to inspect the old town. The quaint antique-looking House of Assembly was one of our first points. Then we wandered through the squares, criticising their queer statues—one of them, the famous dragon—enormous enough. Some of the houses are singular in their ornamentation. One amused us much. Over each of its

* Some years ago the skull of an extinct rhinoceros (*R. Tichorinus*) was dug out of the diluvium near Klagenfurt, and preserved in the Rath-Haus there. The common people believed it to be a remnant of their old enemy, the 'Lindwurm.'

numerous windows was carved in relief the head and shoulders of a lion in full front, his fore paws grasping the upper corners of the window, and his hinder ones the lower, so that the window itself appeared to open into the stomach of the animal. The formal, yet varied, expression of such a family of pompous old lions gave a most comical aspect to the physiognomy of the house. Most of the shops have a picture painted either on the wall or a board, representing the sort of articles that are sold within, and these gaily lettered decorations add much liveliness of colour to the streets. Altogether, we think Murray unjust to the old capital in his rather depreciating remarks; and the neighbourhood has attractions which we must return to. At present we have an object in view which becomes pressing. The *Wulfenia* in flower is yet to be obtained, and the Alpine plants are so much more advanced than G—— expected to find them, that we must hurry on to Hermagor.

Hermagor: July 24, 1862.

Dear E——, We left Klagenfurt on the afternoon of the 17th, and at 3 P.M. stepped on board the little steamer that navigates the Wörther See. Twelve miles of water landed us at Velden; and thence a stellwagen brought us to Villach at 9 at night. I will gather for you a few more notices of the Klagenfurt neighbourhood, which, as we picked them out of a Carinthian guide-book, helped to render the voyage on the lake the more interesting. It seems there is a view from the lofty tower of the parish church of St. Egydius, a building dating from the origin of Christianity in these parts, which gives a splendid panorama of Carinthia. Many 'illustrious personages,' and even 'crowned heads,' have descended from the gallery declaring that the prospect is one of the most remarkable in the Empire. One may well imagine it to be so, with the

Noric Alps on one side, the graceful Karavanken on the other, the Lake in the midst, and the curious plateau of Satnitz diversifying the plain. Then, away some six miles to the north, there is Karnberg, the oldest castle in Carinthia, near which is still seen the stone pedestal on which all the Dukes of Carinthia sat for installation; while at a short distance is the equally venerable 'Herzog's Stuhl,' where they received the homage of their subjects. This custom is older than the thirteenth century, and continued down to 1597, when, on January 28, the Emperor Ferdinand occupied the Stuhl on the last occasion of the kind. Still more interesting, however, is the Church of Maria Saal, on the ridge above the 'Stuhl,' a little more to the east. The two towers may be seen from a great distance. This is the oldest church in Carinthia. In A.D. 754, St. Modestus, with four priests, arrived here as missionary bishop, sent by the Archbishop of Salzburg to instruct the people in the Catholic faith. There is a small cottage below the church where he is reputed to have lived, which still bears the name of the '*Modestistöckl.*' He lies buried in front of the altar in the church. Here always the Duke, after his installation at the Karnberg, came to hear high mass in presence of all the dignitaries of the country. Here too he partook of a meal, while his cupbearer, carver, and others were solemnly installed in their turn; and then betaking himself to the neighbouring 'Saal' or 'Zollfeld,' he received the homage of his vassals from the 'Stuhl,' and took oath to dispense justice to all applicants. The ducal chair is but roughly constructed of old hewn stones, and, during its thousand years and more of existence, has suffered much from weather. It is close by the road, and in 1834 was inclosed within iron railings. Composed of two seats with a common back; there is to be seen on the edges of the back, cut in two perpendicular and opposite lines of Roman letters, a question and its answer. 'Has he the Holy Faith?' the one, and the other, 'The Faith'—so at least they are rendered.

Yet another interest attaches to this neighbourhood. Near the little castle of Töltschach, not far to the north of the Maria Saal, is a small pine wood, which conceals excavations that for hundreds of years have proved a mine of Roman antiquities. These identify, beyond a doubt, the site of Virunum, the oldest and most important city of Roman Noricum, whence the Roman roads, still visible in their traces here and there, streamed out in all directions. No wonder that this elevated plain, universally known as the Zollfeld, should be chosen by the early dukes as the seat of their power, and should be considered the classic ground of Carinthia.

This Wörther See, which now helps us so pleasantly on our way to Villach, is one of several long and narrow lakes in Carinthia. Near Villach is another, the Ossiacher See; and I may as well relate one other historical incident of which this is the scene. On the border of the lake is the former abbey of that name, claiming a higher antiquity than any other in the country, but now only used as a place for rearing army horses. Here, about the year 1060, resided the great Boleslaus, King of Poland. His lawless life had brought down upon him a sentence of excommunication from Pope Gregory XII. In retaliation, he issued an order forbidding mass to be said in Cracow, and, detecting the bishop of the city performing mass in secret, slew him by the side of the altar. Struck with remorse, he repaired to Rome to sue for absolution and the removal of the Papal sentence. The journey led him through the soft and peaceful-looking scenery of Ossiach, and its attractiveness so dwelt upon his mind that he finally resolved to enter, unknown, the abbey walls as a common house servant, trusting, by the performance of menial drudgery, to achieve a sufficient penance for his misdeeds. He passed nine years in this manner, and only on his death-bed discovered his name and rank to his confessor, intrusting him with the royal signet-ring in proof of his assertions. The ring, unfortunately, was given some years afterwards to a Polish traveller on his way to the Holy Land, in exchange for one made exactly like it.

Surrounded by scenes of so much historic interest, and by a landscape sweet as well as grand, it was a pleasant sail that afternoon along the Wörther See. At Villach we went to an inn, recommended as the best by a person in the stellwagen. There were bedrooms of vast size, but only dry bread and very bad coffee for a meal, and we lost no time in ordering a small carriage for Hermagor the next morning. By seven we were off; and, to our surprise, instead of turning immediately up the Gail Thal, to our old quarters, we ascended by a high mountain road at the back of the Dobratsch, and through a district producing a larger quantity of lead from its mines than any other in the Empire. For two or three miles the signs of this industry were seen all along the mountain side, and on the sunny slopes, numerous cottages of the miners, with here and there the handsome villa of an official or a proprietor. Pleasant quarters might be found by any one wishing to visit the mines, at Bleiberg, the chief village; and at Kreuth some miles beyond, is a comfortable inn, where we baited an hour before descending by a steep road into the Gail Thal. We reached the well-known valley at last, getting fine views as we dropped into it of the creamy-coloured walls of the Julian Alps in front, the same we penetrated from Tarvis last year, and of the great masses of the Dobratsch, now revealing itself behind us. True to our former experience of this region, a storm gathered blackly round us when but an hour or so from Hermagor, and the driver, halting for another bait, drew under the broad eaves of a house. Yet, notwithstanding this delay, and the rolling up of heavy clouds which promised a deluge, it did not burst till we were safely sheltered in our pretty Hermagor. Short it was, though sharp; and in the evening, strolling up the Gitsch Thal, we enjoyed the exquisite fragrance of the freshened air, and the beauty of a scene in which, as a twelvemonth ago, the Dobratsch in evening light, suffused with the most tender tints—silver, blue, and faint vermilion—was the chief feature of its loveliness.

We have spent several days in this retreat, where we find every comfort and not a few luxuries. Among the former, large basins, instead of pie-dishes, to wash in, and, wonderful to say, delicate pink soap! and for the latter, an elegantly arranged toilet-table, with pin-cushion and hand-bell, and some fair oil paintings. The room, which opens from a small antechamber upstairs, is small but cosy; two windows, shaded by curtains, look upon the church, up flights of steps, opposite; and another shows the vista of the long street, closed in by a green mountain slope. The old Kellnerin, who was both a trouble and an amusement last year, has given place to a clean, quiet, and obliging 'Kammer Mädchen'; and there is a very accomplished cook, whose resources, as far as a week's trial has tested them, seem inexhaustible. Is it not strange to meet with all this in a Carinthian country village? Perhaps we owe it to the botanists who come for the *Wulfenia*.

The *Wulfenia*! Of course a visit to the Gartner Kogel is our great event. At half-past six, July 19, the mists low in the valley, but the day promising to be fine, we started with a guide, hoping to see the wood slopes blue with the beautiful spikes of the longed-for flower. I need not describe the ascent; you heard about that and the character of the mountain last year. Our impatience increased as we approached the alp shoulder—the Kühwege—which is the habitat of the plant. Alas! instead of the purple hues, there were only myriads of stalks, brown and bare, rising out of the broad green root leaves. The glory had departed—we were a week—only a week too late!

Not to lose a chance, however, G——, a few days afterwards, started for the Watschacher Alp, a little higher up the valley than the Gartner Kogel, which it adjoins. It is the only other known habitat of the *Wulfenia*, and as G—— intended to visit the Gartner also before descending, the expedition was beyond my powers. We drove together in a little light carriage, about an hour and a half, to the village of Watschíg, where the ascent begins. It was a morning of cloud and mist. A pleasant, dark-eyed Italian woman came out of the village Gasthaus to offer civilities, who spoke of the mountain as 'sehr steil,' 'sehr schwer,' and shook her head at the look of the weather. G—— and his guide, however, took the hill undaunted; and on my return drive to Hermagor, I was happy to see the sun penetrate the mists with promising good will. The day, indeed, proved beautiful. The pedestrians, though not more fortunate in their search for the *Wulfenia* in flower, which yet grows in such abundance that when in bloom the alp must be quite a sight—found many good plants. The woods, too, were rich in ferns, both in species and in individuals, and G—— had nowhere observed single pine trees so tall and massive. From the Watschacher they passed on to the rocky summits of the Gartner Kogel, by its southern face, where the view in that direction was very fine. Six distinct ridges could be counted, one behind the other, the last being the snow fields of Monte Canino, part of the great platform at the foot of which Flitsch stands. The Luschariberg, the holy mountain of our last year's pilgrimage, was conspicuous with its tiny white cluster of buildings at the top—a mere speck; and the road to Italy, below the Pontebba, could be seen running southwards for miles, through a narrow defile, and in close fellowship with the torrent, till lost at the base of a fine chain of mountains stretching east and west. The sky was brilliantly clear towards evening, except that upon every near peak was a wisp of mist, as if each were giving out its own smoke.

This disappointment about the *Wulfenia* is almost ludicrous, after having come so far to see it. It is certainly not a little mortifying, and all we can do is to come again next year. Meanwhile, I will translate for you part of an account given by a more fortunate botanist, Professor Vulpius, of his visit to this mountain in 1850, which will amuse you no less for his misadventures than for the enthusiastic delight he manifests at his floral acquisitions. It is a contribution to a botanical periodical published in Vienna:—

'At six o'clock in the morning,' says he, 'I arrived at Mayer's Inn at Watschig, and enquired my way to the Kühwege Alp. Mayer is a good fellow, but, like most Carinthian peasants, is fond of drinking glass after glass of schnaps the day long; so that you must catch him early if you want any rational conversation with him. He told me that the *Wulfenia* was even more abundant on the Watschacher than on the Kühwege Alp, and he advised me to proceed thither at once. At the huts there, one of which belonged to him, I was to enquire for the "Repp," an alp richer than any other in the district for plants; while from it I could return to Watschig, by way of the Kühwege.

'I followed his directions. In the field close to the

village, *Galiopsis versicolor* grew abundantly; and in bushy places, upon sandy soil, *Thalictrum angustifolium.* Two thousand feet higher in the wood I found *Homogyne sylvestris* and *Senecio cacaliaster.* But how delighted I was when, emerging from the forest upon the open alp, I saw, for the first time in my life, a crowd of the rare and beautiful *Wulfenia carinthiaca* before me! So beautiful were all of them, that I could not determine which I should gather first. The large, bright-green, scallop-edged and lettuce-shaped leaves, and the numerous flowers, all turned in one direction and packed close one above another, like tiles on a roof, forming a compact blue floral spike—both contributed towards the beauty of the plant.

'At the hut my reception was not so pleasant. In front of the first stood a well-grown maiden, whose only answer to my enquiry, whether this were the Watschacher Alp, was "wohl!" Hoping for more civility within, I entered the doorway, and enquired of a man putting on his Sunday clothes the way to the innkeeper's hut. The huts of these alps are separated by several deep ravines, and the man pointed out one of the most distant. Arrived there, I found a woman drinking milk from a bowl. "Guten tag," said I. No answer. "Guten tag," I repeated. Still no answer? "Don't you speak German here? Is it impossible to get an answer here?" At last the woman turned, with "We have nothing here for you." Gracious, this, thought I, and went to some huts further on, hoping to meet with more friendly people; but every door was closed. I then returned to the first group of huts, though with a shrewd suspicion that I should now find these also forsaken; and true enough they were. Not a man was to be seen on the whole alp side. I sat down in the shade to lay out my specimens, and presently spied the sulky maiden coming round a corner; but as soon as she noticed me she turned and ran away. There was not a soul to ask a question of; and after packing my plants, I ascended the long lines of debris to the peaks and precipices that bound the alp towards the south and east, and whose highest point is the Gartner Kogel. While climbing, I heard shepherd-boys shouting to their cattle. I will have a try at these fellows, thought I. But as soon as they saw me steering towards them, away they went, driving their cattle quickly downwards, over knoll and ridge! I now began to be seriously uneasy. How shall I find the "Repp" or the Kühwege, or a shelter for the night, if all doors are shut against me and everybody runs away? Yet for a time my attention was diverted; for there bloomed abundantly around me in the grass, *Homogyne discolor, Linum alpinum, Achillea Clavenœ, Thlaspi rotundifolium, Scrophularia Hoppii, Cerastium latifolium, Papaver alpinum, Pedicularis rosea.* In the chinks of the precipices, *Arabis pumila, Laserpitium peucedanoides, Sesleria sphœrocephala*; and at their base, *Rhododendron chamœcistus* and *Potentilla nitida*! Still eager in my quest, I directed my steps to the highest points of the Kogel, where grew *Saxifraga Burseriana,* and a multitude of the beautiful and rare *Gentiana imbricata.*

'But again came the question, What was I to do? I climbed the ridge between the Gartner and the nearest neighbouring summit, and then downwards over debris, to the precipitous face of the mountain, for a passage to some alp below. But the lower I got, the less I seemed to approach human habitations, and the more to be involved in the depths of a frightful "Tobel." The slope was so steep and the forest so difficult, that nothing remained but to take to the bed of the stream and clamber down the rocks. In this way I slid over wet slippery slabs, and let myself drop from ledge to ledge. The stream splashed over me, and once swept out of my hand my map, full of precious plants; I was fortunate, however, in recovering it. At last the stream took a leap which forbade my accompanying it any further; I was compelled to work my way through the wood, and, as evening was coming on, my position became almost desperate. Seeing presently that the bed of the stream below me had become less steep, I descended to it again, but in a short space the sides of the ravine closed in, the stream once more threw itself over an edge, and worse than ever, the ravine itself seemed entirely closed by a wall of felled trees belonging to the sluice of a timber slide. It was night, and every chance of getting out of this frightful "graben" seemed denied me. In the midst of my distress I suddenly caught sight of a small block hut among the scrub at the foot of some rocks. Words cannot express my joy at this discovery. I crossed the stream and found the hut closed only by a wooden bar. Within, a bench ran along the wall, covered with fir branches, and upon this, evidently the sleeping place of some woodcutter, I lay down and spent a quiet night. My clothes were much damaged and I had nothing to eat, but I was reassured in mind, for there was certain to be a path from the hut in some direction or other.

'At dawn of day I lost no time in reconnoitring my position, and soon discovered a tree thrown over the stream to serve as a bridge. As I expected, a path led from it on the other side, and after two hours of hard climbing, I reached the ridge of a wooded mountain, and heard the voices of shepherds. Further on, I came upon a woman and a child tending cattle, who to my great joy did *not* run away. They belonged to the Kühwege Alp, but the huts she told me were at a considerable distance. She was full of wonder as to whence I had come, and I related to her the events of the last twenty-four hours, begging her to show me the way to Watschig. The child went a short distance with me for this purpose, and then a tall bearded chamois-hunter—Martin of Watschig—took me in hand, and by ten o'clock, with a wolfish appetite from twenty-eight hours of fasting, I found myself again in the village.'

You will see that the poor professor would be very likely to endorse Goldsmith's line about the rude Carinthian boor. The professor has left his name in the botanical history of these parts, for a *Serratula*, a plant allied to the thistle, and found by him at Auf der Plecken, our favourite retreat last year, has been designated *Serratula Vulpii*.

G—— has made another ascent during our stay at Hermagor—that of the Reiskofel. It is one of those prominent and isolated peaks on the north side of the Gail Thal, which answers to the Gartner Kogel and others on the south. The first part of the way is up the Gitsch Thal to Weissbriach, the village where we dined last year on our excursion to the Weissensee. I went so far with G—— in a carriage, and was recognised at once by the people at the inn, and not by them only, but by the surly fellow who left us in the lurch at Raibl, soon afterwards. It must have been rather a surprise to him. This evening, the last of our stay, we have taken a farewell walk from Hermagor, down the valley about four miles, to the Preseler See. The little lake is beautifully set. It seemed as if the brilliant green meadow formed a basin for the steely blue water. Beyond it glistened the white spire of a village church, perched upon a gentle slope, with a pine wood for background, and to the left rose the bulky mass of the Dobratsch in profile, its own rich tints intensified by the vermilion hues of sunset. The whole scene was a perfect picture, and we turned from it only when sober twilight reminded us we were a long way from our inn.

How sorry we shall be to leave our pleasant quarters; eight days have made us quite at home in them. The sweet sounds of the singing at daily service in the church, wafted over to my room, where a sprained foot has kept me much a prisoner, have been very pleasant to listen to. I have borrowed the service book to make extracts. Most of the music is by Gregor Riharja of Laibach, the same composer whose 'sacred songs' (*Sveti Pesmi*) I obtained last year from the organist at Veldes in Carniola. At night there is the chant of the watchman, immediately at the striking of every hour. It runs thus:

'Alle meine Herren lasst euch sagen,
Der Hammer hat Zehn geschlagen.
Bewahret das Feuer und Licht,
Dass uns der liebe Gott behüt.
Bitt bei Gott für uns, O Maria!
Hat Zehn geschlagen.'

To-morrow we leave for Villach and Klagenfurt again—a week only remains before the meeting time with our friends at Tarvis.

Tarvis: August 2.

Dear E—, We left Hermagor last Saturday, July 26. Our driver, cheery and talkative, was an old acquaintance of last year. A splendid waistcoat was donned for the occasion, and his hat was ornamented with yellow everlastings, carnations, and a lemon-scented geranium, to say nothing of three feathers stuck bolt upright, plucked from the tail of a Cochin China. A cosy little carriage and a capital horse carried us along at a great pace till we climbed behind the Dobratsch into the Bleiberg district again. Now, as before, the distant precipices of the Carniola chain—or Julian Alps—were seen sharply cut out against the blue—so hard and yet so soft! I noticed in my last letter the mining works of the Bleiberg, but did I mention the enormous stacks of wood piled ready for their use? Every cottage has, of course, its stack hoarded for winter, but those provided for the lead smelting are on a scale so gigantic as to make one tremble for the forests.

This mountain road brought us down upon Villach, where we spent a night on our way to Hermagor. It is a pretty town on the banks of the Drave, in a plain varied with hill and dale, and on three sides girt in by mountain peaks. Eastward the plain extends towards Klagenfurt. Our driver, who dashed very spiritedly into Villach, greeted by several young Frauen of his acquaintance, here completed his engagement with us. The humbler stellwagen conveyed us in three hours to the Wörther See, and another three on the boat, brought us to Klagenfurt. We had stayed before at the 'Post,' an inferior inn; now we went to the largest in the town—the 'Kaiser von Œsterreich,' which is deserving of our commendation. The windows of our spacious room face the large square or platz, of which the centre ornament is an old-fashioned monument of many figures, quaint and crumbly, surmounted by the statue of Saint Florian. The custom of the house is, morning—coffee in the bedroom; dinner by carte at half-past twelve in the salle; and supper, which is dinner over again, at eight. There is a large bevy of officers, white-coated, or in blue and silver, and once, at dinner, a General, with a young wife and children, graced the occasion, and so dazzled the waiters, that no civilian could be attended to, much to the disgust of an irate old gentleman near us—always very particular about his dishes.

With all this company the Visitors' book shows not one English name; but as the railway will be opened next year from Marburg, tourists will probably soon make their way to Klagenfurt, which is central for excursions to every quarter of Carinthia. In the remote east we see our old friends the Sau and the Kor Alpe of Wolfsberg. To the south-east, the Gross Obir of Kappel memory, looking on this side like a Lion Couchant, while to the west is the Dobratsch with which Hermagor has made us so familiar.

We took the opportunity of being at Klagenfurt again to visit that plateau of Satnitz, which is so marked a feature in the scenery. It rises, a continuous terrace of coarse conglomerate, more than 500 feet above the plain, and with cliff-like edges, extending for many miles. The summit, varied with slight hill and dale, is covered with woods, cornfields, and meadows, and as I mentioned before, is inhabited only by Slovenes. A carriage from the hotel took us down a pleasant avenue of lindens, across the plain to the village of Ebenthal at the foot of the cliffs, and leaving it there, we made our way through woods and past orchards and farmsteads, to a little open place at the edge of the cliff, called the Prediger Stuhl, from which there is a very extensive view of the plain of Klagenfurt, and the lovely lake, upon which that afternoon we were to glide once more on our way to Villach. In the distance opposite, was the old historical site of Karnberg and the church of Maria Saal.

Our destination now was Wurzen, Sir H. Davy's favourite retreat in the Upper Save Thal, and for this, it was necessary to return to Villach. The lake, with its pretty slopes to the north, dotted with hamlets, and its vistas of 'delectable mountains' southwards, looked its best as we sped across its waters for the last time. Nine o'clock brought us to our old quarters at the Post in Villach.

The next morning, early, we were off, first entering, and then crossing the Gail Thal, to the point where the zigzags left the road to climb the ridge which separates the valley of the Gail from that of the Save. Near the entrance of the Gail valley are tokens of the earthquake which on Jan. 25, 1348, brought down there a portion of the mighty Dobratsch. The ascent of the ridge we made on foot, striking into grassy and shady side paths, which cut off much of the distance. The hot sun brought out multitudes of butterflies. The tawny spotted Fritillaries, large and strong of wing, hung on the thistles by scores. We often see the *Camberwell Beauty*, a rich dark maroon with amber-coloured border to the wings; the *Apollo, Peacock, Painted Lady*, the three sorts of *Swallow-tail*, and once, near Hermagor, met with the rarer *Purple Emperor*. At the top of the pass is a boundary post, marking the entrance upon Krain (Carniola). Upon this spot we all stood last year looking down over the then unvisited Villach country. Now, we hoped for better fortune than we had then experienced at the little Wurzen inn. The burst of the Save mountains as we descended, was really glorious. This time we were lucky, and not only in quarters, but in breakfast, though it was nearly twelve before we got it. Then out upon the grassy slope for a sketch of the Philosopher's 'haunt,' and in the evening we followed his favourite walk to the source of the Save. The pool, or small lake, where the river rises, extends some distance by the side of the road, and our steps disturbed a multitude of brilliantly-marked malachite-green frogs. They went hopping and plopping into the water in succession, just stopping a moment on the surface for another look before the final plunge. The evening light upon the Stou Berg, and other mountain profiles at the lower end of the valley, was very beautiful, but the west was lurid with something else than sunset glow. We returned only in time to shelter from a storm which made a night of it, and detained us prisoners part of the following day.

'*August* 1.—The thermometer was down to 48° in the night, a fall of eleven degrees, so the air felt quite keen as we started in the usual little car for Raibl. It was a very different arrival from the dark, stormy, and inhospitable one with S—— and her husband, when soldiers filled the inn. Now there was plenty of room. In course of the day we strolled up the Predil Pass, botanising successfully. The showy bright-blue *Aquilegia pyrenaica* was in great abundance on the rocks, and by the edge of the lake we surprised a black salamander. On our return we called on the old lady who sheltered us on that not-to-be-forgotten night. She was overjoyed to see us—such shaking of hands and clacking of Deutsch! The kind little wife of the commissary was gone with the soldiers. To Tarvis we drove in the pleasant afternoon, taking possession of most comfortable rooms at the 'Gelbfuss,' in the upper village; and yesterday, August 3, accomplished a happy meeting with our friends and fellow-travellers, J—— and S——.

* * * * * *

'Yours affectionately,

'A——.'

CHAPTER XIII.

MOUNTAINS OF FRIULI, OR CARNIA.

Plan of Journey—Diligence from Salzburg to Villach—Old Times at Villach—Ober Tarvis—Descent of the Pontebba—Resiutta—The Tagliamento and Tolmezzo—Adelaida—Arrival at Rigolato—Forni Avoltri—German Colony of Sappada

'Six o'clock on Saturday evening, August 2, at the inn-door of Ober Tarvis.' With those words Churchill and his wife parted from us in England; then and there we were to keep our tryst. This village is excellently situated for command either of the Drave, the Gail, the Save, or the Isonzo valleys; but the advantage it offered to ourselves at this time was its position at the head of the Pontebba Pass, leading directly to Friuli, a district into which we had not yet set foot. Through it we might approach the Dolomites from quite a new direction; while at the same time we traversed a line of mountainous country which, though forming part of the distant horizon of Venice, is absolutely unknown to the ordinary tourist.

Our plan was to keep southward of our former course, as well as to reverse its direction—travelling now from east to west, as then from west to east. In a good map the chain of the Carnic Alps is very distinctly marked. It is that portion of the great range which more immediately overhangs the plains at the head of the Gulf of Venice. Our previous journey, after leaving the chief

Dolomite group in South Tyrol, had carried us along the northern face of this Alpine barrier, where it sinks into the long trough of the Gail Thal. Our intention now was to explore its southern, or Italian face, of which we could learn nothing beyond what the maps could tell, and their rather conflicting indications left the tracks uncertain. For this region, Tarvis and the Pontebba offered, as will be seen, the precise avenue of approach.

In due course we should reach on this line the Ampezzo district, where, taking Cortina for a centre, we might make up for former deficiencies, especially as respected Auronzo, to the east of it—the Gader and Gröden valleys, to the west—and the neighbourhood of the Sasso di Pelmo, on the south. Our final object was farther southward still, where, midway between Belluno and Trent, but apart from the lines of communication, lay concealed the remarkable Dolomitic mountains of Primiero. From this sketch of our intended course, a programme which was exactly fulfilled, it will be seen that we propose to lay open a considerable amount of new country to the reader.

S—— and myself, leaving England a month after our companions, reached Salzburg on Tuesday, July 29 (1862). There we found that the diligence for Villach, in Carinthia, carried passengers but twice a week, and would not be available till the Friday. We had thought at one time of travelling to Villach by means of the small single-horse carriages of the country, hiring them from day to day; but this plan appeared to involve too much time, too much expense, and too much trouble. We were, therefore, well content to await the diligence, which, leaving Salzburg at six o'clock on Friday morning, would arrive at Villach in the afternoon of Saturday, in time for us to join our friends at Tarvis, four or five hours farther, pretty nearly at the hour appointed. An excursion to Berchtesgaden and the Königsee pleasantly filled up the two days at our disposal; but on our return to Salzburg it was vexatious to find that the hour of departure had been put several hours later, so that, not reaching Villach before ten on Saturday night, it would be impossible for us to fulfil our tryst.

The afternoon journey from Salzburg—an afternoon so gloriously hot as to make amends for all the chilly summer months in England that year—retraced, as far as Werfen, the earliest of our tours—through Golling—through the the grand pass of Luegg. At Werfen, just as dusk was falling, we turned to the left out of the Gastein road, working through many dark hours, rendered darker by the dark woods, towards Radstadt—a small walled town on the borders of Styria. Not far beyond, commences the 'Radstadter Tauern,' the first of two passes which open the way into Carinthia. How long we had been ascending I do not know; but after a drowsy consciousness for some time of exceedingly slow progress, and a queer rattling of chains, I discovered that the road was tilted at a very steep slant, and that four patient oxen were harnessed in front of the horses. When morning broke, in a sky of exquisite purity, and the ascent still continued, it was time to turn out into the fresh air, and enjoy the rosy tints which touched the mountain tops. Behind, in the distance, was the serrated line of the Dachstein, near Halstadt; around, bare summits, not remarkable but for the glorification of dawn; and immediately about us, alpine meadows and sparse pine and bush. This pass is over the subsiding portion of the Noric range, and is reckoned a five hours' business. The descent on the south, though for a long time uninteresting, displays one fine view over the upper Mur Thal, before the road drops into it at St. Michael.

Before noon that day, a second ridge, the Katschberg, of

less height, but of great steepness, had to be surmounted. It is the frontier of Carinthia, but all view into that pleasant province was as yet denied. The mountain was covered with thick woods. The small post-house of Rennweg gave us dinner, and then came endless descent in a sort of ravine, intolerably hot as the sun got lower. One welcome deliverance from this confining gorge was granted at Gmund, but no striking effect occurred till about five, when we descended once more into the noble valley of the Drave at the town of Spital. Here, daylight did not serve long to display the wide, commanding scene, dignified by the river, and adorned by villages and orchards. Five weary hours separated Spital from Villach, which we entered soon after ten, tired and stupid with the two-and-thirty hours of diligence-shaking.

Altogether, no one entering Carinthia by this route would be much struck by the scenery till he reaches the Drave. It is wanting in variety, and the solitariness, not being associated with grandeur of feature, only adds to the monotony. 'Ah, you are English—there is a letter for you,' was the greeting of the honest 'hausknecht' of the inn at Villach. There was life in the sound: news from the friends we were impatient to meet. But the letter was in the post-office, and could not be obtained before the following morning, nor then till after eight o'clock, which prevented our being off betimes. We learnt from it that the Churchills had passed through Villach three days before on their way to Wurzen, and thence to Ober Tarvis, where at the 'Gelbfuss' they would await our arrival.

Till the plain is seen from the hills, the great battle of Villach, in 1492, cannot be understood; but then the splendid arena it offers for a mighty struggle is displayed at a glance. The Drave passes through its midst, receiving the Gail from the right, the Ariach from the left. To the south rises the long line of the Karavanken, overtopped by some of the higher summits of the Julian Alps beyond. The wooded Carinthian hills close round on the north and east; and westward rises the Villach Alp, culminating in the Dobratsch. Defended by the Drave and Gail in front, and backed by the Karavanken range, the vast encampment of the Turkish host might spread for many miles, and be a convenient depôt for the plunder and prisoners of all the radiating valleys. But there, as in a net, they might be caught; and there, attacked by the Carinthian chivalry, assisted by the Emperor Maximilian, and under the command of Kevenhüller—a name famous in these wars—they were, after a terrific contest, broken and destroyed. Few would regain the Hungarian frontier through the numerous intervening defiles or mountain passes, whichever way they fled.

By reason of this momentous battle, the name of Villach yet lingers in the ears of the nineteenth century. Formerly it was known through Europe, in connexion with Venice, as a great emporium of Eastern traffic. It was the commercial city of Carinthia. St. Veit was famous as the seat of the Ducal Court, Friesach for its military strength, Villach, yet more, for its commerce. In Roman times it was known as 'Villa ad Aquas,' from which the derivation of its present name is obvious. In A.D. 878 it is mentioned, and its boundaries described, in a grant from King Karlman to the monastery of Oettingen. The Emperor Henry II. gave it to the bishopric of Bamberg, founded by him, and to this it remained attached for 700 years. By the rights and liberties obtained, the city grew in riches and importance, attracting artisans and traders from far and near. At that time, when the roads of Tyrol were less practicable, merchandise from Germany generally went by way of Salzburg to Villach, and thence through the

Canal Thal—now known as the Pontebba Pass—to Venice. From Vienna and Upper Austria also, the traffic came this way, on account of the unsafe condition of the roads through Carniola. Down to a late period, Villach kept up an intimate connexion with Nuremberg, Augsburg, and Ratisbon, which cities maintained commercial agencies in Venice. Villach boasts, in fact, to have been at one time concerned in the carrying trade of three quarters of the globe; for which enormous transit the Gail Thal and the Katschberg district supplied the draught and pack horses.

In the products of the country also, viz. iron, lead, planks, timber for the masts of ships, &c., a most active trade was carried on; in which the Jews, who were numerous in Villach and the neighbouring villages, took a lively part. Nor did the knights and nobles of the country round disclaim to make a profit by supplying an armed escort for the trade caravans, and by manning the town walls in times of danger. Many of them erected in Villach palatial residences, and became patricians of the city. The Kevenhüller, now princes; the Grotta, subsequently counts; the Seenusse, afterwards barons; the Leiningen, and others, were among its magnates. But a greater name than that of either prince or count illustrates the annals of Villach. Here lived the father of Theophrastus Paracelsus, practising as chemist and physician. His renowned son succeeded him for a time, but died at Salzburg, where his tomb is to be seen in the churchyard of St. Sebastian.

We were too soon out of Villach, and it was too soon hidden among the trees of the broken plain in which it stands, for us to retain much impression of this old and historical town. It was filling with peasants for the Sunday, and the sun was blazing in its open streets. Besides, as our little carriage cleared the crowd and the houses, the shapes of the glorious and familiar hills in front—the Mangert in their midst; and presently, as we crept round into the valley of the Gail, the long scarped flank of the mighty Dobratsch, quite filled our thoughts and set our pulses going with delight.

For some distance our road bore southward, skirting the western side of the hummocky plain; then, crossing the Gail, and reaching the foot of the Karavanken hills, it bore off to the right, towards the opening at Tarvis, by which it penetrates the great Carnic chain of Alps, and descends upon the Venetian provinces. This was the road which made Villach great. Before the Trieste railway it was still the grand route between Venice and Vienna; and the readers of Mendelssohn's delightful letters will find that it was by this road he first entered Italy. The road to Wurzen, on the Save, so highly prized by Sir Humphry Davy, and described in A——'s letters, a few pages back, strikes directly up into the Karavanken, soon after the Gail has been crossed.

Two hours from Villach we baited at the picturesque village of Arnoldstein—picturesque from its situation at the outrush of a stream from the broken foot of the hills, from its castle on a rock, from its view of the soaring Dobratsch across the valley—a scarred line of precipice. Scarred, I say, and truly; for it bears witness to the terrible earthquake of 1348, already referred to in our account of the Gail Thal.

That castle on the rock was then a monastery, built by one Arnold and his wife Matilda at the time of the great dispute between Pope Gregory VII. and Henry IV. as to the right of investiture. On the 25th of January, in the year named, the abbot Florian was standing at one of its windows observing, not without forbodings of evil, the murky atmosphere. Suddenly, the Dobratsch opposite seemed bodily to fall. The blast of wind it caused, threw him backwards; and so violent was the movement of the rock beneath, that he believed himself and all his monks to be sinking into the bowels of the earth. The buildings of Arnoldstein were covered with dust; and the space lying between it and the mountain—perhaps three miles—was heaped with mounds of rubbish, under which many villages and castles lay buried. The parish church of Villach fell, many houses, and part of the city walls—damages which the Prince Bishop of Bamberg came forward generously to repair. A portion of the Gorlitz, a mountain by the side of the Ossiacher See, was thrown into the lake. In the far distant valley of Primiero, as we shall have occasion to tell, the earthquake wrought similar mischief; but in all that spasm of terror few could have been more advantageously situated for the spectacle than the abbot of Arnoldstein. To us the scene was lovely, though still above was the scarred mountain side, and below the mounded plain.

There were yet two hours of continual ascent before little Tarvis showed itself. Our progress up this road last year had been amidst clouds and rain, with the Königsberg, Alboin's mountain, in a gloomy shroud of storm. Now, it was clad in a vesture of light, and light and heat flooded all the landscape. It was two o'clock before we stopped at the quiet door of Herr Gelbfuss's inn; from open windows above we heard familiar voices, heads were popped out, and there was a bustle within; but before any one else, a little woman rushed from the door, and almost hugged us in the warmth of her welcome. It was Amelie, now settled in Tarvis with her husband (advanced to a higher grade in Commissaryship), and able to live comfortably in their own house. Churchill and his wife, sunburnt and healthful with their month among the mountains, were close behind; the landlady, the

Kellnerin, the Commissary himself, quickly followed, and so, surrounded by friends, and under a battery of greetings and questions, we mounted to the cheerful upper floor. Such an arrival made a happy ending to our ten days' journey from England.

Ober Tarvis is far better situated than the older village below, which we visited before, and the inn supplies very comfortable quarters. Herr Gelbfuss at this time was absent with the inspector of forests, on his annual visit; and the selection of him for this, is proof of his intelligence, position, and knowledge of the country. His wife had that ladylike appearance which we often found united with the character of landlady in these Carinthian inns. We were rather amused, however, with her reply, when asked the number of her children, 'Oh, fünf stücke'—five pieces—which seemed rather lacking in the maternal sentiment. From near the inn an old road, now disused, runs back round the face of the hill at a considerable height above the present route. It forms a charming terrace walk, commanding all the fairest prospects—downwards towards the Gail; opposite, to the noble Save mountains and the Mangert, towering grandly; and southward to where the Königsberg fills up the gap of the Predil Pass, and the Wischberg frowns behind him. On this terrace road our evening stroll was prolonged till dusk, and almost all Monday was spent there also; we gave ourselves that day for various final preparations before diving into Italy, and the recesses of the Friuli mountains.

Tarvis offers to the tourist in these parts the most important advantages. On the crest of the pass, it commands both the northern and southern slopes of the Carnic chain. The Julian Alps commence just beyond it to the east, and the Gartner Kogel (the *Wulfenia* mountain) is in near neighbourhood on the west. A day's excursion will show you the beauties of the upper Save, or Davy's favourite solitary lake at the foot of the Mangert. The Dobratsch, and the Luschari Berg, especially the former, afford from their summits magnificent panoramic views. Southward, between Tarvis and the back of the Flitsch mountains, there is scenery of almost unsurpassed picturesqueness and grandeur. Indeed a chapter might be devoted to the description of the country of which Tarvis forms the convenient centre; while historical interest is added to the scenic: here Massena wrested from the Archduke Charles the key of Carinthia: here Napoleon, fresh from the passage of the Tagliamento, halted for a night.

It was like leaving home again as we packed the carriage on Tuesday morning for the descent of the Pontebba. Amelie was there with tears in her eyes, and her husband in his uniform to do us honour. Frau Gelbfuss vied with the busy Kellnerin in care and kindness; the 'fünf stücke,' were clustered on the door-step, and the clean house within looked twice as clean as we thought of the doubtful 'Albergos' and 'Osterias' over the frontier. Little Tarvis, bright and German, gave us a farewell as cordial as its welcome had been warm. Our carriage was hired of the Postmaster for Resiutta, at the foot of the Pontebba.

The Pilgrimage Church of the Luschari Berg shone aloft as we passed the base of the hill. This time the silver-winged angel beckoned quite in vain. No sledges were flying down the mountain side, and S—— and A—— could not recognise the course of their own descent, which at the time, they had little leisure to note as they sped through the air. The water-shed, where the Fella begins to flow, occurred not long after Saifnitz, with a grand view up a valley to the left.

I can say more about this valley now than any of us knew then. The Churchills have since explored it, and report that no other valley in the district. can compare with it in scenery. It leads to the base not only of the Wischberg to the left, but of a mountain variously named the Balitza Spitzen and the Jof di Montasio, on the right, which is not known as it deserves. We have frequently observed it since from far-distant points, and it always held a proud supremacy among its neighbours, including even the Mangert. Captain Holsmay gives, in the Proceedings of the recently-formed Vienna Alpine Club, the height of the Montasio at 8,736 English feet, but does not mention his authority. It stands at the meeting-point of three valleys—the Seisera Thal, that just referred to; the Raccolano, which we passed lower down; and the Canale di Dogna.

Soon after, the fort of Malborghet showed its white walls. This is smaller than the Predil, and does not look so strongly situated. Its capture at the same time with its sister fort has been already mentioned; and, in memory of its similarly heroic defence, the same monumental lion is sculptured at the entrance. Perhaps the repetition is a little too suggestive of art by contract on the part of the prudent Emperor. At Pontafel, or Pontebba, the valley, which has been running due west, makes a right angle, and turns directly south. Here the *Wulfenia* mountain, or Gartner Kogel, is not far off to the north; but only wild white peaks and precipices met our view, and its front in this direction probably consists of the like. This valley gives its name to the pass; and the bridge over the Fella in its midst separates a German from an Italian population, and forms the frontier between Carinthia and Venetia. Murray speaks rather disparagingly of this pass; but the startling grandeur of the glimpses continually occurring on the left, first, as I have said, towards the Wischberg and the Balitza Spitzen, and afterwards as we descended southwards, towards the sky-piercing summits which guard the Raccolano Thal, are enough to redeem the unimpressive features. The cheerful Alpine look is certainly gone. No bright cottages sparkle on the slopes. Some few houses are shovelled together at the openings of the glens—their walls the colour of mud, their roofs flat and dilapidated, their casements unglazed—yet Nature, in her mercy, has flung over their wretchedness green masses of the vine and the gourd in careless and abundant beauty, and a porphyritic redness in the soil reflects a glow of colour. A sombre picturesqueness is the ruling impression. No one, however, could think of a possible sleeping-place in any of the villages, and Resiutta, as we approached, looked dismally like them; while a train of artillery wagons ranged without horses along the road, and soldiers in siesta under every rag of shade, spoke plainly of a full inn, whatever else it might be.

There was time to reach Tolmezzo, on the Tagliamento, two or three hours farther; but the situation of Resiutta at the entrance of the Resia valley, penetrating towards Monte Canino and the back of the awful Flitsch mountains, tempted us to stay there if we could—a point which was soon settled by the absence of any means of farther conveyance; and though officers and soldiers thronged the house, two decent rooms within its rambling walls were still at our disposal. The regiment was en route for Klagenfurt; the day's march, commencing at four in the morning, had finished by ten o'clock—an arrangement which left the long hours of heat for the sprawling repose in which nine tenths of the men were indulging.

While we could spend our time—too short for a visit to the Resia—in the shade of trees, on a trellised hillside, the forlorn and crowded inn could be forgotten. Below, was the flat-roofed town, fringed and threaded with greenery; beyond it the broad white bed of the stream—the Fella; and then tier above tier of olive and violet-coloured mountains, with the splintery peaks of Dolomites more distant, filling up the intervals: or, climbing higher as the sun sunk lower, to a small chapel on a knoll, we looked into deep purple hollows among sterner mountains behind, where the Resia bored its way, to issue at Resiutta into the broad and burning valley.

On these military roads Theodore Hook's amusing description of the perplexities of a wedding party in the wake of a marching regiment came frequently to mind. The Churchills had to seek their bed-room through the officers' supper party, and, shut in for the night within hearing of the lively sallies of the mess-table, found themselves in company with pounds of candles, boots, and beetles. Artillery horses champed and stamped in the stables underneath: at four the trumpet sounded, and the ado which followed must needs have awakened any sleeping soul whose slumbers had survived the restless night.

No horses still! The landlord and his steeds had all gone off together, and we must wait their return. The heat was almost blistering; S—— and A—— closed every shutter, and perched themselves for the morning on isolated chairs in the largest chamber; but Churchill and I started, nevertheless, to obtain some notion of the Resia valley through its deep portals. Our discoveries were rather negative than positive. The path along the sunny northern side of the valley was carried, for the most part, upon a treeless and block-scattered slope. Certain massive, slab-faced mountains, hidden in the sun-glare, rose opposite on the south; but it was long before Monte Canino, the culmination of the Flitscher Gebirge, was fairly seen at the valley head. To our surprise it bore little trace of the peculiar Flitsch character; and it was clear that the Resia valley approached the tamer side of that great knot of mountains of which the Prestelinik is so remarkable a member. The Raccolano Thal, the next above the Resia, would probably introduce the explorer to a far finer scene.

The landlady at Resiutta had hitherto been little in our good graces. During our absence, S—— and A—— altered their opinion of her; she had endeavoured to amuse them by displaying all the stores of her wardrobe; then, closing the drawers with a sigh, 'I have no pleasure in them now,' she said; and, sitting down, she opened her woman's heart, and the story of the loss of her only daughter—a loss that left herself and husband, strangers from a distance, alone in this Italian village, and without care or hope for the future. The master returned in the afternoon, and we thought the great sorrow had left its traces even on his solid German features. There was still time to reach Tolmezzo with the capital horses he could now supply, and we were soon swinging at speed down the high road towards the still more imposing valley of the Tagliamento.

The bridge over the Resia at Resiutta marks the limit at which Austrian money will be received. The Venetian territory obstinately prefers its own gold; and a spiked gate, jealously watched at the south end of the bridge, bars passage to all gulden and kreutzers. There seems to be a spice of national assertion in the way they flout them, if they happen to be produced. Napoleons or Venetian silver will alone clear that barrier. A singular scene displays itself as you shoot down the slanting road, cut in the face of the rock. The valley below, on the right, is a level sheet of bleached stones from one mountain foot to the other, nearly a mile apart. There is no shore to the dazzling desolation, and sometimes it is one mass of raging water—a terrible sight. One such occasion our driver described with a shudder; it was in 1851, and the boiling surge rose to the surface of the road, thundering on its way to the sea-like waters of the Tagliamento. The vast trough remains, waiting for such another flood—a spectacle the more impressive when it is recollected that here is that region of heaviest European rain-fall, whose borders only we touched the previous year. Tolmezzo is that dark spot on the map; and we could not but look upward at the now pure and peaceful vault of heaven, as if its stores of storm must be held suspended near.

How different is this southern scene from any on the northern Alpine slope! Yonder is a town upon a hill—Moggia Sopra. On the German side it would have been all roof and timber; here it is all stone and wall. Northward, the bleak hills would have been sombre brown and grey, interspersed with the vivid green of grass; here, trellised vines hang upon ledges of bare and bakey rock. There is savagery in both, but there is a subtler terror in the south. The landscape is scarred with passion, and its smiles look dangerous.

Not far below, we turned off to cross the dreary waste by a long embankment, at a point near the junction of the Fella with the Tagliamento. The wind, tormenting every wretched bush, revels upon this plain, and shakes the sheds upon the long bridges, in the breaks of the embankment, which protect the melancholy-looking toll-collectors. A heavy toll it is; but nature here so wars upon the works of man, that one does not wonder if they are maintained at great cost. Entering now the great valley of the Tagliamento, we turned toward its upper course, where, descending from the north-west, it drains by many affluents the south side of the Carnic Alps. The main road continues onward to Udine, the capital of Friuli, soon leaving the mountains for the plain, and those scenes of the great Napoleon wars, which make the Tagliamento famous.

Tolmezzo lies a few miles above the junction of the Fella with the Tagliamento. At that point stands Monte Mariana, the dividing bulwark between them; and along the flanks of this mountain the road to Tolmezzo is carried, for a considerable distance, over an enormous fan-like débris, a congealed deluge of small stones, looking, in the whiteness of its expanse, like the ice-field of a glacier. This phenomenon is another testimony to the water-power which is yearly sweeping down and pulverising the mountain masses of this district. We had never seen a more striking instance of its destructive action. Tolmezzo, in the flat bed of the valley, is so much buried among mulberry trees, vines, and Indian corn, that its situation could hardly be perceived as we approached; and its deserted streets, open spaces, and tall melancholy houses, raised the notion that it was not only out of sight, but out of mind, in these busy days of progress.

We had arrived so much sooner than we had expected, that when we drove through the vaulted gateway of a large inn, into a courtyard, dreary and disorderly, we were debating the possibility of reaching Rigolato that night. Rigolato appears in large letters in the maps, far up amongst the recesses of the mountains. All day, and all the day before, Rigolato had been the first question in our catechism; but people only shook their heads, and suggested every other likely name they could think of; and if we thrust the map under their faces, their eyes wandered over it in a hopeless way, and they were only more puzzled than ever;—or they would close the matter by saying it was two hours—it was three hours—beyond Tolmezzo, and so turn the subject with a sigh of relief. We began to think we should be not only the first travellers, but the first natives, in the place—if we ever reached it.

Rigolato, therefore, was again upon our lips, as we descended hesitatingly from the carriage in the inn-yard at Tolmezzo. A crowd of people, gathering as we passed through the town, now filled up the gateway behind; the mistress, her three daughters, and a crowd of helps, beset us in front—all on the tip-toe to see and hear. For the moment there was silence; but the instant the colour of our thoughts was known, 'Rigolato' was shot at us from a dozen different quarters, in a dozen different voices, and in all the tones of deprecation. In the rattling discharge of vocables, it was difficult at first to distinguish more than a few cardinal facts—'Six hours;' 'Seven hours;' 'Bad road;' 'Up, up'—and everybody slanted their hands very much up indeed. Amidst the babel of sounds we might have been still in doubt, when another and a more weighty voice joined in—thunder! All uncertainty was at end as this warning sound reached our ears. Looking through the gateway, a blackening sky was seen at the head of the valley, and we had no desire that our first experience of a rain-storm in this region should be without the shelter of a roof. So they triumphantly escorted us up heavy flights of stone staircase, two stories high, to a couple of bare but very habitable rooms, where each bed was big enough for three people at once, though too high to be clambered into without help of a chair. M. Esquiros discusses somewhere national articles of furniture: England, he says, elaborates the fender and fire-irons; France dotes upon the sofa; Italy expatiates upon the bed. If so, the huge contrivances in our chambers afforded, at least in respect of size, another indication that we had crossed the Alps—and there was still another.

Among the crowd of faces in the vaulted archway, one had rivetted our attention from the first moment of arrival. Such a face! If I say it was that of an angel, you will fancy the fair, insipid thing of modern pictures. This was the angel of Michael Angelo! Dark hair, tossed up from the forehead as if the figure had just alighted from the clouds; eyebrows lifted over full dark eyes; expanding nostrils; a mouth both sweet and powerful; and a neck set with massive muscles superbly on the shoulders;—such was the head. Yet with all its noble lines the expression was neither refined nor thoughtful, but full of luxury and laughter. The dress, a loose blue tunic, slightly girded round the ample waist, suited the easy gait and figure. The feet, alas! were thrust into a pair of most ungainly slippers. She was Adelaida, the second daughter; Philomela and Mariana were her sisters. With some circumlocution, we suggested to Adelaida our wish to secure her portrait for our sketch-books; but our modesty was needless; the damsel threw herself at once easily upon a seat, and presenting her profile, told us that was her best point.

The large corridor, dimly lighted at the best by round-paned windows at each extremity, became darker with the storm. Soon, shutters and doors rattled under furious gusts of wind and rain, and the blue light of lightning glimmered from end to end. Neither of the sketches succeeded to our wishes, and the sitter was not satisfied either. She was right enough about her profile; as she stood against the lurid window-light it was almost grand —much finer, to our minds, that that of a fashionable Beauty in an engraving, that she explained was like her own. However, she asked for copies of our performances, and we for a second sitting. But that bored her; she preferred cracking nuts from a large basketful in the corner. Alas, my angel! Everybody was at the nuts; and Mariana, kind creature! cracked a score or two in a trice with her fine teeth—all on our behalf!

As the storm passed it left a streak of twilight in the west, and there, under the arch of a cloud, a line of purple peaks—densely dark against the orange glow of sunset, and set sharply, like the spines of some monstrous fish—filled the distance of the valley. They were the Dolomites of Cadore—Titian's country. I transferred them to my sketch-book in the morning, but they were then almost as cerulean as the sky. That was certainly the most tempting prospect within our view, and as Cadore was our ultimate destination, and this part of the valley of the Tagliamento appeared to point directly thither, it may seem singular that we should choose the circuitous route by Rigolato. More than one reason decided our course. By approaching closely to the great range we should ascertain the southern aspect of the mountains about Auf der Plecken, and should be led also into the neighbourhood of Auronzo, where magnificent scenery was to be expected. But a third argument was conclusive. A char-road did exist by Rigolato, if the map might be trusted, while none appeared to ascend the course of the Tagliamento. That might not be strictly correct, but the track was emphatically banned by our hostess, who described that by Rigolato as '*bella*' in comparison. *

We breakfasted in a small den parted off from the kitchen, in which blackened chamber a huge hearth occupied the middle of the floor, raised a foot or two, and furnished with benches round the wood-fire, whose smoke, ascending to the roof, escaped by a funnel aperture. We were nearly 'deaved' by the shrill voices of mother and daughters, as they encompassed our table. Adelaida's fine throat sent out volleys of sound, and Philomela's no less, but of no nightingale sort. Here again there was Italy,

* A new road is now carried up the Tagliamento and across the mountains, thus connecting Udine with Cadore.

for no northern lungs could give forth notes of such ringing intensity—enough almost to split the northern tympanum.

The crowd that had seen us arrive assembled again under the gateway to see us depart on our incomprehensible errand to Rigolato; and the driver, as he mounted the box, muttered 'Mother of God!'—in prospect, I suppose, of the truly '*cattiva strada*' which led there. Just beyond the town, a long bridge crossed the stream—or rather its wasteful bed—which, descending from Paluzza through the Val di St. Pietro, here joins the Tagliamento. This is the course of the old Roman road from Aquileia, leading to the pass of St. Croce, upon which last year, at the farm of Auf der Plecken, we spent three pleasant days. The valley had an attractive aspect, and a visit to the isolated colony of Timau, at its head, we were sorry to omit a second time. Our course lay yet westward for a while, before turning northward to the great Alpine range; and a second broad stream-bed, this time without a bridge, and where the carriage perilously surged and swung, explained something of the often-repeated '*cattiva*.' We are, however, perhaps the last travellers who will encounter the same difficulties, for a new road is constructing along the base of the hills, furnished, wherever necessary, with solid bridges.

But if the road were '*cattiva*' in one sense, our Tolmezzo hostess had rightly styled it '*bella*' in another, especially after leaving the Tagliamento. At the village of Villa—where a single rocky hill, like Dumbarton, bears on its summit a small church, seen from afar down the valley—we turned away northward. Then the road was often like a sequestered English lane—only that the hazel-nut hedges were lined by a peculiar wattling, which made them look neater than ours—and the scenery possessed an harmonious richness very soothing to the eye. A soft drapery of bush and wood fell over all the mountain-sides, and drooped over the faces of rock; and though villages or houses were few, they were perched prettily on promontories, or nestled in umbrageous hollows. Seen near, they were squalid, and of very little interest. Girls were winding silk here and there, under the shade of a wall; and once, suddenly turning a corner, we found ourselves in presence of a tall gaunt man fiddling, in a glass-less window, to some laughing lasses below. He bowed to us as Don Quixote might have done, and looked quite as lunatic as he.

In about three hours from Tolmezzo we stopped at a village, Comeglians, no better than the rest; and, becoming very doubtful of Rigolato, made what dinner a wretched inn could give. About here, however, the scenery was bolder, and one village, jutting out on the forest-sided hill, displayed a substantial house, with a bright, green-tiled, conical roof, which looked as if it belonged to a Signor Somebody. Yet, after Comeglians, the road was no more a road. It forfeited that character by throwing itself up steep stony places, which even the empty carriage surmounted with a world of trouble, only to encounter a more frightful descent on the other side. These ups and downs were so incessant that we walked the whole of the remaining distance, about two hours—the last twenty minutes on a sort of terrace, ash-bordered and shady, which introduced us very pleasantly, and sooner than we expected, to Rigolato; sooner, too, than was expected by the driver, for his knowledge evidently did not extend much beyond half way.

A few straggling houses, and a church on the top of a rock—that was Rigolato! Not for the first time we discovered that a name printed large on a map is no reliable indication of present size or importance. Drawing up under the eaves of a house, for it began to rain a little, after a very fine day, our driver disappeared in search of an inn, returning presently with a large-nosed woman, who, we were rather relieved to find, had only one room to spare. Again the driver dived into dingy recesses, and issued next with a man, pipe in mouth, who did not trouble himself further than to nod assent to our enquiries. We went to see what the nods meant, and found a small house in a back yard, with upstairs a small whitewashed room, very tolerable in our present state of chastened expectation. Behind the tenement, over an outhouse, and approached by crazy outside ladder-steps, was another room, smaller, and less tolerable; yet we thought ourselves on the whole well lodged.

Before the door of the house, on a worn piece of soil, three or four men, sipping occasionally from jugs of wine, were playing at bowls—their 'custom always of an afternoon.' One of them was a priest, showing very long legs in rusty black, as he gathered up the tails of his coat with one hand, to make a fling with the other. Another priest sat looking on; and having nothing else to do while the rooms and a meal were preparing, we sat also, to watch what appeared to us a very mild amusement. But without book or newspaper, or cricket, or rifle drill, what could the poor fellows do during the long hours, but just haunt the old corner, meet their old acquaintances, and knock the old balls about? At half-past seven the Angelus bell sent its trembling tones through the air. Then the priest dropt his coat-tails, his companion rose from his seat, and the party broke up; but none for church except the reverend gentlemen.

Rigolato hangs upon one of several promontories thrust from the side of a valley, so steep and deep below, so steep and high above, that you cannot readily walk either up or down, but only lengthways along the narrow terrace; while the opposite side again might be that of a round world with a wealth of woods upon it, looming up against you, shutting off light and air. But those woods are the glory of the scene; not sombre pine, but hazel and beech, they fall fold upon fold, drooping from the sky, and looped up over every knoll. There is a power of greenness, melting into soft purples, broken here and there by red-coloured rock, or the white walls of villages, which crest the ridges far up to where, just now, the evening sky is shedding golden light.

Rigolato must have been once the chief village of the district, but all the life of it has gone to Forni Avoltri, at the upper end of the valley; and the old place is left sequestered among its beeches, and toppling up and down its rocky bluffs. Forni, had we known it, would in every respect have been preferable to stay at, for it commands access to the adjoining chain of Alps, which its situation denies to Rigolato; the latter, although immediately opposite the Kollin Kofel and the crest of the Santa Croce Pass, being cut off from all view of them by the vast mass of hill in front.

The next morning there was, as might be expected, much discussion as to vehicles and prices. When in the memory of man had four travellers arrived from 'Inghilterra' to be conveyed over the mountains? Yet there was small choice. One voluble personage had it pretty much his own way; a light vehicle with two horses was assigned to S—— and A—— and the baggage, Churchill and I walking.

Sappada, a village on the further side of the Col, here dividing the tributary waters of the Tagliamento on the east from those of the Piave on the west, was our destination. We had not supposed that wheels could cross this Col, but there proved to be a passable track. Large sunny spaces in the sky encouraged hopes of a fine day, though clouds hung about the upper peaks, especially on the north; and if at various openings the Kollin Kofel and others of his brethren might have been visible, they were not so to us. To our left, that is, southward, we were more fortunate. A remarkable peak, high and grey above the wreathing vapours, stood early out to view—first in front, then alongside, and then behind—Monte Tuglia. '*Sempre, Monte Tuglia, sempre,*' said our peasant driver, an amusing fellow, who had soon contrived to ingratiate himself with his lady passengers.

By stream and through forest, we penetrated at length to the head of the valley and foot of the pass, and there found Forni Avoltri. Its situation at once commended itself. There was a great opening northward to the Gail Thal mountains, and the Kollin Kofel, or Monte Collina, as it is here called, rises directly in its rear. For a visit to the Wolayer See, for exploring the Collina, or its neighbour the Paralba, or southward, the grand group, now beginning to display itself, of which Monte Tuglia is a conspicuous member, Forni Avoltri is excellently situated. In the strategy of any tour to the south of the Carnic chain, it must take a prominent place; and the 'Cavallo Bianco' seemed as if it might offer fair quarters.

It was now that the Monte Tuglia mountains became, *par excellence*, the spectacle of the day. As we rose towards the Col, they rose beside us, an entire range of bare peaks and mural precipices, grand enough for any Alpine landscape. It might have been the clouds, or it might have been the slant of the plateau, that hid their greater neighbours on the north; but certain it is, these last did not come into competition. About half way up the ascent, the path fell into a lovely basin of verdure, out of which the woods, now chiefly pine, climbed as high as they dared upon the awful dominating slopes by which it was encircled—more merciful, perhaps, than they looked, if they bore the brunt of storms which might otherwise despoil the green recess. A second steep ascent led through these woods to the ridge, and then a valley, of totally different aspect from that we had left, opened to view. Instead of the rich forest-curtained slopes and romantic glens, there was bare alpine pasture and dark alpine wood bristling upon the knolls through the long perspective of a vale which should be Swiss or Tyrolean rather than Italian; and all the more that instead of white-walled and tattered-roofed villages, there appeared clusters of those brown, broad-eaved châlets, so distinctive of the German Alps. Yet on the right there still stretched the mighty dividing range—though hidden in clouds—shutting off all the northern world; and this scene was as certainly comprised in Italian territory as that we had left. The summit of the pass divides the province of Friuli from that of Belluno.

The absence of Italian character was soon explained. A miller, short and square, and of jovial countenance, joined Churchill and me as we were descending upon Cima, the first of these red-timbered villages. Our wives and the vehicle were far out of reach, and with them our stock of Italian; but we were doing our best, when we bethought ourselves to ask whether he spoke German. 'Ja, ja,' was his quick reply, 'we are all Germans here;' and he threw his hand over the map-like valley below, and pointed to the little nests of cottages right away to where the church of Sappada was just sinking out of sight, claiming them all, with a patriotic chuckle, for German property. This was, in fact, one of those Teutonic colonies which have intruded south of the Alps, subsisting under severer conditions than the Italian temperament is willing to accept, and warming up the waste with a scene of genial industry. Our companion had travelled far from this remote valley, selling woodware even to as great a distance as Hamburgh, through which city he concluded we had come, having no knowledge of any other route from England.

The mountains on the left, or southern side, were still a continuation of the Monte Tuglia group, but developed into still grander and severer forms, culminating over Sappada in the Terzo Grande—a noble rocky mass. These mountains rise so abruptly as to overshadow the valley, and must materially intercept the winter sun. The Germans leave that portion of their domain to the dark forests, and build and cultivate far up on the opposite slope. Sappada is a cheerful village. In the church the Italian masons have had a hand, and there are two or three houses of tolerable dimensions, and shining in white walls, one of which is the inn, where two shy sisters made us very comfortable.

Near the village is a height, crowned by three large crosses. The figures upon these are carved and painted with a rude vigour, betokening a northern hand. The greatest effort is concentrated upon the impenitent thief, whose tongue, hanging several inches out of his mouth, is a thing to dream of. Lower down is an extensive representation, after the manner of Madame Tussaud—only in painted wood, instead of wax—of our Saviour in Gethsemane. The disciples look very sound asleep indeed; Judas—with a bag upon which thirty is conspicuously marked—very villanous; and the bandy-legged soldiers very truculent, like supernumeraries at a country theatre. The sacred central figure I will not speak of. A more interesting object was a small death-picture by the side of the road. The landscape, under snow, was excellently given—the only instance of fair landscape art I remember to have seen in these memorials. In the foreground was represented a poor fellow in snow-shoes, carried by 'a dust storm' into the black stream.

The immediately superincumbent mountains on the north are Monte Rinaldo, Monte Paralba, and Monte Antola, one behind the other, and abutting upon the upper Gail Thal. These form the highest summits of the Carnic range; so that, with the Terzo and its neighbours on the south, Sappada is situated amidst the loftiest and wildest mountains of this part of the South Eastern Alps.

CHAPTER XIV.

TITIAN'S COUNTRY AND THE AMPEZZO.

Auronzo, and the Drive there—Wet Days—The Auronzo Dolomites—Approach to Titian's Country—Cadore—The Titian Tower and Titian House—Cadore Landscape—Entrance to the Ampezzo—The Four Dolomites of Ampezzo—Mr. Ball's Ascent of the Pelmo—Cortina and the Ghedinas—The Festa—A Tyrol 'Gavarnie'—Lago di Misurina and Val Grande.

AURONZO! It had long been a fixed purpose of ours to visit Auronzo. The very word rolls richly over the tongue, and conjures visions of grandeur. The single sentence of 'Murray' in which the name appears, raises great expectations. 'East of Cortina is a track leading by Monte de' Tre Croci to Auronzo. The north side of the Croda Malcoro is one of the most singular and wild combinations of crag and glacier to be seen in the Alps.' A glance at the map stimulates no less the curiosity of the explorer. Auronzo is a cul de sac, so far as any road is concerned, and the stream of traffic, whatever it may be, passes unvisited its narrow entrance. Within, Dolomites of mighty name are seen encircling it on every side. The excursion is among those which may be made from Cortina; but the proper access lies between Cadore and Sappada, where the last chapter left us.

Saturday, the morning of our departure, left no doubt as to the intentions of the weather, which the night before had been sufficiently ominous. We were shut down by clouds, whose murky roof rested upon the pine woods, while white masses of vapour, rolling up from below, entangled themselves in the very branches. Very soon a pitiless rain blotted everything from view. We left, packed in a narrow four-wheeled cart, under a rough matting, stretched over three hoops, and open at both ends like a brewer's dray. Our luggage formed the seats, but, crouch as we might, we were so knocked against the low roofing, that S—— and A——, dismissing their hats, tied handkerchiefs over their heads, and might have passed for peasant wives going to market.

A new road will soon reach Sappada. At this time, for about an hour, we were threading the unfinished works, among blocks of stone, over temporary and uncomfortable-looking bridges, and balancing perilously on the edges of depths where the white surf was thundering. Emerging upon the finished road, it was an easy bowl down its well-managed gradients into the heart of a deep ravine, where the Piave is wearing its way at the base of that great southern range which, under various names, accompanied us all yesterday, and will end to-day in the massive buttress of Monte Cornon. Grand it must be, though the precipices which rise like a wall on either hand are battened down under the leaden roof of cloud, and our only prospect is below, where the Piave is struggling, not only with the rocks which savagely straighten and bar its passage, but with enormous quantities of timber logs, huddled up in heaps that choke the stream for fifty yards together, waiting for a 'fresh' to hurl them thundering on.

At St. Stefano the valley opens, and admits a road from the north. A pass exists there over the Carnic range into the Sexten Thal, and so to Innichen; and a place on the ridge named 'Mauth Haus' implies the levying there of an ancient toll. The district on this southern side is called Comelico, and is populous with villages which we could see crowning the heights. We knew nothing at this time of the fine scenery which—leading, as it does, to the rear of the Dolomites of Auronzo—this pass displays.

A large fresco of the martyrdom of St. Stephen, outside the church, is one among other tokens that the Italians claim St. Stefano. Again the road plunges into a wall-sided gorge. This time it is Monte Cornon that bars the way southward, and compels the Piave to rush through the narrowest of grips, till river and road together can issue into the more open valley which descends to Cadore. There, abruptly turning upward to the right, we found the entrance to Auronzo—a gorge like that we had just left. Beyond, the first object in the valley, was the white-domed church of Villa Piccola—the lower village—containing the official buildings of the district, but no inn. For that we were referred to a farther group of houses, styled the Villa Grande, dignified with a piazza, and an older church. But the inn had ceased to exist, and our disconcerted driver, followed by a crowd of Auronzians, led his horse through a lane of straggling houses, till a wisp of shavings before a humble tenement brought him to a stand-still. Within, some German gutturals from a German-looking girl struck gratefully upon Churchill's ears; but the entrance to the small bedrooms was through the accumulated droppings of roosting fowls, and a most disheartening odour. One other chance remained: there was another inn at a little distance. Every feature of this was Italian—a large kitchen, with hearth in the middle of the floor, spacious chambers, huge beds, and general dishevellement. On a comparison of smells, the verdict was decidedly in favour of the poultry droppings; and an Italian maid, whose stately figure did not make amends for her sulkiness, sent us back with a unanimous preference for the good-humoured German girl, whose tact had in the meantime set the entire strength of the rival establishment

—namely, three old women—to clear the obnoxious landing with spade and broom, and to scrub all the floors. That done, the little rooms were positively snug. In the matter of provisions, it was 'nix, nix,' at first, to every enquiry; yet with the dinner, composed of one small fish a-piece, preceded by thin soup, and followed by poached eggs, we were well content. Still, when, at the end of a long wet afternoon, the evening meal consisted of nothing but dry bread and black coffee, butter and milk being equally unattainable, we felt rather in need of consolation.

Oh that rain! It seemed likely to clear as we entered Auronzo, and, believing we saw almost all there was to see, we exchanged glances of dismay at the tame aspect of the valley. Where were the wonderful rocks that should guard the vale? No trace of them appeared, and maps and Murray were alike visited with reproaches. Just before dark, a suspicion of a peak or two appeared at an inconceivable height among the clouds, and with that slight encouragement we were fain to go to bed—the rain still falling with heavy and ceaseless splash. Sunday, and it was still the same. We read till we were tired, wrote till we were tired, talked till we were tired, visited each other's rooms, went down-stairs, went up-stairs, and stood profoundly meditating at each separate window, till lines of roof, and wall, and paling grew odiously familiar. Evening was again upon us, when, lo! a light in the west. It still rained, but, throwing cloaks and shawls over our shoulders, we all turned out, and, clearing the houses, beheld a wondrous scene of boiling mists and shivered pinnacles, all glory-tinted, and suspended in air half-way towards the zenith. Moreover, as each bald top showed itself for a moment, it was crowned and belted with fresh snow—a sure promise for the morrow. We returned to dry bread and milkless coffee with the best humour in the world.

That promise did not fail. A cloudless dawn was followed by a cloudless day, and the grand buttressed towers—that ranged where we least expected them, along the eastern side of the valley—stood clear and sharp, with the yellow morning streaming from behind, pale and dreamy in the noontide heat, and in solid redness as the sun went down. A grassy alp, Monte Melone, rises to a sharp panoramic peak opposite Auronzo on the west; upon this we spent our day. The hill itself was a cheerful scene, rising ridge above ridge, and covered with parties of haymakers, each with an iron pot set among smoking embers. As we appeared, they shouted to each other from height to height, and stood for a moment resting on their scythes, all willing to be friendly and helpful in any way they could. The actual summit, very steep to climb, and very narrow at top, contained one solitary hay-cutter, who, extended on the grass, with his face towards the blue illimitable vault, was singing a song to himself. Coming up behind him, we stood amused and silent, till at some slight sound he turned, started, stared, and sat transfixed as if four beings from another world had stepped out of the sky to visit him!

Any one coming to Auronzo—and every one wishing to acquaint himself with Dolomitic scenery should come—must also ascend this hill. From the valley, the scene of grandeur is entirely on the eastern side, where that magnificent array of towers, such as might guard a very fortress of the giants, impends over the village, and stretches northward, ending, at the extremity of the valley, in two solemn peaks, set side by side like Egyptian Colossi—these being no other than portions of the Drei Zinnen, referred to at p. 159, here seen on the contrary side, and known, under another name, as the Cime di Lavaredo. From our panoramic hill these 'Cime' are the only missing features, all the others are displayed from base to crest, admitting the searching eye to their unscalable recesses, and strangely riveting the fancy. The principal of them, beginning with the most eastern, are Monte Najarnola, Monte Giralba, Monte Popera, and Coll' Agnello. So far, the view has only gained from greater elevation; but now on the *western* side of the valley a range of summits is disclosed, whose mere outline is so jagged and singular as to challenge equal attention with those on the eastern. They are what the student of the map has been expecting from the first, and those to which Murray alludes, but they are hidden from below by the green alp shoulders, one of which now gives us this vantage-spot of prospect. They are, in fact, the Cortina range of Dolomites seen from the opposite side, and consist of the Croda Malcora, the Marmarolo—not to be confounded with the Marmolata—and the Froppa. Towards the entrance of the Auronzo valley the view is closed by that Monte Cornon which forms the final spur of the Sappada mountains, and round whose base flow the imprisoned waters of the Piave. The prospect from this hill is quite remarkable for the profuse display, on almost every side, of characteristic Dolomitic forms—stately and massive on the east, wild and fantastic on the west, while between them the green, islanded alp lies tossed into hills and glades, and smiles with rural life. At this time it was curiously striped by the labours of the mowers, who were cutting in bands and ribbons down the sides and into the hollows, storing the hay in small châlets up and down the knolls. The populous Auronzo valley lies deep out of sight; the few dwellings scattered upon the sward around are lifted into the pure ether, and solemn companionship with the pale Dolomites around.

We remarked, on descending, numerous horizontal cracks,

as they seemed, in the grass, sometimes extending a long way round the hill-sides. These were the work of ants, whose original covered-way had, by action of weather, become exposed and widened till it assumed the appearance described. We did not remember to have noticed anywhere else so curious an effect.

There is a path over to Cortina, following the course of the Anziei, the main stream of the valley, upwards. It passes the village of Palu at the foot of the Marmarolo, and then ascends by the side of the Croda to the saddle of the Tre Croci pass, whence it is an hour and a half's walk to Cortina. This saves a very long détour, but, though our destination was Cortina, we had a reason for preferring the carriage-road, however round about: it passed through Cadore, the birthplace of Titian! This place is not more than three hours' drive below Auronzo, and the latter may claim to be included in Titian's country, not only in virtue of neighbourhood, but from the fact that it has only recently been separated from the Cadore district. It was pleasant to remember this the next morning, as, just before losing sight of the valley, a turn of the road showed its grand features, which on Saturday had been entirely lost by weather. Deep in the foreground was the stream, issuing to join the Piave; beyond, the domed church and the roofs of Auronzo; and on high the Titanic towers of Dolomite, with the twin peaks of the Laveredo closing the vista, as if a pair of Titans, turned to stone, had been left among the snows to preside over their desolated citadel. If the next visitor to Auronzo enters the locked-up valley under favourable conditions of weather and light, he will not think we have exaggerated its awesome features.

The actual country of Titian displays itself very soon after leaving the gorge of Auronzo. The road joins that coming from Sappada through the defile of the Piave; and here again, now that the roof of cloud was removed, we saw how much grandeur had been lost to us in passing through its portals three days before. The enormous mass of Monte Cornon, the last buttress of the Sappada range, is here the dominating feature. After a glance at its northern side, and passing under its western end, we opened upon the whole of its southern front, where the mural precipices are almost equally remarkable. The Piave was thundering in its deep bed, and at the point

AURONZO.

where the Auronzo stream joins it, the skill of the road-engineer was displayed in a triple bridge, the three arms meeting in the middle upon a single lofty pier. The place is called 'Tre Ponti,' and the effect of the bent roadway, carried at such a height, is rather chilling to the nerves as you swing over it in a carriage. Beyond this, villages are seen adorning the hills in Italian fashion, with their slender white campaniles; and to the east, a range of genuine fantastic Dolomites soars above everything. These are especially striking from the village of Domeggè, which was rebuilding, after having been destroyed by fire. Two or three miles farther, on the summit of a long ascent, is Cadore.

A rocky hill, crowned with wood, and boldly projecting into the valley, holds the ruins of a castle; a narrow saddle connects this hill with the western side of the valley, and upon this saddle is placed the town—thus challenging observation from every direction. It is small and Italian-looking. The church is domed and modernised, but the Pretorio, or town-house, in the Plaza, boasts an ancient tower, upon which the figure of the venerable painter, some dozen feet in height, clothed in his well-known robes, is depicted in strong colours. He points with one hand towards the cottage in which he was born, but the merit of the work falls far below the intention. It was presented to the Commune a few years ago by an artist commissioned to paint a picture for the church. The Pretorio itself is a quaint-looking building, and the ceiling of one room, divided in heavy wooden panels, is richly carved with fruit, leaves, and Cupids. 1590 is the date inserted. The bare walls of whitewash, sadly out of keeping, bear witness to a ruthless destruction by the peasants, before the strong hand of Austria grasped the Venetian provinces.

The house of Titian's birth lies a little way to the left, the last out of the town upon the lane, which, passing round under the Castle hill, and through the village of Sotto Castello, must have been the ancient entrance to Cadore. It is a very unpretending spot; but when is the birthplace of a great man anything else? We are apt to forget that a great man is born in all senses little, and that he has to grow into the space he fills in history. A tablet in the side of the house, now occupied by an artisan, contains this inscription:—

NEL MCCCCLXXVII.
FRA QVESTE VMILI MVRA
TIZIANO VECELLI
VENE A CELEBRE VITA
DONDE VSCOVA GIA PRESSO A CENTO ANNI
IN VENEZIA
ADDI XXVII. AGOSTO
MDLXXVI.

The house, upon the death of his elder brother, came into Titian's own possession, and he is known to have resided in it occasionally during the last few years of his life.

TITIAN'S HOUSE.

A fountain close by is surmounted by a figure of St. Tiziano, the bishop and saint of the family, from whom the young Vecelli derived his world-renowned name. In the church is a picture, duly curtained as a treasure, of which a portion, the head and shoulders of a Madonna with the

Child, is ascribed to him. It is not a worthy representative of the great painter in this place of his birth.

The castle, under the walls of which the Vecelli cottage was snugly ensconced, must have been a building of some mark, judging from the representations of it which remain. It furnishes the arms of the town in the shape of two towers and a fir-tree. A certain Canon is writing a history of Cadore; when it is published, we may learn something of the, at present, obscure fortunes of the castle. Like some other strongholds in the neighbourhood, it may have been first raised as a defence against the ravages of the Huns under Attila, at the time of the siege of Aquileia. A singular crucifix, accidentally discovered a quarter of a mile from Cadore, in 1540, and now preserved in a small church on the spot, is supposed to have been buried at that time of terror. Whatever its origin, however, the castle seems always to have been a government building. When the Patriarchs of Aquileia were the rulers of Friuli it was held in their name. When the Venetians conquered Friuli in 1420, the castle passed into the hands of the Republic, and was always in charge of a noble Venetian captain. In the decadence of their power it was let to any one who would inhabit the building and keep it in repair. Its destruction is due to those indefatigable despoilers, the French, who, under Massena, seized the Cadore country on the advance of Napoleon to the Tagliamento in 1796, and reduced the castle to its present state of ruin.

The view from it will repay a climb. Northward, the valley, sprinkled over with villages, stretches up to the base of Monte Cornon, which in picturesque variety of outline fills up all the prospect in that direction. Southward the valley falls through abrupt gorges, by Perarolo and Longarone, into the rich Belluno country. An abrupt mountain range, peaked above, and wooded below, walls in the eastern side of the Piave Valley. It conceals in its recesses a wild Dolomitic chain, which startles the sight at intervals—as from Domegge, already mentioned, and lower down, where the weird form of Monte Duraino, its loftiest member, overhangs Perarolo. To the west, the landscape is more varied. The most striking mountain outline immediately about Cadore lies north-west; and is best seen in the glow of evening, from the field immediately behind Titian's house. There the spires of Monte Marmarolo appear shooting marvellously into the sky, in true Dolomitic fashion, and surely made their mark on the boy's observant mind. Directly west of Cadore rises Monte Antelao, so imposing from the Ampezzo Pass; here it is for the most part hidden by shoulders of hill. There is a fine peep, however, of the tower-like Pelmo beyond; though but the corner of one topmost turret, it suggests enormous height; while a little to the south a vast grey mass is none other than Monte Civita. This back view of the Civita is so different from that of its many-pinnacled front, as displayed at Caprile, that we did not recognise at first our old acquaintance, but there is no doubt of the identity. Below Cadore, as you look from the castle hill, numerous villages, with white campaniles, deck the hill-sides, and make a sparkling vista,—especially in the direction of the Boita, which enters the Piave from the west, and gives access to the Ampezzo district.

Thus, long before their geological peculiarity was known, or their singular appearance noted in guide-books, the Dolomites were familiar to the eye of Titian. They were the mountains of his boyhood, and helped to educate his artist-soul. Certain it is, that whatever changes may have taken place in the near features of the Cadore scenery, those strange shapes remain as he saw them, and the Dolomitic outline becomes additionally interesting from the fact that it was the earliest mountain form he knew. It was also tenaciously retained, for it appears in many of the landscape portions of his pictures.* But, indeed, through his long life they were familiar to him. During the heats of summer he frequently, like Venetian artists of the present day from the same neighbourhood, repaired to his native mountains—often certainly to his country-house near Serravalle. Domegge boasts a standard painted by his hand for use in processions. A village in the Val di Zoldo, four hours south of Cadore, possesses the remains of an altarpiece by him. Santa Lucia, near Caprile, claims his hand for a now defaced fresco of St. Christopher, which tradition says they owe to a winter visit, when, snowed up for a fortnight at the curé's house, he repaid the hospitality by this specimen of his art. All this district must have been well known to him, and how well—to return to the Castle hill of Cadore—this prospect of the Piave Valley! Yet, wait till evening drapes it with her solemn shadows, before you attempt to realize the country of Titian. Then, when low tones possess the sky, illumined, perhaps, by one or two white masses of cloud, and the mountains are shapes of gloom, and colours melt into sombre harmonious tints—then may you best recognise the landscape of the great 'Cadorino.'

On this occasion, a few hours were all we could spare for Cadore—we have since bestowed upon it many days. A poor inn gave us dinner; neither horses nor vehicles were to be obtained. Fortunately, our Auronzo drivers, whose engagement ended here, consented to extend it to Cortina, more than twenty miles farther. A short distance out of Cadore on this side, the town appears to most advantage. Its larger buildings front the south, and it rules the situation

* If I am not mistaken, a distant mountain in the celebrated picture of Christ at Emmaus is taken from a portion of Monte Marmarolo.

J. Gilbert, del.t Hanhart, lith.

SASSO DI PELMO FROM MONTE ZUCCO.

well; while the tossing forms of the Cornon range make a charming background. A mile of swift descent, and then you reach the 'Strada Allemagna,' the great Austrian road which connects the Tyrol with Venetia through the Ampezzo. At the point of junction is the village of Tai Cadore, and there we marked for future use a tolerable looking inn. The road descends southward by many sweeps and zig-zags into the gorge of Perarolo; but in the other direction towards the Ampezzo it climbs in long ascending reaches. This was our course, and while still in the Cadore district the scenery attained its most romantic aspect. There is scarcely another spot in our remembrance so strikingly picturesque as the village of Valle resting upon a precipitous ridge, amid the most varied lines of hill, and rock, and wooded steep. Above, to the right, a sudden opening shows the shivered summit of the Antelao, and the great Pelmo begins to darken the west with his bulk.

As you turn northward the landscape interest changes. You feel that it is indeed northward you are going. Italy is behind, the Alps are in front. Vast pine forests sweep upward on either hand, and the four great Ampezzo mountains gradually disclose themselves.

This Ampezzo valley, offering the only carriage route through the Dolomites, may be traversed by the reader any summer's day on his journey to or from Venice. We are anxious he should appreciate it; but he will not do so, unless he has apprehended the position and character of its four great mountains—the four guardian Presences of the valley. Knowledge wonderfully helps eyesight. It has been mentioned elsewhere, how, on passing this way several years before, I either did not notice, or quickly lost the recollection of one of the most remarkable—the Pelmo—simply from not knowing anything about it; and I have met with others who, from a similar cause, while sensible of a general grandeur of scenery, entirely failed to observe its peculiar features, and were unaware that they had passed under anything so singular as the Pelmo, or so striking as the Antelao. We should like to enable any future traveller upon this road to greet each of these mighty brethren—and not less their neighbours the Croda Malcora and the Tofana, as they step forth to view—with due appreciation, and intelligent interest.

Perhaps I may best introduce them as they successively disclosed themselves to us on the present occasion. The Antelao, occupying the apex of the fork between the Ampezzo and Cadore valleys, commands them both. We had been winding round his base for half the day, and had sent many a searching glance up the dark hollows of his subject hills for a glimpse of his rocky walls. At Valle, where the road cuts into a deep ravine, occurred the first satisfactory view. Then, though still close upon our right, as we turned northward into the Ampezzo, he was hidden from sight. It was the Pelmo on the left that now absorbed all attention. His tower-like form has been often mentioned, and the vast bulk of this, as we entered the Alpine scene, smote us with wonder and awe. His form was cut out in shadow against the western sky; a cloud hovered over the broken summit, and the horizontal lines of bedding, which most singularly mark the sides, looked like a gigantic staircase ascending to the mysterious cloud-filled hollow. Yet to judge rightly of the Pelmo, he should be seen from various points of distance; the road is too near, and too low, to allow his true character to be understood by those who are not already aware of it.

The declining sun, which cast the Pelmo into shade, threw into brief illumination the Croda Malcora on the opposite side of the valley. His multitudinous peaks and long line of gigantic wall were all golden and vermilion

—a dazzling vision. This mountain is a considerable distance up the valley, and seems from this point to stretch almost across it. The Pelmo is one rock; the Croda, on the contrary, is a piled-up heap of rocks, with enormous basement lines of débris, a total contrast in every respect. The village of St. Vito is seen at its foot; and arrived there, the Antelao is at last fully and nobly in view. Unlike either Pelmo or Croda, his long clear lines stand out sharp and snow-defined. What a spot is St. Vito! In front the Malcora—to the right the Antelao—on the left the Pelmo!

ANTELAO, FROM ST. VITO.

I have not yet introduced the fourth great Ampezzo mountain, the Tofana. He is still far to the north, and, like the Pelmo, on the western side of the valley. If you stay at Cortina you will soon know him well—that breeder of storms—that murky pitiless form!

Before reaching St. Vito the desolate tract is passed where the Antelao, in a fit of wrath, some fifty years ago

(1814), destroyed two or three villages by rolling down upon them a vast fragment from his sides. These mountains are Powers, of whom it is well to retain a wholesome dread. After St. Vito it became chill and dark, and stars twinkled above the distant head of the Tofana; while a friendly little red spark, high on the mountains to our left, marked the sheds where the year before we were regaled with milk, on our way over the Gusella from Caprile to Cortina. Should we find the 'Aquila Nera' all it was then? The week of rough quarters since leaving Tarvis had sharpened our appetite for clean rooms and decent fare; and we looked to Cortina for both. Scarcely a ghost of its campanile was visible in the darkness as we approached, and but a few lights shone here and there in the Plaza. At the well-known inn, a little woman in a round black hat peered out, holding a candle over her head. We were recognised in a moment, as we could not fail to recognise the sharp clever little Kellnerin in the hat that was never off her head. Old Ghedina and his wife, the son, and all the servants, came out to add their welcome, and the four 'Engländer' soon took possession of chambers as 'fair' as any Mr. Interpreter, or the House Beautiful, could boast.

We spent a week at Cortina, but the first morning after our arrival took advantage of the returning vehicles to go back as far as St. Vito. Three such sights as the Pelmo, the Antelao, and Malcora, all at once, are not to be seen every day. There is a small but tolerable inn there, and the master is intelligent, with much knowledge of the country. As may be supposed, few mountains look so inaccessible as the Pelmo; yet a President of the Alpine Club, Mr. Ball, once achieved the ascent, winning some rare plants for his pains. Murray says none but an experienced cragsman should attempt it; but as the St. Vito landlord assured us that only the final ice portion was difficult, Churchill and I intended to have made the trial, had weather served. Unfortunately, it was very unsettled during the time we were in the neighbourhood. A few details, kindly supplied by Mr. Ball, will explain the character of the ascent.

Mr. Ball started from Borca, a little below St. Vito, on September 19, 1857, at three, A.M., with a guide who had accidentally discovered a way to the summit. In two hours a châlet was reached on the alp at the foot of the Pelmo, and beyond lay long lines of débris, that abutted against the precipitous walls forming the eastern face of the mountain. Arrived at the summit of this débris, a nearly horizontal ledge was followed, until, at a considerable distance from the point where it was entered upon, it was intersected by a channel that descended from the upper plateau. The ascent up this channel was long and steep. Arrived at the plateau, a glacier, slightly inclined, was found to cover it. To the north-west it was bounded by a sheltered ridge of nearly vertical rocks, forming the highest crest of the Pelmo. Ascending by the névé, Mr. Ball found no difficulty in reaching the ridge at a point where it commands a view on two sides—the one overlooking the Val di Zoldo, and the other the valley of Ampezzo. On gaining this point, the guide declared that they had reached the top. Mr. Ball pointed to a ridge, probably eighty or one hundred feet higher, that shut out the view to the north. To ascend this, the guide declared was utterly impracticable, from the shattered condition of the rock, and earnestly deprecated the attempt. Mr. Ball, however, without much difficulty, made his way to the extreme summit of this ridge, and from it enjoyed an admirable panorama, in which the Gross Glockner on the one side, and the Marmolata on the other, were conspicuous. The Antelao seemed to be about one hundred feet higher than the Pelmo; and some of the peaks in the ridge beyond Auronzo, as well as the Croda Malcora, appeared to be very nearly on a level with it.

Mr. Ball left the summit at 1, P.M., reached the châlet at 5, and after halting a quarter of an hour, arrived at the inn at Borca at 6.15, P.M.*

We were told, though we distrust the information, that the Antelao has never been ascended. St. Vito would be the best point of departure for that, as well as the Pelmo. A Pass—the Forcella Piccola—to the summit of which Churchill climbed, leads over between the Antelao and the Melcora into the Cadore country; and another, the Forcella Grande, which may be expected to display extraordinary rock scenery, crosses between the Malcora and the Melcora at a high elevation, through a Pyrenean-like Port, into the upper Auronzo valley. On the other side again, St. Vito may be taken as a starting-point for the Val Fiorentina and Caprile, by a path passing under the Pelmo; as the Val di Zoldo may be reached by another lower down. This part of the Ampezzo affords a distinct circle of excursions, such as Cortina itself can scarcely equal.

I have mentioned the desolation caused by the Antelao between St. Vito and Borca; a sadder desolation may be witnessed at the latter village. There has found a refuge Signor ——, one of the heroes of Venice in the eventful year '49. He was a man of high culture and noble aims, and shared with Manin in the brave defence of the city. The fatigues of that terrible time, and the sad results, over-

* The height of the Pelmo, as given by Mayr in his 'Alpen-länder Atlas,' is 9,910 Paris, or 10,838 English feet, while that of the Antelao is stated at 10,012 Paris, or 10,950 feet English. Another height for the Antelao, but without indication of the authority, appears in the first volume of the Vienna Alpine Club, where it is incidentally mentioned to be only 10,297 Vienna, or 10,678 English feet.

threw his intellect; and now, a wreck of his former self, he lives with his brother, an innkeeper in the village. Still the busy brain is active, and he deems himself to have made great discoveries in physiology, which, alas! no one appreciates.

We reached Cortina again by starlight, and again the Tofana showed his head amongst the stars. By day he was always shrouded with mist, and the first rain ever broke from *his* dark sides. By night the snow-streaked shape stood awful and bare, and seemed to regard us with an evil smile. He is a wicked mountain, but a great one. In 1863, the Tofana was for the first time ascended by a member of the Vienna Alpine Club, who determined the height at 10,721 English feet above the sea. It is the Tofana that, placed at the head of the Ampezzo, overhangs Peutelstein, shooting out towards it a cold tongue of glacier, and making himself every way a very uncomfortable neighbour.

Ghedina the old Jäger, and landlord of the 'Aquila Nera,' was proud, as he ought to be, of his son, the Venetian painter. It has been told how on our former visit we admired the pictures by his hand, which adorn the walls of the inn. Now, we took an early opportunity of visiting his summer studio in an old mill belonging to his father, among bright green fields. Unluckily the bird was flown. He had started for Venice the morning of our arrival, and left his studio bare. Yet several specimens of cartoon drawing remained—subjects for pictures in hand, or intended. Most of them were destined for churches, and showed great delicacy of feeling, as well as skilful drawing. In the latter particular he reminded us of Mulready, especially in his free and graceful rendering of those difficult matters, 'the coats, the hosen, and the hats' of modern costume. A large design representing, if I recollect rightly, the laying of a foundation stone for a church, was full of groups which the illustrator of Goldsmith might have owned; while, as regards expression, there was much of Ary Scheffer's pure and tender thought. A very sweet portrait of his mother, in which he had dispensed with the otherwise indispensable low-crowned black hat, was a specimen of this latter quality.

Two of his younger brothers are also artists—one a painter, chiefly of portraits, and the other a sculptor in wood. The workshop of the latter was in the village, and what we saw of his carving was full of the genius of the family. That day we were at a loose end, and spent another hour in a third studio of the place. Cortina is a resort for painters. Was not Titian born next door—and who knows? A Signor Semprone, also from Venice, had borrowed the armoury of the Town-house, to finish a large altar-piece for a chapel at Vienna. We will not say more than that this work increased our respect for Ghedina's.

The day was one of episodes. In the afternoon, half a dozen reverend gentlemen, in long black coats, black stockings, and bright buckles, and one cowled and sandalled monk, trooped without warning into the Churchills' room. A—— fled, laughing, to us. Loud sounds of greeting sent us in to see what had happened, when the monk turned out to be the Franciscan Professor of Natural History at Botzen, whom we met last year at Ratzes. He had been let out for a fortnight to hunt for beetles on the mountains, and, quite ignorant of our proximity, was going round the house with the clerical party to see Ghedina's pictures. Great was the fraternisation of the two 'Scientifics.' Unluckily, the Franciscan was at the end of his tether, and obliged to be off in the morning.

The presence of such a body of divinity in Cortina was

explained the next day. It was the great autumnal feast of the Virgin, and from early morning strings of peasantry were coming over the hills and crowding into the village at all ends. The street was lined with booths; and a lively trade was afoot in handkerchiefs and petticoats, rosaries, pictures, and hats. The women, as they should be, were the prettiest sight of all; but more for the gay kaleidoscope bits of colour they made, streaming down over the green grass, than for face or figure. Large aprons of a deep blue, over a black dress, edged with red; white sleeves, red stockings, a bright handkerchief of a well chosen tint, put like a ruff round the neck, a sprinkling of lace and ornaments, and the little black hat at top of all, set off many a homely maiden to great advantage. One girl on the hill, hurrying down alone, was so wonderfully decked out, and so conscious of it, as to be almost too shy to pass us. The women touch their hats to you, like men, and in church take them off, when steel or silver pins are seen ornamenting their braided hair behind.

This was Friday; the fête lasted three days, and on Sunday the crowd at church was immense. All the Ampezzo must have been there. Dense masses of white-sleeved women upon the floor, were streaked with brown throngs of men, and all wedged like the blocks of a pavement. The host was carried round to at least a dozen altars in the large church; lanterns, like those of the Lord Mayor's state coach, preceded, with banners and several priests, and everybody sung or responded with lusty vigour.

They are a kindly, honest folk, and many a cordial welcome we met with in our rambles. Sketching one evening the galleries and gables of a mountain hamlet, the good people came down upon us from their upland work; the women with huge bundles of hay on their backs, the men guiding sledges, similarly laden, down the stony paths. These sledges, drawn by a horse or bullock, ran upon a single pair of wheels in front, but slid upon two long tails of timber behind, worn sharp by friction. Out danced a merry little kitten from one house, and a frisky small dog from another, to welcome their respective households, who fondled and petted and rolled them about in the hay, with all the glee of children. Then, before supper, came the serious business of storing the hay in barns, which were, in fact, the comfortable, roomy garrets of the dwellings, bespeaking snug winter shelter. This done, they gathered round the strangers, diffident but curious. They examined our sketches and maps, were delighted to identify the mountains round, and to write the name of their own hamlet—and a pretty name, too, 'Lacedell'—in our books. Then, when they saw symptoms of departure, they fell into a solemn circle, and all uncovered, as if grace were to be said. Our gravity scarcely survived the occasion.

Another evening, caught in one of the Tofana rain storms, we were perforce conducted up the outside staircase, along the gallery under the eaves, and so into a little peasant parlour—warm, and brown, and clean, with a wooden ceiling, walls and floor of wood. A few sacred pictures, crucifixes, and holy water glasses, were the decorations; a stove, a bed, and bench, the furniture. They wished to offer us coffee: they would not be denied a dish of hot beans, which made their own supper, and which were very sweet and palatable. On these occasions, if they talked about England, it was generally of Lord Palmerston!

Murray says, of Cortina, the 'scenery is bare, and not agreeable.' Certainly it is not rich and broken like that of Cadore, and I can imagine a passing traveller concurring in the verdict. We must help him to a juster conclusion.

Let him stroll across the valley,—he will find footpaths through meadows of emerald greenness,—then turn and view the prospect up and down. It is bare, but grand. Northward there is a closing in of savage-looking masses around the lonely, rock-perched Peutelstein; and most likely the Tofana, on the left, will be darkening it all with his mantle of cloud. That will suit the traveller's Byronic mood, should he happen to be in one. To the south there will be sunshine and beauty, as well as grandeur—beauty in the upper regions, if not in the lower. I know not what is beautiful if the Antelao, here a serene and lofty obelisk, soft in all the tints of the sky it pierces, be not so. The Pelmo is out of sight; but a fine enough mountain, Monte Rochetta, takes his place; and at the extremity of the valley certain fine peaks of the Val di Zoldo will, if the hour be favourable, shine lustrously among the clouds. Over Cortina will be seen the embattled turrets of the Malcora; and if the traveller knows a secret we can tell him, he will find those turrets very fascinating. Behind them is Gavarnie!

'Gavarnie!' you will say, 'that is in the Pyrenees.' True; but here is a cunning copy of it, of which no Frenchman dreams. Churchill and I have the key. One fine day—there were but few—we started alone up the sloping hollow behind Cortina, and by the side of the Malcora, so to speak, though he lies back some distance on the right. To the left is a line of precipices, and, as we rise, appear the higher ranges of Monte Cristallo. For two hours the path is all ascent, through meadow, sparse wood, open stony spaces. Then, on the ridge—the saddle —appear three crosses, which we have been looking for; the pass is named the 'Tre Croci,' and leads over to Palu, in the Auronzo country. Now the path dips into a deep forest—dips, and drops, and wanders. There are fine gleams of bare Dolomitic spires through trees behind—hints of the Cristallo—but the recesses of the Malcora, which we want to see, will not open at all. From the summit of the pàss, the Marmarolo, beyond, had shown well its glacier-burdened masses; but now, in the depths, we seem losing everything. Two hours from the summit, and in the middle of the confusing woods, we find a bare and sloping space of green, with a group of cattle-sheds; from this spot the Malcora stands clear before us, and opens to its very heart. A vast amphitheatre of wall, with snow on each terrace-ledge, rises to the sky. A glacier lies gleaming in the midst; and a cascade, supplied by a tarn hid behind the precipices, tumbles out below into a dark blue depth among the pines.

Now, of course, one great feature of Gavarnie is wanting. There is no mob of French tourists. No ladies are to be seen with satin slippered feet—*chaise à porteur*; no gentlemen with polished boots and marvellous whips, on horseback. Those huts will yield no champagne and soda water; the grass is strewn with no pic-nic fragments. The real Gavarnie is a much gayer spot than this. Here, not a figure passes on the stretch of lonely sward. A lad or two may be left about the huts, but the herdsmen will not come down till supper time; a rude cross, leaning from the winter winds, planted in the midst, bespeaks their natural piety.

I am free to admit that the 'Pyrenean Cirque' possesses other and less doubtful advantages. In its numerous waterfalls, in the height of the principal one, in the level floor within the circle of precipices which so much enhances their effect, Gavarnie excels. Its Dolomitic rival is not the same sort of 'oule' or pot. But in grandeur of proportion and solemnity of aspect, it is we believe quite equal if not superior. The general resemblance

J. Gilbert, del^t. Hanhart, lith

"CIRQUE" OF THE CRODA MALCORA, NEAR CORTINA.

must be considerable, since we both exclaimed on the spot, 'Here is another Gavarnie!'

From the ridge of the Tre Croci, Churchill subsequently made an excursion to a lake hidden between the flanks of the Cristallo and Cadino. Passing this lake, and ascending the slopes to the summit of Monte Piana on the north, the traveller will find himself in the heart of a Dolomitic world. Directly opposite, to the east, are the Drei Zinnen, so close that a stone's throw would seem to be sufficient to bridge the interval—looking none the less wonderful for their nearness. To the north are the rock wildernesses, lofty cones, and sheer precipices of the Bürken Kogel, Bull and Pizzo Schwalben, separated from him by the deep gorge that opens out at Landro. Peeping over this wilderness is part of the Drei Schuster, the giant of the Sexten Thal, whose middle and loftiest peak is 10,350 feet high. To the north-west, a long vista, between the Dürenstein and Geiselstein, lets the eye into the smiling basin of the Pragser Bad, and beyond, to the Welsberger Alp, in the Pusterthal near Brunecken. From no other point is the Geiselstein, which last year we baptised the 'Mount of Sacrifice,' seen to better advantage. To the right is the jagged lateral line of the Cristallo; to the left, four rugged series of bosses, forming the rocky mass of Monte Campedelle. Below, in front, lies the pleasant Lago di Misurina, occupying the meeting-point of the green lines sloping down from the Cadino and the Cristallo. Southwards, and filling up the whole space left open by the Misurina Alp, is seen the grand rock-world of the Marmarolo and Malcora, fully developed in all its intricacy and extreme of wildness. A lofty col between the two is the Forcella Grande, and nearly filling it, rises up beyond, the sharp snowy peak of the Antelao. The Misurina Alp is very extensive, affording pasture for

800 cattle. It belongs to the commune of Auronzo. In the lake are large trout.

Again, from near the Tre Croci, on the Cortina side, may be found a path—rather a difficult one—to the summit of that line of precipices which skirt the pass on the north. Thence is a fine view southward, including the Pelmo, the Civita, and the Marmolata. Churchill and I devoted to this excursion the last day of our stay, descending from the point of view described, through the uninhabited valley of Val Grande, upon the Ampezzo road at Ospitale. In this descent the ruined castle of Peutelstein appears with new and striking effect below, upon its isolated rock, surrounded by the heavy superincumbent masses of the Tofana and other Dolomitic mountains at the head of the Ampezzo. One of them, of a singular red hue, reminds one that the blood-stained mount of sacrifice, the Geiselstein, is in close neighbourhood below Ospitale.

It was on this occasion we found the path, which, leaving the road before it reaches Peutelstein, crosses the gorge on the left by a bridge suspended over dizzy depths, and shows the ruin in its most romantic aspect. It makes a short cut into the Ampezzo valley, about five miles above Cortina. The great route down the valley, of course, takes its Imperial way in straight lines and easy gradients. If, full of the sentiment of the old castle, you would enjoy the scenery as it was in days of yore, you may take the ancient pack-horse track, lying more in the bottom of the valley, and so return to Cortina. In it you will come upon the remains of another defensive work of the olden time—a square enclosure, with towers at the corners, evidently once the chief place of the valley. It was destroyed, they tell you, by the French.

CHAPTER XV.

THE CRESPENA JOCH AND CAPRILE COUNTRY.

From Cortina to Buchenstein—The Livinallongo—Finazzer's Inn—The Castello—An Expedition concerted—We leave our Wives 'at Home'—Corfara and the Priests – Plan and the Englishman—Castle of Wolkenstein — The Lämmergeier — The Jäger's Failures — The Crespena and its Weird Sights — St. Leonhard and Evangelistas' Inn —Buchenstein again—Reception at Caprile—Sta. Lucia—Val Ombretta—Excursion to Val di Zoldo—Tourists at Caprile—The Fisher Girl of Alleghe—The Timber 'Leap'—Agordo.

THE valleys of the Gader and Gröden, the one striking southward from the Pusterthal, the other eastward from the valley of the Eisack, meet at a Col bearing due west from Cortina, and distant about one long day's march. Though more visited than any of the Dolomitic valleys, except that of the Fassa, we had not yet seen them, and to do this, determined to shift our quarters to Buchenstein, in the Livinallongo, six hours west of Cortina.

On Tuesday morning, August 19, with three stout fellows carrying our baggage, we left the Aquila Nera. Everybody said the path to Buchenstein was very boggy, and S—— and A—— had dismal forebodings of sticking in the mud; we had waited, therefore, a day to let it harden, if it would; yet, as the track lay along the flanks of the Tofana, there was little chance but that it would be kept well watered.

The promise of weather was fair enough at first, and up the green pastures which command the Ampezzo valley it was pleasant walking; but from these slopes we passed to the track that has given a bad name to the pass. It is a confused labyrinth of water-courses, all descending from the Tofana; every twenty yards we had to dodge about for a crossing over some boggy streamlet, and the odious Tofana became more odious still. His precipices on the right were black under cloud, as usual, and a mizzling rain soon added to our difficulties. These wet green hills, the rain blotting out any distant view, wore an unhappy likeness to the grassy highlands of Scotland. A herdsman's hut was welcome; still more a gleam of sunshine, which sent us on rejoicing, and in hopes of eluding the Tofana before he could fill his rain-bottles again. We were not to escape so easily. In an hour he was down upon us, and this time with a pour that drove us to what shelter we could find—under the roots of an overhanging tree, to sit with legs dangling over a torrent, or squeezed against the lee-side of a pine trunk. We had lost the porters and the track; an hour passed before we hailed one of them in search of us. He led the way to a deserted hut, the last on this side the Col, where his comrades had raised a cheerful blaze with pine chips. Here, as long as we could stand the blinding smoke, we toasted our feet and dried our clothes.

To reach Buchenstein by daylight, however, it was necessary to face the storm again, and we made up our minds for a three hours' soak. But we were nearly beyond the evil influence of the Tofana. There was light a-head over the Col, and in half an hour, when we stood upon the ridge, all the Scotch-like mist and streaming hill-sides were behind; and in front, all the romantic richness and grandeur of the Italian Alps. Changes so magical are the delight of the mountains. The rain on the Cortina side certainly enhanced the contrast which awaited us on the other; but I am inclined to think that it must always be striking. The Cortina side is dull. The precipices of the Tofana may be fine, if they are ever free from cloud; in other directions there is, I suspect, a tameness and monotony of scenery, and pretty certainly a monotony of mud. The pass crosses the same range as that from Caprile to Cortina by the Gusella; the latter, our track of the year before, is far superior.

The path was now among slabs and blocks of rock. Scrambling down in haste to reach lovely glades below, we were suddenly stopped by a gate—an odd impediment in so wild a spot. It marked the limits of the Ampezzo district, and would have mattered nothing to us, but that the porters took advantage of it to strike for wages. I am sorry to record this of them, and it was indeed all the work of one grumbler, who had never liked the job. Seizing some of the luggage he carried, transferring it to our own backs, and upbraiding them all for breach of contract, Churchill and I soon stopped the mutiny, which for a moment looked awkward; once through the gate, and they would willingly have relieved us of our self-imposed burdens, if we would have let them.

According to the map, we should now soon arrive at Buchenstein; and very puzzling it was to dive deeper, and still deeper into the endless depths of valley, and find it not. A castle-ruin, yellow-white as the Dolomite fragment on which it was perched, shone through the trees; we followed still the torrent, that tumbled adown rocks, woods, and meadows, and sometimes far outstripped us by a headlong plunge. A village, Andraz, appeared near the opening upon the Livinallongo, the central valley of the district; and here the path divided—descending on the left to reach Caprile,—on the right, keeping high upon the mountain side. This terrace walk was ours; it commanded prospects the most enchanting. Opposite, across the deep valley of the Livinallongo, and over an intervening ridge, rose the Marmolata, white with snow and glacier; at the upper end of the valley stood the Dolomitic mass of the Sella Spitze, closing it entirely in that direction; and at the lower, filling up the vista, the noble shape of the Civita, soaring clear and free, with lovely Alleghe set like an emerald below. Woods and crags, and jutting cottage-roofs, formed the nearer view.

You must climb the bleak pass through hours of rain, and turn upon that terrace-path as the western sun is flooding all the valley with lustrous amber tints, to appreciate that view as we did; but it must be always beautiful.

Buchenstein is on the level of this path, and appropriates almost all its advantages of view. The village hangs on the very steep northern side of the Livinallongo, about 5,000 feet above the sea. Pieve is the name in most maps; and where, in the same maps, Buchenstein is placed, there is certainly no village at all. There are two inns—the best, Finazzer's, is a small shop at a small corner. At the head of the stairs you will see upon the wall ancient spears and halberds, spoils from the 'Castello,' as the ruin on the Dolomitic rock is called—what other name it had is lost. From the landing a ladder takes you to an upper floor, and at the top of the ladder you run your head against an ugly life-size figure of a man, painted on the wall, who points the way to two adjacent chambers. They are queer little dens. Every odd bit of space is used as store for groceries; pyramids of sugar stand white in the corners, and cases and sacks peep from under the beds. But they are snug, which is what you most want at such an elevation; and then from one of them, through the small hole of a window, what a prospect! The house, like most in the village, is built at the edge of a cliff. From this the valley falls away so suddenly, and so deep, that you cannot see the bottom; but far away, through the vista of overlapping hills, the eye, as if from the watch-tower of some lofty castle, pursues the wondrous view right on to the Civita. Draw back the curtain as you lie in bed when morning dawns, and you can watch the purple edge with gold as the mountain ridges successively catch the sunbeams.

A small room on the first floor serves for a salle, and has the same view, if you could see it, for the plants and double casements that fill up the apertures of windows. Like the rest of the house, the salle is clotted up with all sorts of stores, and much tawdry church rubbish besides, the relics of bygone festivals, all contributing to a certain musty smell pervading the place. More interesting objects are a Jäger's shooting gear—wonderful rifles, with crooked stocks—ranged on the walls; and a picture, representing the proud occasion when their owner returned from Innsbruck to his native village, the winner at the yearly shooting match. The hostess is his daughter—an active little body, and a very fair cook. The Jäger himself, now an old man, keeps a small inn at Andraz. His name, also spelt 'Vinazer,' is a renowned one in the Gröden Thal. A family, to whom no doubt he is related, lived at St. Ulrich in the eighteenth century, and became celebrated as artists both in Spain and elsewhere.

We differ about the merits of Buchenstein. Some of us cannot forget the grocery smells; others retort about the wonderful view. It would, indeed, be difficult to find one more beautiful of its sort than that from the hole in the wall, which serves as window to the little eastern bedroom. In the morning the Civita is a dark silhouette; in the evening it is all a-glow. Nay, you may sometimes see a sight more solemn than the mountains. Below, across a deep ravine, lies the village cemetery. One early morning a group of men and women were waiting there at the gate, beside a small coffin on the ground. The priest, in surplice and cap, arrived; and the bare-headed procession, reciting prayers that floated far in the still air, followed him up the grave-covered hill. In front went a cross of flowers and ribbons, carried by a boy; while another, from a pail of holy water, plentifully aspersed the sacred soil around. At the grave the men stood in a cluster; behind them, at a little distance, knelt the women; two only among them, in Sunday white sleeves, distinguished in any way as mourners. The grave was entirely filled in before the service ended; a cross was planted at the head, and, for the last time, the rain of holy water fell upon the group. Then they left the sleeper till that other morning when the rocks and hills shall disappear, and the little child awake! One of the white-sleeved women remained behind; she paid the sexton, sprinkled once more the grave, and, as it seemed with special care, some other graves around. Morning and evening, so long as we stayed, the same figure was to be seen there, turning for many a lingering look each time as she stole away.

The church stands upon a ledge near the village plaza, the terrace walls impending over the depth of valley; and in the dusk you may compose there what elegies you will. The draping woods hang before you as a pall; the Sella Spitze and the Civita you may liken to the old world's tombstones. When the Angelus bell has ceased, no one will disturb you; but the black figure of the *Geistlicher* will perhaps come out on a narrow shelf of garden below, pacing backward and forward, his day's duties over, and carrying a tiny red spark at the end of his pipe.

The Castello, said to be of Roman origin, but whose present ruins date back only from the middle ages, lies in a lonely spot, an hour and a half from Buchenstein, on the path to Cortina. It is one of the most characteristic of the

Dolomite castles, built on the top of an isolated fragment, half toppling over on the slope of a hill. I spent a morning there. Two sides of the rock overhang, and carrying up a wall under one of these, they obtained a sort of huge cavern, useful, no doubt, in many ways, besides preventing an enemy from sheltering where they could not 'prod' at him. There are the remains of a drawbridge over a torrent that rushes past the foot of the rock, and of various battlemented outworks. The castle itself above, clings to every inch that could be made available, and looks like a strange

CASTELLO.

half-destroyed fungus that had grown upon the grey rock fragment. Northward lies a sterile Dolomitic range, peak above peak, with old Tofana in their midst. Darkness, rain, and thunder gathered upon him, as usual; and a spurt of his wrath drove me under the caverned rock for shelter. It was a freak worthy of the spot to build there a Place of strength.

The expedition to the Gader and Gröden valleys, Churchill and I were to make alone. In the angle between them stands a huge mass of mountain, possessing no designation, as a whole, in the mouths of the country-people in either valley, who have contented themselves with bestowing names upon the peaks or bosses that stand immediately opposite them. Thus, that part of it forming the western boundary to the upper Gader is called the Guerdenazza Berg; the name Geister Spitzen is attached to a portion of the north-west wall; while the Crespena Kofel rises aloft on the south-east border. On its western side it is cut into by two ravine-like valleys, the Tschister Thal and the Langen Thal, by which access to the plateau is gained, and which, running north-east, are in line with two others starting from the opposite border. In this manner the plateau is naturally divided into three sections. Baron Richthofen has selected the Guerdenazza as the designation for the whole mass. The entire area amounts to about twenty-two square miles, and the level of the plateau must be at least 9,000 feet above the sea.

We proposed to cross this plateau by way of the Langen Thal, in the Upper Gröden, passing over the Crespena Joch to St. Leonhard, in the Gader Thal. Ascending, we should see the mountains of the Gröden; descending, those of the Gader, and see them far better than by merely passing through either of the valleys.

With a man to carry our knapsacks, we departed one bright morning, S—— and A—— accompanying us for an hour. Then, rather forlorn, they left us to return alone as their own wits and our best instructions might serve, and not to expect us at Buchenstein till the third day at shortest. Meanwhile the Jäger's daughter had promised to take care of them, and the painted man would stand sentinel at their doors. Three hours over rolling, grassy, and rather boggy hills, redeemed by massive Dolomites lifting their grey and yellow sides in all directions, brought us to the solitary inn of Corfara, at the head of the Gader Thal—a spot dreary enough. Yet six priests, out for a '*lust reise*'—or, say 'a lark'—had made it their rendezvous for the day, and, in a very lively clatter of talk, were approaching at the same moment with ourselves. Brown, honest, mountain-looking men they were, and withal, cordially good-natured. While we lunched, they dined, and, it is certain, discussed something other than theology. The best bedroom in this out-of-the-way place had a carved ceiling of remarkably rich design, and the panelled walls enclosed no end of roomy cupboards; yet commend me to the stuffy little dens at Buchenstein the rather, for the windows here looked out only upon mud.

On again, and with improving landscape, up a rather steep pass between two vast bulks of mountain, all bare and awful rock, the upward abysses filled with surging cloud. The mass on the right was the Guerdenazza, that on the left the Sella Spitze—the same that, from Buchenstein, divides the honours of the view with the Civita. This Sella Plateau stands between the heads of the Fassa, Gröden, and Gader valleys, a wilderness in itself, and, excepting the Guerdenazza, differs from most other Dolomites, showing neither pinnacles nor towers, but long terrace ridges, amazing bastions, and flattish cones rising up out of its interior. We learnt to regard this mountain with great respect, though the pretensions of its neighbours—the Schlern, Marmolata, Lang Kofel, and others—had at first obscured its merits; and we were not for some time aware of its singular Orographic importance.

The Col we were ascending divides the Gader from the Gröden Thal, and the descent into the latter lay through smiling hay slopes, broken into numerous lovely glades by rocky fragments, and clumps of the picturesque *Pinus Cembra*—a tree dark and rich in foliage, but in sadly too much request for the carvings that make the Gröden Thal famous. The Lang Kofel and the Schlern, now showing themselves in front, pleasantly linked our present ramble with last year's wanderings. We were to sleep at Plan, described in 'Murray'—for to this portion of the Dolomites he devotes a page or two—as 'an inn of the humblest description;' and so we found it. Butcher's business was

VIEW OF THE SELLA SPITZE FROM THE GRÖDEN THAL.

going on below; in the room assigned us, one bed was shoved into a recess where the roof sloped down from within eighteen inches of one's nose, to within two of one's toes; and the other was mysteriously developed out of the thickness of the wainscot.

But the best room was occupied—and by whom? Positively, an Englishman! Remember that through all these regions, both last year and this, we had never chanced upon a compatriot, and you will understand the curious sensation caused by the discovery. What President of the 'Alpines,' or learned Professor of the 'ologies,' was this, prowling within the charmed circle of the Dolomites? Well, we never learnt the name of our friend, but he was certainly neither a Kennedy nor a Murchison. For one thing, it was clear he did not know where he was. From his own account — knowing no language but his own, and bound to walk, except on Sundays, so many hours a day—he had started on a direct line from somewhere in Italy, to somewhere in Germany, and that straight line brought him here. This eccentric specimen of our eccentric nation was in high condition; brawny, bull-necked, and sunburnt, he might have stood for a portrait of St. Christopher on his travels—he had all the saint's goodnature—and knew as little of the Dolomites. The next morning he was off on his straight line again—northward, for the Gader—his knapsack carried by a porter at twice a fair day's wages.

Hitherto we had not been able to learn anything about the Crespena Joch; but the late landlord of Plan was a Jäger in his day, and his son, Alois Perathoner, a jaunty young fellow, proud of inheriting the family rifle, went into raptures about the black cock, ptarmigan, chamois, and *lämmergeier*, to be shot there. 'Lämmergeier!' we exclaimed. 'Ja, ja,' cried our young host, stretching his arms to express the enormous spread of wing of this vulture-eagle of the Alps—ten or twelve feet sometimes from tip to tip. It is, perhaps, scarcely necessary to explain that this formidable bird is now very rare, both in the Alps and Pyrenees, though, perhaps, more frequently to be met with in the Grisons than elsewhere in Europe. Yet what better refuge could the fierce marauder find than the Guerdenazza and its neighbours? To climb the Joch was now an enterprise more than ever tempting. Our sporting friend intimated, with a patronising air, that he would accompany us. Far too magnificent to talk about terms, he would have left that matter to arrange itself; but his old mother struck in with a stout refusal to let the rifle go without a definite understanding, which it cost some trouble to arrive at with the strong-fisted dame.

Plan is at the foot of a pass—the Evas Joch—leading to Campitello, between the Sella Spitze and Lang Kofel, and likely to partake of the grandeur of both mountains. The Lang Kofel cannot be seen well, till lower down the Gröden Thal than we were able to reach the evening we were at Plan; but the shadow of him rested upon the white ghostly mass of the Sella, and told of his presence.

No morning could be more brilliant than that destined for the Crespena. Our young friend stepped forth wonderfully accoutred with pouches and belts, a fowling-piece, rifle, and, as he professed himself a mineralogist, a geological hammer to boot. Too much burdened with all these, his younger brother was summoned to serve as henchman; and our porter, to whom the affair was no joke, gravely followed with his load. At the village of Sta. Maria, half an hour down the valley, whose church is celebrated for a pilgrimage-picture of the Madonna, we turned up the Lang Thal, a delicious green glade, flat and lawny, guarded on both sides by singular towers of rock, or, rather, an avenue of towers, 2,000 feet in height—their summits steeped in sunshine, their bases in cool shade. The effect was quite novel, for again the contour of rock differed from the usual Dolomitic forms.

But where is Wolkenstein? Wolkenstein was a castle of the valley, in the family of Oswald the Minnesinger, and when the poet lived at Hauenstein, under the Schlern, was occupied by his brother Michael. It was the original seat of the family. Tradition asserts that it was built by an Italian Count, who fled from the invasions of Attila into the mountains. In very early times, however, it came into possession of the Lords of 'Villanders,' (a castle near Klausen,) who took from it their title of Wolkenstein. Well may it be named 'the stone in the clouds,' wrapped, as it must often be, in mountain mist. From an early date it served to protect wayfarers over the pass of Campitello into Italy; though at the same time its garrison is said to have often inflicted great cruelties upon the surrounding peasantry.

We had looked vainly for the ruin up this glen the night before, picturing it on some airy height. We were amazed when now, stuck against the side of the loftiest boss of Dolomite, appeared a patch of yellow clay—nothing more—and that was Wolkenstein! It is niched into the wall of precipice rising sheer 2,000 feet above, and partly leaning over, so that no enemy, should he ever reach the summit, could even shoot down the chimneys—if chimneys there were, for smoke that could never live in face of such a cliff. 'How terribly afraid of each other they must have been in those days,' said Churchill; and it was the most appropriate comment. Why else should anyone build his house, like a swallow, against the wall of rock? It is possible that, like one or two castles in the Val di Non, interior caverns, natural or artificial, where armed retainers might lie like maggots in a cheese, may have been the inducement. We had no time to climb and see.

Further on, in the depths of the glade, stood a small chapel, as old as the castle, they said, and containing one or two pictures brought from thence, as well as ancient frescoes, now obscured by whitewash. A more recent interest lay in a memorial of the death of a girl who fell over the Wolkenstein precipice a few years ago, while keeping sheep upon the summit. Coming out into the air again, we turned to look up at those awful salmon-tinted battlements, aloft in the blue sky—the dizzy height from which she fell. At the moment, 'Geier, Geier!' shouted our young guide, and two stately birds, with no perceptible motion of their outspread wings, sailed slowly across the sunlit face of the rock, and into the blue again. Their enormous size might be calculated from the height at which they crossed the front of precipice. In a frenzy of excitement, Alois seized the already loaded rifle from the hands of his brother, and rushing nearer the base of the rock, fired almost directly upward. The height was too great; one of the creatures swerved perhaps for an instant, but did not appear to quicken its moveless flight.

Our friend was mortified at this failure, and as we pursued our way up the sloping bottom of the glen, now widening into sunny spaces, now narrowing into a rock-strewn gully, had much to say in explanation. At last pointing to a pine-tree stem, clear in the midst of a grassy opening, and about 600 yards distant, 'Now,' said he, 'I will show you that I can shoot.' He fired, and we all walked on, nothing doubting the result; the marksman quickening his pace in his eagerness to point out the scar. He looked long with a face of deepening gravity; none of us could help him to a feasible hole, and muttering something about 'an ass,' and 'the devil,' he turned away, very crestfallen. Presently he shot a grey crow of which he was not very proud; but these repeated discharges brought down wonderful rolling thunders from the rocks, if nothing else, and enlivened the walk considerably.

We were all this time ascending; but the stiff climb was postponed till at the end of the glen, a very steep funnel of débris crossed by innumerable faint zigzags, offered the only means of further progress. These were wide enough to hold one foot at a time, but no more, and cost an hour and a half of steady stepping. When we touched the summit we found ourselves immediately looking down an opposite ravine, which nearly cleft the mountain in two, and left us standing upon a narrow neck —a deep funnel on either side. Advancing a short distance to the left, and the vast Guerdenazza platform was displayed, several square miles in extent, a picture of the sternest desolation. It is set round with lofty bosses, and in the midst rise conical towers like the ash-surrounded orifices of extinct craters. The white, storm-washed rocks are terrible in their solitude. One might suppose the scene a piece of Spitzbergen. Among the jagged ridges near the southern front of the mountain, lies a small tarn, dark as if it were a pool in snow; on our way to this tarn, suddenly, before our faces, rose a Lämmergeier! He was within a few yards of us, but by ill luck the rifle had been left with our porter at the ridge. With fowling-piece only, away dashed our sportsman, endeavouring to get beneath the circling bird, rising slowly into the air, and with the same even steady flight as the others. At the shot, the Geier seemed neither hastened nor impeded, only slanting his course towards the gully we had left. Alois perhaps watched longer and more keenly than we, for presently shouting, 'he has fallen, he has fallen!' he rushed off white with excitement, and we saw him no more till, returned from the tarn, we found him, without the Geier, indeed, but staring still into the gorge, where, wounded or not, it had disappeared.

The passage across the Crespena Joch is not marked by any path. The desert of scarred and broken rock, the slabs, fissures, and ridges, all bleached and shattered dolomite, admit of none. The course of the hunter or herdsman is directed by the bearings of certain of its towers and cones. At the widest it would take two or three hours to pass from edge to edge. Numerous deep cracks were pointed out as caused by lightning; and in a recent-looking hole we were assured a thunderbolt had buried itself not a fortnight since. When caught in these storms, the Jägers hide their rifles under one slab of rock, and themselves under another, lest their gun-barrels should prove fatal lightning conductors. One shelf of bare rock was singularly marked with circular indentures, as if a dozen donkeys had danced over it, leaving for ever the petrified prints of their hoofs. No explanation offered itself to our Scientific, though he would not admit the supposition of mysterious donkeys. But among the weird sights of this thunder-smitten place, were here and there a lovely gem of Nature's setting. In secret cracks and holes were nestled delicate little ferns, mosses, and occasionally a brilliant Alpine floweret, such as *Gentiana imbricata, Arenaria ciliata, Armeria alpina,* and *Pæderota Bonarota.* The Crespena Joch, though unknown to the tourist, is not so to the botanist of these Alps. Churchill had long had the name in his note-book.

The view! To the north and east we were shut up by the white masses of the plateau itself. Westward some fine 'shrieking' looking peaks were identified as the Geister Spitzen. More to the south lay the Schlern (of glorious memory) and nearer, the towering Lang Kofel, but early obscured by clouds which grew upon the splendour of the morning. Directly in front was the wilderness of the Sella Plateau, the companion of the Guerdenazza, which it much resembled in conformation; and beyond to the south-east shone the glaciers of the Marmolata—the noblest sight of all.

Yet the riven summit of the Sella, dark with tormented cloud, was the more interesting at the moment; a darkness, not of cloud only, but of mystery and murder hung over it. Alois, clashing his gun-stock upon the ground, and pointing with an impressive finger toward one of those livid rifts, 'That,' said he, 'is the Forbidden Way,' and then with rapid pantomimic action, he poignarded his stomach and pistolled his ear. It was very dreadful, but what did it mean? The best we could make out was, that a path existed there over the Sella to the Val Fassa, which either on account of the smuggling facilities it offered, or from certain robberies and assassinations of which it had been the scene, had been closed by the authorities. That these mountains were not entirely free from the latter danger we had afterwards reason to believe; but the 'Forbidden Way' looked tempting as other forbidden ways, though for no earthly reason than that it *was* forbidden.

The clouds in that direction began to look malignant, and an occasional low rumble sounded as if the lurking lightnings were finding here and there a victim. Our young host of Plan had engaged to conduct us to the edge of the descent into the Gader Thal; and was now anxious to fulfil his task and be gone before the Guerdenazza itself should become the scene of a tempest. He showed us the deep valley into which we must descend; assured us we could not lose the way when fairly off the summit; and then with his companion turned at a rapid pace towards the advancing gloom. We, as rapidly, plunged downward, and in three minutes were utterly lost among edges of impossible precipices. They fell in terrace after terrace on every side. At the same moment a curling cloud lifted itself over the top, and stretched after us long wispy fingers like a pursuing ghost; should it reach us, we could only huddle together under a rock and wait—all night perhaps. That adventure did not happen. With much backward and forward work, skirting and craning over no end of precipices—always another when we thought we had cleared them all—scrambling down 'chimneys,' and squeezing through clefts, helped at last by a shepherd shouting from a rock islanded in mist—helped to better purpose still, by an old woman returning with an empty 'creel' to the valley—we reached the bottom. For full two hours our cloudy foe, unable to overtake us bodily, pelted us mercilessly with rain.

There was only one inn to make for—Evangelista's, at the village of St. Leonhard. It was difficult to find; and when we did find it, the good man was far too good to allow us any meat on a Friday. A piece of dry bread and cup of coffee at five in the morning; another piece, and a couple of eggs for dinner, had left us sharp set now, for supper. More eggs and more coffee, however, did very well for us, as for others who had sought the same shelter; and meanwhile Evangelista, in black skull-cap and lean breeches, quaint in costume as in name, sat by each guest in turn, putting benignantly the quaint questions of the olden days. 'Whence come you to-day? and whither going?' 'Ah! yes; and how have you found it on the way?' And so each man's story comes out, and is commented upon. Later than ourselves, as tired, wet, and hungry, came in a German mineralogist, with a bag of fossils from St. Cassian, and shared our bedroom; there were four beds in one large chamber. His toilet was delightfully simple—off with coat, waistcoat, and trowsers, and he was ready for bed; on with them in the morning, and he was ready for breakfast. His pouch of fossils and an umbrella were his only encumbrances! St. Cassian is a village two hours from St. Leonhard's, celebrated for the enormous richness in fossil shells of certain beds in the volcanic ash of its vicinity,—not far from the summit ridge between the Gader and Livinallongo, and north-west of the Dolomitic peak of the Set Sass.

Of the scenery at the head of the Gader Thal we could scarcely form an opinion. The rain that fell all night, fell still in the morning; and the Guèrdenazza on one side, and the Heiligen Kreutz Kogel on the other, showed only their piney flanks. Yet the latter can, we fancy, boast an array of jagged peaks when the sky is clear above. The season, this year, they said, had been 'always rain.'

We were ready to start at six, hoping to reach Buchenstein for dinner; but it was not till after ten that a few wandering sun gleams drew us from Evangelista's roof. At St. Cassian we stepped into the curé's house to enquire the way. His housekeeper will entertain a traveller when need be; and the smell of dinner was too potent for men who had fasted on the Friday so rigidly as we. A portly priest, on a visit to the curé, was one we had seen at Cortina; and while their reverences dined at one table, we did the same at another, under a lively fire of questions. The ascent behind St. Cassian was almost one quagmire; the soil in many places had slipped, and the turf lay in folds and wrinkles down the slopes. Nothing could be more tedious, and successive storms of rain overtook us from the ever-gloomy Tofana, now visible to the east, outtopping its more western neighbours. Yet once upon the ridge, and the valley of Livinallongo, with the Civita in the distance, opened to sight as lovely as ever; and at five we entered Buchenstein, to find our wives gone up the wrong hill to meet us! From the little window in the wall they were soon seen returning. Their three solitary days had passed tolerably; but they were clearly rather tired, both of the Finazzers and themselves. We enjoyed the welcome Sunday's rest upon the alpine meadows, an hour or so above the village; while the Marmolata, bright with snow, and the Civita, crowned with spires, chaunted us their psalms.

A week at Caprile was in the programme of our journey. It lay at only three hours' distance; and having sent word of our approach, we moved down there on the Monday morning. A rich and picturesque descent it is; but Caprile does not show, till the steeple is exactly under your feet, and just at that interesting moment our unfortunate mule tumbled over a rock, which blocked up the deep-sunk path, and lay wedged and groaning under a heap of baggage. The misadventure caused considerable delay, and rather spoiled our first greeting to Caprile. When we made our appearance in the narrow street, hasty messengers were seen flying to the 'Pezzés'; and father, mother, son, and daughter, were quickly grouped at their door to give us a right kindly welcome. Cortina received us graciously, but Caprile affectionately. The rooms had all been freshly swept and garnished. Two large bouquets, which no Caprile garden could have furnished, ornamented the salle, and an enormous cake, made expressly for the occasion, was placed upon the table. Every little want of last year had been remembered and provided for, with an anxious care that was quite touching, and especially an ample supply of meat had been obtained, so that we can no longer speak of the Caprile larder as ill provided. A few little presents, brought from England for this worthy family, were accepted as the gifts of friends; and like friends we were treated during the five days that Caprile was our home.

There were three or four things to be done at Caprile. The first was to get the Pelmo into the sketch-book, as seen from Sta Lucia. This village we had passed on our way over the Gusella the year before, and it may be remembered as that which once held Titian prisoner for a fortnight during a storm of snow. On the afternoon of our arrival I started. No chance of catching the Pelmo in his naked majesty was to be neglected in this unsettled weather. How anxious is the moment when, after a hard climb, your mountain should appear within the next few steps,—and there may be only white masses of cloud instead! That afternoon he was tolerably gracious, baring first one shoulder and then another, lastly unrobing his hoary head. The peasants, busy in the last labours of their harvest, collected, as usual, to witness the strange processes of art. Of course, apropos of an Englishman, there soon turned up the name of Lord Palmerston. 'Ah, he is a wonderful man. "Sehr kräftig." Whatever he wills must be.' Thirty years ago Borrow heard the same story from the peasants in Spain. Two or three houses in the village looked like relics of a time when, spite of its isolated and airy situation, it may have been of more importance than now. Upon one was carved armorial bearings, with the date 1601, and upon a tablet was inscribed: 'Fabt—15 + 85—Renovta 17 + 96.' Churchill, with S—— and A——, arrived just in time to observe one of those wonders of colour which sunset sometimes works among mountains. The Pelmo glowed vermilion through a drapery of clouds, and reddened with reflection all the landscape round. Where was Titian's hand to dash the splendour in? Though darkness follows quick upon these sunsets, we could not leave the spectacle till it had faded quite away; then hurried for the descent. Caprile's steeple could scarcely be distinguished among its score of roofs when we reached the nearest overhanging shoulder, but its vesper bell-sounds came swelling up from the gloom.

Under the southern precipices of the Marmolata is the Val Ombretta—'the valley of shade.' From the description of a German geologist, it should be one of the grandest things to be seen hereabouts. 'Shady' it must be, between those frightful walls of rock on the one hand, and the masses of the Sasso Vernale on the other. On an expedition to the Ombretta, Churchill and I were accompanied by Pellegrini, Herr Grohmann's guide, 'of inexhaustible humour.' Our own deficiencies in Italian no doubt prevented our appreciating the finer points of his wit, and perhaps compelled his drollery to expend itself chiefly in certain capers and pantomimic performances.

Away we trudged on a bright morning; at first on the track familiar to us, through Rocca, and through the 'famous' gorge of Sottoguda. We were curious to verify our impressions of the spot by a second visit. Morning, instead of evening light, and ascending, instead of descending, made a difference certainly; and perhaps there was something on our first passage through it due to unexpectedness. We used to speak of dozens of bridges—there are, I believe, just twelve of them. The distance is under, rather than over, a mile; and there are some wider spaces than we remembered. All this for accuracy, but we hold, nevertheless, to its being a gorge grand enough for anybody, and if Herr Grohmann calls it 'famous,' and speaks of it as 'a crack a thousand feet deep,' others must think so too.

Once through the Sottoguda gorge, instead of turning up towards the Fedaia on the right, we kept on directly for the face of the Marmolata. Of two modes of access to the Ombretta we chose the shortest. Pellegrini said indeed something about a ladder; but we understood it metaphorically of the steepness of the path. After an hour's scrambling, however, we suddenly ran our noses against something too like a ladder, and too little like it, to be pleasant either way. Upon a face of rock were two long beams of wood, with, instead of spells, notches cut in the timbers at irregular intervals. The first alarming supposition was that our unaccustomed feet were to go into those notches; but after Pellegrini had gone up, cat-like, it appeared that the notches were for the hands only, while the feet were to do their best with the rock below. It was easy enough when we tried it, and as for getting back again there was another path for the cows, and we were confident of being equal to cow-practice at least.

Not long after this we entered the Ombretta. It is a mere cup hoisted up upon the side of the Marmolata, and at such a height that the south precipice which drops into it, loses much of its expected effect. If the Ombretta had lain as deep as we supposed, then that precipice must have been prodigious. Still, on a more favourable day it might answer better to the description of our geological precursor. When we were there it went straight up into a line of cloud. On the side opposite to the Marmolata rise dark snow-patched rocks, and the whole boulder-sprinkled hollow is a perfect specimen of dreariness. A cluster of black sheds in the midst shelter the cattle which come here for their summer feeding, and their 'banished lord' who tends them ; he answered with a far off *jödel* to Pellegrini's call, which we took for permission to use his bowls, drink his milk, and poke his fire ; but we never saw the solitary man.

The return path showed us by far the finest scenery. From it the structure of the south-east corner of the Marmolata, a marvellous piece of natural architecture, is admirably seen; and the views outward embrace the summits of the Pelmo, Civita, and many other jagged tops. The excursion would be worth making for the sake of this portion of it alone. It was dusk as we hurried through the deep portals of the Sottoguda gorge, which was all itself at such an hour. Dim figures of returning peasants flitted across the bridges, filed along the ledges, were darkly seen here and there against the white torrent surf,—just where they were wanted.

One more excursion from Caprile I must put before the reader. That spiry wonderful Civita, which looks like one vast shattered wall: is it really a wall? or is there a long slope at the back by which it could be ascended? Pellegrini said it was unscalable. The St. Vito landlord, on the contrary, thought it might be ascended from the Val di Zoldo. This valley, opening at Longarone towards the Belluno country, penetrates by various choking gorges and platforms of verdure, to a point midway between the Pelmo and Civita. We had seen every side of the Pelmo but this; we had seen no side of the Civita but that from Caprile; it was an object therefore to explore that portion at least of the Val di Zoldo. It might be reached in four hours over the Col Dai from Caprile.

Dear mother Pezzé there was no doubt would take abundant care of S—— and A—— during our absence, and on Wednesday afternoon, with lively hawk-nosed Pellegrini, and young Pezzé, as a volunteer, we took—not the road but the path,—first to Alleghe, accompanied so far by S—— and A——, and then up the ridge by the side of the Civita. There was a saddening soapy look in the sky, and before long, it began to rain, while heavy volumes of mist rolled down upon our Col. A few glimpses of the Civita upon our right—peeps into the wild heart of him—and now and then a backward glance into the depths of Alleghe, were all we got before entering the body of cloud, which left nothing visible but scattered rocks, and forlorn slopes of grass. Yet on the Col itself, we were lucky. At the moment of reaching it, the mists tucked up their skirts with a magical swiftness, parted right and left, and the Civita close on one hand, the Pelmo more distant on the other, and the long descending Val di Zoldo in front, were simultaneously displayed. It was but for the moment, then cloud and rain enveloped all as before.

On the descent, a sloppy hole in the grass was pointed out in which a cow had disappeared a week or two before, beyond all reach of plumbing. Of course every one that passes pokes his stick down as far as he can, and wonders, but will never know, where the cow has gone to. In the valley our observation was confined to the string of dirty villages we passed through—dirty and wretched-looking enough; yet several of the houses showed faded colours on their walls, remnants of frescoes—Scripture pieces very literally, here an arm and there a leg of sacred personages,—while not unfrequently a small glassless window would show a Venetian column, or a balcony of rusty but elaborate iron-work hold pots of straggling carnations.

It would have been much more convenient to find quarters at one of these villages, but we could readily believe young Pezzé's assurance that the inn was '*cattivissimo*'—'most bad'—though scarcely his accompanying assertion that at St. Nicolo there was one 'most excellent.' Such it proved, however; a tidy, bright-looking country house, with a clean kitchen for a very noticeable fact. They would have served us supper on the third story in solitary state among the best bedrooms, but we preferred descending to the company of a priest, the landlord and his wife, and our two guides. Doubtless they preferred it too; all that evening the three former never took their eyes off us. The landlady for a long time stood fixed to the middle of the floor, till at last she accommodated herself with a chair, still intent upon our every movement. Without our wives we had small means of conversation—nobody spoke anything but Italian, and after parting with the few words at our disposal, we resigned ourselves to sup with silent and regal composure.

The rain still continued in the morning, and would have rendered hopeless any attempt upon the Civita, from which indeed we had been sufficiently discouraged from what we had seen of its back premises in descending the Pass. There was no practicable slope, only jagged ramparts in all directions, and it was clear that it was in reality almost as much of a wall as it seemed from Caprile. During a temporary clearance this morning, among the clouds, we verified that discovery, ascertaining also that the ascent would require a considerable circuit so as to attack the spiny ridge at its south-west extremity, whence it might be followed till the brink of the great precipice over Alleghe should be reached. A good climber on a fine day would be rewarded.

That temporary gleam and space of drifting blue did us one rare service. For an hour the Pelmo, far more striking here than the Civita, rose clear above the near green slopes of the valley northward—rose like some dream of Martin's —all but the very battlements free from cloud; a pale salmon-tinted, glistening mass, shooting upward from its hidden base below into the eddying mists above; a spectacle not of the earth but of the sky, in its cerulean tints and aërial architecture. St. Nicolo is a straggling village, its red-spired church occupying the edge of one of the abrupt descents so common in Alpine valleys. Below, at about two hours' distance, is Forno, the principal village of the Val di Zoldo. Here again a (more stately) church, with a frescoed façade, is placed upon a commanding platform, and the houses are jumbled together at the bottom. It is the centre of a busy nail manufacture, carried on in sequestered humble-looking sheds. Scraps of old iron of every description are brought up on muleback from the Venetian towns, and, beaten into nails, are carried down again on muleback, through the almost continuous gorge of ten or twelve miles between Forno and Longarone. This gorge—for we explored it the following year—offers some fine scenery, especially in glimpses to right and left, of Dolomitic precipices aloft. Near Forno there rises, in closely-fretted tiers, something like a gigantic imitation of Henry VII.'s chapel, another illustration of Dolomitic caprice.

The hope in the sky was soon gone; and after waiting half the day for another chance, we started to return, marching in wet, wet, wet; hour after hour over the Col; finding scant shelter now and then under a rock or tree. Towards evening there was a lift and a swirl among the masses of vapour, and suddenly beneath our feet—for we stood upon a jutting grassy pyramid—lay lovely Alleghe, and opposite, reared the bare-naped neck of Monte Pizzo, in whose throes of trouble the lake was born. Two hours afterwards we entered Caprile.

An immense event had happened in our absence. At noon that day five Englishmen trooped into the village, and were, as our wives informed us, at this moment penned in the lower salle. Mother Pezzé was in great excitement, rushing up and down stairs, conveying scraps of information now to the ladies, now doubtless to the gentlemen. '*Dio, Dio*!' said she, 'how shall I understand them?' for our countrymen were evidently ill provided with Italian vocables, while, drenched and hungry, they had much need of them. No diplomatic intercourse had as yet taken place, but was supposed to be imminent; and, in fact, ten minutes after our arrival, an ambassador of very engaging address appeared at the top of the stairs to arrange an exchange of civilities. They were an Oxford party, abroad for the first time, and making their way, somewhat hedge and ditch fashion, for Venice, had tumbled thus into the Dolomite country. The weather had prevented their seeing anything of it; and as on the following morning they split into two parties—the one for the Ampezzo, the other for the Adige—they would be speedily out of its labyrinthine recesses. In the early daylight their cheerful English voices made the street jocund for a few minutes, as, with guides and mules, they took their different ways. Perhaps they saw enough that day to carry away a favourable report; for the following year, when we were again in the neighbourhood, seven more happy 'knapsacks,' as we heard, invaded the village, and Caprile, which had scarcely seen an English face before our visit, can now, no doubt, look at an Englishman with more composure.

If the second party were like the first, they never saw Alleghe, and missed, let me tell them, not only one of the finest bits of scenery in Europe, but as pretty a fisher-girl as they might wish to see. In a round hat and knitted jacket, she was sculling about the lake that day, and of her own sweet will rowed home, and back again, to land some chairs for us as we sat by the side of the soft lapping water; then, resting on the gunwale, she occupied her pretty fingers in breaking wriggling worms to pieces to serve for bait,—a fisher-girl *is* a fisher-girl, you know. In the afternoon one more clamber to Sta. Lucia, and in the evening one more chat with dear mother Pezzé and sighing Ursulina. We were all getting sentimental, and the parting in the morning was rather more than that—the poor woman and her daughter were fairly in tears, and we, for our parts, were in anything but a joyous mood as we filed away from the hospitable door. We were bound for Primiero, far off among the southern mountains, towards Feltre and the Val Sugana. It will presently be seen what led us there. To reach it we must now descend the Val Agordo to the town of that name, a walk of six hours.

Civita looked its grandest. At the lake, the fisher-girl and her father waited for us, by appointment, to save the long circuit of its shores. Standing with a light foot in the bow, beside her brown, wrinkled sire, her supple figure bent gracefully but forcefully to the oar, and sent us too swiftly past the changing forms of cloud-capped precipice and wooded steep. The freshness and brightness of a coming September were in air and sky; and not Lucerne itself can boast a finer combination of scenery than this little lake afforded, as we looked across its level floor of waters towards majestic Civita. Landing at the farther end, our pretty oarswoman lifted her hat like a sailor lad, and waved us a good-bye. We have not seen fair Alleghe since, nor those merry eyes again.

It was quite a new country that we now entered. The waters of the lake tumble over the vast rocky dam formed by the fall of Monte Pizzo across the Val Agordo, here circling round the base of the Civita on the west. We had never yet looked round that corner—never seen the western flank of the Civita. Well did the mountain sustain his character as we now skirted him for miles; and at Cencenighe, a fine valley breaking off to the right, opened up the mountains immediately south of the Marmolata.

At Cencenighe we exchanged the mule-track for a road. We had not met with that evidence of civilisation for a fortnight, and almost resented its easy-going inclines. After a rest and dinner at the small Cencenighe inn, the afternoon walk was delightful. It was a stretch towards Italy; warm and tender tints filled the downward vista, though all about was savagery. Enormous boulders—blocks as big as houses—lay piled on either hand. One of them gave rise to a curious sensation. It had fallen a-tilt, propped against another, and shrubs and grass were growing upon its under surface, upside down! It had clearly descended quite within the historic period—nay, possibly within the period of last week. We reflected that another event of the same kind might be disastrous to our journey, and, with a scrutinizing glance above, passed on.

A lively scene succeeded. The stream—known, after leaving the lake, as the Cordevole, whence the valley sometimes bears that name—now flowed deep on the right, and heaps of yellow pine logs lay piled and torturing in its bed. Such we had often seen before; but here, on both sides of the torrent, gangs of men, barefooted, to cling the better to the wet rocks, and armed with long poles, spiked and hooked, were working with a 'Heave, O!' at log after log, to launch it from its fellows. The roaring of the water almost drowned the shouts of the men, leaping from slab to slab of rock, clustering perilously upon ledges over the white foam—some above, some below, some upon isolated surf-surrounded blocks. For minutes together the masses of timber would refuse to disentangle; then some huge log, slipping, sliding, would give with a rush; and, once fairly caught in the whirling water, how madly it plunged and danced! sometimes swallowed in the creamy foam, and then shooting up on end, till lost to sight in the distant scurry of the waters. The shadows were falling fast, and the pot for supper was smoking among the rocks behind; so, when a great bulk of timber had been dislodged, the long poles were dragged ashore, and the scattered groups of men gathered round the redly-glowing spot. Lifting our hats as we left the high bluff from which we had watched the work, twenty caps were instantly in the air to acknowledge the salute; but the din of the coursing torrent between, overpowered the interchange of a cordial '*buona notte*.'

Agordo was soon in sight, on a small sloping plain, rich with Indian corn and open meadow, and groves of chestnut, beech, and oak. Dolomite mountains, in still new forms of grandeur, surround it on all sides; yet set so spaciously about, that it is open to the sunlight. The south beams full upon the gracious scene, and the west, in turn, sheds into it gold and crimson.

A domed and double-towered church gave the town an important air as we approached. Yet it is a small, scattered place, just a shell round a large Plaza, itself a space of grass, shaded by trees for the most part, and bordered on one side by an Italian nobleman's Casa, with its outbuildings, a strange specimen of dilapidation, yet gay with rows of statues, columned arcades, quaintly carved and twisted chimneys,—gay and picturesque. Our hotel, built upon heavy arches, nearly filled the upper end of the square. It is the shabbiest-looking pile you can fancy, but offers, at the top of three dirty flights of stone stairs, two large and decently-furnished apartments, with a view over the open green Plaza to the mountains beyond.

CHAPTER XVI.

PRIMIERO.

Agordo—The Path to Primiero—The Bonettis—The Valley of Primiero and Castello Pietra—The Dolomites of Primiero—Its Commerce and Curiosities—Its History—Storms Without and Within—Passage of the St. Martino Col—Hospice of Paneveggio—A Drowned Road—Predazzo—Vigo—The Sasso di Damm—The last Col and the Porphyry Gorges—Botzen.

Two sunny days we spent at Agordo, the pleasantest little mountain town we know—Sunday, the last day of August, and Monday, the first of September. Seldom, at this season, are there other than serene skies over the Alpine ranges, while the summer's heat is tempered by a delicious autumn freshness. One final week of weather like this, we said, and we should be content.

A wooded hill rises close to Agordo, crossed by many footpaths, and beyond it lies a grassy down, adorned with clumps of trees like a natural park. On all sides rise the mountains. Could there be a more charming spot for a quiet Sunday? There is but one blemish. Southward, the mead tilts down towards the narrow gorge by which river and road find their way to Belluno; over that corner there hovers always a bluish vapour; it looks suspicious, and is deadly—arising from quicksilver mines at the foot of Monte Imperina. All else is lovely. The chestnut and oak-covered steeps, with white cottages nestled among them, are picturesque beyond compare. Those should be ideal homes; but ideal homes are seldom fitted to ideal scenery. Around, above, part and parcel of the sky and cloud, pale Dolomites shoot upward. To the south they fall into a confusion of sun and vapour-hidden summits. East and north they stand clear and sharp, the spines of that range which ends in Civita, and guards the Val di Zoldo. Westward stretches an opener prospect, over hills abounding with village life. But north of west is the wonder and pride of Agordo. I have said enough of the inexhaustible variety of Dolomite forms: here was yet another instance, and not the last. Two enormous towers, buttresses of the Palle di St. Lucano, stand there impending over Agordo. Twin cathedral towers, one may call them, but that they are ten times as lofty. The mass they belong to—the Cima di Pape—reaches to 8,250 feet; and, aided by tint and cloud, they look any height you like.

Quiet may be had on a Sunday outside the town, but not inside. Crowds are pouring in, and knot and tangle in the upper Plaza, round booths and shops and inns, the fountain, or a strolling raffle for cakes and sweetmeats. Now and then they surge into the church—the women mostly—and loud organ-notes pierce the summer air. Towards evening, the game of 'Morra,' with its rapid ringing shouts, sounds deafeningly from low-arched rooms; and the few notables turn out for a stroll round the grassy Plaza. One horseman, issuing from the gates of the Casa Monzoni, canters round a dozen times, and in; and one carriage of fair Monzoni dames drives a mile or two out and home, with a circuit round the Plaza for a finish. On week days it would be still enough, but for the splash and clatter at the fountain, where the town's wash goes on.

The beauty of Agordo was a surprise to us, for we had thought of it only as a halting-place on the way to Primiero. Primiero! Why must we go there? Among the rude wall-pictures at the Campitello inn, we had all noticed—Churchill in 1860, and the rest of us the following year—a very strange one, where a castle stood high among the wildest-looking peaks, which could be none other

PALLE DI ST. LUCANO, FROM AGORDO.

than Dolomite. The landscape was labelled 'Primiero.' In the map the place was found—two days or more to the south, shut up in a very mountainous and secluded region. Churchill afterwards passed one of its entrances at Predazzo; and, sure enough, there were pinnacles up there that might well answer to the picture. And so, with one thing and another—slight hints from time to time—Primiero became the spot of all others we must not fail to visit—reserved as the final *bonne bouche* of the journey.

It lies, one may say, in the heart of that roadless country which is bounded, northwards by the Val Fassa; to the south, by the Val Sugana and Val di Mel; and on the east, by the Val Agordo. Coming from the Ampezzo, the latter must needs be our starting point, and from Agordo it lay distant eight or nine hours over a mountain track. There was a choice of two paths; but as one passed through the scorched and bare neighbourhood of the quicksilver mine, we preferred that which, mounting over the cheerful-looking hills west of Agordo, led by the side of Monte Agner, and, as we hoped, within view of the great central block of those parts, the Sasso di Campo.

Two ponies carried our baggage, and on Tuesday, September 2, a clear though cloudy morning, we were on the march soon after six. Rising for some hours out of the basin of Agordo, its noble sweep of mountains through east and south could not be better seen; but Monte Agner, to the north, retired behind the near green hills, and the Sasso di Campo never showed at all. Villages, woods, grassy slopes, and rocky ravines, succeeded each other. Gosaldo appeared the most prosperous of the hamlets, and a large church was building there. A path for pedestrians strikes off here for Primiero, and crossing close under the Campo, is probably well worth exploring. Our guide preferred for his ponies a charming terrace sort of lane, winding in and out among thickets of hazel, but seldom losing sight for long of the deep valley on the left, where lay Sagron, one of the most ancient settlements in the district. The route from the quicksilver mine, which our's joins by-and-bye, lies along this valley; and down a gorge to the south, a tempting thread of a path lay loosely over bluff and shelf, wandering into blueness, and the Belluno country.

Our track, now lane and now path, still skirted the hill, and the beautiful valley of Mis opened fully to sight below —beautiful in the softness of its dwarf woodland, and the strings of cottages hanging to its sides. At the further extremity lay the Col, and before mounting it, at a glittering spring we sat down to dinner. Through thicket and meadow and pine clump, by foot-path, horse-track, and water-course, we toiled to the smooth alp meadow at the top; and then, with less toil but more trouble, along an endless descending trough or grip, more woody, more watery, and much more stony. Where it was field, it was bog, where path, it was water, where neither, it was loose rattling stones;—nothing on either hand above, but monotony of pine wood, and jutting edges of rock. It was not the sort of descent we had expected, and when the view forward began to open, and there was still no hint of peak or pinnacle—nothing but the tops of round-backed hills, we ruefully said it might be Devonshire out there.

No landscape is more sudden in its changes, more abrupt in its surprises, than the Dolomite. In a moment a depth opened below, the walls of a ruined building glimmered through the trees, and soon stood clear—a castle on a crag —with, behind it, such an apparition of cloud-wreathed shapes, sharp, shattered and riven, some purple, and some orange where tinged by a western gleam, as quite satisfied our appetite for the wonderful.

In the distance, in the valley bottom, was something like a town; that was Primiero. Nearer, lay the village of Tonadigo, and slanting down under the castle crag, a path, horribly stony, led in half an hour into its street of dingy houses. Here and there the walls were warmed up with old frescoes; one house arrested us by a picture of the Virgin of the Luschari Berg—the far-off mountain of the sledges—a record of the proprietor's pilgrimage; and almost all showed a motto inscribed on their fronts, 'Christus nobiscum stat,' 'May Christ stay with us;'—every house the same. We were fallen, it seemed, among a pious people.

Twenty minutes from Tonadigo, across a small plain full of Indian corn, and over a wide rushing torrent by a wooden bridge, brought us to Primiero. Our Caprile friends had obtained for us the name of the best inn, and the Agordo landlord had furnished a letter of introduction. To our perplexity, now that we compared the two, there was difference enough to raise a doubt as to their identity; and as the ponies and their driver had gone a-head by an hour or so, we had no means of previous enquiry. On approaching the town it was evident that the arrival of the baggage had created a sensation, and that in most people's opinion, the evening cigar and twilight stroll might as well be taken in the direction whence the four '*forestieri*' might be expected to appear. Of course it *was* rather remarkable that a party of ladies and gentlemen from England, with sticks and umbrellas, should be just that day walking into Primiero. Casting eyes up and down for an inn sign, we went on through a street of well-built respectable houses, and everywhere, as at Tonadigo, the same inscription, 'Christus nobiscum stat,' in large letters, ran along the walls. Presently a denser crowd of the inhabitants was seen round an object at a door-way, which proved to be the most conspicuous of our bags, judiciously placed there as a token that the remainder were within; taking the hint, we found ourselves immediately in charge of a blandly-smiling Signor Bonetti, his three delighted daughters, a grinning, barefooted hag, and a miscellaneous assortment of youngsters, not one of whom was content without something in particular to carry up stairs.

Somehow we felt that we were 'done.' The small rooms were a contrast in every respect to those of Caprile and Agordo, but the eagerness to retain us was beyond belief. They shouted, demonstrated, beleaguered every step; bundled an unfortunate man out of his chamber, the better to accommodate the illustrious strangers; and at last, though by this time we had become aware that there was a better inn in the place, we weakly yielded, thinking that people so anxious to please might make up in willingness what they lacked in means. It was a great mistake, and the more unfortunate since days of stormy wet ensued, shutting us up in our unsavoury quarters. The best inn, and a good one too, as our experience the following year enables us to say, is the 'Aquila Nera,' also a Bonetti's. The two landlords are brothers, but there is a feud between their families, which may account in measure for the passionate rivalry of the inferior house.

As to the town, we speedily found we were in a singular place;—a town with no road to it;—a town where no wheel mark is to be seen in the streets, no sound of wheels is ever heard, and the daily mail comes in and goes out on the backs of donkeys;—a town almost as silent as Venice, and which, small and secluded as it is, still possesses houses of nobility among its humbler tenements;—a town where at night people go about with twinkling lanterns, as in the old days before them. But I must first describe its situation.

Not till the afternoon of the following day could we sally out to obtain a notion of the Primiero country, and then the mountain forms were so cloud-tormented, that I must make use of later-acquired knowledge to describe its very interesting features.

The Primiero valley is closed at both ends, the town

J Gilbert, delt. Hanhart lith

CASTELLO PIETRA, PRIMIERO.

being near the upper extremity where it turns off northwards, as the Val Castrozza, towards the desolate Col of St. Martino. The lower end narrows, and sinks into a deep gorge, winding for several miles through savage scenery till it makes exit into the Feltre district. The valley itself is as pleasant a scene as you would wish to see, with several villages—sisters or daughters of Primiero—surrounded by plots of Indian corn, and rejoicing in the abundant shade of Spanish chestnut groves on the steep heights above. These are principally on the side opposite to the sun ; on the other, green Alpine hills swell into knolls and sink into glades, to receive many a cottage home, all fenced off at last by a lofty line of precipices, far enough away not to interfere with southern air and light.

The striking effect lies in the direction whence we came. There, backed by masses of Dolomite, stands on a single unpropped crag the ruined castle of Pietra—the original of the Campitello picture. Among the Dolomite castles, this must stand preeminent for size, situation, and history. It rivals in romantic position the castles in Calabria, or the monastery of Meteora, in Greece. No possible means of entrance can be seen in front, for the rock appears perpendicular on all sides ; behind, it is of less height, but still unscalable. Working round, however, to the northern corner in this direction, the remains of a large tower are discovered ; and passing through, hopeful of finding here the ancient passage-way, you suddenly stand on the brink of a chasm, which has been scooped out in the débris on which the rock-mass rests, within the last half-century.* Across it, and possible to reach by an

* The rushing torrent far below is the agent in this destructive process ; and now that the hand of man leaves the ruin to the natural influences at work around, there is nothing to prevent the stream from undermining the loose foundations of the rock, and, in course of time, tumbling both rock and ruin into its bed.

expert climber, is the actual entrance, but still far below the basement of the building, which, we were assured, has been long inaccessible. Of its history I will speak presently.

The rock itself is not Dolomite, but a mass of limestone, about 150 feet in height, resting upon an enormous mass of loose débris, with which the entrance to the glen is filled up. Behind, as already said, and circling round to the north, are reared the Dolomite peaks which give to the scene its peculiar wildness. Penetrating into the glen at their foot, at about half an hour beyond the castle, a flat

COUNT WELSPERG'S JAGD SCHLOSS.

green meadow is suddenly disclosed, where you would expect nothing but a chaos of rock and débris. Here Count Welsperg, descendant of the Lords of that name, who for many generations held the castle, has built himself a small house, to which he retires in the summer months. Once a distinguished officer in the Austrian cavalry service, ill-health, and, it may be, love for the rude cradle of his ancestors, has brought him to this most secluded spot, where the giant Dolomites stand round him like pillars of the sky, and the jackdaws chatter, and the eagles scream.

From Primiero itself, this amphitheatre of rock-towers and peaks is not seen; but they end in a fantastically-shaped mountain immediately opposite the town, which is the principal feature in the valley. Nothing in Dolomite is like it for the singular variety of the horns and pinnacles fringing its sides. It soon passed with us for the 'Procession Mountain,' since in some directions it appeared as if troops of draped figures were ascending to the often cloud-invested summit. The summit itself rises in three great towers—the centre and hindmost one, of huge bulk and height, out-topping the others. Its name, the Cima Cimedo, seems intended to express its character—'peak upon peak.'

The Cima forms the corner buttress, so to speak, projected towards Primiero, of a Dolomite mass stretching, northward, in magnificent array, by the side of the Val Castrozza and the San Martino Pass, in a straight line towards the Marmolata; and eastward, toward its dominating peak, the Sasso di Campo—a mountain we never succeeded in distinctly recognising—ending beyond in Monte Agner, the narrow towering crest seen in face from Agordo. The whole block is, therefore, of great extent. The triangular space lying between these two diverging lines opens out towards Cencenighe, and must be a region of wild and lonely desolation, since it is almost uninhabited. In the distant view obtained of the group, when we afterwards crossed the high ridge separating the Canale St. Bovo from the valley of Tesino, we could discern large sheets of snow among the bare forms behind the girdle of peaks.

The scarped precipices which, as already mentioned, shut in the valley to the south, are probably not Dolomitic. Over them, at a point called the Colle di Luna, is a high hunter's path, nearly 8,000 feet above the sea. The fine view from this col was frequently extolled to us. The beautiful Val di Mel—the Belluno country—lies beneath; and on a clear morning, the sun-gleams upon the Adriatic, distant some fifty or sixty miles as the crow flies, can be distinctly seen; while to the north-east, over Primiero, the Castrozza Dolomites must be grandly displayed. The ascent to the col should be made while the flocks are yet on the alp, and night quarters can be found at the huts; the final climb is then taken before daylight. Another pass, lower and more practicable, over this chain, lies farther to the east, at Monte Fenestra, but is said to be much inferior in view.

Immediately behind Primiero, on the north, but concealed from view by a lower range—the same that has been spoken of as picturesquely diversified with groves of chestnut and steep slopes of grass—behind this range of hills, rises the panoramic mountain of the entire region, Monte Arzon (8,700 feet above the sea). It was not spoken of as such to us; but having, on a second visit to Primiero, climbed one day one of the peaks of Monte Scanaiol, more to the north, we saw at once that it must be so, and regretted greatly that we had lost the opportunity of verifying our belief.

In the depression between Monte Arzon and the ridge that overlooks Primiero, lies a small lake—the Calaita See—a bare Alpine spot. This depression, the Val di Luzen, containing a village and several hamlets, circles round Monte Arzon towards the west, in a curve parallel to that made by the Primiero basin, but at a much higher level, and sinks into a valley, the Canale St. Bovo, included in the Primiero administration, and which has always followed its fortunes. Here is another and considerably larger lake, in a narrow, sterile, fearful-looking hollow. So late as 1823, this lake was formed by a tremendous land-fall from the mass of the Cima d'Asta, on the western side of the valley, which, with the accompanying floods, swept away Canale di Sopra, the upper village. The name, Lago Nuovo, is a token of its origin. What we saw of this spot in 1863 reminded us somewhat of a desolate Highland scene. The rocks are of grey granite, and lie tumbled down the abrupt sides of the hills in dark and terrible confusion.

Now, having brought the reader round by the Canale St. Bovo to the lower end of the Primiero valley, opposite to that by which we first entered it, let us return by that route to Primiero itself. The communication between the St. Bovo valley and that of Primiero is not by the course of the stream; it would be a long circuit, and through two deep gorges. There is a path over the high dividing tongue, which, as it descends into the larger valley, commands a charming view. First notice, however, to the right, the rift, a perspective of black depths, by which the Primiero river, the Cismone, escapes southward, to join eventually the Brenta.

Through that rift, and by the side of its boiling stream, runs the path by which Primiero once held politically, and still holds commercially, to the outer world. Six hours down there, is Fonzaso and the rich Feltre country. Along that path, stony, steep, and tortuous, goes the mail in panniers, and up that way come goatskins of wine, fruits and all foreign produce. The valley grows corn, and especially maize, but does not cultivate the vine; timber it has in abundance, yielding a large revenue to the government, and the Cismone floats down great quantities to Italy.

Primiero butter, too, is famous, made so well, they tell you, that it will last a year, and is exported to Verona and Venice. And something, too, more precious than butter once went that way. Silver mines in the middle ages were worked in the Primiero valley, and the ruins of the smelting furnace are still to be seen there. They were abandoned at last in consequence of the many earthquakes, that of 1600 especially, doing great damage. Iron and copper have since superseded the silver, bringing great destruction upon the woods, but great profit to the proprietors. During the summer the men are engaged in preparing charcoal upon the mountains, and the works were silent at the time of our visit.

So, despite its singular isolation, Primiero has contrived to make itself of some importance in the world; and its mountain paths, particularly this of the Cismone, have at all times been the scene of more or less traffic. The frontier between Tyrol and Venetia crosses the Cismone gorge about an hour below the entrance of the Primiero valley, and there the ruins of a tower mark the place of an ancient toll. This gorge, like the ways into Primiero, is so solitary that, on entering the valley, one is astonished to find such a population; it is estimated, with St. Bovo, at 12,000, which may well be understood as the prosperous-looking villages salute the eye. Commencing at this lower end, Masi, where the toll now is, Imer, and Mezzano occur in succession, before Primiero — Fiera, as it is locally called—is reached; and beyond lie Transaqua, Ormanico, Tonadigo, and Siror. Near the latter village was the ancient silver mine, and between it and Tonadigo, just at the foot of the Cima Cimedo, once stood the village of Piu Baco, which in the earthquake of January 25, 1348—that which shook down the cliffs of the Dobratsch in Carinthia, and did so much injury to Villach—was destroyed: overwhelmed by a slip from the Cima of part of its lower flanks. The marks of the catastrophe are still visible.

Approaching Primiero from the south, the first object is the church, which stands outside the town in this direction, with two or three other buildings of importance,—the Canonica, the Fürst Amt, &c. Accustomed in all these parts to Italian architecture, one is surprised to find in the Primiero church a grave gothic building of the thirteenth century, lofty and imposing in its interior. The tall windows filled with small round panes of dull glass, and guarded outside by ornamental ironwork, cast a solemn light within, and on the walls of the chancel are faded frescoes, the arms of the chief families of the district, said indeed to be those of the workers of the mines, to whom the erection of the church was due, and who, being German, adopted for it a German style. A curious crucifix in dark walnut wood over one of the altars was found, with a bell, among the ruins of the buried village; but the great boast of the church and all the valley is a *monstranz* or hand-shrine for exhibiting the Host. It is of solid silver, two feet high, in shape like a gothic spire, sheltering three figures in gilt of St. Peter, St. Paul, and St. John. The centre, of Bohemian glass, forms a sort of lantern, and the whole weighs eleven pounds. It is accounted to be 650 years old, having been presented by the silver workers at the time the church was built; and became an object of such notoriety, that the Venetian Republic, we are assured, desired to make it their own, by purchase—or even otherwise, if the Signori are not belied. They seem to fear no thieves now: remarking upon the insecurity of the sacristy, we were told that no robbery had been known in the valley within memory of man. The priest of this church is the ecclesiastical superior of all others in the valley. Yet it is not the oldest church; a small ruined building was pointed out near Siror, in ruin, they said, for 600 years, which, as the church of St. Giacomo, claims the highest antiquity; some remains of frescoes are yet visible.

Nor is the little church of Transaqua, a village across the Cismone, without its treasure. It is dedicated to St. Mark, a fact explained by the singular circumstance that this remote spot was at one time an apanage of the Doges of Venice, who presented a portrait of the saint by Titian for an altar-piece. They do not say, however, that more than the head and hands of the figure can be attributed to the great painter, and there is not much in them to sustain his reputation. A screen with triple arches, Lombardic columns, and groined ceiling, gives entrance to the chancel; this ceiling is covered with Scripture subjects enclosed in circles, and painted in fresco with considerable artistic skill, though they have been perhaps coarsely retouched in places, especially in the borders. On the front of the screen, above the arches, is painted a copy of Tintoret's great picture of the Crucifixion, in far from despicable style. Such was the church of Transaqua in 1862. Alas! in 1863 there were woful changes; whitewash had invaded the frescoes, and it was even said that the entire screen was coming down, in order that the chancel, in which great alterations were in progress, might be better seen from the body of the building. It was the doing of the Heads of the commune, and the Primiero priest and his brethren did not expect that their remonstrances would be of any use.*

I have mentioned two or three buildings of mark in the open space surrounding the Primiero church. One of these,

* The interval between our first and second visits witnessed, also, the destruction of most of the inscriptions along the walls of the houses in Primiero—a fit of plastering and whitewashing had almost everywhere effaced the 'Christus nobiscum stat.'

the Fürst Amt, is a tall fortified house with eyelet holes under its eaves for the cross bowmen, odd looking oriels projecting at its corners, and armorial bearings painted across its front. It is another relic of the silver workers; they built it for their officers and for a place of strength. The date is uncertain, but an inscription tells that it was renovated in 1558.

All these things declare that Primiero has a history. How often one vainly speculats upon the annals of some remote corner of the earth; certain that events of some sort have gone over the heads of the generations there, and that the great world without has surged more or less upon the little world within, but wanting in opportunity or means for learning how or when! At Primiero, the Castello Pietra, frowning and forlorn on its worn rock, the old churches of Fiera and Transaqua, the quaint Fortalice of the silver workers, the toll-house Schloss, the ruined St. Giacomo—everything bespeaks a history; and fortunately the wet days of our first visit enabled us to learn something of it. An invitation came from Signor Sartori, the post-master, to visit his museum, and we found there not only a collection illustrating the natural history of the district in all its branches, but in Sartori himself, a very intelligent man, informed upon all points respecting his native valley. From him we gathered the particulars that follow.

Primiero has always been in close relations with Feltre, and Feltre—upon what authority we do not know—is stated to have been founded in the year 750 B.C., and to have been conquered by the Romans in 219 B.C. During these ages, however, and long after, history is silent about its mountain neighbour. The earliest tradition respecting Primiero relates that the valley was peopled A.D. 452 by refugees from Friuli, escaping from the destruction caused by Attila, and who, in remembrance of their native city

Primerianum, gave the same name to their new home. They came by way of Belluno and the Val di Mis, and made it their first care to erect the Castello Pietra to command the pass by which they entered the valley.

They speedily organised a simple form of government, dividing the valley and its neighbourhood into four districts, and appointing a head man over each, who was styled the Marzolo, because elected in the March of each year. The first section consisted of Transaqua and Romanico, now called Ormanico. The second, of Tonadigo, Piubaco (afterwards destroyed), Siror, and the outlying Sagron in the Val di Mis. The third, of Mezzano, Imer, and Masi. The fourth, of the offset, Canale St. Bovo, with its tributary, the Val di Luzen. A proof of the early date of Piubaco is found in the inscription on the bell belonging to the buried village, now preserved in the church of Primiero; it is marked 'Anno Dom. vvv.' And the local chronicler further supposes, that the village of Sagron derives its name from *Sacrum,* itself a record of the consecration bestowed by the fugitives upon their first place of shelter. A trace of their early Republican liberties remained so late as the year 1723 in the annual election of the 'Marzoli.'

The Goths, and afterwards the Lombards, who possessed themselves not only of the Italian plain, but also of the mountains, included Primiero in the countship of Feltre. After the fall of the Lombard power, the Emperor Conrad disposed of this as a '*Grafschaft*' to the Bishops of Trent, A.D. 1027, and as this brought Primiero more into connection with the north than the south, the Bishops soon after erected a monastery and Spital, dedicated to St. Martin, for the succour of travellers on the long and difficult pass into the Val Fassa. No longer a monastery, but known as San Martino, it is still a noted halting-place for all who pass that way.

The jurisdiction of the Bishops ceased a little later than A.D. 1300, when Primiero came with Feltre under the rule of the Verona Scaligers, who confirmed all the old statutes. But in 1355 we find it made the centre of administration under a certain Boniface Von Lupi, by Prince Charles of Luxembourg, called also King of the Romans, in the reign of the Emperor Charles IV. In 1373, by an arrangement between this same Lupi, Francis of Carrara, and the Archduke of Austria, Primiero—with the singular exception of the village of Transaqua, which had been at one time presented to the Republic of Venice, and was still regarded as their property—was for the first time separated from Feltre and attached to the domains of the House of Austria. On the occasion of this transfer, a toll-house became necessary, and the Schloss was erected for that purpose, whose ruins now hang on the side of the ravine of the Cismone at the frontier of Tyrol.

The Archduke Friedrich pushed on the working of the silver mines, which in those times rendered Primiero a valuable possession; and it is recorded that they brought him a revenue of more than 80,000 florins yearly. It is even stated that in the year 1400, the royalty paid to the archduchy amounted to 114,000 florins, besides a further sum of 160,000 florins, which was handed over, perhaps as a share of the profits, an arrangement which holds in some portions of the Prince of Wales's Cornish possessions. In connection with these mines many Germans were introduced into the valley, for whom a German priest or Cooperator was provided; and the place became so important that several so-called 'palaces' were built in and about the town of Fiera (Primiero).

The war of the league of Cambrai, which broke out between the Venetians and the Emperor Maximilian in 1509, was very disastrous to Primiero. The toll-house

Schloss, and many houses in the valley, were burnt, and a battle was fought at Transaqua, of which tokens have frequently been found in the bones of men and horses, arms, rings, coins, and the like. In this war the Castle of Pietra was thrice besieged by the Venetians, but does not appear to have been taken. It had, in the year 1401, passed into the hands of the Welspergs, who purchased it from the Archduke for 4,000 Hungarian ducats, together with the right of jurisdiction, to which, in 1600, was added the *jus gladii* and *jus gratiandi*—in other words, power of life and death in the valley. This power, during a re-building of the castle after its destruction by fire in the year 1670, was exercised with great cruelty to compel the service of the peasants, so that the pile is still pointed at by them as having been built with their blood. The family of Welsperg derive their name from the valley of Welsperg, in the Pusterthal, which was given to the founder of the house, Rubertus, A.D. 1150, by the then Emperor, in reward for services.

Under the Emperor Charles V. the church was enlarged and ornamented as it now appears; and at this time, probably, was built in the chancel an imitation of the celebrated silver *monstranz*, in which specimens of all the materials used in the construction of the building were introduced. It resembles, in character and situation, the *Sacramentshauslein* in the church of St. Lorenz, in Nuremberg, but cannot vie with that masterpiece either in design or workmanship.

After this, Primiero seems to have dropped out of the grasp of history. The extinction of its silver mines probably so diminished its importance, that no one cared to meddle with the secluded spot. We did not hear of any French incursion. If *they* had penetrated the valley, the silver shrine would not now have been among its treasures. Yet Feltre supplied a title to one of Napoleon's marshals in the campaign of 1796, when the tide of war must have swept past the narrow entrance to the valley, onward to Belluno, where Cadore and the Ampezzo were not so fortunate. The last event recorded is the fire which, about sixty years since, a second time laid the castle of Pietra in ashes, since which its bare walls have alone remained, rendered inaccessible from a subsequent fall of rock and débris. Twenty years ago, by means of ropes and ladders, Count Welsperg and several Primiero people succeeded in reaching the ruin; but that is the last time it has been visited by foot of man.

From this glance at the fortunes of Primiero I must now return to our own. Any one who gets into Primiero must immediately set about considering how he is to get out again. The ways are difficult, and the means scanty. Feltre was out of our line of route, and so also was Borgo, in the Val Sugana — a twelve hours' march. There remained only the track to Predazzo, in the Val Fassa, over the pass of San Martino—also reckoned at twelve hours. The Primiero people necessarily, when they leave their valley, either walk or ride; but to sit on horseback astride, or sideways like sacks, with nothing to hold by, did not suit our ladies, and a twelve hours' walk was rather too much for them. Fortunately, the Hospice of Paneveggio—a solitary house on the other side the Martino pass—offered an opportunity for breaking the journey.

There was wild weather during the three days of our stay. Night after night the sound of drenching rain, exaggerated by the spouts that poured cataracts into the streets, made night hideous; by day, if we were able to sally forth for an hour or two, the continuous low rumble of the Cismone told that rocks and stones were grinding and thumping along the bottom; and all the streams were swollen so as to check and limit our rambles. On the morning of our departure, a storm inside the house succeeded to that which had raged outside during the dark hours. The refusal to pay an extortionate bill, the first we had met with in these valleys, transformed the three Misses Bonetti into gesticulating and defiant furies; fortunately, the threat of appealing to the Syndic, and the mediation of the post-master, induced them at last to yield to a compromise. The Fates were certainly against us during that visit. We left, vexed in spirit, turning up the wet and stony path which led through Siror and the Castrozza valley towards San Martino. The pass a-head was dark with mist, and rain soon beat in our faces. In four hours, wet and miserable, we reached the Hospice—a cluster of buildings upon an open pasture, where several men and mules were resting. The excellent coffee they gave us there, is a warm and comfortable thought even now; and as the rain had ceased, and the driving clouds let in some gleams of sun, we started gaily for the desolate and tedious climb before us.

The burdened beasts,—a pony with donkey as 'tender,'—could move but slowly over the wet ground, and we soon left them and their conductor far behind. At first, a broad track through a pine wood left no doubt of the road; but the trees thinned away and diminished to scrub, and the track broke into numerous wandering paths, all disappearing in the cloud above. We might have been in difficulties but for a pleasant old man, whose alert figure and wizened features confirmed his assertion, that by birth and lineage he was a Frenchman, though he had nearly forgotten his native tongue. He was crossing the Col, and constituted himself our guide *pro tem.* To him the mountain was horrible; many, he said, perished there every year; and truly it seemed an easy thing to happen, as we entered the confusing clammy cloud. A few glimpses had been vouchsafed, as we climbed, of the wonderfully fine Dolomites, the Cima della Rosetta, Cimon della Pala, Il Cimon, and others which line the eastern side of the valley and guard the pass; they even gained in effect from the rapid play of light, and obscuring cloud, over their stark sides, of which it was difficult to say whether it rendered them more beautiful or appalling. From moment to moment the towering Titanic walls glowed as if a-flame, and then vanished utterly from sight in the swift white vapours, to appear again as suddenly in startling patches of red at some unimaginable height. The redness, which might be either metallic or lichenous, was very remarkable in these Castrozza Dolomites. Below, looking backward, arches of cloud, like ribs of iron, stretched across the Castrozza valley; beneath which, at an immense distance, shone a sunny bit of the south, seen as if through the wrong end of a telescope.

On the Col, the circuit of vision comprised only a few yards of slippery grass, stones, and mud; but on the northern side the prospect cleared again, and we found ourselves on long descending downs, perplexed by a labyrinth of streams and boggy tracts. To avoid the worst of these, our old Frenchman led us by a long but easier route than the usual one from the summit, not bidding us adieu till he could point out below, the lonely Hospice of Paneveggio. It seemed near, but a long and painful descent remained, through a forest torn by water-courses, before the welcome but dreary refuge was attained. Vast woods enclosed it on every side, and, as at St. Martino, there was not another house in sight. It stands 5,200 feet above the sea level; St. Martino is lower by about 300 feet.

The place of resort for all comers was the kitchen, where a fire on a raised dais of stone sent up its column of smoke in the midst, and into a huge dark hollow overhead. This stone dais, or hearth, filled the whole of the rounded end of the room, which was indeed one enormous chimney, lighted by one or two small windows. Behind the fire ran a semicircular bench against the wall, giving ample accommodation to all and sundry wet and tired folk, of whom some half-dozen, cattle and mule drivers, were there already, stretching out their legs towards the fire in the centre. We soon ranged ourselves amongst them, stretching out also our shoeless feet to the fire that cooked our supper, and enjoying all the snugness and warmth of this best of chimney corners. A pair of tall iron-dogs supported a strong cross-bar over the fire, from which hung various pots steaming with victual. The sturdy maid—Kellnerin and cook in one—poured out hot messes for each party—stews, or broths, or polenta; and one of the guests—perhaps a strolling shoemaker—took our boots in hand, to clean and dry, round the glowing embers. Our baggage-man arriving an hour later, reported having crossed several deep torrents on the course he had taken, and we were all the more grateful to the old Frenchman.

The bedrooms up-stairs were forlorn curtainless dens; and all that night the fearsome landscape without was lit up with the brightest and bluest of lightning—pine-tree tops and desolate peaks clear for the instant as at mid-day.

The house, in its loneliness—the one poor shelter in these wilds—might have been a ship at sea in a dark tempestuous night, and, if it did not reel in the waves, it rocked on its base, as the blasts rushed down upon it, and the thunder crashed among the hills.

Morning broke with the dull light of a heavy downpour; and though the hurly burly had ceased above, the hills were all in a roar with torrents. From six to nine we waited before a brightening sky encouraged us to start. It was Saturday, and we must, if possible, reach Vigo that day, or at least Predazzo, in the Val Fassa. But, oh! the water! The grassy slopes were smooth sheets of water, rippling over the track; the woods were full of ominous rushing sounds, and seamed with the white streaks of streams, pouring from unknown heights — hurrying to unknown depths. Movement and noise were everywhere, and filled us with an undefinable dread. We had crossed streams without number, slushing through as we might, when among the thick trees there gleamed a broader, whiter mass of foam, and the next moment a turn in the path showed a torrent, fierce and tawny, careering through the wood. It was rushing over the remains of a timber bridge, and flooding on both sides, so that further progress was impossible. When our animals came up, the driver stood dumbfoundered, as we had done, and then we all turned to retrace the miserable way.

There was hope that in a few hours the waters would abate, and several men immediately left the Hospice to see what could be done in restoring the bridge. The large party assembled by the bad weather the night before, had so lowered the stock of provisions, that a thick rice soup was all they could afford for dinner, and the possibility of being shut up at Paneveggio for a day or two was not pleasant to think of. Luckily, by one o'clock the water was down and the bridge practicable. We pushed on with all speed, amazed to notice the change that had taken place in three or four hours; sheets of water had diminished to streams, streams to rills, and for the first hour or two there were few difficulties to encounter. Yet marks of devastation were plentiful; and at one spot, a black deluge of soil had poured down a hill-side, destroying for years, if not for ever, many acres of what had been velvet slopes of mown grass. Where the people lived to whom it all belonged it was difficult to say, for I do not remember that we passed a single hamlet, and scarce a châlet, for miles along this valley of woods and meadows.

There was soon rain again, and soon the noise of watery movement in all directions. Paneveggio would be cut off behind us, and Predazzo was our only chance. We had sheltered under trees while our driver went on, and were surprised to see no donkey when we overtook him, though the donkey's load was lying in the middle of the path. 'Where is the donkey?' cried we. The driver shook his head, and gazed moodily at the load, in front of which we perceived, at last, long ears and a pensive countenance just protruding from the mud—all the rest of him gone! With the assistance of a muleteer, who luckily chanced to pass at the moment, the load was lifted, and the donkey, hauled up by head and tail, was got upon solid ground, a wretched, plastered object, looking as if his legs had been sucked to sticks. 'He will never carry more!' said his master, as we stood in silent dismay over the catastrophe. If that was a thing desired by the donkey, he had better not have begun to nibble actively the grass under his feet. At sight of that, his burden, lightened as far as we could, was immediately readjusted, and we floundered on again.

In three hours from Paneveggio we reached a road, and thought ourselves safe, but in several places torrents were pouring over it, and it seemed as if Predazzo, whose steeple we could see below, where our valley struck into the Fassa Thal, would be cut off from us no less than Paneveggio. A hay-wagon lay wrecked and abandoned in the midst of one of these streams, and at another spot masses of stones and rubbish covered the road for many yards. Through all these difficulties we pressed, sometimes circumspectly pursuing the coping-stones of a wall, sometimes scrambling over rocks and bushes—and so it came to pass, we scarcely know how, that at last we reached Predazzo, and the comfortable inn of Jacomelie, and the unaccustomed sound of wheels, and the strange sight of an omnibus in correspondence with the 'Strada Ferrata,' at Trento. A few days after, at Botzen, we learnt, that storm and inundation had been general through the Alps—that the river Inn had risen twelve feet at Innsbruck, and much damage had been done. We congratulated ourselves at having escaped so tolerably from the Primiero mountains, but had no wish to encounter their watery perils again.

Predazzo is a great centre of attraction to all German mineralogists. It is to them, what the head of the Gader Thal is to palæontologists, and the Seisser Alp, with its rim of Dolomites, to geologists. As we descended the last reaches of road, every wall showed varieties of melaphyr, porphyry, syenite, and granite. Dolomite and limestone were out of sight upon the heights to our right, and it was plain we were surrounded by quite other geologic conditions. At the inn a large table was covered with specimens, and a mineralogist from the north of Germany had made it his quarters for some weeks.

The little town stands at the north-eastern border of a wide, level, alluvial opening—fertile, but block-strewn here and there. It is the centre of the Trias Crater, whence the great variety of eruptive rocks have emanated. They run up steeply on all sides, and prevent any distant view, except in the direction of the valley we had just descended. Outside the circle occupied by these rocks we find Dolomite mountains again, standing in isolated masses at three separate points, on a basis of lower trias beds.

The late hour at which we reached Predazzo, and our

wayworn condition, put Vigo out of the question for that night; but letters were waiting there from which we had been debarred for weeks, and we ordered a carriage to be ready early the next morning. Vigo is that village in the Upper Fassa Thal where, at Antonio Rizzi's inn, Churchill spent some days in 1860. Arrived there, we should be upon the western limit of the Dolomites once more, having traced them to and from the far east. By touching upon the neighbourhood of our earliest experiences, the circle would be completed. Val Fassa is, by reputation, so pre-eminently the Dolomite district, that most tourists must be disappointed, we suspect, as they ascend the valley. At the village of Moena the scenery first begins to promise something, in portions of the range to which the Rosengarten belong; but from no part of the road in the valley would a stranger understand the true nature of the Dolomite region. Now that we had seen so much of it, we felt this strongly.

None of us, excepting Churchill, had ever seen Vigo, and he had promised much for Rizzi's inn. The village stands high upon the slopes that face the east, and, leaving the carriage to wind its slow way up, my friend and I struck across the fields, reaching the cheerful hamlet just as the people were streaming from early mass. Among them was Rizzi himself, who, at once recognising his guest of two years ago, led the way to his house, behind its gay little garden of sunflowers, dahlias, cockscombs, and marigolds. All its rooms were at our choice, and selecting one commanding the upward, and another the downward valley, we felt happy in securing for a few final days so pleasant a home in the Dolomite region.

If anyone wishes to picture the spot, I must refer him to the description in the third chapter, of the spacious, prosperous alp, the scattered substantial houses, the two churches—sombre St. Johann down below, and bright little Juliana above, with a big St. Christopher painted on its walls. And if the reader desires to understand the situation more particularly, let me remind him that, of the two grey masses now sprinkled with snow, that peer up at the head of the valley, one is our old acquaintance, the Lang Kofel, and the other is the Sella Spitze, of which, with its 'Forbidden way,' so much was said in the last chapter. Not visible from Vigo, but from some of the heights near, the shining villages are seen specking the valley right up to Campitello itself, only six or seven miles of distance remaining to complete the circuit of our wanderings.

The Rosengarten had struck Churchill as the grandest spectacle he had seen in his solitary excursion of 1860; how would they strike him and us after our late more ample experience? On Monday morning—which, with a sharp north wind, ushered in weather brilliantly clear, but cold—he led us, by the climb he has described, to the crags among the pine woods, whence the amphitheatre opens abruptly on the sight. He waited for our votes, and, sitting down among the heathery rocks, we compared the view before us with all the comparable and incomparable scenes in our remembrance. I think the verdict satisfied our friend. The cloven precipices that form the vast circle are worthy of the Genius of Dolomite, and of what the imagination pictures to lie behind the Rosengarten, as seen from Botzen. Yet other spots of the same character show, perhaps, a greater unity of effect; and the woods, which here creep to the very bases of the crags, detract from the arctic severity which other Dolomite scenes possess. The, view, page 75, taken from a distance, explains the general character, yet gives but a feeble notion of the Rosengarten.

The next morning, hunting up Churchill's old guide,

Grazzioli—a droll little fellow, whose short legs, though they put him at disadvantage, could do a deal of work—we three started to ascend the Sasso di Damm. It lies on the eastern side of the valley, nearer to the Marmolata than the Monzoni ridge, formerly ascended by Churchill. Of two or three ways to reach the alp, which is well known to the peasants, that from the Pozza Thal is, perhaps, the best. There is the usual wooded shoulder to surmount, and then a long narrowing ridge to follow, till it ends in a rocky summit scarcely more than two yards square. The air was perfectly still, and we found ourselves in the centre of a circle which included all the great Dolomite mountains of the district.

Had we intended to select a spot which should bring into one panoramic view the greatest number of familiar peaks, we could not have chosen better. The Marmolata, difficult always to see to advantage, here rose superbly, offering the profile of his southern precipice.* None of the others did themselves justice, but the Platt Kogel, Lang Kofel, Sella Spitze, on the one side of their monarch, and the Sasso Vernale, Sasso Val Fredda, Campo Ziegelan, and Monte Rocca on the other were all clearly recognisable; while in the opposite direction soared the Rosengarten, and in the further distance to the south-west, the crescent of the Latemar. The view well accorded with the theory which places the mountain upon which we stood—itself composed of eruptive ash—in the centre of a vast extinct crater, of which the Dolomites occupy the rim. Geologically, topographically, pictorially, the view was alike interesting. Four hours did not exhaust its attractions, and though a thin veil of snow fell from time to time over some portions of the prospect, and the point we

* See the View given, page 70.

occupied was not less than 9,000 feet above the sea, there was no chill in the air.

The only signs of human life were a few distant hay châlets, and wreaths of smoke where the hay cutters were finishing the last work of the season; and—on the ridge and summit itself, curious rows of stones wandering round and about, with openings here and there, very inexplicable, in such a place, to the uninitiated, but showing the cunning labours of the Ptarmigan hunters. Ascending from below, they drive the birds upward, which entering at the spaces, are foolishly caught within, as in a trap, though they might hop over the mimic wall in a trice if they had the wit to do so. There we gave good-bye to the solemn silent Dolomites; and with the first step downward felt that it was home now, to England.

Vigo is 5,000 feet above the sea, and with the north wind blowing, became bitterly cold. In the morning the Lang Kofel and Sella Spitze showed white with snow, and in the evening we sat shivering under all the cloaks we could muster. Having seen the 'Cirque' of the Rosengarten, and climbed the Sasso di Damm, it was time to leave Winter to do his will among these wilds. So, settling the bill, chalked on the door-posts, and carrying away as keepsakes from Miss Rizzi, four little pictures of saints, with two huge cakes presented by her mother, we left the cordial people. Rizzi himself undertook to conduct us over the Caressa Pass as far as Welschenofen, on the way to Botzen, a walk of four hours. The Col lies behind Vigo, and reaching it in the fresh of the morning, we were fortunate in obtaining one more view of the Dolomite region, even the Primiero Dolomites stood on tip-toe in the far east to see the last of us. Then, with the Latemar Spitzen, on the right, the Rosengarten on the left, and in front the distant glittering peaks of the Oertler and Œtzthal ranges, we dropped down the western slopes into the porphyry country.

Vigo had been disturbed the night before, with rumours of banditti, who having crossed the frontier from Italy, were lurking somewhere near the head of the Fassa Thal. At Welschenofen, the first village on the Botzen side, we found a company of soldiers in pursuit, and leaving them en route for the mountains, we the more willingly descended towards the plains. At Welschenofen, the horse track ended in a wheel-road, which had been carried thus far from Botzen since Churchill's journey in 1860, and the pony, which had hitherto shared our luggage with a donkey, was now put between shafts to run us down the remaining fifteen miles.

People talk of the terrors of Alpine roads who only bowl down easy gradients in a vetturino's carriage. They would gain a much more vivid impression of danger on this road through the porphyry gorges. Slight and rough in construction, it is carried on narrow shelves round sharp corners; or it shoots across dark gulfs by slender bridges; or is suspended over the depths on wooden brackets, showing an ugly tendency to slant outwards. The drag broke soon, and with all the force we could put upon the break, Rizzi's pony, though an excellent one for mountain work, proved unable to control the long awkward vehicle borrowed from Welschenofen, down the many steep pitches that occurred. Its hind legs constantly slipped, and sitting down upon its tail, the shafts went up into the air. Though pressed for time, we abandoned the carriage at last as too great a trial of nerve, if not absolutely perilous, and could then spend a little more observation upon the scenery, which did not need the sense of danger to render it in the highest degree impressive. It consisted of a series of narrow and deep rifts through the porphyry rocks. These, unlike the Dolomite, are extremely favourable to vegetation, which in some form or other, creeps up every cranny, enriching, while adding to the sombre depth of colour due to the black and red tints of the rocks themselves. Entering the gorges, we entered into darkness, heightening the effect of the white tumbling stream at the bottom. Looking backwards through an opening at one of these dark corners, we saw again the Latemar precipices, which we had lost sight of since leaving Welschenhofen. They stood high in air, and bathed in sunlight, their front worn into singular resemblance to the pipes of a gigantic organ. Near the gloomiest of these spots the robbers had recently murdered a peasant, and carried off his mules. Altogether, we breathed more freely when passing under the tall towers of Schloss Karneid, reared aloft above the last of the gorges, we found ourselves in the sunny and verdurous valley of Botzen; full of villages, campaniles, and castle turrets, and terraced on every side with vineyards.

It was evening, and Botzen saluted our approach with the sonorous notes of its cathedral bell—that bell no doubt which a former proprietor of one of these castles—Haselburg, upon the porphyry slopes—never heard without wincing. Like his neighbour, Oswald of Wolkenstein, and many others, Hugo von Küepach had departed for the Holy Land, but unwilling to leave his treasures of gold and silver in charge of his young wife, he first poured them into an iron ball, which was then, as worthless, flung into the moat. Unluckily, before his return, the priests of the 'Dom' came collecting for a new bell, and his wife Kunigunda, pleading that in the absence of her husband she was short of money, offered the old castaway ball as a contribution in metal. Melted down, the gold and the silver ran mingled into the mould, adding a marvellous sweetness to the bell tones, as all ears acknowledged—excepting his, whose money went clanging in the belfry!

After an interval of six years we were all once more at Botzen. The railway in the interval, had pushed its way up from Italy. The outskirts of the old town had been cleared to make space for a roomy station. The old pathway to the Calvarienberg had been diverted. But there was still the rich red porphyry landscape, and still the distant jagged line of the Dolomites in the east. It was not with curiosity and wonder that we now looked at those shapes. They no longer screened an unknown region, they belonged no longer to hope, but to memory, and *that* they filled with many happy pictures of scenes and days among the Dolomites.

OUT-OF-THE-WAY SPOTS:

A SUPPLEMENTARY JOURNEY IN 1863.

CHAPTER XVII.

OUT-OF-THE-WAY SPOTS.

Old Kärnten again—Friesach and its Castles— St. Veit, the old Court City—Hoch Osterwitz—The Zollfeld and the Herzogstuhl—Virunum—The Maria Saal—Klagenfurt—The Loibl Valleys—Villach and the Landskron—Night Ascent of the Dobratsch—The View at Sunrise—Last Visit to the Wulfenia—Passage of the 'Kirschbaumer'—The Lessach Thal and Legend of Lukau—The Sexten Dolomites—Tai Cadore—Excursion to Brags—Forno and Signor Cercena—Belluno—Feltre and Primiero.

ONCE more to Old Kärnten. People wondered at our pertinacity,—that year after year we should take the same route, and now again, in 1863, should be off as usual to our Dolomites. But the Churchills must needs make captive the beautiful *Wulfenia* that had twice eluded them, so they started early, not to fail a third time; and we that remained, could not rest long contented, as we heard of glorious days in the Gail Thal; of Frau Claus's hospitable welcome at Auf der Plecken; of Tarvis, and the worthy Gelbfuss; and of new researches among the Karavanken. By the end of July we were en route to join them, and to cover as much fresh ground as possible, entered Kärnten for this, the fourth time, at quite a different point. From Ischl, travelling on the romantic high road through Styria as far as Rottenmann, and then over the Rottenmanner Tauern to Unzmarkt in the Mur Thal, we crossed into Kärnten at Neumarkt, and within the venerable walls of Friesach, once more met our friends.

We purpose in this chapter to pick up a few dropped

threads, and to disclose two or three more secrets of the Dolomites. To be frank, we have hesitated whether we should not keep these to ourselves. We have told of Ratzes, and Caprile, of Auf der Plecken, of Wurzen and the 'Caldron,' of cheerful Tarvis, and secluded Primiero; is not that enough? May we not fairly retain for our own use one or two later discoveries, nor, before it must be, let the world of tourists in? It was a temptation, but we have resolved to be generous, and make a clean breast of all we know.

Carinthia was our first word, and Carinthia shall be almost our last. We love the old country. It has mixed itself up with our proper subject perhaps rather more than it ought, but it is so little known, that the digression may be pardoned. It was the ancient historical centre of the country that we now visited for the first time.

Just before entering the small plain in which Friesach stands, you pass under a lofty rock, and catch sight of castle towers on its summit. That is Dürrenstein or Dürnstein, the first prison of Richard Cœur de Lion, who was arrested near Friesach. Friesach itself is a striking place, and striking in its history. Roman remains exist not far north of it, and Mediæval times have left abundant memorials in walls, gateways, towers, churches, monasteries. It has stood sieges, and has heard the sound of battle from the sunny plain below. It was long the seat of power for the Prince Archbishops of Salzburg, from whom the Dukes of Kärnten sometimes tried to wrest it. The Emperor Conrad III. stayed here on his return from the Holy Land in 1149. King Ottokar in 1276 made it a heap of ruins, and the same fate befel it thirteen years later at the hands of Duke Albert. But—greatest misfortune of all—it became a prey to the Turks, and from 1479 to 1490 those ruthless foes continued to ravage the district.

On the craggy heights above the town rise heaps of towers from no less than three separate castles. The centre one, the Schloss Petersberg, is the proudest. The coining chamber of the archbishops, black with mediæval smoke, is still to be seen among the ruins. Thence issued the coins of Carinthia, curious square pieces of silver stamped on the obverse with a portrait of the Archbishop, and in a circle round it, the legend 'Sancte Rudberte ora pro nobis;' the reverse side gives his name 'Leonard de Keutsch, Arc. Sal.,' the date, '1513,' and his arms. In one of the shields is a full portrait of the famous 'Keutschach' turnip—a worthy rival of Mr. Skirving's—which the Archbishop Leonard was so proud of having introduced into his dominions, that he took care its portrait should be everywhere seen. In some of the rooms of the old Schloss of Salzburg, and even on a fine earthenware stove there, it is to be found. In 1490 he restored the fortifications of the Schloss Petersberg, and over the principal entrance affixed his shield, in which also a representation of the much-prized root appears. Here, too, in the castle church, is a quaint picture, by Albert Dürer, of the Virgin, comfortably tucked in bed, and drinking veritable caudle, while a homely washtub on the floor waits for the holy child, reposing in a homely cradle. Respect its honest truth! In the same church they will show you a strange outcome from that humble beginning, in church vestments 600 years old, all glistening with rich embroidery,—to be worn by that child's ministers.

From this castle height you might formerly have looked down upon no less than twelve churches within the small walled town; you may still see their ruins. One of them was dedicated to St. Virgil, the canonised Bishop of Salzburg, the same who commissioned Modestus in the year A.D. 754, to convert the Slovenes of Carinthia to Christianity. An Irishman by birth, St. Virgil, was sent by Pepin, the father of Charlemagne, to Odilo Duke of Bavaria, and was by him appointed to the then bishopric of Salzburg. Nor, among the hints and glimpses of times long gone by, must I forget to notice the inscription on a slab in the ancient Church of the Dominicans, 'Hic stabat Thomas Aquinas.' So they recorded a six months' visit from the great 'Angelical Doctor.'

Two days were scarcely enough for romantic and venerable Friesach; but on the afternoon of the second, we started southwards with a brilliant project in our heads. The Churchills had seen in the museum at Klagenfurt a picture of a lake and a castle, with, in the distance, a splendid prospect of the Julian Alps. It lay somewhere up here; while 'Murray' spoke of another castle in the same direction, Osterwitz,—on the summit of a lofty rock—the seat of the famous Khevenhüllers—as the finest in Carinthia. What if we could find an inn at the lake for night quarters, and visit both castles on our way to Klagenfurt?

There *was* an inn, and away we went in the early afternoon through a landscape all golden with sunlight and harvest; great mountains rising distantly in front. Diverging after a couple of hours from the Klagenfurt road, we turned upon a country track, through woods and open fields, and suddenly dropped upon a small lake, with a large pile of buildings, formerly the monastery of St. George, on its banks; but not a vestige of a castle, and scarcely a vestige of the mountains. Sequestered among trees was a farm-house, serving also as an inn, and the landlord, busy and brown with harvesting, came out to meet us. 'Castle,' said he, 'there is no castle here.' And after putting it in all sorts of ways, we were obliged to believe our own eyes, and him. There was a mistake somewhere.

We must push on to St. Veit five miles further, regaining the high road there, through another rough country way. But if we left the lake disappointed, our spirits soon rose again, for in a mile or two there shot unmistakably into view the famed 'Hoch Osterwitz' on its conical hill, with a crown of towers glittering in the sun. That was clearly the excursion for the morning.

Next to Friesach, St. Veit is the oldest town in Carinthia, once its capital, the court city of the old dukedom. While the orange glow of evening lasted, we hastened to the Calvary, a hill with three crosses on its summit, and shrines dotting the ascent. Below, lay the town, like Friesach, girdled with walls; around were pine-covered hills, one behind the other as far as we could see, and on almost every hill a castle ruin; princely Osterwitz in the east, outshining them all. This was the most knightly district of Carinthia in the days when its chivalry was needed to fight the Turks. Down these hills have streamed pennons and pikes to meet the invader, or, on many a high-day to the gathering of the people on the sacred Zollfeld below. Southward there opened a more distant horizon, and those who know what a mountain passion is, will appreciate our delight on recognising the peaks of the Julian range—the Mangert—the Prisinig—of other years; and, topping them all, the snowy Terglou itself.

After an early breakfast we took the road to Osterwitz, lying five miles to the east of the direct Klagenfurt route. It is not seen till within a couple of miles, when it strides into view, a commanding place of strength. The hill, of limestone, appears conical on this side; on the other it falls in one precipice 900 feet deep. The ascent, through fifteen towered gateways, and over three drawbridges, wind round the hill to the walled and turretted top, after the manner of ideal castles in old pictures. At a farmhouse we left the carriage; no guide appeared to accompany us up the hill, and the iron-plated gates were all ajar, or easily pushed open. The bars, bolts, and curious locks, were most of them in their places, and the little hanging door with iron-rimmed peephole, still swung in the midst of each heavy gate. The machinery of the drawbridges was gone, and only planks remained over the deep chasms which successively barred the progress of an enemy, should he attempt the path, that winding round the rock had always the precipice on the right. Each gateway was a small fortress in itself, and each bore upon its front a marble tablet, exhibiting either the arms and titles of the family, invocations to the Trinity, or texts of Scripture, all in Latin. On the uppermost of the fifteen was inscribed 'Deliver me, my God, from mine enemies, and the hands of bloody men,'—a fearful suggestion of the terror which may have sometimes reigned within. Here, one of the spiked portcullises remained suspended. Doors and vaulted passages accumulated towards the summit, and gave entrance at last to a battlemented terrace, supporting the lofty walls of the actual castle.

Within the building is a court—the ancient tilt yard. A chapel, overhanging the depth of the precipice, occupies one side, and shelters the remains of some of the Khevenhüllers; several rooms open upon it on the other, and at one end is the armoury. The interior has been spoiled of almost everything but portraits of the Khevenhüller family, whose gaunt figures still line the walls of their desecrated chambers. The French it was—always the French—that gutted the building, carrying away twenty wagon loads of trophies and valuables. Yet in the armoury are some curious things; among them a suit of mail for a man nine feet high, quivers, cross-bows, &c., and especially the coat of chain mail worn by Margaret of Tyrol, 'Maultasch,' or Mouth-poke, as Carlyle calls her, who was here besieged. Her 'war hat,' an enormous conical broad brim of stout leather, in shape like the traditional beaver of the witches, lies beside it, and in a corner stands the speaking trumpet, ten feet long, through which perhaps 'Mouth-poke' herself parleyed with her foes. This good lady it was who brought Tyrol to the House of Hapsburg. Two wells, deep as Hades, supplied the garrison, and in a corner of the guard house an orifice, just large enough to force a man through, opens upon a pit, the dungeon of the castle; let us hope that the wrong man was never fitted into that square hole.

Here lived the Khevenhüller who commanded the Christian army at the great battle of Villach in 1492, and he of the same name, the redoubtable general of Maria Theresa. They were a noble race that fledged their wings on this Carinthian rock. The view from it is not remarkable. It is placed in an amphitheatre of low hills, their tops all wooded; their sides partially arable, and with a few villages distributed about. No English names were inscribed in the visitors' book, as far as we saw; now that the railway reaches Klagenfurt, they will probably soon be found upon its pages.

In A——'s letters from Carinthia, p. 340, mention is made of the antique stone chair still standing in the field where the Dukes of Carinthia were installed with feudal homage. That was our next object. On leaving Osterwitz we regained the high road in a few miles, and presently reached the open common, browsed over by herds of cattle, which as the ancient Zollfeld—Saalfeld—is so sacred in Carinthian eyes. It is surrounded by hills similar to those about St. Veit, excepting on the south, where it is open to a glorious view. In descending from Osterwitz we had it all before us. First, the pale Dolomitic forms of the Julian Alps, set round the far horizon; next below them, the rolling masses of the Karavanken, sweeping along in great waves of wood and rock from east to west, lost in distance at either end; then in front of these, the range of low hills with a precipitous edge, covered with wood, and with not a village, scarcely even a cottage visible upon them, which constitute the singular Satnitz plateau, inhabited by the shy Slovenes. Klagenfurt, immediately at the foot of this, cannot yet be seen. These three ranges, beginning at the first, come successively into sight, and are all finely in view from the Zollfeld, which thus offers the noblest of areas for a national ceremonial, as it once did for a Roman city.

At the foot of a wooded hill to the right is the Karnberg, where till this present year remained the stone—'Der Fürstenstein'—upon which the duke, as prince only, received the first rite of investiture. It is now in the Klagenfurt museum, and proves to be simply the defaced capital of a Roman column! So, the new civilisation seated itself upon the ruins of the old. To the left, upon another of the surrounding hills, is the venerable church of St. Maria Saal, where the second portion of the ceremony—high mass by the bishop, and his benediction upon the newly-created duke—took place. And here, in the midst of the open common, is the weather-worn but stately double chair of stone itself, on a rude stone platform, where in face of all Carinthian nobles and people, and of the far-off ranges of the Carinthian mountains, tier above tier, sat the Duke, back to back with the Count of Görz, and received the oaths of fealty. Only within the last few years has a strong railing been placed to protect this most interesting monument, and in front of it the traveller passing on the road can plainly read in large letters the words, 'Kärntens Herzogstuhl.' *

STONE CHAIR OF THE ZOLLFELD.

The principal portion of the ruins of the Roman city of Virunum have been discovered a little to the north of the Herzogstuhl; but others have been found in every direction in and near the Zollfeld. Even on the summit of the Magdelensberg—a high hill behind that on which the church of Maria Saal stands — many antiquities have been disinterred; amongst them was the bronze statue of Antinous, a noble work of Roman art, now one of the most valued treasures in the Museum of Antiquities, at the Palace of the Lower Belvidere in Vienna.

* There are two original narratives of the ceremonies observed on the day of inauguration. These—with a discussion of the differences existing between them; the meaning of each portion of the ceremony, arising out of peculiarities in the history of the Slovenic dukedom; the presumed Slovenic inscription, to be seen on a stone supporting one of the seats of the Herzogstuhl; together with woodcuts of the 'Stuhl' and the 'Fürstenstein'—are to be found, by those who take an interest in such matters, in a little pamphlet by Max Ritter Von Moro, 'Der Fürstenstein in Karnberg und der Herzogstuhl am Zollfelde in Kärnten,' published at Vienna in 1862.

Virunum was the most important Roman colony in the ancient province of Noricum. It stood at the junction of the road from Juvavum (Salzburg) with that from Ovilabis (Wels), and served as the link to connect the military posts on the banks of the Danube with the city of Aquileja,—itself the meeting-point for the whole of the Illyrian trade with the West, and the military station best adapted for watching the movements of the tribes to the north and east of Italy. Virunum is mentioned by both Pliny and Ptolemy, and appears in two inscriptions that have been found in Rome. Its fate is left in darkness; but it is supposed to have been abandoned at the time of Attila's great movement towards Gaul in A.D. 451 against the Romans and Visi-Goths, when it was laid waste by the left wing of his vast army. The route of this portion of his forces was through Pettau, Cilli, Juena (now the Jaunthal, in south-east Carinthia), Virunum, to Salzburg, and Augsburg; from which point it advanced to attack the Burgundians, then settled in the neighbourhood of Basle.

With Osterwitz for the morning, and the Zollfeld for the afternoon, this day's journey teemed with historical interest; but it was not till the day following that, returning from Klagenfurt, we visited the Maria Saal. The old church is not the least interesting of these ancient sites. The present building dates from the beginning of the fifteenth century, with the exception of the lower portions of the two towers, which are older. The original church of Modestus was founded in the year A.D. 754. A chapel in the churchyard is evidently of much earlier date than the church, and between the two stands a pillar, supporting a lantern of some size, all richly carved in stone, looking very old, and in some parts much worn. It bears the remains of a Sclavic inscription in old German characters.

In the walls of the church are inserted numerous slabs

and reliefs, remains from the Roman city, whose Pagan devices appear in odd association with Christian emblems; and before the porch, in memory of a far different phase of history, hangs by a chain a stone cannon ball shot by the Turks against the sacred edifice. In front of the altar is the stone, covering the sainted remains of Modestus, which, though we did not verify the fact, moves every day nearer to the altar! When it touches it the last day will have come;—but there appears to be time enough yet. A picture in the church represents a fearful 'Storm on the 13th of August 1843,' when the Virgin miraculously protected the building from lightning, while a neighbouring house was destroyed. They have since afforded her the valuable assistance of Sir W. Snow Harris, by putting up a lightning conductor. The cottage, or 'stöckl,' of Modestus lies a short distance down the hill, differing but little in appearance from the farmhouses about. Its walls, however, are said to show great age.

Klagenfurt is about five miles from the Zollfeld. To the Churchills the old city was familiar, and to us almost as much so from their descriptions. We arrived on a splendid evening, and repairing to the gardens of the Kreuzberg, westward of the city, enjoyed a lovely prospect —one with which the Klagenfurters say their Emperor was well pleased when he visited the city in 1856. An inscription marks the spot where he stood, and the gardens have received the name of 'Franz Josef's Anlagen.' The hill, crossed by many winding walks, is a favourite evening resort. Unfortunately, the Wörther See is not a feature in the view; but the plain of Klagenfurt, eastwards, the wooded plateau of Satnitz, the dark Karavanken mountains, with a few peeps of the Julians above them, form a noble landscape.

Klagenfurt itself has a sleepy stateliness about its squares and streets, which render it pleasing, if not striking, as a city. And who that looks upon the terrible dragon in the Neu Platz can doubt the story of its origin? For my part, I am quite of Mr. Kingsley's opinion, that the 'Scientifics' call the mud monsters in their museums by long Greek names, just because they have pooh-pooh'd the old stories so long, that they are ashamed to call them dragons. The Klagenfurters religiously believe in theirs. The Land Haus, or Hall of Assembly for the Carinthian Estates, is perhaps the most interesting of the public buildings. In its 'Wappen Saal,' covered, as Murray describes, with coats of arms, we were especially amused at recognising among them one with a Dolomite mountain for device. We have ventured to appropriate it for ourselves.

We did not neglect to visit the Prediger Stuhl, on the edge of the Satnitz plateau. The road to it across the plain is bordered with fine elms, which, with the view from the 'Stuhl,' including a long stretch of the lake, make it a most agreeable excursion. A finer view, however, would be afforded from the pilgrimage church of the Ulrich's Berg, a hill five miles to the north of Klagenfurt, overlooking the Zollfeld. A violent storm turned us back on the ascent, and we did not reach the summit. The Hungarian leader, Görgey, it may be interesting to some to know, occupies, with his wife, a small house about the same distance on the other side of Klagenfurt, in the direction of the Loibl pass, surrounded by charming scenery—in which one may hope his wounded heart finds solace. A few of his countrymen are still detained under surveillance in the city, and, at the time of our visit, English tourists were so rare that we heard ourselves more than once designated as Hungarians as we passed along.

Before our meeting at Friesach, the Churchills had made a short visit to three of the more western valleys of the Karavanken—the Loibl Thal, traversed by the diligence to Laibach; the Boden Thal, more to the west; and the Bären Thal, still farther in the same direction. In the Loibl Thal they stayed at a little way-side house, not far from the entrance, called 'Deutscher Peter,' where German is spoken. It is much frequented by the hunters of the chamois, which are still numerous upon the Gross Gerlouz—a huge rocky mass, rising abruptly in the line of the north Karavanken ridge. The valley is filled with short spurs from its sides, so that any general view is impossible until the height of the pass is gained. From the summit they looked down into a narrow deep valley, formed by a curious duplication of the main ridge. Looking up it westward, there is a fine profile view of the precipices of the Stou, the Seleniza, and other peaks. The next valley, the Boden Thal, is open and clear, from Bleiberg, with its numerous lead mines, situated at the entrance, to its head, closed by the precipices of the Vertača. A track ascends under these to the summit of the lateral ridge separating the Boden from the Bären Thal, and thence along the main ridge to the summit of the Stou, 7,326 feet above the sea—the highest peak of the western Karavanken. The easiest approach is made by this track. The other is by the head of the Bären Thal, but by both some laborious climbing among boulders and *geröll* is necessary. The Bären Thal has scenic attractions far surpassing its sister valleys, with the advantage also of a very good inn at Windisch Feistritz—where, too, German is spoken. This picturesque little village, on the lower edge of the mountain slope, overlooks the valley of the Drave, while the long line of the Satnitz plateau bounds the view to the north. Near the village are the extensive wire-drawing works of the Count von Egger. The inlet to the valley is by a long, narrow, broken, and varied ravine, down which the Feistritz flows to join the Drave. At two hours from Windisch Feistritz a farmhouse called 'Kranoutz' is reached, capable of affording tolerable head-quarters to an explorer of the valley; but only Slovenic, or 'Krainerisch,' as the Germans call it, is there to be heard. A little farther, near Senidar, the first view of the Stou is obtained; but the fine effect of his precipitous face is much enhanced by taking a circuit to the little church—the only one in the valley—perched at a considerable height upon the slopes, and commanding the whole. A track leads from the church round the shoulders of the Matschacher Vrh, and thence above the ravine by which the valley is entered, back to Windisch Feistritz.

On the afternoon of the third day of our stay at Klagenfurt, the fussy little steamer on the Wörther See carried us away westward. Here and there it called at a rough wooden jetty belonging to some peasant village. Not a single villa, or house of any pretensions, adorned the shores of a lake as beautiful as many that tourists crowd to see. A diligence, waiting at the farther end, conveyed us to Villach, over high ground, showing well the long rolling range of the Karavanken, and, near Villach, the scene of the Turkish defeat, with the mass of the Dobratsch rising above it.

A fine ruin, almost rivalling Heidelberg in its lengths of wall and rows of eyeless windows, overlooks the plain from among the wooded hills to the north, near the outlet of the Ossiacher See; and, being nearly as much castle as mountain-mad, we marked it for an excursion the following day. It is the 'Landskron,' belonging to another branch of the Khevenhüller family; and had not the interior been destroyed by fire some years ago, it would have borne comparison with Osterwitz. Steep alleys, through dense woods, lead to deserted grass-grown terraces, whence the view is magnificent over the plain of Villach—perhaps it was too magnificent on the day of the great battle, when all the fluctuations of the fight could be traced along the banks of the Drave. The steeples of Villach quivered in the noontide heat some five miles away; and southward, the abrupt defiant outlines of the Wischberg, Mangert, Spik, and Terglou, proud members of the Julian range, stretched along the horizon.

But our principal object just now lay farther to the west—not at Villach, but at the Villacher Alp, otherwise called the Dobratsch. This mountain has been so frequently referred to in our pages that we hope it is not merely a harsh Sclavonic name to our readers. Commanding the point of junction of the Drave and the Gail, and opposite the pass over the Carnic chain southward, it is the corner-stone of this portion of Carinthia. Once a year the Sclavonic population makes pilgrimage to the summit. Frau Klaus, of Auf der Plecken, had when a girl, upon one occasion, accompanied thither some of her Sclavonic acquaintance, and her description of the ascent and the view, combined with our interest in the mountain, determined us to witness, if possible, a sunrise from its top. After spending the morning, therefore, at the 'Landskron,' we drove in the afternoon to the mining village of Bleiberg, at the back of the mountain. We ought to have reached this place in time to climb the Dobratsch—a matter of three hours, according to local calculation—before dark; but the fascination of the 'Landskron,' the sultry afternoon ascent of the Bleiberg, and the preparations necessary for spending a night on the mountain, brought us to seven o'clock in the evening, before, with a guide, a lantern, and a bunch of candles, we were ready to start. Yet the mountain, a mass of rock and débris, towering before us, was still luminous in the western glow; and the hut which was to furnish a night's lodging seemed almost near, notched against the clear sky. Who could think of night, darkness, and difficulty, in the splendour of such a scene, and the glee of such an adventure?

Darkness, however, came down quick; but supposing that the path up a pilgrimage mountain could not fail to be a well-worn way, we made little of that matter, and 'lighting up' in the middle of a thick wood, enjoyed the flitting glimmer among the tree stems, expecting soon to conquer the steepness, and find smooth walking on the alp. But above the wood was no grassy alp—only a frightful stony trough or gully, shooting down from top to bottom of the mountain, and the path became nothing but footsteps, set backward and forward along the loose *geröll*, skirting ledges of rock, twisting upward in fact any way it could, towards a pale streak of snow above—just the awkwardest path possible for people to be taking by candlelight. The single lantern was handed to the hindmost, and the guide, lighting one of the candles, advanced in front, protecting it in the hollow of his hand. After a while we found ourselves abreast of the snow, shooting into nothingness below, at a pitch steeper than any house roof; and while each one rested up and down, where he or she happened to stick, the guide scrambled sideways with the lantern for lumps of snow to suck. The stillness upon all the mountain side was wonderful. We might have been hanging on a ladder to the stars. At a vast depth below, there twinkled a few lights in the Bleiberg village, and far away, at a great height on the opposite mountains, here and there, like red sparks, shone the fires of shepherds. By-and-bye, a deeper blackness gathered in that quarter, and then a blaze of blue lightning rose, now and again, into the sky, and every jagged rock at hand took sudden shape, and vanished. To our comfort the distant storm seemed to die away; but quickly it flared out again, and thunder, rolling like a chariot over the dark Noric hills, sent through us a thrill of alarm. Every peal urged us onward; for the climb was now not only exhausting, but perilous. Presently a wind began to draw down from above—a welcome sign that the summit was not far distant. Unluckily it blew out the guide's candle; no efforts could protect it; and at last lantern and candle were blown out together. A little further on S—— became so distressed as seriously to alarm us all. We were climbing against time on account of the storm, but a halt was absolutely necessary, and to our great relief the black mass which was blotting out the stars northward edged away, and the thunder sounded more distantly. Another quarter of an hour, and the tinkling of a sheep-bell showed that the grassy alp was near. Even that was stony when we reached it, but the hut was now visible in the faint starlight, and at eleven o'clock, after four hours of toil and darkness, we reached the door.

Fumbling for the latch, we entered, and the guide helping us up a ladder into a hay-loft, led into a small inner room, where six men lay asleep upon straw, all in a row. A stove in a corner sent out a stifling heat. A narrow bench ran round the walls, and upon a small table were the remains of a meal. It turned out that an engineer visiting the mines, the forest inspector, and two or three others, from Bleiberg, had arrived some hours before ourselves on the same errand, and it was their slumbers we had now so unexpectedly disturbed. In a few minutes the master of the hut, a most polite old fellow, appeared at the top of the ladder, and was soon sent down again to blow up a fire and boil water for tea; among our equipments we had taken care to include a teapot. It did us all a world of good, and then, before sharing the straw with the rest of the company, we stepped out to look at the just risen moon, shining over the Ossiacher and the Wörther lakes in the distance—a lovely sight. The storm had quite died away, and there was every promise for the sunrise.

Excitement, fatigue, stove-heat, and more than all, fleas, quite prevented sleep ; and when the small window-panes began to redden with the stealthy light of dawn, we gladly said 'good morning' to each other as we rose from the straw. Those who first reached the outer door returned quickly to say the sight was too beautiful to lose. Indeed it was. The crimson glow in the east was as if that half of the globe had taken fire, while the moon, not yet paled, was still ruling in the west. In short time everybody was out upon the narrow ridge of the mountain, about five minutes above the hut. Familiar as we were with the vast apparent bulk of the Dobratsch, it was amazing to find it thinning off to this knife-like edge, almost as precipitous on the one side as on the other; on the south especially, falling away from where we stood, in absolute walls of rock, fearful to look over. Here it was that the earthquake of 1348 had scooped out the bowels of the mountain, leaving it sheer and bare. Two small chapels occupy the ridge, the smallest of them planted on the western end, belonging to the Slovenes; both impinging perilously upon the edges of the precipice.

Is there any spectacle in this world comparable to a sunrise from a mountain top? We stood, a row of shivering mortals, exclaiming that nothing could be more glorious—glorious for the mere colours, as in every clear sunrise, flung into the sky; glorious here for the landscape it illuminated. The Julian Alps, bare Dolomite walls of stone—as if creation had been arrested in its earliest stages—line the whole south, as seen from the Dobratsch. They were marvellous in the flush of the first half hour. Terglou, Spik, Prisinig, Mangert, Wischberg, Balitza Spitzen—all a-glow—the Mangert, immediately opposite, taking the chiefest place of honour; the central, if not the loftiest member of the range. North and west, a glittering fringe of snow-points marked where the Gross Glockner and his fellows held sway among the Norics. Between these two opposite sources of attraction lay a world of mountain and valley, diversified by shining streams, or broad surfaces of lakes—a landscape which, during the last three years, we had crossed and re-crossed on many different lines. The course of the Drave went away mistily to the east, at the foot of the interminable Karavanken, and from beneath our feet the straight valley of the Gail cleft its course towards the west. The tops of the *Wulfenia* Mountain (the Gartner), Polinik, Kollin Kofel, and what else of the Carnic range, early caught the sunbeams in that direction, and Hermagor and the sparse Slovenic villages brightened cheerily as they shot along the valley. But what is the use of a list of names upon the page, which to the reader can be little else than names? A panorama cannot be painted with the pen—very poorly with the pencil.

After wizening with cold for an hour, we ran down to the hut for breakfast, rejoicing in having brought with us some portable soup; and after a second visit to the summit, started at eight, when the day seemed already far advanced, along with the Bleiberg party, for the descent. By their advice we took a circuitous route, at least an hour longer than that by which we had ascended. It is altogether over the alp, and is easy walking, with magnificent views over the plain of Villach and course of the Drave.

On these accounts it is the one to be recommended,—perhaps also for another reason still, that it passes over a natural strawberry bed in the woods, the most prolific we have ever seen. Everybody gathered handfuls, and many handfuls were poured into our ladies' laps by the Bleiberg gentlemen, to whose courtesy and kindness we were all much indebted.

We had intended to drive on to Hermagor that afternoon, but the conveyances promised were not forthcoming, and we were not sorry to have nothing to do but go early to bed. The next morning we were off in good time, reaching Hermagor at noon.

Does the reader remember that, when we visited the Gail Thal two years ago, we left the upper Gail — the remote and roadless Lessach Thal—unexplored? We discussed the matter one evening on the hills above Kötschach, after returning from Auf der Plecken, and in view of much other work in hand, agreed to leave that end of the valley to some other explorer, with the warning, however, that after all we might be beforehand with him. We were now about to justify that warning. The Lessach Thal was our next object; and it is one of the dropped threads that this chapter must pick up.

But once more in the Gail Thal, and under the Gartner Kogel, we could not resist paying a final visit to the *Wulfenia* beds. The Churchills had this year gone direct from England to Hermagor, and on the 26th of June saw for the first time the plant in abundant bloom on the Watschacher Alp, subsequently visiting its other site, the Kühwege. It was now far too late for any flowers, but Churchill and I arranged to give a day to an excursion which should include both alps, ascending by the Kühwege on the eastern side of the Gartner, crossing over the mountain near its summit, and descending by the Watschacher. These two alps form two opposite spurs of the mountain; upon these two alone the *Wulfenia* grows, and upon the northern slope of each only; so that the plant (capricious thing!) is not only particular about its mountain, but particular about its place thereon.

To me the Gartner was new ground; I need not repeat the details of the ascent, which have been already given. It took us three hours to reach the Kühwege—the eastern spur. We sat down at one of the few springs on the mountain. 'Are we near the Wulfenia?' said I. 'It is close behind you,' replied my friend. Starting up hatless in my haste, a dozen steps brought me into the midst of its rank luxuriance, covering the ground like—large lettuces, shall I say? or like a thick bed of strawberries?—any way, triumphantly spreading itself over acres of soil, and defying apparently all the laws of extinction. It is still better seen on the Watschacher, the western spur. Climbing the steep col, noticing on the way the gradual disappearance of the plant, which seems not to grow below 5,000 nor much above 6,000 feet of elevation, and enjoying the splendid prospect on the Italian side, over a heaving sea of mountains, we descended upon this western spur, where the *Wulfenia* covers several rocky terraces with its vivid green, and where, in the pride of its bloom, the effect must be charming. It was near these terraces that A——, a month earlier, made a careful drawing of the plant. Any one visiting the mountain had better take it as we did on this occasion, ascending on the eastern, and descending on the western side, to the village of Watschig, where, if he chooses, a car from Hermagor, five miles distant, may be appointed to meet him.

Herr Gelbfuss was at Hermagor, and his account of the path through the Lessach Thal, crossing, as he said, sixty 'Graben,' together with the heat of the present season, rather daunted S—— and A——, and instead of continuing up the Gail Thal, we crossed over by the Gitsch Thal and the Weissensee—old ground—to the Drave at Greifenburg, reaching Lienz the next morning. The plan was for Churchill and myself to cross over the Lienz Dolomites alone, dropping down upon the middle of the Lessach Thal at Sta. Maria Lukau, and rejoining our wives in a day or two at Innichen in the Puster Thal.

These Lienz Dolomites were the first specimens we ever saw of the mountains that have cost us so many tours. They looked as imposing now as ever. Apart from the main Dolomitic field, they form the western end of a range in itself separate and singular, dividing the Drave from the Gail, and terminating eastward in the Dobratsch. The Reiss Kofel, midway, is also Dolomite, but the *mass* is at this Lienz end. See it towering in the purple twilight as you come up from Oher Drauburg, and confess the grandeur of Dolomite. An honest, cheery fellow from Leisach, three miles from Lienz, accompanied us, as, early one morning, we crossed the Drave near that village, and assailed the western flank of these mountains. The path is familiar to the people of Leisach, for it leads to the Kirschbaumer Alp, their summer grazing-ground. Do not expect to find *cherries* there; it is named, not after a tree, but a man. There was the inevitable climb of three or four hours through all the sternness of an Alpine forest, and under dead walls of rock—upward, upward, through the cleft where a stream dashed down, till the alp expanse was reached, with its one low hut, where the lad in charge supplied us with a pail of milk, and two wooden spoons to skim off the cream. Botanists know this alp as well as herdsmen, but it was too late in the season for any specimens of *Ranunculus parnassifolius*, or the other rare plants this locality has the credit of possessing. Another hour put us on the summit ridge, a smooth, innocent surface of shale on this still day, but the very playground of the storm.

Northward lay distant Noric peaks, and the near Dolomitic masses, savage in repose. Southward was the more striking scene, not into the Lessach Thal—that was too deep a crack—but over it, to the Carnic range, where the Kollin Kofel justified the importance recently assigned to it.* The view was narrowed, however, by a mighty shape, apparently not Dolomitic, projecting on the left, and forming the eastern side of the short lateral valley descending into the Lessach Thal. This valley we must gain. Our guide, not so much at home on this side as on the other, warned us to expect something, but no warning could prepare us for the strange and wonderful descent through a rift that had torn its way downward, from top to bottom of the mountain. Falling from depth to depth, and closing with relentless grip, it soon shoved the path—if path it might be called—into the bed of the frantic stream, which, fighting with the rocks, had forced many a curious passage through them. Through these we also had to squeeze, and it cost nearly two hours of scrambling before, wet and battered, we reached the bottom of the trough. Looking upward, no one would suppose that deep and jagged cleft could ever serve as staircase to the alp. Every peasant of the valley, when he found we had crossed the Kirschbaumer, had a shrug and a smile for the 'Graben.'

The Lessach Thal opened with great loveliness when we reached, an hour or two below the 'Graben,' the shoulder of the last hill. Farm-houses on every knoll, yellow harvest patches, green meadows, woods, interlacing hills, and a village spire or two, formed a picture of sequestered

* See 'The Vienna Alpine Journal,' vol. i.

rural beauty. Secluded enough, geographically, the want of a road has made it more so. Footpaths along its steep slopes afford the only communication from village to village, and the numerous ravines that score the slopes cause many tedious circuits in the paths. The people are reported to be very simple in their manners, and remarkable for great 'religiosity,' which may be partly due to their possessing a famous shrine, that of Santa Maria Lukau, visited by pilgrims from Tyrol and Italy, as well as all parts of Kärnten. A monastery is attached to the shrine, and the story told of the origin of so remote a place of pilgrimage is as follows :—

'In the year 1513, a poor but God-fearing woman of the neighbourhood, slumbering in a field of wheat, was instructed by a vision to build on that spot a church in honour of the Queen of heaven. To test the reality of the commission, she placed a lighted candle in the middle of the field. "If," said she, "during three days and nights the candle is not extinguished in the strong alp wind, the will of God will be declared." The proof was granted, and Helen—that was her name—procuring a small picture of the Virgin, begged with it from house to house. Contributions were slowly collected, and at last, not without strong opposition from the owner of the field, a wooden chapel was erected on the designated spot, and received a wooden statue of the Virgin. The report of the good deed drew so many worshippers to the humble building, that in two years the means were forthcoming for a larger church, which was completed and consecrated by the Bishop of Aquileia, in 1562. Eighty years later, a monastery for Franciscan monks was erected. It was subsequently transferred to lay brethren, but in 1640 a fire destroyed both the roof and the bells, and the present building is due to the munificence of Cardinal Christopher, Count of Widmann. The princely family of Porzia, to whom much of the Gail Thal belongs, have always patronised the shrine, and the church became noted for the richness and value of its gold ornaments, which, in the troubled time of 1809, were removed to a place of greater safety.'

Where there is a shrine there will also be inns, and the place has become the most important in the valley. It happened that we arrived on the eve of the great Festa, extending over several days ; but we were fortunately able to secure a good room in the principal inn, belonging to the 'Guggenburgers,' people of some condition. Their arms, and a sketch of the family history, from which it appeared that some few centuries ago they had migrated from Bavaria, hung upon the wall. Busy preparations for the fête were in progress ; and of the three beds in our room, one was a receptacle *pro tem.* for church decorations, wreaths, crosses, and ribbons, making a gorgeous display.

The mountain-paths were full of people, and every vacant space about the village. Among the groups the queerest costumes abounded, raked up out of holes and corners, where the fashions had not changed for the last five hundred years — the oddities themselves that wore them seeming all unconscious of their antique guise, though one could almost fancy some of the younger men felt a trifle sheepish in their greatgrandfather's garments. The old Tyrolese costume prevailed, but with nothing of the opera-like smartness one has seen in Tyrol Proper, and there was a dullness of expression which obliged one to confess that mind as well as things might be rather stagnant in the valley.

'The Kloster' is a good-sized building, with ranges of

cheerful windows facing the south. Its garden walls enclose the small gothic church and churchyard, entered by a picturesque gateway. It was too dark that evening to judge of the interior, and in the morning there was too great a crowd. The whole occupies, with the village, a kind of terrace on the side of the valley, with a pleasant view up and down, and opposite, where an opening showed a rocky 'cirque' like those in the Pyrenees. This last was the only striking piece of scenery, and successive openings of the same kind southward are the chief characteristics of the valley. The higher mountains, whether to the south or north, are seldom visible, and so far our expectations of the scenery were disappointed.

The Guggenburgers—father, mother, son, and daughter—appeared successively at our breakfast-table in the morning; indeed, some one of them duteously sat by at every meal. The masses in church began at five, and were continued every hour till nine, the family, their guests, and servants, attending one or the other, as most convenient; and no doubt, on such a busy morning, our early departure was not regretted.

Our course lay westward, straight up the valley, the scenery gradually losing its embosomed character, and becoming bleak and open, with still here and there a striking glimpse southward of dark and snow-flecked ranges—the backbone of the Carnic Alps. Companies of pilgrims from Tyrol met us from time to time, filling the way with a murmur of prayers; the large village of Tilliach was full of them. The Gail, which above Lukau had run sparkling among bushes and round bluffs, was now shrunk to a brook in the open field—now it was a single runnel,—now an oozing from the grass. We had reached the Source. Then a marshy meadow swept from side to side of the shallow pass, and we stood upon the dividing ridge, where, right before us, lay the Pusterthal; and the Kärnten country ended.

One last word upon its history. The Lessach Thal is said to be at present exclusively occupied by Germans; but the names of some of its villages, such as Tilliach, and that of the Kartisch Thal beyond, indicate the former existence of a Sclavonic population. And there is evidence that, not only in this valley, but through the whole of the Pusterthal as far as the Brenner, Sclavonic laws, customs, and language prevailed from about the seventh century, A.D. until the time of the Emperor Maximilian, when German manners and institutions gained the upper hand. A few scattered Sclavonic names about Lienz and the Pusterthal, confirm the historical evidence. One of the Lienz Dolomites has the name of 'Rudnik;' Dölsach, Amlach, and Tristach, are the names of villages near Lienz; Liesach lies west of it, and Reischach to the south of Brunecken. These are all Sclavonic names.

The descent into Tyrol through the Kartisch Thal was full of landscape beauty, the distant view stretching along the Pusterthal, and the ruined towers of a castle near Sillian marking the junction of the Kartisch with that larger valley. The last part of the descent was rapid enough, and then the bridle-path ended in the broad high road. Parting from our Tyrolese guide at Sillian we took carriage for Innichen, where S—— and A—— had arrived that day from Lienz. They had been left in charge of our old friend Amman; years had gone by since, on this road, spruce and gay, he drove us Botzenwards,—years had dimmed the spruceness and damped the gaiety. Things were not well with the poor man; and now his son, a gentlemanly lad, took his place upon the box behind but one sorry representative of the pair of steeds that used to rattle out of Lienz. No doubt seven years had told their tale also with his 'vier Engländer.'

Had seven years, or seventy times seven, wrought any change upon the spiry crest of the Drei Schuster? Doubtless none. Whatever wear and tear had seamed its sides or scooped the débris at its foot, that sharp proud shape still cut the sky as in centuries gone. The valley of Sexten pushing round this mountain on the east, and skirting the eastern side of the Tyrol Dolomite region, as that of the Eisach does the western, was the next of our dropped threads.

After a Sunday at Innichen, passed in the deafening noise of the minster, monastery, and parish church bells all the morning, and of rifle practice all the afternoon, we gladly left the Festa-crowded village in the fresh of the following day. The entrance to the Sexten is concealed by the tongue of that low wooded hill—itself nothing else than the subsiding end of the great Carnic range—upon which stood the Roman city of Aguntum, keeping its outlook upon the Pusterthal. The spot has been described in our sixth chapter. A pleasant road winds upward by the stream that descends from Sexten, and passes, buried in a depth of woods to the right, a bath-house, 'Wild Bad,' which we did not visit. Soon after, a footpath leads across charming meadows set about with 'parky' clumps of trees—a short cut to Sexten—and here the Schuster, from crown to base, comes royally into view—a very picture of a mountain—the Queen of the Dolomites, one should say, from its slender symmetry, did not its ugly German name compel one to call it rather the King of the 'Cobblers.' An hour further is the village of Sexten in an open, blithe, Alpine-looking valley. Two or three inns afford choice of accommodation; ours, the one nearest to the church, though rough below, has two comfortable little rooms above.

The flanks of the Schuster rise immediately above the village to the west, but in a merely rugged characterless wall. The unexpected grandeur of the Sexten valley is due to a range of Dolomites now coming first into sight, which, we are inclined to say, beats everything dolomitic in our experience. They stand in line with the Schuster, and belong, as the map will show, to the Auronzo block of mountains. A short lateral valley—the Fischelein Thal—breaks away into the heart of them from Sexten. At the

THE SEXTEN THAL.

near corner stands the Schuster, at the farther, Monte Popera, and in the midst, the Zwölfe Spitzen point their fingers skywards. These two—the Popera and Zwölfe Spitzen—rule the scene with an Arctic, haggard grandeur, that, once beheld, will never be forgotten. Rain, snow, and biting wind, a funereal blackness alternating with glares of sunshine, gave to this scenery its wildest aspect, while we, storm-bound, remained at Sexten; but in the peacefullest sunshine such shapes can never lose their native savagery; and it is for this particular quality we would rank them so highly among their Dolomite brethren.

The wild weather prevented any excursion. A path over to Auronzo, another, striking westward by the side of the Schuster, and eventually under the Drei Zinnen to Landro on the Ampezzo road, and a track encircling the entire mass of the Zwölfe Spitzen, would each be worth exploring for anyone with a mountain passion; while, should he add to this the zest of a botanist, Herr Gander, the 'Co-operator' of the village, can lead him to spots where some of the rarest specimens of the Tyrol flora may be found. From accidental circumstances, there is a curious link between this Sexten village and the Roman Catholic African missions. A tablet in the church records the name of a clerical brother who left this village on a mission to Central Africa, and perished a few years ago at Khartum; and Herr Gander sends specimens of his Alpine flora to cheer the hearts of some Tyrolean members of the mission still labouring in Egypt. The Sexten Bad, a small rough place at the entrance of the Fischelein Thal, might offer tolerable accommodation in summer.

After four days' delay at Sexten we crossed the low pass, the Kreuzberg, which separates the Tyrol valley from the Italian district of Comelico. It is a char road, six hours to drive, climbing and descending all the way at the back of the Auronzo Dolomites on the west—the low bare hills on the east giving no token of the Carnic range in that direction. A solitary inn, the Mauth-haus, though no longer a 'Mauth,' marks the summit, and the descent is very fine into populous Comelico, where, in consequence of recent fires among the villages, they have rebuilt the houses in a scattered uncomfortable way along the ridges of the hills. As usual, the change from a German to an

Italian population is not at first sight to the advantage of the latter, though when you taste their fine white bread you may acknowledge that the Italian after all knows a thing or two better than his neighbours.

If the reader has any notion of our whereabouts, he will know that our road comes down at St. Stefano upon the route by which the previous year we crossed from the

TITIAN'S TOWER.

Tagliamento country to that of Cadore, and he will not expect us to describe old ground. Yet upon that occasion the low clouds, and pouring rain so much obscured the scenery, that, to us, the present afternoon drive through the magnificent gorge of the Piave under Monte Cornon was almost new. Then came the opening into the Auronzo valley; and then, following the Piave southward, the ridge of Cadore came in sight. It was dusk as we passed through the Plaza of the little town, which the old robed Titian on the tower seems to claim as his own. A mile beyond we pulled up at Tai Cadore on the high road, at the inn of Giovanni Tommas.

The coarse plaster floors and rude furniture, the landings filled with flour sacks, the noise and bustle of a place where all the teamsters of the Ampezzo bait their horses or stable them for the night, filled us at first with regret for snug and cleanly Sexten; but the splendour of the scenery made amends, and after nearly a fortnight's stay, we were quite reconciled to our quarters, which the people did all they could to render tolerable. It was at this time that 'Titian's country' became thoroughly known to us. As much probably as most readers will care to know, has been told in the fifteenth chapter. The weather had settled into autumn stillness, a glorious moon illuminated our nights; every footpath brought us to some new point of view, and Cadore dwells in our memories, a picture richly framed.

The view from the Castle hill has been already described. I will mention two other points that will well repay the climb required. Opposite the inn is a hill covered with wood, rising towards the western end to a lofty crag. This is Monte Zucco. Along the ridge are striking views down to Perarolo and upward towards Cadore; but from the final crag a noble prospect is displayed up the course of the Boita which glistens at a vast depth below. The eye is led along the valley, bounded by the Antelao on the right, to the overshadowing bulk of the Pelmo, to which all the scene is subject. The second view is thoroughly panoramic, and requires a steeper and a longer climb. Opposite Monte Zucco, between it and the Antelao, shines in air a small white chapel: that is St. Dionigi. Perhaps three hours from Tai through the village of Nebiu will put you on the narrow summit. The sweep of view, west, south, and east, is magnificent. It is filled with jagged forms that you will soon recognise as belonging to the Dolomite family, and especially in the east, where a line of very characteristic aiguilles marks the last range of Dolomites in that direction. The hill is a spur of the Antelao, which frowns darkly on the north.

One section of the Tyrol Dolomite group had all along escaped us. It is that abutting upon the Pusterthal between the exit of the Ampezzo road and the mouth of the Gader Thal. Nearly in the midst is a mountain bath-house, like those of Ratzes and Sexten, but of older date than either. This is Brags (pronounced 'Prax'), for a knowledge of which we were indebted to the Sexten curé, and during our stay at Cadore the Churchills, availing themselves of the diligence running every other day through the Ampezzo, made an excursion to visit it.

They describe the bath-house as standing on a pleasant open alp, an hour's drive from Niederndorf, in the Pusterthal. After penetrating for some distance southwards up the lateral valley it forks into two; one branch, the Inner Brags Thal, continuing southerly, and the other, the Ausser Brags Thal, turning south-west and west. The old establishment is in a corner of the former valley, sheltered from cold winds by the precipitous sides of the Bad Kogel, while the fine peaks of the Dürenstein and Geiselstein—the latter our blood-stained 'Mount of sacrifice'—shut in the view towards the south, yet leaving abundant space for sky and sunshine, a wide expanse of velvet slopes, and tracts of forest. A narrow outlet between these leads into the Ampezzo route, about half-way between Landro and the Peutelstein Schloss. Far-reaching views are not to be looked for in a basin like this, yet noble prospects are attainable if its walls be climbed. From the Flodinger ridge, a branch of the Dürenstein, the eye overlooks a long reach of the Landro road, and sees, close opposite, the lofty rock-masses that separate that road from the Sexten Thal, the peaks of the Schuster rising into view behind. To the south the Drei Zinnen and other wild-looking peaks of the Auronzo valley, and even the Marmarolo, are visible. If an excursion be made to the Ausser Brags, a noble view is presented there of the massive square-edged wall of the See Kogel, impending over a small lake, and rising to a height of 9,200 feet. Its upper beds belong to the Jura formation, and are stained with red, as are portions of many of the neighbouring peaks. Its dark grey form, as seen from Cortina, when backed by storm clouds, looks marvellously like a gigantic elephant uprearing itself. The Herstein portion of the mass which separates the two valleys, also shows some fine bosses above the lake. From this point the valley under another name turns westward, and leads up to the Col dai Latsch, overlooking the upper Enneberg, a branch of the Gader Thal. Not far from the lake is the small village of St. Veit, in which is a more modern bath-house of a humbler character. Many Botzen people regularly visit the older establishment; among others, Baron Hausmann, the author of a 'Flora of Tyrol.' Patients come also from Cortina and villages more to the south on the Ampezzo road. The newer part of the building is of wood; the bedrooms are small, but clean and comfortable, and the Saal will dine a large number. A good dinner is served at 11.30 A.M., and supper—another dinner—at 7.30 P.M. The people of the place can be recommended for their civility, attention, and moderate charges. Among these Brags mountains, the rare fern, *Woodsia glabella*, has been lately found—its first Tyrol locality. Hitherto it had been known only as an Arctic and North American plant.

Our Dolomite tours are winding up. One glance at the Val di Zoldo, lying over the ridge there, south of Cadore—one more peep at Primiero, whose far-off peaks can be seen faint in the west from the Dionigi chapel—and our work will be done.

On Friday the 4th of September, disencumbered of baggage, which went southwards by diligence, and once more on foot, with a Cadore man for guide and porter, we struck off the high road at Valle, across the deep Boita, by a single-arched foot-bridge; and ascending by the village of Cibiana, and a long verdant scoop in the hills, reached in about four hours the ridge which gave the last view of Cadore, and the first of the mountains of the Val di Zoldo. They are those which, stretching from the Civita southward, form the eastern rim of the basin of Agordo; our present point of view was entirely new, but the haze of a sunny day reduced them to shapes of mist. A long descent, becoming rich and broken at the bottom, brought us to romantic Forno, the chief Zoldo village. One glance there was of the Pelmo, on this southern side of him, up the glen which, on one of its steeps, holds the little village of Zoppe, boasting a Titian picture; and down in Forno, which we reached when evening had cast it into shade, a crimson light was reflected from some lofty tiers of Dolomitic rock that guard the narrow outlet of the valley.

'I have seen you at Caprile!' cried a shrill voice from the top of a garden-wall not far from Forno. The greeting came from a lively old lady, with a smiling girl at her side, soon recognised as a daughter of our kind friend Signora Pezzè. She no longer smiled when we confessed that Caprile this time was out of our route. We had hoped the good signora would never know that we had been within a day's journey of her house, and now could only send all manner of messages, and a promise of a letter from Belluno.

The inn at Forno is a dark old house, in a street so narrow you might shake hands across it, or pluck from your window the flowers in the pots over the way. The kitchen is the hall of entrance; a wood fire slumbers on the hearth in the middle of the floor, and a bench is carried round the grimy walls behind. The spare wavering figure of Signor Cercena, the owner, rose to welcome us as we entered, and, with abundance of apology and depreciation of his poor means, ushered us into two dark chambers above, whose floors, one should say, had never known a scrubbing-brush. Yet the beds and furniture were of an antique, solid goodness, and we could not hurt the feelings of the poor man by asking for a broom. A good supper—or dinner as it was to us—was served, after a couple of hours of busy preparation, in a long and narrow corridor, where, in the feeblest illumination, the old man flitted about, like a ghost of other days. That over, raising a temporary floor of chairs round the enormous beds, we were not long in climbing into them.

Such is the kind of accommodation at Forno. Were it better, the scenery of the place might tempt anyone to remain for a few days to explore the path to Agordo over the Pramper Gebirge; to scramble up to Zoppe and test the genuineness of its Titian, or touch the base of the Pelmo in that direction; or, last not least, to wander up and down the Val di Zoldo itself. Its upper end we had seen last year when we crossed the Col Dai; now we took the first of the morning to descend its lower reaches. These form one almost continuous gorge of ten miles; trains of mules laden with iron to and from the rude forges of Forno keep it alive with traffic, or it would be solitary enough. The manufacture of nails is the business of the valley.

At Longarone there is the high road again, and a two

hours' drive brings us to Belluno. This city, so rarely visited by tourists, stands in a broad valley, rich with orchards and bowery lanes, bright with farms and white-walled villas—a graceful, grateful region, bounded southward by soft hills, like English downs; guarded northward by an illimitable range of Tyrol's proudest mountains.

Primiero lies shut in amongst them, under the glowing west; and, after two days at Belluno, we drove eighteen miles down the spacious Val di Mel to Feltre, as the readiest place of entrance to that difficult spot. Feltre, where we slept, is a strange old town, desolate upon a hill, because deserted by the road, upon which, at the hill-foot, a new town has gathered. Eight miles further is Fonzaso, a village at the mouth of the glen, through which the Cismone has cut its way from Primiero.

For a third of the distance, the walk up that glen—helping two overloaded donkeys along the stony undefended path, expecting one or the other every moment to roll down headlong—was tedious enough; the sun hot, the landscape dreary. But the landscape rose into grandeur, the heat moderated, the path became smoother, the donkeys bore their loads better. A solitary Osteria, in the depth of the gorge,* supplied coffee and bread, and soon after, the valley of Primiero opened to the right, and the pleasant

* In this gorge Churchill gathered some specimens of that rare fern, *Asplenium* (*Acropteris*) *Seelosii*, which, first detected by Bartling in 1843, lay unknown in an herbarium until other specimens were, in 1855, found by Seelos, and named after him by his friend Leybold. It is figured at p. 348, in the vol. for 1855, of the Ratisbon 'Botanische Zeitung' Since its discovery it has been found in four distinct localities, not very remote from each other, among the Dolomites of South Tyrol. The gorge of Primiero will add one to the localities already known. Its nearest allies are *Asplenium Septentrionale* and *Germanicum*. It peeps out of narrow chinks of rock, from which its extraction in an entire state is rather difficult. Sir Wm. Hooker, in the third volume of his *Species Filicum*, designates it as 'assuredly the rarest and most circumscribed in locality of any known European fern.'

evening saw us threading its villages, one by one, till dusk fell upon us entering Primiero itself. Donkeys and all, we footed it softly through the silent street. Bonetti (the other Bonetti) received us right gladly to his comfortable inn; and the postmaster, five minutes after, rushing in with a packet of letters, crowned the welcome in a torrent of German, Italian, and French.

Six days of sweet, unclouded sunshine we spent at Primiero; learnt all its secrets; climbed every hill-side. How attentive was Bonetti, how active Sartori, how polite the Burgomeister, how courteous the Count, we have no room to relate; but when our caravan filed out of Primiero again, it was with the recollection of a happy week. An afternoon walk of four hours took us to Canale St. Bovo, to sleep at a small inn there, breaking in that way the long journey to Borgo, in the Val Sugana. Next day, winding skywards, high on a mountain-side, the Primiero valley slid softly into sight beneath, asking for one more adieu. The castle of Pietra shone, a white speck, upon its rock; the grey Dolomites—the last we were to see—stood in clear array behind; then the path turned round a green shoulder, Primiero disappeared, and the Dolomites were gone!

We dined on the alp in a hut which its owners were that day closing for the season. In the afternoon we reached the almost Spanish-looking valley of Tesino, a scene, it might be, among the stony 'Sierras.' At the village, Pieve, there was a road, but no vehicle, and we were fain to walk five or six miles farther; descending into the splendid scenery of the Val Sugana, and dropping at last by an extraordinary staircase almost a quarter of a mile deep, into Strigno.

There was just light enough to see Borgo over the mulberry and walnut trees, distant another hour. Not another step could be got out of S—— and A——; not a carriage could be had at Strigno. 'Will you ride upon a carro?' cried a friendly by-stander. 'A carro! what is that?' said we: 'a carretta?' 'No,' said our friend, laughing. 'A carrettina?' 'No, no!' and he laughed the more. 'You had better come and see.' The carro stood in the street—a dray with no bottom to it, an open raft in fact, laden with half-a-dozen flour-sacks. 'Will you mount upon the sacks?' 'Certainly,' said S—— and A——; and in a few minutes we were all holding on for bare life, as three stout horses clattered down the rough road out of Strigno into darkness. Yes, into darkness! Our story is ended. From the top of the flour-sacks we wave to our readers a last farewell.

PHYSICAL DESCRIPTION OF THE DOLOMITE REGION.

BY G. C. CHURCHILL.

PREDAZZO, S

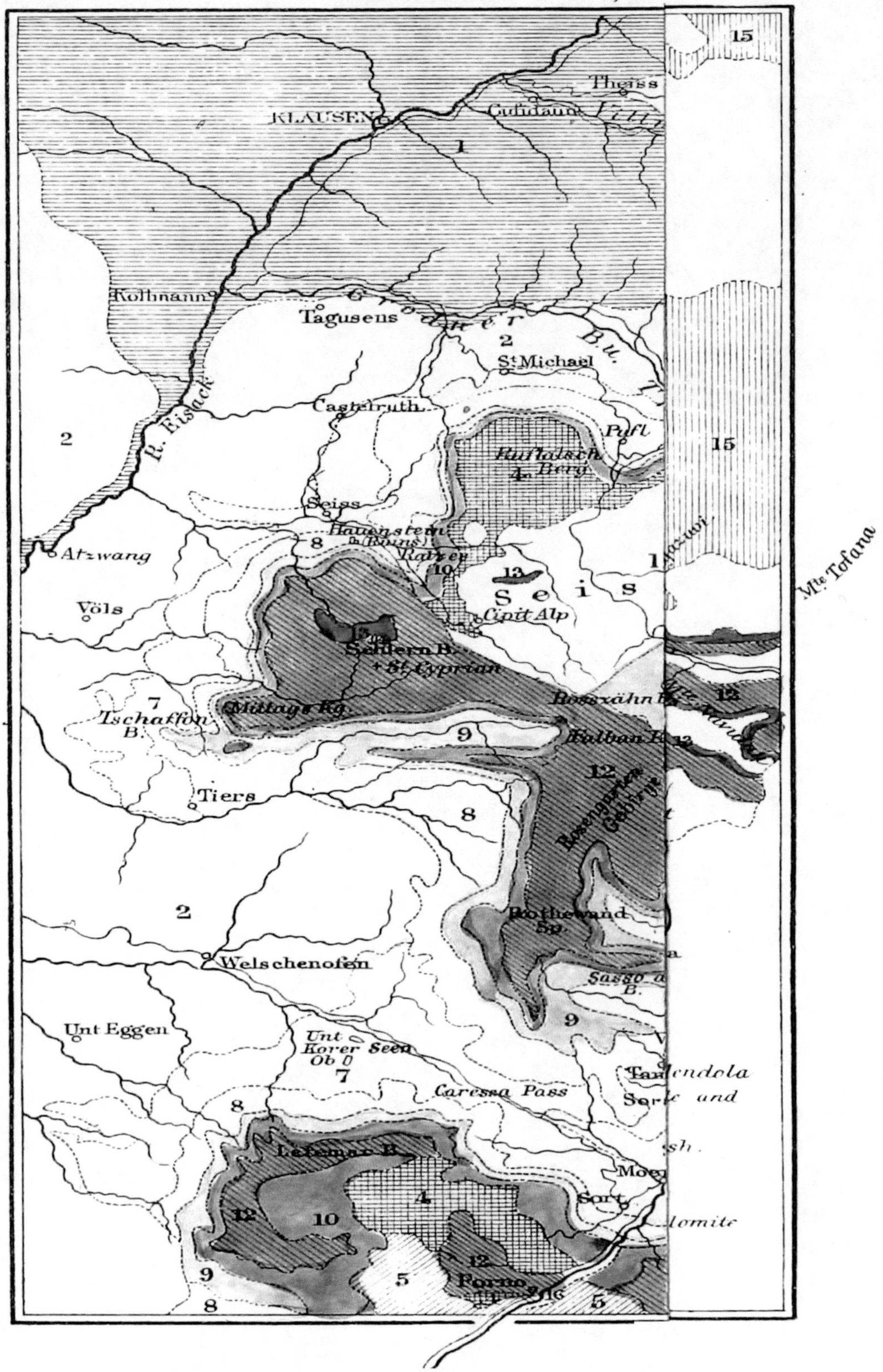

KLAUSEN
Theiss
Gufidaun
Kolhnann
Tagusens
St. Michael
R. Eisack
Castelruth
Pufl
Seiss
Atzwang
Völs
Seis
Cipit Alp
Schlern B.
St. Cyprian
Mittags Kg.
Tschaffon B.
Rosszähn
Tiers
Rosengarten Gebirge
Rothewand Sp.
Welschenofen
Unt Eggen
Sasso B.
Unt Korer Seen Ob
Caressa Pass
Latemar B.
Sort
Forno
Mte Tofana
1
2
4
5
7
8
9
10
12
13
15

CHAPTER XVIII.

PHYSICAL DESCRIPTION OF THE DOLOMITE DISTRICTS.

Modern Conception of the Structure of the Alps — Position of the South-Eastern Limestone Zone—Its four included Groups—Relief of the Western Dolomite District—Its two great intersecting Ridges—Its four radiating Valleys—Porphyry Plateau—Tuff Plateau—Dolomite Plateau—Relief of the Carnian District—Its Lines of Depression—Its Series of Basins—The Canal Socchieve—The Sauris Basin—Relief of the Ampezzo District—List of its intersecting Lines of Elevation and Depression—Features of the Julian Alps and Karawanken—Geology of the Western Dolomite District—Richthofen's Work — Table of Trias Beds of South-Eastern Tyrol — Historical-Topographical Description of them—Features of the extinct Craters of the Upper Fassa and Predazzo—Richthofen's Coral-Reef Theory of the Origin of the Western Dolomites—Origin of Dolomite as a Mineral—Biography of M. Dolomieu.

We propose to bring together in this chapter a few observations upon the Physical features of the country traversed in our excursions. Without any intention of offering original information, we think that clearness of view is best consulted by this mode of presentation, and our narrative is left unburdened by what might often prove to be incongruous. The material thus offered for the reader's consideration will, we believe, be welcomed by many as a needful complement to the succession of pictures afforded by our narrative.

Before, however, asking attention to the special features of the Dolomite regions of the Alps visited by us, it seems desirable first to point out its position in the general system of which it forms no inconspicuous a portion.

What are its neighbours, and how does it stand related to them?

The time has long gone by when the Alps were represented as one great chain of mountains stretching in a vast sweep from Nice to Vienna; but if we abandon the conception of a chain, and substitute for it that of a zone or 'belt' of mountain land, there is truth in the representation. The conception of a chain receives an apparent support from the vision of the long line of peaks that reward a spectator when he ascends some well-posted outlier either on the north or south side. Further observation shows this to be an illusion of perspective in the case of the Alps; in the Pyrenees, on the other hand, as seen from Toulouse or from Pau, the illusion is much closer to the reality, that range being much more simple in its formation.

Another view, put forth at a later date, presented the Alps as consisting of a central chain, flanked by a lateral one on the north, and another on the south. It appealed for justification to the Eastern Alps, where a greater regularity is observable among the mountain masses. But it had no root in geology, and was sure, sooner or later, to be proved inapplicable to the entire Alpine zone.

The later researches of the Swiss and Austrian geologists have provided the geographer with the truer conception of the Alps as a great system of '*Mountain Groups*,' '*Massives*,' or '*Gebirgstöcke*.' Each 'Group' is characterised by a crystalline nucleus of some form of granite, which is overlaid to a greater or less extent by schistous or slate rocks, constituting an oval with a long or a short axis. A band of sedimentary rocks, (limestones, sandstones, shales, or marls) surrounds this schistous covering, and isolates the 'Group' more or less completely from its neighbours. In or near the middle portion of these ovals or ellipsoids rise up the highest peaks of the 'Group,' sheltering between them the glacier masses, and from these peaks,—ridges, and valleys run out as radii in the direction of the circumference of the ellipsoid. This is the ideal type—where the orographic features happen to harmonise with the geologic structure. The *relative position* of the three elements—nucleus, schistous covering, and sedimentary band—varies, however, in each case. Sometimes, owing to the manner in which the schistous covering has been affected by the upheaving force, the culminating peak or peaks of the 'Group' are to be found, not in the nucleus, but among the schists, and even, as in the case of the Œrtler Spitze, in the sedimentary band. In these instances, the result may have been brought about by the *lateral* pressure exerted by the elevating action in neighbouring 'Groups.'

The greater number of these 'Groups' lie in or near the line of axis of the whole Alpine zone, in moderately close proximity to each other, the axis of each cutting the main axis at different angles. In this way an almost continuous line of peaks is presented to the eye throughout the length of zone of mountain-land, giving rise to the illusion of a single chain. No single 'Groups' lie on the north side of the main axis of the mountain zone, but several are to be found on the southern border, and it is on this side also that almost all the outbreaks of eruptive rock—porphyry, melaphyr, and basalt—occur.

The varied deposits of sedimentary rock accompany the crystalline nuclei in a broad band on the north and south sides, pressing in, however, towards the interior spaces wherever an interval allows. A striking instance of this is to be met with above the Lake of Constance, in the valley of the Rhine, which is completely occupied with tertiary and secondary rocks, the latter indeed extending in patches nearly *across* the Alpine zone as far as Chiavenna. Another instance occurs on the Brenner

Pass, where, close to its western border, large masses of limestone rising into lofty peaks extend southwards as far as Sterzing, the remains of a broad sedimentary band that once separated the Œtzthaler 'group' from that of the Tauern.

This relation between the central zone of crystalline nuclei and schists, and the band of sedimentary rocks on its north and south borders, is general enough,—notwithstanding the existence of isolated nuclei on the south side,—to enable us to speak with tolerable accuracy of a northern limestone zone and a southern limestone zone.

Now, our Dolomite region, the region which includes the Dolomitic scenery, *par excellence*, is comprised within the southern limestone zone and within the eastern section of that zone. The division between the Eastern and Western Alps will be marked by a line running up the valley of the Rhine from the Lake of Constance, as far as Chur, and then letting it follow in a southerly direction the western borders of the Selvretta, the Œrtler, the Adamello, and Monte Castello groups, until it issues into the Italian plains at Brescia. Or, looking at the two zones of country they separate, rather than at the 'Groups' themselves, we may say that, while the *western* slopes of these 'Groups,' belonging politically to Switzerland and Lombardy, may be treated as part of the Western Alps, their *eastern* slopes, almost entirely within the boundaries of Tyrol, may be comprised within the Eastern Alps.

The South-eastern limestone zone will thus have its boundaries on the west and north determined by the line of the Castello, Adamello, Œrtler, Œtzthaler, and Tauern 'Groups,' which follow each other along the line of a great arch, sweeping round from Brescia as far as the peak of the Ankogel south of Gastein.

We must now call attention to Four groups that exist *within* this boundary, and narrow the space to be occupied by its sedimentary deposits; two of them, comparatively unimportant for us, appear to be merely lateral appendages to the larger 'Groups' near to which they stand; while the two others are isolated and independent masses, intimately associated with the geologic history of our zone. The two former we mention, because the southern border of their schistous covering provides the slope upon which rests the lowest bed of the sedimentary masses of our district. These are, first, the Penser 'Group,' lying to the south-east of the Œtzthaler 'Massive,' and occupying the country between Sterzing, Brixen, and Meran; the lofty Iffinger Spitze behind Meran being one of the peaks of its granite nucleus. Secondly, the Teffereggen 'Group,' immediately to the north of the Pusterthal, and filling up the zone of country between the Penser 'Group' and Sachsenburg on the Drave below Lienz.

Of the two remaining and more important 'Groups,' the first is that of the Cima d'Asta, which rises up in the form of an ellipsoid, and fills the space between Primiero and Borgo, in south-east Tyrol. It culminates in the Cima d'Asta (9,200 feet) at once the highest peak of the granite nucleus and of the entire 'Group.' Its position is a remarkable one, being placed almost midway between the extremities of the great arch we have referred to, and exactly opposite the apex of this arch, at Meran. The great Porphyry Plateau of Botzen runs in unbroken continuity from its northern border to Meran.

The last, or fourth group differs in character from its neighbours. It is in fact a chain rather than a 'Group.' In it the crystalline rock which constitutes it a 'Group' only comes to light in small patches at distant intervals, and the schistous covering is everywhere absent, except at its western termination, where it abuts on the Teffereggen group. Sedimentary rocks compose almost its entire mass, and run in lines more or less parallel to the general direction of the chain and to each other. We may call it the Carnic-Karawanken chain. For though the two designations are ancient and of historical importance, yet, in an orographic and geological point of view, the two parts constitute but one chain. The depression near Tarvis, where the Carnic Alps are usually supposed to end, and those of the Karawanken to begin, though considerable, and filled up with tertiary deposits, is no real solution of continuity. Politically, this chain is the boundary line between Carinthia on the north, and Venetia with Carniola on the south. Commencing at its western end at Innichen in the Puster Thal, it runs in a nearly south-east direction as far as Cilli in Styria,—probably beyond, and forms the northern boundary of the Laibach plain. The highest peaks of the ridge are not formed of granite or schistous rock, but of limestone or Dolomite.

Such are the Four 'groups' that exist in the area occupied by the South-eastern limestone zone.

The remainder of the area, though we have designated it as limestone, is not exclusively composed of that rock. Two beds of sandstone, one belonging to the *lower* Trias, the 'Gröden sandstone,' and the other to the *upper* Trias, the 'Raibl beds,' are present either as long lines of outcrop, or in patches, throughout the whole of the area. Beds of sandstone also of the lower Keuper are to be met with to the north of the Canal Socchieve in Carnia. Eruptive rocks, too, not resolvable into the nuclei of 'Groups,' occupy on the western border of the area a considerable space. Many square miles are covered by red and brown coloured porphyry, between Botzen and Trent; another large space is taken up with the eruptive rocks and volcanic ash that have been evolved from the crater at the head of the Fassa Thal, and from that at

Predazzo, lower down. Masses of diabase are found near Rigolato in Friuli, and of a variegated porphyry immediately to the south of Tarvis in the Julian Alps. With these exceptions, limestone is everywhere, either in its ordinary forms, or as Dolomite.

For the purposes of this chapter, however, we dismiss from consideration that portion of the great limestone zone that lies between the line of the Castello, Adamello, and Oertler 'Groups,' and the great trough of the Adige. This we did not visit, and our district will thus form a triangle, with the Adige-Eisack trough for one side, and the straight line of the Puster-Kartitsch-Gail-Drave valleys for the other; the apex being at Mühlbach, north of Brixen; and the base being given by the Laibach, Friulian, and Venetian plains as far as Verona; along with the intervening band of plateau country. Yet of this district we do not by any means aim to describe the whole, but only such parts as are more immediately connected with our subject.

In the first place, then, we propose to draw attention to some of the principal features in the *Relief* of the district thus bounded, and then to point out some of its more interesting *Geological* specialities. We shall proceed from west to east.

The Cima d'Asta 'Group,' which rises up from amidst the sedimentary deposits at a greater distance from its neighbour 'Groups' than any other in the whole Alpine zone,—being at least thirty-five miles from the apex of the line of arch formed by the Castello, Adamello, Œrtler, Œtzthaler, and Tauern 'Groups,'—forms a most important element in the history of the development of South-Eastern Tyrol. Two great lines of *ridge*, both of porphyry, with a line of depression between them, owe their existence to this 'Group,' and run in a curved line parallel to it and to each other. The one nearer to the Cima d'Asta starts from a point south-east of Paneveggio in the Travignolo Thal, and curves round to Pergine and Levico in the Val Sugana. In it the loftiest mountain is the Cima Lagorei (8,567) feet. North of this ridge is a parallel line of *depression* formed by the Travignolo Thal from Paneveggio to Predazzo, and the lower half of the valley of the Avisio from Predazzo downwards. Beyond this again is the second porphyry *ridge*, which, beginning with Monti Aloch, Bocche, and Lusia, that bound the Travignolo Thal on its northern side, and interrupted by the subsequently formed eruptive and Dolomite mountains of Predazzo, reappears westward in the Zangenberg, Schwarzhorn and Pass del Gaso, and thence becomes the northern boundary of the valley of the lower Avisio to its outlet at Lavis. Thus we see that the great porphyry plateau, the beginning of all geologic history for the western Dolomites, has been considerably affected in its relief by the action of the 'Group' standing near its south-eastern border. Both porphyry ridges have their escarpments facing or opposite to the Cima d'Asta, reminding us of a corresponding relation in the northern limestone zone, where the great escarpments are found to face the central Massives along the borders of which they run.

But among the dominating lines that may be said to govern the general conformation of the country, the two lines of ridge we have next to describe are the most important.

Directly or indirectly the influence of these extends over a considerable portion of the western part of our district, and they condition the existence and direction of its principal valleys. The first, runs nearly due N. and S. from Mühlbach, north of Brixen, to Fonzaso, near Feltre; many of the western Dolomites stand upon it—not causing it, for the line would exist if they were removed. It runs underneath the Guerdenazza and Sella Plateaus, the Marmolata, and Sasso di Val Fredda, and the long range of the Primiero Dolomites. There are interruptions in it, of course, but the general direction is clear. The second line runs from ENE. to WSW. It commences near the western termination of the Carnic Chain with the Kreuzberg in the Sexten Thal, where it forms a junction with Monte Silvella in that chain. Its course is marked by the Poper Kofel, Drei Zinnen, Krystal Köpfe, Monte Tofana, Set Sass, Sella Plateau, Lang Kofel, Monte Palatscho, Rosszähne, Mittags Kogel, and Tschafon Berg, where it dies away in a porphyry ridge close to Blumau, in the Kunter's Weg, east of Botzen.

The Sella Plateau stands, as will be seen by reference to the map, at the *point of intersection* of these two lines. And yet its removal, as with a razor, clean from the green slopes from which it rises, would not affect the intersection. This independence of position must not be forgotten when we dwell upon the circumstances connected with its history.

The existence of these lines has been considered as due to the action of the crystalline 'Groups' that bound our district to the W. and N., that is to say, to the line of the Castello, Adamello, Œrtler, in the one case, and to that of the Œtzthal-Tauern in the other, to which these sedimentary ridges are respectively parallel, or nearly so. But if this be true, it is singular that their escarpments face the E. and the S., that is to say, *away* from their crystalline neighbours. The reason for this requires investigation.

On the northern border of this ENE. and WSW. ridge, is a line of *depression* that runs from Moos or St. Joseph in the Sexten Thal, up the right branch of the Fischelein Thal, and over the watershed by the Patern Kogel down to the Düren See at Landro. From this point, as far as the Peutelstein Schloss, it is occupied by the road of the Ampezzo Pass. Leaving the Schloss behind, it constitutes the trough between the Fanis Gebirge and the Tofana 'Massive,' coming out near St. Cassian, in the Gader Thal. It then crosses the N. to S. *line of ridge* at the Grödner Jöchl, between the Guerdenazza and Sella plateaus, and follows the Gröden Thal to its termination in the gorge of the Eisack. It is interrupted by three lines of watershed, that may possibly be the result of later upheaval; and appears to be turned out of its direct course by the subsequent formation of the plateau of the Seisser Alp.

From the four angles, formed by the intersection of these two lines of ridge, arise as many *valley systems*, the waters of which flow in contrary directions. The Gader and Gröden, to the N. and NW., and the Avisio and Cordevole to the SW. and SE., carry away all the waters of the Western Dolomite district. Their sources so closely adjoin each other, that a half day's walk, commencing at the Fedaia See, near the origin of the Avisio, would amply suffice to visit the three other sources. We will take these in the order we have named them. A glance at the general map will enable the reader to trace the relative position of the intersecting ridges and of these four valleys.

The upper basin of the *Gader Thal* lies in the eastern half of the Tuff Plateau, a frequently saturated gathering ground. The higher valley descends along the western border of the North Ampezzo Dolomites, which have the Tuff rock as their base. Further to the north, the beds of the lower Trias emerge from under the Tuff, with patches of igneous rock bere and there breaking through. The lower valley is hollowed out of the gentle mica clay-slate region bordering the south side of the Puster Thal.

The *Gröden* has its source in the union of many streams that break away from the steep north slopes of the Seisser plateau through deep rocky ravines, that lay bare the whole series of the lower trias beds, with others that emerge from the wilderness of the Guerdenazza plateau. Most of its course lies in a deep-seated ravine out of the influence of the direct rays of the sun, which gives the valley a colder climate than that of the Gader Thal. There are, however, three points in the upper half of its course where the valley widens out a little, and in these openings the three villages of St. Ulrich, St. Christina, and Santa Maria stand. In picturesque effect and wild character of background it far exceeds the Gader Thal. In ascending the valley, the traveller catches sight, in the distance, of the enormous Dolomite pillars, at least 2,000 feet high, that stand at the entrance of the grassy level of the Lange Thal crowned with the salmon-coloured Raibl beds, and at the end of the mile-long vista between them, discerns the lofty plateau of the Guerdenazza. The ruins of an old Schloss, the primitive castle of the Counts of Wolkenstein, perched upon the summit of a debris-slope at the base of one of these Dolomite walls, is crushed into the extreme of littleness by the contrast. This combination of lofty Dolomite walls with level grassy valley-bottom, leading up to the heights of a vast plateau 9,000 feet high, is unique in the whole region of the limestone Alps. In the lower part of its course, the Gröden falls into the region of the porphyry plateau, and finds its way to the gorge of the Eisack through the jaws of a deep defile.

The two remaining streams have a much longer and more varied course than their northern brethren.

The *Avisio*, the only stream of the four that is glacier-fed, runs along the N. border of the Marmolata, while the

Duron coming to meet it at Campitello, from the opposite direction, coasts along the north border of the Rosengarten Gebirge. In this way the two branches draw off all the water that can be collected along the steep escarpment of the south face of the Tuff plateau. After a gentle course in the nearly level alluvium, that surrounds the base of the slopes of eruptive rock, occupying the centre of the Fassa Thal crater, it escapes through a wide gap in its southern wall. Soon after, at Moena, two lateral valleys, the one communicating with the porphyry plateau by the Caressa pass on the right, and the other with the Cordevole district on the left, contribute their waters. The beds of the lower Trias have suffered much denudation here, and even the red porphyry, which underlies them, is exposed on each side of the river, and for some distance up the lateral valley to the right. Here, too, the upper Avisio, or Fassa Thal, terminates. The second portion of the valley, called the Fleims Thal, commences with the narrows of Forno, where the stream has cut a course for itself through the varied eruptive rocks of the Predazzo crater, until it reaches the town of that name, standing in a wide and fertile alluvial opening. This opening was the former mouth of that crater. At this point, the Avisio falls into that line of depression between two porphyry ridges already described, and the remainder of its course is continued along that line to its end at Lavis. From near Altrey, downwards, the valley is a cleft—nothing more, and the numerous lateral valleys that pour into it on either hand from the porphyry slopes, are also clefts or cloughs. The physical characters of this section are so distinct from those of the Fleims Thal, that it has obtained a separate designation as the Val Cembra. The number of lateral clefts is great enough to render easy transit down the valley impracticable, and the active and well-to-do people of the Fleims Thal have, therefore, sought a more rapid means of communication with the great high road of the Adige trough, by a route across a depression in the porphyry ridge at St. Lugano, terminating at Neumarkt and at Auer, both stations on the Botzen railway.

The *Cordevole*, the fourth river of our district, may be said to be an alternation, thrice repeated, of gorge and valley-opening. It rises at the base of the Pordoi bastion belonging to the Sella plateau. The upper valley—the Livinallongo—skirts the south-eastern portion of the Tuff plateau. As far as Cherz, the slopes are gentle and the valley wide, lying entirely in the Tuff; but between Cherz and Caprile, it cuts deeply and sharply like a saw into the lower Trias beds which underlie the Tuff; and the valley in section has literally the form of a V. The villages and hamlets are, therefore, all perched on the heights, and the paths coast along the steep slopes. The river rushes at a great depth below, and is generally invisible. Buchenstein is the chief centre of this, the upper Cordevole. To this succeeds the middle section of the valley, possessing too the double character of valley-basin and gorge. Caprile is its principal village, nestled under the steep slope that hides it completely from the upper valley, and at the point where two lateral valleys fall into that of the Cordevole. The débris brought down by the three streams, together with the obstruction caused by the slide, in 1771, of part of Monte Pizzo, have created the level basin, and produced the lake at its southern end, intensifying the scenic effect of the grand escarpment of Monte Civita, which rises in a double tier of precipice to a height of nearly 7,000 feet above the waters of the lake. A gorge succeeds the lake, coasting southwards for miles along the roots of the Civita Massive, until it issues in the wide basin of Agordo, where the third section of the valley commences. The rock forming the fertile soil of this basin, is the same red sandstone that gives rise to the rich pastures of Vigo in the Fassa Thal; but the clay slate underlying it also makes its appearance in a long strip, in the line of pass between Agordo and Primiero westwards. This rock is a portion of the schistous mass of the Cima d'Asta group, and forms the long slope and double saddle separating the Agordo basin from that of Primiero. To the north and south of this schistous rock it disappears from view, under the base of the limestone and Dolomite precipices which accompany the pass on each side, but it reappears *in mass* in the Primiero basin.

At the apparent junction of this rock and of the red sandstone, and at the point where the mountains close all exit to the south, except by the deep narrow gorge, that winds out of the Agordo basin into the hill district of Belluno, there is an ancient quicksilver mine. The mountains set round the basin are much varied in form and aspect; the Palle di St. Lucano has two lofty towers like those of a cathedral, and Monte Agner, with its thin crest and tapering peak, is a noble member of that great rocky mountain mass, almost uninhabited, except by chamois and other game, of which the Primiero Dolomites form the western face.

Another feature worth notice in the character of the mountains that encircle the Agordo basin, is the contrast between those forming its southern border, and the others to the east, west, and north of it. With their escarpments facing Agordo, and rising in massive hummocky stages up to a smooth sky-line, those on the south run in unbroken continuity from E. to W., interrupted only by the very narrow gorge through which the Cordevole has cut its way. The rock is in colour a clear opaque white, brought out by a sprinkling of vegetation which heightens rather than obscures the colour of the surface. All these features are opposed to the bare, cream or ochrey-tinted precipices, isolated masses, and jagged, ruinous-looking pinnacles presented by their neighbours on the north. It would be natural to suppose that here we have the boundary between one geological formation and another, and yet we see the well-known red sandstone cropping out at intervals along their base. This southern ridge is prolonged in both directions beyond the Agordo basin; that is to say, both to the north-east and to the south-west. It is possible that the ridge of which Monte Sfornioi is the culminating peak, lying south-west of Cadore, may be its continuation. But with greater approach to certainty we may treat the ridge shutting in the Primiero basin on the south, similar as it is in its characters, as identical with it; while possibly the line of elevation that bounds the Val Sugana on its southern border all the way to the Adige trough, and which culminates in the Cima Duodici, opposite Borgo, may be a further continuation, and the whole may have been raised by the upheaving force of the Cima d'Asta 'Group.'

Having traced the four main valleys that radiate from the point of intersection of the two principal lines of elevation, and indicated some of their distinguishing characteristics, we will now describe the two plateaus that form so striking a feature in the scenery of the western Dolomite district. The larger one is the *Porphyry Plateau*; the smaller, placed upon the other at its north-east corner, is the *Tuff Plateau*.

The *plateau* character of the enormous mass of porphyry near Botzen cannot well be recognised without ascending to some high point on its border. If we climb the Schlern or the Latemar on its eastern side, or the Mendola Pass on its western, we shall then look down upon a gently rolling country mostly covered with pine forest. To the north the plateau rises gently to its limits in that direction, and then plunges with a steep face down to the slopes of the clay slate country beyond it, lying between Meran and a point south-east of Brixen. On its southern limits it preserves the same character in a gradual ascent to the summit of the ridge of the Zangenberg, Schwarzhorn, Pass del Gaso, &c., the steep slope of which faces the south. This ridge, thus bounding the plateau to the south, we have already pointed out as one of the two great Porphyry ridges that face the Cima d'Asta Ellipsoid. On its east and west borders its red or reddish-brown masses disappear under the base of the pale wall-like lines of Dolomite ;—under the Mendola escarpment to the west, under the Schlern, Rosengarten, Latemar, and Weisshorn escarpments to the east. Its average height above the sea may be about 4,000 feet, but it sinks below 2,000 feet in the neighbourhood, and to the south of, Meran. It is the result of several eruptions which have originated at various points of the district. A series of narrow cloughs that generally preserve a WNW.—ESE. direction, cut deeply into it, and at right angles to the main direction of the Eisack-Etsch trough between Brixen and Trent. In their depths these cloughs are often not more than wide enough to contain the stream that has created them. Their walls rise upwards of 2,000 feet above the stream, and in their upper portions gradually open out in a series of stair-like stages, increasing in breadth as they ascend, their face sometimes worn into perpendicular columns, until they merge into the wave-like surface of the plateau.

The average height of the *Tuff* plateau is 2,000 feet above that of the porphyry mass on which it rests ; in other words, it has a level of about 6,000 feet above the sea. It includes the upper portions of the four valleys of the Gröden, Gader, Fassa, and Cordevole. The villages of Seiss and

Castelruth lie at the foot of its western face, and it stretches eastward with a constantly increasing breadth until lost under the line of the Heiligen Kreutz Kofel, Tofana, and Rochetta. The mass of the Civita partly rests upon it; that of the Pelmo entirely. Two stages are observable in its surface. The *higher* one to the south is separated into three segments by the erosion of the upper Avisio; but if the traveller ascends to the summit of the Sasso di Damm, a ridge belonging to the most southern of the three segments, and midway between the Rosengarten and the Marmolata, their oneness will come out to view with great clearness. The northern boundary of the higher stage runs along from the Rosszähne, over the Sasso di Capell on the N. side of the Marmolata, as far as the Col di Lana behind Pieve in the Livinallongo. The *lower* stage includes the Seisser Alp, the bases of the Sella and the Guerdenazza plateaus, and the whole upper Gader. The surface is irregular and hilly, mostly covered with alp pasture, while the lower plateau of porphyry belongs to the forest zone.

The impression of the Tuff district as a connected plateau is, however, somewhat disturbed by the Dolomite Massives which rise up here and there, thousands of feet above its surface. Thus we have the Schlern with its western face stretching down to the porphyry plateau, and its eastern resting upon the higher Tuff land. Further to the east rise the gigantic masses of the Lang Kofel and Plattkogel. Beyond them, again, are the Guerdenazza and Sella plateaus, and the small mass of the Cima Pasni; all three standing exactly in a line running due north and south. And finally the wet pastures of the upper Gader are shut in to the north-east and east by the Dolomite masses of the Drei Finger Spitze, Eisengabl, Heiligen Kreutz Kogel, Monte Lagazuoi, Set Sass, and Monte Nuvulau.

It has been seen how plateau-like is the summit of the

Schlern, and how this character is continued in the wildernesses of the Guerdenazza and Sella. We may consider them as the commencement of a *third* and *highest plateau* which has its greatest extent in the rocky deserts to the east of the Heiligen Kreutz Kogel.

The Orographic features of the crater of the upper Fassa and of the smaller one of Predazzo, have as yet only been incidentally referred to, and this would be the place to describe them, but we shall pass them over for the present, along with those of the secluded basin of Primiero, until their geology is noticed.

We propose now to draw attention to the lines of elevation and depression in the Ampezzo and Friulian, or rather, Carnian districts. It will be more convenient to take those of the latter first.

In the Carnian district—the basin of the Tagliamento and its tributaries—the lines of depression are more remarkable than those of elevation. The *main* lines of depression run from east to west; the subordinate ones north and south. The one which runs through the centre of the country is the more important, inasmuch as it extends beyond its own district into the Ampezzo to the west, and among the Julian Alps to the east. *Within* the Carnian boundary it commences at Paularo to the north and east of Tolmezzo; and after crossing four intermediate low saddles, which are not more than five or six hundred feet above the level of the intervening cross valleys, it debouches into the main valley of the Piave near Lorenzago. But *westward* it may be traced further, in the Oten Thal, which crosses to the north of the Antelao by the Forcella piccola, beyond which its course extends across the ridge between the Pelmo and the Rochetta, down the Val Fiorentina past Caprile, until it terminates in the Val Ombretta on the south side of the Marmolata. And to the *east* of Carnia its further course is obvious. If we ascend the saddle to the east of Paularo, we shall see, stretching out before us in an E. by S. direction, a long line of depression, occupied by the Pontebba torrent to its junction with the Fella; by the Fella from the water-parting at Saifnitz; from Saifnitz to Ratschach in the Save Thal by the narrow *cross*-basin of the Gailitz; and lastly by the valley of the main or Wurzen Save. It is probable that this enormously long line may be rather the result of the blending of several partial lines coinciding in direction, than be due to the action of a single set of forces. It may be compared and contrasted in its features with a line of depression in the northern limestone zone of corresponding length; namely, that extending from Rottenmann and Admont in the Enns Thal, to Zill in the Ziller Thal, east of the Brenner Pass.

The *second* line of depression, the one to the north of that just described, is intimately associated with the structure of the south face of the Carnic Alps. While the north slope of these Alps, overlooking the Kartisch, Lessach, and Gail Thals, exhibits a very regular series of spurs and cross valleys running out at right angles or nearly so, from the main ridge, like the processes of a series of vertebræ, the south face, or counter-slope, is occupied with a system of *narrow basins*, whose longitudinal axis lies, not north and south, but *east and west*, that is to say, in a direction nearly *parallel* to the main chain. The streamlets running down the east and west slopes of each of these basins, unite at their foot to form a main stream, which then makes its escape from the basin in a southerly direction through an opening, having a more or less ravine-like character. As many as *seven* of these basins fill up the wide space between Monte Germula, north-east of Paularo, and the Sexten Thal. In the second of the series proceeding westward, the ancient road from Auf der Plecken takes its course down to Timau on its way to Paluzza. The third and fourth, owing to a great northerly bend in the main chain of the Carnic Alps at this point, between its two loftiest summits, the Kollin Kofel and Monte Paralba, lie, in descending order, to a considerable extent below the fifth basin. The waters of the Degano have, therefore, to find their way out of the most northern of these three basins into the fourth, and out of this again into the third. Rigolato is situated just below the third, and Forni Avoltri stands at the outlet from the fourth basin. The sixth basin is noticeable from its supplying the main portion of the head waters of the Piave, and as having Monte Paralba on its eastern rim. It is also the largest of the series.

The *second* line of depression may now be traced through the first, second, and third of these basins to Cima and Sappada; then by a bend to St. Stefano, across the low spurs south of Monte Najarnola to Auronzo, up the Auronzo valley, over the Tre Croci saddle to Cortina; and finally, over the saddle of the Tre Sassi, past the foot of the Set Sass, and up the higher portion of the Valle di Livinallongo to the eastern base of the Sella plateau.

A *third* and shorter line of depression is traceable from Monte Quaterna, on the borders of the Sexten Thal, through the seventh, sixth, and fourth basins. It then crosses over to the *north* side of the main chain at Monte Wolaya, and, further east, over a saddle into the Valentiner Thal, and thence beyond Auf der Plecken and the Pollinik. This feature—an apparent *duplication* of the main ridge—exists also to the east and west of the Loibl Pass, in the Karawanken chain.

But the *great longitudinal valley* of Carnia is the Canal Socchieve, lying to the south of our first-mentioned line of depression. It is the main valley of the Tagliamento, which rises at its extreme western limit. From Amaro, at the foot of Monte Mariana, the valley gradually ascends westward, and as far as the village of Socchieve is wide and open, with far too much of its surface occupied with a sea of dazzling white geröll, in the expanse of which the waters of the river are almost lost to view. At Amaro the valley is about 1,000 feet above the sea; at the source of the Tagliamento, at Mauria, it rises to about 4,200 feet. But the line of depression does not cease at Amaro; it is continued *eastward* in the Valle del Ferro, which ascends to Resiutta, and then forks into two valleys, the Canale della Resia and the Canale di Roccolana. The former ascends to the base of the great Flitsch plateau, while the latter rises to a watershed almost overlooking the Raibl Lake, and about the same height above the sea as the watershed at Mauria, at the extreme west. The waters of the Fella and Tagliamento unite near Amaro, and then make their way south through a cleft of very modern geological date by Venzone and Ospidaletto into the Friulian plain. Nearly all the waters of Carnia are drained through this cleft. This great basin of the Tagliamento and Fella but repeats, on a much larger scale, the characters of the basins that we have described as occupying the south escarpment of the Carnic Alps.

No streams are contributed to this important basin by its southern boundary-wall; all come from the north, along the north and south lines of depression referred to at page 534. That most to the E. contributes the Fella itself; the next one, westward, opens out at Moggio. The third, opening out at Tolmezzo, is twofold, one of its branches descending from Paularo, the other from Timau and Paluzza. The furthest in this direction, owing to the gradual retreat northwards of the Carnic Alps, is the longest of these lines. It descends from Forno Avoltri and Rigolato, and opens into the Tagliamento basin at Villa.

This intersection of Carnia by great E. and W. lines of depression, with subordinate lines running N. and S., separates the mountain-land into a system of more or less rectangular masses. Its relief does not exhibit those striking features present in the district of the Piave to the west, and in that of the Isonzo eastward.

Another feature worthy of notice before we pass on to the Ampezzo, or Piave district, is the *basin of Sauris*—again a *depression.* It is a high Alpine basin in the centre of Carnia, elliptic in form, and shut in on all sides by high mountains. The river Lumiei escapes from it through a long narrow gorge into the Canal Socchieve at Ampezzo—not to be confounded with the Ampezzo of the Piave district. A track accompanies the stream through the gorge; but for the most part of the year, either from freshets, avalanches, or falls of rock from the mountains, is impassable. The usual path—a mule-track only—leads over Monte Pura, nearly 4,800 feet above the sea, to Ampezzo, which is 1,860 feet above that level. The inhabitants of the valley live in four villages, all occupying an alp on the south slope of the Morghendleit, the highest, Sauris di Sopra, being but 300 feet lower than the summit of the Monte Pura ridge. They are Germans, isolated from their neighbours, and distinguished by their greater cleanliness and thriftiness—qualities very apparent on entering Cima and Sappada, north of Sauris, two other isolated German settlements in Carnia.

In the *Ampezzo* district—the basin of the river Piave and its tributaries, to which we now proceed—the features of elevation and depression are *equally* prominent. The great fork made by the meeting, nearly at right angles, of the valleys of the Boita and the Piave at Perarolo, at the foot of the Antelao, is the key to the structure of the whole district.

The valley of the Boita runs NW. and SE., that of the Piave NE. and SW., and the Antelao—a mighty corner-stone—stands within the angle produced by the junction of the two valleys. Several lines of elevation and depression run parallel with the valley of the Boita; others run parallel with the valley of the Upper Piave. These two sets of lines partially intersect each other. But the NW.-SE. lines appear predominantly on the *west* side of the Boita; while the NE.-SW. lines are most distinctly marked on the *east* side of the Piave. The following are the NW.-SE. lines, proceeding westward:—

1. The line of the Antelao, Crodas Melcora and Malcora, Tre Croci ridge, and the Croda di Val Grande; a line of elevation.

2. The valley of the Boita from the south foot of the Seekofel; a line of depression.

3. A second line of elevation formed by the Heiligen Kreutz Kogel, Tofana, Nuvulau, Rochetta, Pelmo, Monte Pera, Sasso di Bosconero, and Campello. Here it is interrupted by the valley of the Piave at Longarone. But further to the south-east it continues in the peaks of Monti Maggiore, Messer, and Cavallo, with which latter it dies out in the Italian plain at Aviano.

4. The whole course of the Val di Zoldo; a second line of depression.

5. The line of the Civita, Mojazza, Piacedel, Vescova, Pelf, Serva, dying out at Capo di Ponte, a village in the valley of the Piave; a third line of elevation.

6. The Val Agordo from Cencenighe, downwards to its opening into the Val de Mel, opposite Belluno; a third line of depression.

7. The short line of Monte Pizzo and Monte Alto, which terminates at the Val de Mel; a fourth line of elevation. Here we abut upon the Primiero district. The

second and *third* of these lines are the most important of this series.

The series of the NE.-SW. lines proceeding westward are:—

1. The line of Monti Dolada, Dignona, Cornetto, Barbano, Turlon, Premaggiore, Cinnacuta, and Lagna, where it is lost in the mountain masses which shut in the Sauris basin. This line lies entirely on the *east* side of the Piave; a line of elevation.

2. The line from Longarone up the valley in which Erto is situated, upwards to Cimolais, and along the Val Cimolina to its head at the base of Monte Monfalcone. This line also lies on the *east* side of the Piave; a line of depression.

3. The line of the Palla, Pelf, and Pizzo Cimon. Here it is interrupted by the valley of the Piave at Longarone, but further to the NW. it is continued in the peaks of Monti Borga, Duraino, Monfalcone, Lavinamondo, Terza Piccola, Rinaldo, the Scheiben Kofel, and Monte Paralba; a second line of elevation. This line commences on the *west* side of the Piave valley, and crosses it to go eastward.

4. The valley of the Piave from Longarone upwards to the western base of the Paralba; a second line of depression.

5. The line of Monti Pavion and Fenestra, the south wall of the Primiero basin; Pizzon, Corno di Valle, Piacedel, Mezzodi, Sfornioi, dying away in the little isolated spur called Monte Zucco, that stands immediately to the south of the Antelao and Pieve di Cadore; a third line of elevation.

6. The main valley of Primiero, with those of Sagron and Mis, into the Agordo basin; over the Duran saddle down the Val di Goima to Forno di Zoldo; and over by the Val Cibiana to Valle, near the confluence of the Boita and Piave; a third line of depression.

7. The line of Monte Feldrajo, at the foot of which is Tonadigo in the Primiero basin; Monti Agner, Framont, Pelsa, Col Dai, Pelmo, Antelao, Tranego, Bagion, where it dies out at Lozzo, in the valley of the Piave; a fourth line of elevation.

The *third* and *fourth* of these lines are the most important of this series.

These great intersecting lines give to the Ampezzo district a special aspect, strongly distinguishing it from that of Carnia to the east, and the Tyrol Dolomites to the west. It attains its climax at the south foot of the Antelao, near the junction of the Boita with the Piave.

Several exceptions to the regularity of the relief are observable. The Civita, for instance, is an escarpment facing in a direction contrary to any of its neighbours, so far as observed; and instead of the NW.-SE. ridge, against which its *sloping* side abuts being continued on the escarpment side in a NW. direction, as is the case below Agordo, the ridge suddenly ceases, and we see instead, a trough—the Caprile basin. This anomaly greatly enhances the scenic effect. Then the bastion-like form of the Pelmo is singularly perched upon the *intersection* of two cross lines of ridge, at an angle not coincident with either of the two intersecting lines. The angle formed by these intersecting lines on the north side is the head of the Val Fiorentina, a valley debouching into the main valley at Caprile; while the angle formed on the south side by the same lines gives rise to the Val Rutorto, opening into the Val di Zoldo at Forno di Zoldo. Longarone, too, is another illustration. It is situated in or near the intersection of two lines of ridge; but, instead of this intersection being elevated high above the level of the sea, it is a *depression*—the valley of the Piave!

Of the triangular-shaped District lying between the

Pusterthal and that ENE.-WSW. line of ridge, in the first system of relief described, on the one hand, and the valleys of the Gader and Sexten on the other—we may say that it is characterised by the presence of the NW.-SE. lines of elevation and depression, together with a tendency more and more manifest as the masses approach the trough of the Pusterthal to arrange themselves in lines *parallel* to that valley. The Ampezzo road from Landro or Höllenstein down to its outlet into the Pusterthal is the most prominent NW.-SE. line of depression. But it is continued southwards by the Val Popena over the saddle of the Lago Misurina down to the head of the Auronzo Thal, and again by a part of the Forcella Grande or Col del Fuoco to the north slope of the Antelao. The main branch of the Bragser Thal is another of these lines. But west of this line, when we arrive at the Seekofel, the culminating point of the district between the Gader and Ampezzo road, we find the ridge to which it belongs running W. by N., or nearly parallel to the Pusterthal. Another point is worthy of notice. All the Dolomite masses between the Sexten Thal and the Enneberg branch of the Gader, dip *to the south*, and have their escarpments more or less facing the Pusterthal; while those forming the ENE.-WSW. line of ridge dip *northwards*, and have their escarpments facing *away* from the Pusterthal. The Ampezzo road, therefore, between the Düren See and the Peutelstein Schloss lies in a *synclinal trough*. This road is the boundary line also between two districts, having different scenic characters.

We have now traced the outlines of the Orography of the south-eastern limestone zone, from the Adige trough eastward, nearly as far as Tarvis. A few words are all that can now be said upon the structure of the Julian and

Karawanken Alps, in addition to the description given in Chapters IX. and XI.

The most noteworthy fact in the *Julian Alps* is the *great break* in the line of its escarpment. First, forming the Roccolana-Raibl trough, it continues its course, in the shape of a great depression, across the Carnic-Karawanken chain; and then, by the sudden sinking out of sight, through enormous dislocation, of the limestone beds of the Dobratsch, under the level of the Villach plain, has allowed the Gail an exit from its own valley to join the Drave below Villach. From Tarvis to beyond the Raibl See, it runs nearly at right angles to the chain—that is to say, from north to south; in the Roccolana Thal from east to west. This variation is, of course, an instance of the blending of the dominant lines pervading the Julian Alp district, with those that stretch eastward out of Carnia. A mass of parti-coloured porphyry, situated between the Luschari Berg and the Königs Berg, with smaller patches of it on the east also of this great line of fracture, may not be unconnected with its existence. The escarpment of the Julian Alps faces the Save Thal, and the line of depression between Tarvis and Pontebba. Running along its base, and forming the frontal spurs, appear thin bands of the lower and upper trias beds; while the line of wall, the peaks, and the whole of the Flitsch and Isonzo country behind, consists of one mass of so-called 'Dachstein Limestone,' and Dolomite of the Lias formation. Here the 'Dachstein' beds arrive at their full development on the south side of the Alps. Dr. Peters, therefore, regards them as the true southern representatives of the great masses of the Watzmann, Tannen, and Dachstein, &c., Gebirge of the north-eastern Limestone zone. While the Wochein plateau, to the south of the Terglou, has, he thinks, a much better right to the appellation of 'Steinernes Meer' than the mass so named, standing to the south-west of the König See. The summit of the Dobratsch makes an excellent stand-point for a general view of these Alps, from the Terglou to Pontebba; but a nearer and more exact impression of the eastern portion, and of the Wochein plateau and basin, may be obtained from the summit of the Mittags Kogl, or of the Stou, in the Karawanken.

The *Karawanken* form a wedge-shaped band of mountain land, stretching on its north border from Tarvis to Unter Drauberg, on the confines of East Carinthia and Styria; and on its south border from Tarvis to Cilli, in Styria. Near Tarvis it consists of but a single ridge, and its breadth at this point, from Arnoldstein in the Gail Thal to Ratschach in the Save Thal, is not more than three miles and a half. But it increases in complexity and breadth eastwards; and indications of a second ridge make their appearance at the Mittags Kogl, which, a little farther, at the Bären Thal, are developed into a distinct *North* ridge, with a series of cross valleys and subordinate ridges filling up the interval between it and the *Main* ridge. The two ridges continue nearly parallel to each other, running nearly due east and west, but uniting again in the Ursula Berg, to the south of Unter Drauberg. The Main ridge, in passing along eastwards, constitutes the north rim of the Steiner Alp Caldron, and suffers only a single interruption in its course, which occurs at Villach, at the north-west angle of the Caldron. The North ridge, on the other hand, is six times broken; and at these points the waters and streams of as many basins find their way out into the longitudinal valley of the Drave. A *third* ridge, however, makes its appearance on the S. side of the main ridge, to the west of Neumarktl, at the foot of the Loibl pass; which, farther east, splits into two, the *northern* branch forming the south border of the Caldron, while the *southern*, diverging considerably, is the boundary line to an immense broken plateau country, abutting, at its northern edge, on the south-east rim of the Caldron. The *Caldron* is the most noticeable feature of the whole chain. It occupies a mid position in the mountain zone, which here, from Sittersdorf on the N., to Stein on the S., has a breadth of about twenty-two miles—not far short of one-third the length of the whole chain from Tarvis to the Ursula Berg. The Karawanken is a great network of basins, and the Caldron but carries the features that characterise them to a climax. The peaks set upon its rim are some of the highest in the chain; the three open, level valleys in its interior contrast well with the rugged precipices overhanging them; and the outlet-gorge is the narrowest conceivable. In form the Caldron is rhomboidal, and its dimensions are about six miles in each direction. With the characters it possesses, it is not surprising to find masses of igneous and crystalline rock coming to light in the immediate neighbourhood. In the depths of the Kanker Thal, for instance, we find a large mass of porphyry; and immediately above it rise the Dolomitic precipices of the Grintouz—the culminating peak of the chain. In the Ober Seeland basin, on the north side of the Grintouz, there is another large mass of porphyry. Then, in the valleys between the North ridge and the north rim of the Caldron, two narrow and adjoining strips of granite and diorite make their appearance, extending from the Ursula Berg to the Obir. And finally, at the north-east corner, we meet with the Smrekouz Berg, composed of basalt; and below it extends as far as Leutschdorf, the first village met with on emerging from the Caldron, a species of rock—described as a 'doleritic sandstone' by one author, and as a 'greenish trachytic porphyry' by others—that has received the name of *Leutschite* from this village.

The outline of the *Orography* of the different districts we visited during our three summers' wanderings, is now completed. Were we to fulfil our programme, we should now point out their most prominent *geologic* features. But, as the space at command does not admit of this being done for all, we shall confine attention to one district only—the Western Dolomite district—which greatly exceeds in interest its neighbours to the east.

The Geology of this region has been most graphically given in a quarto volume, published in 1860, by Baron von Richthofen.* His work comprises not only a detailed description of each portion of the district, in which he brings to bear the experience derived from a study of the igneous rocks of the northern Carpathians and Germany, and of the limestone beds of North Tyrol and the Vorarlberg, but also an outline of the labours of his predecessors in the rich field of South Tyrol. Its value is much increased by a full list, in chronological order, of the treatises, papers, and maps bearing upon his subject, that had appeared prior to the publication of his work. To it we are indebted for the materials for our sketch, and the study of its pages we would recommend to those of our readers who may desire further information.

We have already alluded to the position of the zones of Clay-slate, that bound the Western Dolomite region to the north and south, one of them being the schistous covering to the granite Ellipsoid of Brixen, and the other standing in a similar relation to that of the Cima d'Asta. In the

* The work is entitled 'Geognostische Beschreibung der Umgegend von Predazzo, St. Cassian, und der Seisser Alpe in Süd-Tyrol.' It possesses an excellent geological map, and several geologically coloured sections. The map given in the present work is a copy on a smaller scale from the central portions of Richthofen's.

interval between these zones is outspread the vast mass of red quarziferous porphyry, the most important in a geòlogical point of view, if not the largest continuous area occupied by this rock, in Europe. Von Buch was of opinion, that it was poured out at one and the same date, but Richthofen shows that at least eight different centres have contributed to its formation, differing in age and character from each other. The older eruptions took place on dry land, while the later were submarine. The whole forms a very complex system of extraordinary thickness, the later masses often not only covering, but also penetrating their predecessors in dykes and veins, and being further connected with them by beds of angular or rolled fragments of porphyry, portions of a neighbouring mass. This conglomerate may be clearly seen in the rocks close to the bridge over the Eisack, at Botzen.

From the appearance of this porphyry dates all geologic chronology for our Western region. The first beds deposited upon the porphyry belong to the Lower Trias formation; no trace has yet been discovered of the Gail Thal beds of the previous formation—the *Carboniferous*. To the east they appear to approach no nearer than Innichen, at the terminus of the Carnic Alps; in the west, a small patch of them is to be met with only to the west of the Adamello, between that mountain and the Lake of Como. And not only does the history of the formation of this region *open* with the beds of the Trias, but with a small exception, if we accept the classification of the Austrian geologists, it *closes* with them.

For clearness sake, we will arrange the series of Trias beds in this region in a table, at the same time collating them with some of the equivalent beds of other districts.

The following is the table: the beds are arranged in ascending order.

Table of the Trias Beds of South-Eastern Tyrol.

	Local designations of Trias beds of South-eastern Tyrol, as given by Richthofen	Localities after which these are named	Equivalent beds on the *north* side of the Central Alps, according to Gümbel	*German* designations or equivalents	*North Italian* ditto, according to Von Hauer	*English* ditto
Lower Trias of Richthofen	1. A sandstone, generally bright red and non-fossiliferous. *Gröden sandstone*	After the valley of that name	*Werfen schists*	*Bunter sandstein*, or *Lower Trias*	*Servino schists* and part of the *Verrucano*	Red and mottled sandstones and conglomerates. *Lower new red Sandstone*
	2. Greyish marly beds, containing Posidonomya Clarai, &c. *Seiss beds*	After the village of that name on the porphyry plateau	*Guttenstein beds* of East Carinthia, and of northern limestone Alps	*Muschelkalk*, or *Middle Trias*		Supposed to be non-existent in Great Britain
	3. White and grey sandstones and marls, containing Naticella costata, &c. *Campil beds*	After Campil in the Gader Thal				
	4. Brownish or black bituminous limestone, containing Terebratula vulgaris, &c. *Virgloria limestone*	After the Virgloria Pass, in Vorarlberg, where the same bed occurs	*Virgloria* beds in the Vorarlberg and Tyrol			
[...]hthofen.	5. Non-bedded, crystalline, cellular, white and grey dolomite and limestone, having a rough surface, and containing Ammonites globosus, and Crinoidea *Mendola* DOLOMITE	After the long line of escarpment lying west of Botzen, the upper part of which consists of this rock				
	6. Limestone, containing flint nodules *Buchenstein limestone*	After the village of that name in the Livinallongo				
	7. An alternation of beds of black schist, of volcanic ash, marls, flinty limestones, and of conglomerate, formed of fragments of limestone imbedded in volcanic ash	After the village of that name in the Gader Thal			*Esino limestone*	

Upper Trias of	8. Smoky grey limestone, containing fragments of corals, Encrinites and Terebratulæ *Cipit limestone*	After the Sennhütte Cipit on the Seisser Alp, at the foot of the Schlern	or Bavaria *Hallstädt* and *Wetterstein* beds of North-eastern Limestone zone	*Lower Keuper beds* or *Upper Trias* (part		sum beds of Cheshire, central England, and Ireland *Upper new red Sandstone*
	9. Marly, dark grey, oolitic limestone, rich in fossils *St. Cassian beds*	After the village of that name in the Upper Gader				
	Note. Nos. 6, 7, 8, and 9 are *local* beds, incorporated or connected with the vast mass of *volcanic ash* or *tuff*, about 2,000 feet thick, that forms the Seisser Alp, and its continuation eastwards to the foot of Monte Tofana					
	10. Dolomite, same in character as No. 5, and resting either on No. 5 or on the Tuff. Traversed in parts by veins of augite porphyry *Schlern* DOLOMITE In the Schlern it is 3,000 feet thick In the Lang Kofel, 5,000 feet ,,	After the Schlern, which it constitutes				
	11. Red and white dolomite sandstone, rich in fossils *Raibl beds*	After Raibl in the Julian Alps, where the same beds occur and were first described	*Lower Alp Muschel Keuper* *Raibl* beds of Carinthia		*Dossena* beds of Lombardy	
Lowest Lias of Richthofen	12. Clear grey bedded dolomite *Dachstein* DOLOMITE The extreme summit of the Schlern and the upper surface of the Sella and Guerdenazza plateaus are formed of it.	After the Dachstein, south of Ischl, in the North-eastern Alps, where this rock occurs in mass.	'*Dachstein Dolomite*' of north eastern limestone Alps '*Haupt Dolomit*' of Gümbel	*Middle Keuper beds*, or *Upper Trias* (part)	Lower Lias	*Lower Lias*

To place the reader in a position to form some idea of the richness, from a geological point of view, of the small area under consideration, the list states separately each distinct set of beds; but, for the purposes of this sketch, we shall mass them somewhat differently, so as to bring to view their relation to the scenery of the district.

Our *first* group will comprise the beds numbered 1 to 5, both inclusive.

These beds accompany each other very constantly throughout the district. If we take our station at Primiero, we shall find them cropping out continually, one above another on the green alp slopes, that run up to the base of the wall of Primiero dolomites. Opposite to them, to the west, rise the mountains of clay slate, that form the schistous covering to the granite nucleus of the Cima d'Asta, and constitute the northern boundary of the Primiero basin. They appear on our right hand, as we pursue the path from Primiero northwards by the St. Martino Hospice, nearly as far as Paneveggio. On this route they are generally covered with pasture, but near the summit of the pass the series is laid bare at several points, and with its varied colours of bright red, grey, green, and brown, presents a striking contrast to the pale precipices soaring above. The rest of the Travignolo Thal, until reaching Predazzo, lies in the porphyry.

At Predazzo, at the mouth of the Travignolo, they rise from the porphyry in the form of three great crescentic curves, the horns of the curves touching each other, so as to enclose a space that has Predazzo for its centre. Upon each of these crescents stands a mass of 'Schlern dolomite,' forming the precipices and walls of the Latemar, part of the Weisshorn, and Monte Viesena. The interior of the space is filled with a variety of igneous rocks, that have been poured forth from the Predazzo crater.

At the Caressa pass, separating the Latemar from the Rosengarten, denudation has laid these beds bare down to the lowest, the Gröden sandstone, and at Moena, at the foot of the pass, in the Fassa Thal, has removed them altogether, and exposed the carmine-coloured porphyry beneath. But from the southern terminus of the Rosengarten, they form the base of the Dolomite wall, which runs northwards to the Schlern.* Further on, they crop out successively at the base of the Seisser Alp, and thence, coasting north-eastward and eastward across the Gröden and Gader Thals, as far as the Kreuzberg in the Sexten Thal, they constitute a great girdle on the north to the Dolomite region. Everywhere, therefore, these beds show themselves as a continuous inter-conformable external border-line to the western Dolomite region.

The character of the period during which these beds were deposited was one of slow *depression*, interrupted only at the upper limit of the Campil beds by an accelerated, perhaps sudden, sinking of the sea-bottom. This is indicated by the bank of conglomerate which marks the boundary between the Campil beds and those of the Virgloria limestone next above them, and the changed character of the fauna.

To this quiet general movement in one and the same direction, followed one of an entirely opposite character. A sudden *upheaval* converted a considerable portion of the district into dry land. Only in the Seisser Alp, the upper Fassa, and the other portions of the Tuff-land, was the sea present, in the form of a large bay, with a ramified coast-line of Mendola Dolomite, and opening out to the sea towards Caprile. At this period, a surface of Mendola

* It is from the bituminous beds of the Virgloria limestone, in the gorge behind Ratzes, that its sulphur-baths have their origin.

Dolomite covered the whole of the present porphyry plateau. Most of this has been subsequently washed away; but small islands, composed of our first group of beds, still exist, and diversify the present surface of the plateau. One of them lies to the west of Cavalese, and two others to the east of Neumarkt.

This period—the earlier portion of the upper Trias—was one of great and long-continued *eruptive activity*, with intervals of rest. The beds of the older Trias in the upper Fassa, bearing a covering of Mendola Dolomite, were upheaved, broken through, and a submarine volcano made its appearance in the southernmost ramification of the bay. Its ring-shaped border can be clearly seen from the Sasso di Damm, or any other of the narrow ridges crowning that giant heap of eruptive ash and augite porphyry—the Bufaure Gebirge—that now fills up, to a height of 9,000 feet above the sea, the former crater of the volcano. On the first glance at the scenery from this point, it seems as if the Marmolata, Campo Ziegelan, Sasso di Loch, Rosengarten, Lang Kofel, and Sella Plateau, might be the broken walls of the crater; but this is an illusive appearance. They belong to a *later* period; it is the bed of Mendola Dolomite underlying these walls that formed the rim. The edge of the crater was unequally elevated, its highest point being at the south-eastern corner, where it rises to more than 8,000 feet above the present sea level; at its northern border—the present south escarpment of the Seisser Alp plateau—it was much lower, and was overflowed by the Tuff sea. On all sides of the rim the older beds may be seen to dip more or less steeply towards the interior of the crater, forming a basin-shaped depression; and out of a probably small orifice near its centre the erupted ash must have been ejected to a sufficient extent to cover these sedimentary beds with enormous masses, to be afterwards partially laid bare by the action of streams and weather.

Over the north border of this rim, the finer particles of volcanic ash were carried away by the sea currents, and deposited upon the entire surface of the bay as sedimentary ash, giving rise to the present Tuff plateau of the Seisser Alp. The borders of this bay can still be traced out by following the devious line of Mendola Dolomite to the Upper Gader, where the Tuff disappears under the base of Monte Tofana and the other North Ampezzo Alps.* And to the south-east, where the bay communicated with the open sea, the Tuff may be followed in the masses of the Col di Lana † and Monte Frisolet, and farther in the same direction to the Civita, Val di Zoldo, and as far as the foot of the Antelao. Even now, the Seisser Alp slopes inwards from its borders, and this may possibly be a remnant of the relations of Relief that prevailed during the Tuff period. The tradition existing among the people, that a large lake once existed upon the Seisser Alp, which suddenly burst its banks, and overwhelmed the country about Seiss with masses of débris, is an indication that this character in the surface of the alp has attracted attention.

Abundant evidence of *another* centre of eruptive activity exists in the Seisser Alp itself. Beginning at the Schlern immediately behind Ratzes, the dark masses of augite porphyry are seen to crown the upper edge of the Mendola Dolomite, which forms the west and north border of the alp. Farther on, the whole upper portion of the Puflatsch Alp is composed of this rock. It continues eastward from this point to crown the border of the alp until it sinks

* In this direction it occupies the slopes of the Tre Sassi Pass down to Cortina, and contributes to make that pass as full of springs and as boggy as the upper basin of the Gader itself.

† On this mountain, which rises behind Buchenstein, the thickness of the Sedimentary Ash amounts to upwards of 2,500 feet.

down into the upper Gröden, near Plan. Large dykes of it are also exposed to light on the line of ridge between the Platt Kogel and Rosszähn Berg, and on the descent into the Duron Thal. Their rugged olive-black—often semi-columnar—masses stand out in as striking a contrast to the surrounding green slopes in one direction, as that which the 'ghostly pale' Dolomites, near at hand, offer in another.

Farther to the south—at Predazzo—*a third* centre of eruption was formed. This crater, like that in the upper Fassa, preserves some of its original orographic features, though the Avisio has worn a channel through its centre, and the stream of the Travignolo worked out a bed for itself through the eastern border, to join the Avisio. It occupies a position in the line of depression between the two great porphyry Ridges, which, as already mentioned, follow the curve of the Cima d'Asta Ellipsoid. Out of its funnel-shaped opening streamed forth, lava-like, the masses of igneous rock that now hem Predazzo in on all sides. The town, with its surrounding fertile alluvial level, stands in that opening. The oldest igneous rock is a peculiar kind of Syenite, which has penetrated through the deep-seated and older red porphyry, and overspread the inner borders of the surrounding lower Trias beds. At a later date followed Tourmaline granite, breaking through the Syenite on the east side of the crater, immediately behind Predazzo, and overlying it. In this rock, tourmaline takes the place of mica. Higher up on the eastern slopes lies a rock of still later date, nearly allied to melaphyr, which, as containing crystals of uralite, Richthofen distinguishes by the name of Uralite porphyry. Of subsequent date to these is a very dark Melaphyr, which shows itself as a dyke breaking through the granite, and then, ascending to the surface of the older eruptive rocks, spreads far and wide, over their upper limits of outflow, into all the three crescentic spaces formed by the curves of the beds of the lower Trias. Fully one-half of Monte Mulatto, to the north-east of Predazzo, consists of it. Finally, penetrating the Syenite, and then the Melaphyr, are veins of two other kinds of rock, called Porphyrite and Syenite Porphyry, the latter—not known to occur in any other locality—remarkable, as possessing very large crystals of orthoclase.

A section of the crater, given in the outline on the following page, taken from Richthofen's work, where the dotted lines indicate the probable mode in which the masses of eruptive rock are continued below the level of the alluvium, will explain the relative position of the different rocks better than a verbal description.

The rich variety of material is one of the contrasting features that distinguish this southern crater from its submarine neighbour to the north. In the *latter*, only one form of igneous rock—augite porphyry—made its appearance throughout the entire eruptive epoch; in the *former*, the kind of rock varied with each outbreak. In the submarine volcano, tuff, or volcanic ash, is the most prominent product; in the sub-ærial one at Predazzo, tuff is entirely absent. The relation between the two is compared by Richthofen to that existing between the *central* crater and the *lateral* outbreaks of lava of a volcano of the present day. Their activity was not entirely contemporaneous—that of the northern crater having nearly come to an end before the commencement of the deposition of the 'Schlern Dolomite,' while the principal activity of the Predazzo crater came into play only after that epoch.

The various points of contact between the different forms of more or less molten rock, and the beds of lower and upper Trias lying outside of them, and dipping more

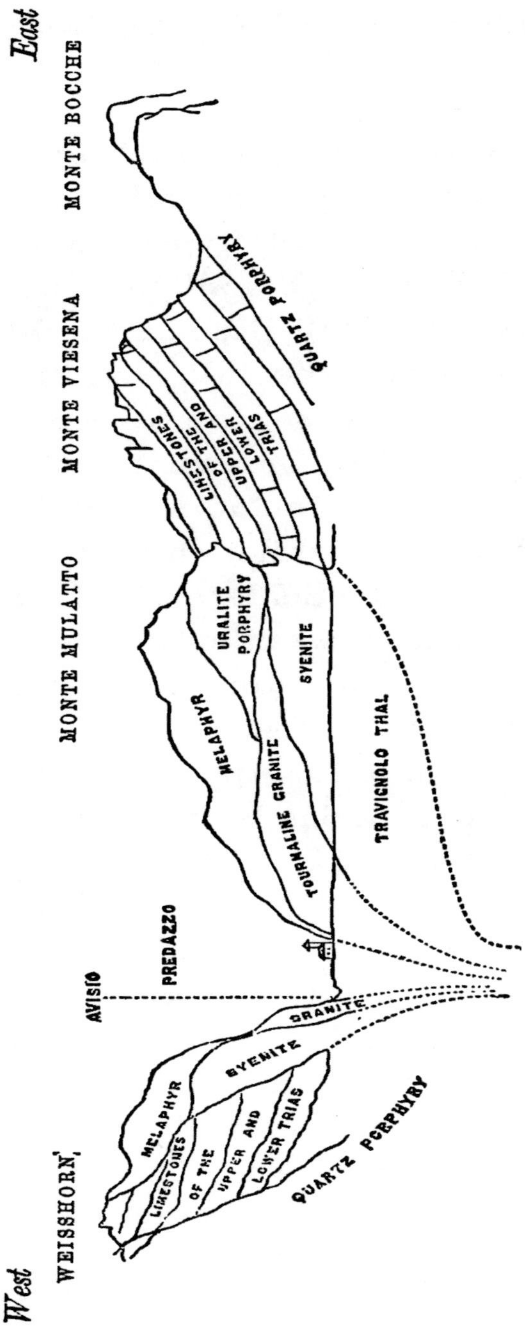

SECTION OF THE PREDAZZO CRATER.

or less steeply towards the centre of the crater, have given rise to a great variety of minerals, that have gained for Predazzo as high a renown among mineralogists as the more general relations of its rocks have procured for it among geologists.

Another outbreak of eruptive rock occurs in a position intermediate between the two craters. A giant mass of syenite, beset with veins of hypersthene, interrupts the continuity of the Dolomitic wall that runs in an E.-W. line from the Sasso di Val Fredda to the Sasso di Loch, opposite Vigo, and forms the so-called Monzoni ridge. It stands, therefore, in the southern border of the Fassa crater. But it must be somewhat later in date, as the whole series of Trias beds, including the Schlern Dolomite, is broken through. For while, on the east of the syenite mass, the base line of the Schlern Dolomite lies more than 8,000 feet above the present sea level, on its west side, opposite Moena, the same line is met with at a height lower by more than 2,500 feet.

During a portion of this eruptive epoch, it is probable that our first group of Trias beds were folded into a series of ridges whose axes had a NW.-SE. direction, implying a lateral pressure from south-west towards north-east. One of these waves is visible in ascending from Moena to the Caressa pass; another, on the south face of the Seisser Alp plateau, between Campitello and Gries. The upper Gröden Thal is cut in one of them, and the stream of the Pissada, descending from the Sella plateau, between Colfosco and Stern in the upper Gader, has laid bare a fourth wave, at right angles to its axis. Evidence of the existence of similar waves may be seen at Campil, lower down in the Gader, and also in the Livinallongo and its lateral valleys. A wave-like surface of Mendola Dolomite must thus have been formed in the bed of the Tuff Sea, upon which the

Tuff, and the local limestone beds connected with the Tuff period, came to be deposited.

The eruptive epoch of South Tyrol was not characterised by the entire absence of sedimentary deposits. Several beds of a *local* character were formed in the Tuff Sea, and these are described in the Table, and comprise the beds numbered 6 to 9, both inclusive. The last beds of this series, designated as the St. Cassian beds, discovered in 1830, have, by the extraordinary number of their fossil shells and ammonites, been a third source of fame for our Western District.

It is impossible, in this sketch, to enter into the slightest detail upon the relative position of these local beds, even of those named after the village of St. Cassian. We must content ourselves with the remark that a great amount of varying scientific opinion has been expressed in reference to their age, which Richthofen discusses in chronological order. He refers these St. Cassian beds to the lower portion of the upper Trias—to the end of the Tuff period; but as continuing also into the following period, when the Schlern Dolomite was being formed.

The existence of the so-called St. Cassian beds, though very local in our western district, is not confined to it. They have been found also near the Lago di Garda and in the neighbourhood of Como, near Bleiberg on the Dobratsch; and on the Obir and Petzen Gebirge, in the Karawanken Alps. In the northern limestone Alps they have been identified by Gümbel with the Partnach beds of the lower Keuper, which, however, are comparatively poor in fossils.

Our *third* group of beds will comprise the remainder of the series—Nos. 10, 11, and 12.

After the principal phase of the eruptive activity had reached its end, the slow upheaval of the land also ceased, and in its place there came a gradual *depression,* which continued for a long period. The change occurred probably towards the end of the Tuff deposits. During this period of depression the 'Schlern Dolomite' and the 'Raibl beds' were formed.

The most striking characteristic of the 'Schlern Dolomite' Formation is its distribution in the form, either of great *isolated massives,* or equally isolated long *wall-like lines or curves.* The Schlern, Lang Kofel, Guerdenazza, Sella, and Marmolata, are examples of the first; the Rosengarten, Latemar, and Campo Ziegelan, of the second, form. Another feature is the excessively narrow *area* within which it is found, and its sudden appearance and disappearance within this area. It is not seen west of the Schlern or Latemar, and it disappears beyond the Tre Sassi pass before reaching Cortina. But in the Schlern its thickness is already upwards of 3,500 feet, and it is probably as much in the Rosengarten. At the Fedaia pass the upper limit of the Mendola Dolomite being met with at 7,000 feet above the sea, a thickness of about 4,500 feet remains for the Schlern Dolomite in the upper mass of the Marmolata. It possesses a similar thickness in the Lang Kofel; but at the Sella plateau it is already less than 2,000 feet. Farther east, in Monte Nuvulau, Set Sass, and Monte Tofana, its thickness does not exceed a few hundred feet.

Another way of grouping the 'Schlern Dolomite' may be made dependent upon the presence or absence of later beds lying upon the Dolomite. The variety in the scenery is closely related to this difference. Hence the contrast between the pinnacles and hatchet-like blades of the Lang Kofel and the level plateau surface of the summit of the Schlern. The pinnacles of the Schlern, fringing its northern border, however, recall the Lang Kofel character. In the group characterised by the presence of later beds are to be found the Schlern, Sella, Guerdenazza, Set Sass, Nuvulau, and Tofana; all the others falling into the other group.

On the Schlern, the presence of the red 'Raibl beds' has protected the Dolomite beneath to some extent from the denuding action of the sea while slowly elevated out of it, and from the later action of weather; but they do not contribute to any landscape effect. But farther to the east they hold a more important place. In the Sella plateau we have a wide outspread massive of unbedded crystalline 'Schlern Dolomite' resting upon the Tuff, and rising up from its surface on all sides in perpendicular walls. Above these precipices, appears a narrow sloping ledge, formed of Raibl beds, and upon this is planted a series of short escarpments, terminating in the background in a multitude of truncated cones, with rocky winding gorges between them, lined with débris, the whole formed of lower Lias Dolomite. The Guerdenazza has somewhat similar features, but on a much larger scale, and it sends out long arms of precipice to the west and north-east. The Raibl beds, by thus interposing a stage between the upper and lower tier of precipices, immensely enhance the scenic effect of the whole mass. This kind of effect may be said, perhaps, to culminate in Monte Nuvulau, a much smaller Massive, that dominates the ascent of the pass from Santa Lucia, by Monte Gusella, to Cortina. Looking up at it from below, seated on the Tuff-land, it strikingly resembles, in its three well-proportioned stages of 'Schlern Dolomite,' 'Raibl beds,' and Lias Dolomite, a mighty Tower of Babel.

The long wall of the Dolomites of Primiero—a line twice the length of the line of the Rosengarten, which in character they strongly resemble—was not visited by Richthofen. From the communications made to him by Herren Foetterle and Wolf, Viennese geologists, he is disposed to consider them as belonging to the Lias Formation. If this be correct, it would appear as if the 'Schlern Dolomite' were all but limited to the volcanic area of South Tyrol.

What then is the origin of this strictly 'family group' of mountain masses? It has formed the subject of discussion among French and German geologists for more than a generation past, and much ink has been shed during the process, without a satisfactory solution having been arrived at. Richthofen is one of the latest contributors to its literature, and he propounds a theory that requires a separation of the question into two parts. We have to ask—First, What is the origin of these *mountains*, as such? and then, What is the origin of the Dolomite *rock* of which they mainly consist?

Leopold Von Buch—in 1822—was one of the first who attracted scientific attention towards the peculiar appearance of the South Tyrol Dolomites. The frequent neighbourhood of augite porphyry; the numerous veins of that rock to be seen penetrating the Dolomite Massives; the aspect some of them possess of having been suddenly elevated from below to their present position; their chemical character, entire absence of bedding, and crystalline, often cellular, structure, were the points that led him to the theory that these mountains had been upheaved by volcanic force and converted from carbonate of lime into *dolomite* by the vapour of magnesia, evolved from the molten volcanic rocks below, and penetrating the limestone above. The publication of Von Buch's letters was the signal for the commencement of a long series of discussions, and led to many scientific visits to the district. The chemist, however, gave the death-blow to this theory, in the proof, besides other difficulties, of the all but impossibility of the production of magnesia in a state of vapour.

Richthofen goes so far as to add, that Von Buch would never have enunciated his theory if he had but allowed himself to examine with care a single Dolomite mountain!

It is impossible to enter into the details of this long discussion, we must confine ourselves to a statement of the hypothesis Richthofen proposes for the explanation of the orographic peculiarities of those mountains, at least, which are formed of 'Schlern Dolomite.' He says, '*The Schlern is a* CORAL REEF, *and the entire formation of "Schlern Dolomite" has in like manner originated through animal activity.*'

The following are some of the facts to which Richthofen calls attention in support of his hypothesis, taking the Schlern as the subject for illustration. First, its form as a mass, falling away steeply on all sides; its isolation from similar masses in the neighbourhood; the improbability of such a form being the result of denudation, as involving—supposing, for instance, the Schlern and Lang Kofel had ever been a continuous deposit—too great a destruction in one direction, and too complete a protection from denudation in another. Then, the undisturbed beds upon which the Schlern rests, and the equally undisturbed Raibl beds upon its summit, imply that the intermediate Dolomite has suffered, since its deposit, no considerable mechanical disturbance. The unequal thickness of the different masses, too, points strongly in the same direction. The Dolomite of the Schlern and of the Sella plateau could never have been higher than at present, covered, as it is in both, with Raibl beds; while the upper portions of the Dolomite of the *more lofty* Rosengarten, Lang Kofel, and Marmolata, have been left exposed to denuding action.

The original *local* character of the 'Schlern Dolomite' formation is implied in another circumstance connected with the mode of deposit of the Raibl beds. Evidence derived from other deposits shows that, during this period the district was undergoing a gradual slow depression, and that no violent catastrophe occurred. Now the Raibl beds—containing fauna of a *shallow* sea—are found, not only on the summit of the Schlern, and of the lower line of precipices of the Sella and Guerdenazza plateaus, but also in two patches *upon the Tuff* at the foot of these Massives, thousands of feet below. These great differences of elevation in an undisturbed bed at very short distances would, Richthofen argues, be difficult to explain without the supposition of reef-building corals.

Richthofen institutes a comparison between the growth and conditions of existence of the reef-building corals in the tropical seas of the present day, as observed by Darwin, Dana, and Jukes, and those of the assumed Trias coral reefs of South Tyrol. The coral animals find an especially favourable ground, without, however, being limited to it, in districts of former sub-aqueous volcanic activity, when a period of slow depression often takes the place of the previous period of elevation. South Tyrol was, during the latter portion of the Trias period in a similar condition, and the sea was filled with the products of the decomposition of volcanic material. They are limited in their growth to a depth of about 120 feet under the sea surface; and yet, favoured by the continual slow depression of the ocean bed, reefs of enormous depth are formed. From soundings made, it is evident that there are reefs in the Pacific Ocean, of a depth equal to the height of the South Tyrol Dolomite Massives. If the Pacific were laid bare, or the reefs in it, with their base, were now elevated above the sea level, would not their aspect, seated upon mountain ridges, and many of them in the immediate neighbourhood of extinct volcanoes, present a similarity to the existing Orography of South Tyrol?

In this comparison between the South Tyrol Dolomites and existing coral reefs, the Raibl beds render a most important service. In those reefs which have the name of 'Atolls,' the reef is generally higher on the windward side; while to the leeward, heaps of coral sand containing shell-fish, and fragments of sea-urchins and coral accumulate. Now on the Schlern there is an inequality in the height of its two arms; for the south-western, which alone supports the Raibl beds, is much lower than the other arm consisting of Schlern Dolomite alone. And there being no evidence of any disturbance of the original horizontality of the whole mass, it is difficult to explain this inequality in height of the two arms, or the presence of the Raibl beds upon the *lower* one only, without the supposition of animal activity.

The fossil *contents* of the Raibl beds offer a strong similarity to those now in process of formation, on the lee side of the present coral reefs. In that position are to be seen masses of coral sand, and fragments of corals, shells, and sea-urchins, that, pounded by the breakers of the ocean, and, swept along by the currents, have been deposited in regular beds in the stiller water on the lee side. These beds then become cemented together into a hard crystalline rock, often white, but also sometimes coloured red with oxide of iron. Now the Raibl beds upon the Schlern are made up of similar fragments, accompanied by the hard shells of Gastropoda, and certain strongly-formed bivalves. And while, on the one hand, there is a complete absence of ammonites, and other shell-fish of a *deep* sea in the Raibl beds upon the *summit* of the Schlern, it is just these forms, and no others, that have been found in the patch of Raibl beds upon the Seisser Alp at its foot.

Evidence of still another kind is brought to bear in

favour of the coral-reef hypothesis, in the peculiarities presented by certain sedimentary deposits, which, in some instances, are found at the base of the Dolomite Massives, and in others not far from them.

On the descent between the Fedaia pass and the narrow gorge that issues out at Sottoguda, on the way to Caprile, there may be seen in the steep and lofty face of eruptive ash—that stands out in such strong contrast to the Dolomite walls of the Marmolata opposite—banks, sometimes of conglomerate cemented together with lime; in other cases, of limestone with fragments of volcanic ash; or of pure lime or Dolomite. None of them continue for any distance; they begin and end abruptly, and are found at various levels, but all in a horizontal position. This phenomenon of short rocky limestone or Dolomite banks imbedded in a mass of volcanic ash, is to be met with elsewhere in the Tuff district, but nowhere do they present so singular an appearance as on the Fedaia pass, where the erosive action of water has laid bare an enormous face of tuff. Richthofen compares these banks with those formed at the present day near the Island of Bourbon by certain species of coral animals.* The banks of conglomerate, consisting of angular fragments of limestone imbedded in volcanic ash, he compares to the fragments of coral, which are continually being torn off by the breakers from the windward side of a reef, and in a state of division, more or less complete, are buried in the sediments that may be forming at its base, or in its neighbourhood.

It cannot be denied that this hypothesis of Richthofen's is fascinating, and offers ample 'room and verge enough' to the flights of imagination; it brings together also to its

* See H. de la Beche's 'Geological Observer' for extracts from M. Siau's description of the formation of detached coral bosses (*pâtés de coraux*) on the bed of the sea, at the Island of Bourbon.

support numerous facts of various orders. But while admitting its plausibility, we decline to put full faith in it until some competent geologist shall have visited the ground, with the express object of testing the accuracy of the observations made by Richthofen, taking care not to overlook any facts that would tell against the hypothesis. If it were right to be guided by appearances only, in these matters, we might refer the reader to a woodcut, at page 622 of Dana's 'Manual of Geology,' 1863, representing a section of a high island encased in coral reefs, where the similarity in external form to that which would be the result of a section of the Sella plateau, is so close and striking, that the one might be substituted for the other.

Fossil corals, well preserved, are frequently met with in beds of coralline limestone in England, Europe, and North America. Dana (page 272 of his 'Geology') mentions an instance occurring at the Ohio Falls, near Louisville, where they ('Favosites') are to be met with five or six feet in diameter, 'nearly as perfect as when they were covered with their flower-like polyps.' But the reef to which these specimens belonged does not seem to be a feature in the landscape scenery. If Richthofen's hypothesis be verified, we have in South Tyrol the *converse* of this—insignificant fragments of individual coral, but magnificent specimens of Reefs, which take on a *mountain* character and become *the* feature in the landscape. Giant carcases they are, indecently left unburied by Nature for men to wonder at ! *

The *second* part of the general question, or, What is the origin of Dolomite rock ? has, as we have said, long been a *questio vexata*. It takes rank with other great questions of a similar kind, such as the origin and conditions of formation of coal, gypsum, and rock salt ; where the aid of

* On the rare occurrence of fossil upraised reefs, see the remarks of Sir Charles Lyell, in the 9th edition of his 'Principles of Geology,' pp. 792–6.

the sister science of chemistry becomes necessary for the solution of the questions raised by geology. And as it is but within a recent period, comparatively, that this aid has been effectively rendered, so it is just this section of the science that has been left somewhat in the rear of the others. It is impossible, therefore, in the present position of these questions to obtain more than a statement of a very general character of the possible circumstances under which Dolomite is formed.

The composition of Dolomite will be better understood by comparing it with that of its two components.

The first, *calcite*, or *carbonate of lime*, has the following composition :—

	Per-centage
In 100 parts it has, of carbonic acid . .	43·87
And of lime	56·13
	100·00

This mineral—so well known—occurs most abundantly in nature, and is to be met with in nearly all parts of the globe from the oldest to the latest formations.

The second, *magnesite*, or *carbonate of magnesia*, has the following composition :—

	Per-centage
In 100 parts it has, of carbonic acid . .	52·38
And of magnesia .	47·62
	100·00

This mineral is not an important one, nor does it frequently occur.

Dolomite, or *magnesian limestone*, is the result of the chemical union of carbonate of lime and carbonate of magnesia. Its *normal* composition has in 100 parts—

	Per-centage
Of carbonate of lime . . .	54·3
And of carbonate of magnesia . . .	45·7
	100·0

In hardness and specific gravity it does not differ much from calcite, but may be distinguished from it by the comparative difficulty and slowness with which it effervesces in acids.

Dolomite is met with in a variety of states, and under different conditions. The proportion of the magnesian carbonate, too, varies almost indefinitely. When a small per-centage only is present—say, less than ten or twelve per cent., the rock is called Dolomitic limestone. Sometimes it has a sugar-like, crystalline structure, at others it is compact, with a conchoidal fracture. To these two states the term Dolomite is often restricted. Again, it is either cellular, schistose, or slaty; or, lastly, earthy. It occurs in a distinctly stratified condition, and, as on the Seisser Alp, without any evidence of stratification. Instances have been met with of masses of Dolomite alternating in the same series with beds of ordinary carbonate of lime. Dana mentions an instance* where certain fossils (Orthoceras), on chemical analysis proved to be dolomitic—containing, indeed, nearly thirty-eight per cent. of carbonate of magnesia—were found imbedded in a rock of ordinary limestone.

Although this rock is most strikingly displayed in the mountain forms of the south-eastern limestone zone, it is by no means exclusively confined to that region. It is to be met with to the west of the Adige trough along the base of the Adamello and Oertler 'Groups;' and in Lombardy a broken band runs westward as far as Lake Lugano, where the Dolomite Monte Salvadore offers easy access to a noble and varied Alpine panorama. In the North-eastern limestone zone, too, the beds of the middle Keuper belonging to a higher stage of the Trias formation, and consisting almost entirely of Dolomite ('Haupt Dolomit'), run in long,

* Page 84 of his 'Geology.'

narrow, parallel, east-west lines from the valley of the Rhine eastwards into the Salzburg territory, and beyond. But it is only in the Vorarlberg and in the valleys of the Lech and Ill, where the bold pyramidal forms of the Hochvogel and Bieber's Kopf, and the precipices of the Mädelergabel and Wild Männel rise above their neighbours, and farther east, in the Kaiser Gebirge, close to Kufstein, that the traveller is likely to be reminded of the more celebrated mountains of the South. Even in the patches of limestone that skirt the western border of the Brenner Pass, Dolomite exists. Finally, in the masses of sedimentary rock that fill up the interval between the Groups of the Selvretta and Oertler, that is to say, in the Trias deposits of the lower Engadine, characteristic Dolomite scenery is to be found.

Fragments of Dolomite, indeed, may be met with as far west as the St. Gothard Pass and even in the Maritime and Dauphiné Alps; yet it remains true that this rock, and the Trias formation to which in the Alps it pre-eminently, though not exclusively, belongs, are almost entirely restricted to the Eastern Alps.

Of the numerous hypotheses that have been put forth upon the origin of Dolomite, several, however otherwise differing, may be classed together by the possession of a condition common to them all, which requires that the sea should, at the time of formation of the Dolomite, be at the boiling point. To complete these hypotheses, the authors of them should have explained how so high a temperature was possible.*

Without requiring such a state of things, Mr. T. Sterry Hunt, of the Canadian Geological Survey, has shown in a

* The 'Chemical News,' for February 6, 1864, may be consulted for a report of one of Dr. Percy's Lectures on Chemical Geology, delivered at the Jermyn Street Museum, in the present year, in which these and other theories are noticed.

series of experiments upon this subject, contained in a paper which appeared in the 'American Journal of Science' for 1859, that the action of solutions of bicarbonate of soda upon sea-water would separate from it, in the first place, the carbonate of lime dissolved in it, and then the magnesia in the shape of a bicarbonate; and that finally, as the result of intermediate changes, hydrous carbonate of magnesia, heated and under pressure, would, if carbonate of lime be present, slowly form Dolomite. 'The union of the mingled carbonate of lime and magnesia to form dolomite is attended with *contraction*, which, in case the sediment were already somewhat consolidated, would give rise to fissures and cavities in the mass. Should the dolomite strata be afterwards exposed to the action of infiltrating carbonated waters, the excess of carbonate of lime and any calcareous fossils would be removed, *leaving the mass still more porous, with only the moulds of the fossils.*'

'The *lowest temperature* at which hydrous magnesian sediments may be transformed into magnesite and dolomite, *has yet to be determined.*'

These experiments of Mr. Hunt show the possibility of the formation of Dolomite by *original deposition from the sea-water*, but we are not aware that he has yet completed the circle of proof by the artificial production of Dolomite in the way he indicates, at moderate temperatures.

But, in some of the circumstances under which Dolomite occurs in nature, we are almost compelled to believe in the possibility of its formation, not only by way of original deposition, but also as the *result of subsequent action, through sea-water, upon the ordinary carbonate of lime*—in other words, through *metamorphic action.* And if Richthofen's hypothesis as to the animal origin of the 'Schlern dolomite' be true, some form of metamorphic action must be resorted to, to explain the change which these so-called coral reefs have undergone.*

From the analyses of Forchhammer and of Professor Silliman, junior, it appears that *recent* corals possess but a very limited quantity of magnesia—varying in different species—in their composition. Specimens, however, of *coral rock* brought home by Dana from the elevated coral island of Matea or Aurora, to the north of Tahiti, were analysed by Hunt, and by Professor Silliman, junior, and found to contain, in one case 5 per cent., and in another as much as 38 per cent., of carbonate of magnesia. Dana did not observe any evidence, in this instance, that the original coral had been subjected to the action of heat. Such facts as these imply an action of the sea-water upon the carbonate of lime of the fresh corals, by which a portion of the carbonate of lime in them is removed, and replaced by an equivalent amount of carbonate of magnesia that had been held in solution by the sea-water. And they also afford some indication that the formation of Dolomite may be going on in coral reefs at the present day. If specimens of the rock from the *lower* and *older* parts of the reef could be obtained and analysed, and compared with analyses of other specimens brought from the *upper* and *newer* portions of the same Reef, it is possible that some light might be thrown upon the question.

Let us apply this to the case of the 'Schlern Dolomite.' Richthofen points out that the *Ammonites globosus* is to

* See a paper by Sir R. I. Murchison and Professor Harkness in the 'Journal of the Geological Society of London,' for May 1864, on the Permian rocks of the north-west of England, where a series of breccias is described, the lower of ordinary limestone, and the upper, magnesian; and the inference is drawn that the dolomitising agent must have acted *from above, subsequently* to the deposition of the upper breccias.

be seen embedded in the Schlern in the form of a regular spiral, containing the usual hollow shell-chambers, lined with crystals of Dolomite; while the division walls of the chambers are a prolongation of the general rock mass. The original substance of the shell—formed of carbonate of lime—has disappeared, and a mould of that shell formed of Dolomite has taken its place! Is not this some indication of what has been going on in the entire mass of the mountain?

Darwin found upon Keeling Atoll, in the Indian Ocean, evidences of changes going on in the structure of the coral. Upon the lee side of the Atoll, fragments of corals were heaped up in great quantity, and cemented together into a firm mass by the trickling of the limestone dissolved by the sea-water. In some parts of this mass the altered coral passed over by degrees into a crystalline sparry limestone—so gradually, indeed, that even with a lens Darwin was unable to distinguish the boundary between the changed coral and the sparry limestone. The cemented mass was very hard, and rang under the hammer. It does not appear that any analysis was made of this sparry limestone. But its great hardness and its clinking character are properties which remind one of the crystalline, cellular 'Schlern Dolomite.' And if it be possible to observe so much change as this in a rock mass now in process of formation, how much more must have been effected in the *older and lower* parts of the Reef? And to what an extent would it have progressed if we could again examine such a Reef, after a period as long as that which has elapsed between the deposit of the Trias and our time?

The *Dolomites of the Future* will probably have to be sought for in the varied coral regions of the Pacific and Indian Oceans, and on the north-east coast of Australia.

Let us indulge a hope that the elevating action may be rapid enough to save their reefs from the fierce ordeal they must pass through on their way upwards to light and air. Leaving the breakers to dash themselves vainly at their feet, they will then display to a distant posterity their manifold bosses, walls, plateaus, and pinnacles of jagged rock; probably as far exceeding in weird grandeur the Dolomites of South Tyrol as these already excel in that characteristic their Alpine neighbours.

At last the 'Coral reef Formation'—if it were such—came to an end, and a period of *slow upheaval* took the place of the preceding period of slow depression. An area of upheaval gradually advanced from the south-west to the north-east, so that the Mendola rose above the waves earlier than the Schlern, and the Schlern earlier than the Sella plateau; while in the Ampezzo the depression still increased. This is indicated by the comparative thickness of the Lias beds. On the Schlern they are less than a hundred feet thick; on the Sella plateau they possess ten times that thickness; while at the Civita, Pelmo, and Antelao, they reach a maximum of several thousand feet.

With this fragmentary and local deposit of lower Lias beds the geological history of the Western Dolomite District closes. The subsequent depressions which, in surrounding districts, gave rise to rocks of later formations, were without influence upon it, except so far as it might be affected by general changes of level that did not bring in the waters of the sea. Henceforth, 'skiey influences' were left to work uninterruptedly towards the wearing down of its surface.*

---

* The Miocene period may possibly prove an exception. There are two small patches of what appear to be Miocene conglomerate in the Traviguolo Thal and in the middle Gader: Richthofen, however, does not regard it as sufficiently proved.

There still remains one point of interest related to the subject-matter of our book—the history of the Frenchman, Monsieur Dolomieu—whose name, slightly modified, we have been compelled to make use of so frequently in these pages. Our readers have already been made aware that it was his name that has been employed to designate the mineral — the rock consisting of that mineral — and the mountains which are made up of that rock. A few particulars respecting him will fitly conclude the chapter.

Deodatus Guy Silvanus Tancred de Gralet de Dolomieu—for our mineralogical friend appears to have had almost as many names as a Spanish princess—was born June 24, 1750, in Dauphiné. Very early in life he became a member of the order of the Knights of St. John at Malta. Having been condemned to death for fighting a duel, the intercession of his friends procured for him, with some difficulty, a pardon from the Pope. He then entered the army, and devoted his leisure to the study of chemistry and geology.

In 1775 he was made a correspondent of the Academy of Sciences, which induced him to relinquish the army, and devote himself thenceforward exclusively to science.

While in Malta, in 1791, he addressed a letter to a friend, M. Picot de la Peyrouse, President of the district of Toulouse, which contains the first allusion to the mineral that was afterwards to bear his name. The letter is dated January 30, 1791, and begins with the observation that he had 'long recognised that effervescence with acids was not always an essential character of limestone, although this property was given by all naturalists as the most certain sign by which limestone might be distinguished.'

He also tells his friend he had noticed that some of the statues of ancient Rome were made of a fine white marble, very hard and heavy, which would only slightly effervesce with acids after some minutes.

Rocks possessing this character he had discovered during the last eighteen months of his travels in South Tyrol, with his friend M. Fleurian de Bellevue. He had met with them on the road between Botzen and Trent, to the south of the Porphyry district. They were found lying in horizontal beds, fossiliferous, whitish in colour, and full of cavities containing rhombic crystals.

This letter was afterwards printed in the thirty-ninth volume of the 'Journal de Physique,' published at Paris.

Upon the establishment of the School of Mines, in 1795, he accepted the situations of Professor of Geology and Inspector of Mines, and soon after was included among the original members of the National Institute of Sciences and Arts, then organised by the French Government.

He also formed one of that band of savants who accompanied the Expedition to Egypt. Being nearly wrecked off the Italian coast at Tarentum, on his return, he only escaped the sea to fall into the clutches of the reactionary party in Naples. He was not lost sight of, however, either by his friends or the Government. While a prisoner, he was appointed Daubenton's successor at the Museum of Natural History; and in the treaty made by the French Government with the King of Naples, after the victory at Marengo, it was expressly stipulated that Dolomieu should be restored to his country.

He died universally regretted, at the family residence at Drée, near Maĉon, on November 27, 1801. His collections became the property of his brother, the Marquis de Drée.

In the year following his death, there was published in Paris a thin 12mo. volume, entitled 'Journal du dernier Voyage du Citoyen Dolomieu dans les Alpes, par T. C. Bruun Neergard.' The author was a Dane, who had very recently travelled with the geologist in western Switzerland, and on both sides of the Simplon and St. Gothard.

On descending the south side of the St. Gothard, the author observes (p. 42)—'Ayrolo is very prettily situated. From this point we made an excursion to the Val Canaria, a league distant. In examining its walls we found gypsum in great masses, mixed with mica, but for the most part affected by the atmosphere. *The Dolomite* was very pure.'

Dolomite is incidentally mentioned in two or three other instances in this book, without any reference to the term as a novelty. It is therefore probable that the name had already been in use some years before—perhaps not much later than the publication of the letter of 1791.

The mineralogist Werner was on intimate terms with Dolomieu, and active correspondence was carried on between them. It is possible that the name was first employed by Werner.

Mons. Fournet, in his 'Histoire de la Dolomié,' says distinctly that Dolomieu's name was given to the mineral through the observations that he had made upon its occurrence among the Dolomitic rocks of Tyrol, and that the new designation soon displaced all the old ones which had hitherto been in but partial use, such as 'bitter spar,' introduced by Emmerling; 'rhombic spar,' by Werner; 'muricalcite,' by Kirwan; 'magnesian spar,' by Bergman; and 'magnesian carbonate of lime,' by Haüy.